Union and Disunion in the Nineteenth Century

This volume examines the nineteenth century not only through episodes, institutions, sites and representations concerned with union, concord and bonds of sympathy, but also through moments of secession, separation, discord and disjunction. Its lens extends from the local and regional, through to national and international settings in Britain, Europe and the United States. The contributors come from the fields of cultural history, literary studies, American studies and legal history.

James Gregory is Associate Professor in Modern British History at the University of Plymouth. Among his publications is *The Poetry and the Politics: Radical Reform in Victorian England* (2014).

Daniel J.R. Grey is Lecturer in World History since 1800 at the University of Plymouth. Among his recent publications is the co-edited collection *Judgment in the Victorian Age* (Routledge, 2018), with Annika Bautz and James Gregory.

D1427315

Routledge Studies in Modern History

For a full list of titles, please visit: https://www.routledge.com/history/series/
MODHIST

Union and Disunion in the Nineteenth Century

**Edited by James Gregory
and Daniel J.R. Grey**

Routledge
Taylor & Francis Group

LONDON AND NEW YORK

First published 2020
by Routledge
2 Park Square, Milton Park, Abingdon, Oxon OX14 4RN

and by Routledge
52 Vanderbilt Avenue, New York, NY 10017

*Routledge is an imprint of the Taylor & Francis Group, an
informa business*

First issued in paperback 2021

British Library Cataloguing-in-Publication Data
A catalogue record for this book is available from the British Library

Library of Congress Cataloging-in-Publication Data
A catalog record has been requested for this book

ISBN: 978-1-138-35430-2 (hbk)
ISBN: 978-1-03-208302-5 (pbk)
ISBN: 978-0-429-42491-5 (ebk)

Typeset in Times New Roman
by codeMantra

MIX
Paper from
responsible sources
FSC   FSC™ C013985
www.fsc.org

Printed in the United Kingdom
by Henry Ling Limited

Contents

Figures

Tables

Contributors

Rachel Egloff is an independent scholar. Her PhD, awarded by Oxford Brookes University in 2019, studied female participation in nineteenth-century discourses on national identity in the context of European international politics, using the case study of the writer Rose Blaze de Bury.

James E.H. Ford is curator at Longleat House and was formerly Consultant Assistant Curator at the Houses of Parliament. His Arts and Humanities Research Council-funded PhD project entitled 'The Art of Union and Disunion in the Houses of Parliament, 1834–1928' (University of Nottingham, 2016) explored the visual representation of the four nations in the New Palace of Westminster.

James Gregory is Associate Professor in Modern British History since 1800 at the University of Plymouth. Among his publications is *The Poetry and the Politics: Radical Reform in Victorian England* (2014).

Daniel J.R. Grey is Lecturer in World History since 1800 at the University of Plymouth. Among his publications is the co-edited collection *Judgment in the Victorian Age* (Routledge, 2018), with Annika Bautz and James Gregory.

Gary D. Hutchison is a postdoctoral research assistant in the School of Government and International Affairs at Durham University. His Wolfson Foundation-funded PhD (University of Edinburgh) focussed on the Scottish Conservative party, 1832–1868.

Margaret Markwick is an Honorary Research Fellow at the University of Exeter and has published on Anthony Trollope. She is currently exploring the relationship between the Anglican thought and the expression of religious belief in the mid-Victorian novel.

Lawrence T. McDonnell is Assistant Professor in the Department of History at Iowa State University and author of *Performing Disunion: The Coming of the Civil War in Charleston, South Carolina* (Cambridge University Press, 2018).

Alison Pedley is a PhD student at the University of Roehampton, studying married women admitted *c*.1840–1890 to Broadmoor Criminal Lunatic Asylum and other institutions for the murder of their children.

Gordon Pentland is Reader in History at the University of Edinburgh. He has published widely on the political and cultural history of Scotland and Britain since the French Revolution, and has co-edited the *Oxford Handbook of Modern British Political History, 1800–2000* (2018).

Pearl T. Ponce is Associate Professor in the Department of History, Ithaca College, and author of *'To Govern the Devil in Hell': The Political Crisis in Territorial Kansas* (2014), *Kansas's War: The Civil War in Documents* (2011), and various essays on Civil War and Kansas history.

Karen Rothery is an independent scholar, researching the implementation of the 1834 New Poor Law in Hertfordshire.

Judith Rowbotham is Visiting Research Professor in Law at the University of Plymouth and a director of SOLON: Promoting Interdisciplinary Studies in Law, Crime and History. Her numerous publications include the edited collection, *The Windsor Dynasty 1910 to the Present* (2016).

Helen Rutherford is Senior Lecturer in Law at Northumbria University, and a doctoral researcher at the University of Newcastle, studying the life and work of the Victorian coroner for Newcastle upon Tyne, John Theodore Hoyle.

Kim Stevenson is Professor of Socio-Legal History at the University of Plymouth. Among her numerous publications are: with D.J. Cox, C. Harris and J. Rowbotham, *Public Indecency in England 1857–1960. 'A Serious and Growing Evil'* (2015).

Emily West is Professor in American History at the University of Reading. She is the author of numerous books including *Enslaved Women in America* (2014) and (as co-editor) the special editions of *Slavery and Abolition* and the *Women's History Review* on enslaved mothers in the Atlantic World in 2017.

Acknowledgements

The editors wish to thank all the contributors for their efficiency and patience in the delivery of their chapters, and for acquiring some of the images in this collection. The images in Chapter 10 appear by courtesy of the Library of Congress and those in Chapter 12 by courtesy of the Berkshire Record Office, Coley Avenue, Reading (with thanks to Mark Stevens). In addition, we would like to thank Ian Rayment for assistance in obtaining images from the Rare Books collection at the University of Plymouth. We are grateful to Rob Langham and Dana Moss at Taylor & Francis for all their support.

Introduction

James Gregory and Daniel J.R. Grey

This collection of essays examines the nineteenth century not only through episodes, institutions, sites and representations concerned with union, concord and bonds of sympathy, but also through moments of secession, separation, discord and disjunction. Its lens extends from the local and regional, to national and international settings in Britain, Europe and the United States. The contributors come from the fields of history, literary studies, American studies and law, and the introduction's first part outlines their themes. Some of the ideals and realities of nineteenth-century union are then explored by the editors.

Part I. The scope of *Union and Disunion in the Nineteenth Century*

The chapters are arranged in five sections. The first is interested in union and disunion in artistic form, through literary fiction and sculpture. We begin with James Ford's chapter on the controversy stimulated by representing in sculpture the barons and prelates involved in Magna Carta in the rebuilt Houses of Parliament. Debates about the validity of including an Irish archbishop in the scheme became the flashpoint for contention between Irish nationalists keen to repeal the Act of Union of 1800, and unionist opponents. The second chapter studies literary representation through Margaret Marwick's discussion of English religious divisions in Margaret Oliphant's *Salem Chapel* and her related novels.

The second part studies promotion of transnational friendship through popular diplomacy and texts on European states. James Gregory's chapter examines public and political responses to the 'English return visit' to Paris in April 1849 in the aftermath of European revolution and Chartist agitation: an attempt to express unions of affection as well as commerce in a more democratic and popular register than the diplomacy of the period. Gregory uses British and French satiric cartoons, graphic journalism and material artefacts. In the next chapter Rachel Egloff studies closely the work of the writer Rose Blaze de Bury, who aimed to forge a literary style that would simultaneously educate the British public regarding German culture and politics, traditionally seen as 'masculine' subjects, while emphasising her respectability and adherence to conventions expected of a female author.

The third part of the book turns to the politics of union and disunion in Great Britain in a variety of forms from national and unionist party politics to 'local politics', beginning with two chapters on political leadership and political parties in Scotland and the United Kingdom. Gordon Pentland looks at Scottish political leadership in the 'long nineteenth century'. Hutchinson's chapter looks particularly at the role of the Conservative party in Scotland from the Great Reform Act to the Representation of the People (Scotland) Act of 1868. A symbolic and practical site for union is the focus of Kim Stevenson and Judith Rowbotham's essay on the three towns of Plymouth, Devonport and Stonehouse in Devon, linked through Union Street.

One of the most prominent expressions of union and disunion in the century occurred in the United States with civil war and secessionist impulses. In part four of the study, we turn to union in Emily West's study of enslaved couples and marriage in the Civil War era. Pearl Ponce's chapter focusses on the Mormon community's experiences with the United States in the 1840s and 1850s. This section concludes in a more biographical vein with Lawrence McDonnell's chapter on the role and legacy of the Democratic statesman (and seventh Vice-President) John C. Calhoun of South Carolina in the period leading up to the war.

The final section of the book examines family division and union in England through the law. In Alison Pedley and Helen Rutherford's chapters, efforts to reunite English families sundered by criminal behaviour, and the disunion apparent in the jury room in a capital case during the late-Victorian period, allow us to see the legal, judicial and penal dimensions to our themes of union and disunion. The book concludes with welfare reform as an impulse for establishing networks of local unions: Karen Rothery studies the creation of administrative 'unions' following one of the most profound legislative interventions of the British nineteenth century, the New Poor Law of 1834.

Part II. Union and disunion in the long nineteenth century: an introductory essay

In a British context, the century begins with the major constitutional act of union with Ireland (1800).[1] In continental Europe union figured politically and in economic terms via such events as the British effort to extend free trade,[2] the Norway-Swedish union (1814–1905),[3] the Italian *Risorgimento* completed in 1871,[4] German unification (a process officially culminating at Versailles in January 1871),[5] customs unions such as the *Zollverein* established in 1834,[6] and currency union schemes such as the Latin Monetary Union formed in 1865 (and comprising France, Belgium, Italy, and Switzerland).[7] External commentators on these tumultuous events and changes held them up as models to celebrate, emulate or avoid.[8] Anglophone writers turned to continental Europe for instances of 'unnatural disunion' in the present or past.[9]

There is a linguistic aspect to union and 'reunion'. In the seventeenth century, Francis Bacon treated the 'confusion of tongues' as the 'first curse of disunion', while Archibald Sayce claimed in 1880 that 'Language begins with multiplicity and disunion, but its end is unity'.[10] In an era of nationalism, the idea of ending 'disunion' among peoples speaking the same language, in continental Europe, could rally support.[11] Others at the end of the century advocated a political union in the Anglophone world. There might even be anticipation of a 'world union'.[12] Advocacy of unity outside political and national entities included efforts to unify science and harmonise technical nomenclature, measurements and a variety of standards at an international level to assist intellectual union.[13] Germaine de Staël hailed a 'union of all thinking men, from one end of Europe to the other', in 1813: scientific unions developed to unite scientists across nations, alongside the creation of less formal personal and intellectual networks.[14]

From the opposite perspective of *disunion*, the United States' federal union was imperilled and saved, generating a flood of print material defending the idea and reality of the union, or promoting disunion of the nation. As Catherine Hall has commented, '[t]he idea of the nation ... was always fragile' in this period.[15] The question of who could join 'national' unions and enjoy political citizenship – who counted, who was excluded and the reasons why – was fiercely debated. This was despite the legal and political decisions of the late eighteenth century that had strengthened the expectation that 'normal' for British citizens was defined as white, Anglican men of the middling sort.[16] Imperialism and colonialism were the creation of, and exploitation of internal disunion and division.[17]

In this introductory essay, we *examine the definitions and usages of the opposing terms of 'union' and 'disunion'* in the nineteenth century, noting traditions of representation and interpretation which had already been established. The theme of *artistic and literary representation* is then turned to.

'Union' and 'disunion': definitions and usage of the words

In 1836, the conservative British *Fraser's Magazine* observed, 'Among the rare phenomena of the day in which we live, are the strange unions that are formed in our country. We have political unions, trades' unions, Protestant unions, and, last and not least, the voluntary unions'.[18] A decade later, the *Coventry Herald* extolled inclination to unite:

> without union there is no strength for anything, – no practical victory for truth, – no security for society, – no progress for individuals or nations ... the greatest hindrance to union is an indiscreet exercise of individual liberty, or the abuse of the Voluntary Principle.[19]

Unions were formed in their thousands for philanthropic, cultural, economic and political aims: from transatlantic labour organisations, women's suffrage, to teetotalism and international telegraphy.[20] These groups might well be reactionary in nature as well as radical, as Madisson Brown has demonstrated was the case for gender-conservative activists in the transatlantic campaigns against prostitution.[21] This section surveys the discussion on union and disunion as ideas in nineteenth-century British discourse.

As a binary to describe political relations and constitutional organisation, 'union / disunion' was not new – 'union' is noted in the *Oxford English Dictionary* in English usage in the fifteenth century, while 'disunion' appears in the late sixteenth century.[22] Ideas about union were an important aspect in Christian theology and sermons. Unsurprisingly an extensive discourse relating to 'union with Christ' continued in Victorian theology whether Catholic or Protestant. The afterlife – after the moment of death which was itself sometimes called 'disunion' – was imagined as time 'without disunion', or indeed an end to 'souls' disunion', for the blessed. But Christianity accepted the disunion of natural humanity from God.[23] Union also figured, as a consequence of their roots, in new faiths like Swedenborgianism and the theosophical movement.[24]

In political discourse, the word 'union' is traced to classical, civic humanism.[25] Its essential presence for political stability was highlighted at moments of crisis: take the comment in a sermon before the House of Commons in 1741, 'Union is so much the Strength of every Society, that without it there is little probability of its continuing long'.[26] As Kersh's research on its prominence in American political language through the war of independence demonstrates, the word was *the* key term for commonality in political discourse from the 1770s 'into the Civil War era and beyond'.[27] Talk of union in politics, Kersh argues, needs to be interpreted as operating within a culture familiar with religious motifs of union and in which union was constantly extolled, as in the words of one prominent writer, the Congregationalist preacher Jonathan Edwards, 'union is one of the most amiable things that pertains to human society; yea, it is one of the most beautiful and happy things on earth, which indeed makes earth most like heaven'.[28] As a term of communal feeling and organisation, 'union' was joined by others in the lexicon of unionism, to describe political, commercial, social and cultural entities in the Anglophone nineteenth century, from 'association' and 'amalgamation', to 'co-operation'.

Society itself being a union, it is natural that among the combinations is 'social union', which appears in Robert Burns's poem of 1785, 'To a Mouse' ('I'm truly sorry man's dominion | Has broken nature's social union'[29]). It was the title for an organisation involving Robert Young, designed to unite 'whatever constitutes the interest, the dignity, or the welfare of society' in April 1799.[30] Social union was described by the English physiologist Thomas Laycock in 1860 thus:

> The desire for union and communion with his fellow-men is the fundamental desire of man as a social animal. And out of this desire arise all those high motives and social efforts, excited by the love of country, and which characterise the patriotic hero.

Laycock traced this through

> ... those infinitely varying combinations of men for a common object, which arise when man is free to carry into effect the social motives which actuate him. It is from this source that the stimulus is derived which, in free countries like Great Britain and the United States, impels men to the formation of all those institutions, companies, associations, clubs, benefit societies, masonic lodges, and religious sects, that so remarkably characterise their social polity.[31]

In a religious age, this social concord was traced back to God's will.[32] The *Eclectic Review*'s essay on Christian union in 1845 argued, 'order and harmony pervade the works of the Deity, so as to constitute the general law of all'.[33] The Liberal writer John Morley observed that Conservative philosophy was that 'social union is the express creation ... of the Deity'.[34] Obviously associated with this is the idea of 'social disunion' – often discussed by Victorians in the context of societies (included the writers') where social unity was absent.[35] The social reformer Edward Carpenter wrote of the 'disunion of the present-day man', in 1889, 'the disunion of the outer self from the inner – the horrible dual self-consciousness – which is the means ultimately of a more perfect and conscious union than could ever have been realised without it'.[36]

The great transatlantic example of political union might act as model, inspiration and warning in the old Europe.[37] But Americans in a century of secession and internecine conflict were obviously aware of the significance of, and challenges towards the ideal of 'union'.[38] Alexander Hamilton told Washington in March 1783, 'The seeds of disunion are much more numerous than those of union'.[39] President Buchanan wrote in 1858, 'In the last age of the republic it was considered almost treasonable to pronounce the word "disunion." Times have since sadly changed, and now disunion is freely prescribed as the remedy of evanescent evils'.[40] 'Union pledges peace at home', commented R.C. Pell in 1863, 'and its invulnerable front frowns off war from without. *L' Union c'est la force* says the motto of Belgium – Union is strength; Union is peace, may America add. It is our very life. It means civilization, progress – all future hope for the continent'.[41] The Englishman Richard Cobden justly observed in 1861, 'each State is in some sense a centre of disunion. Each State attracts to itself a share of political attachment, has separate interests, real or supposed, has a separate set of public men anxious to increase its importance'.[42] The spirit of union and disunion was depicted by Nevin in *Harper's Weekly* (see Figure 0.1).

The many other areas in which union and disunion could be examined include the phenomena of natural and human sciences (such as the relationship between sexual, family and social unions[43]) and policy in state and inter-state relations, as most famously represented by the German *Zollverein* and discussion of British imperial unions.[44] Those British workers uniting in trade unions had international parallels, as might organisations for social

Figure 0.1 J.M. Nevin, 'The Spirits Abroad – The Spirit of Disunion', and 'The Spirits Abroad – The Spirit of Union', *Harper's Weekly*, 28 July 1860, pp. 472–473. Image courtesy of James Gregory.

policy and welfare such as Poor Law Unions.[45] The Scottish philosopher George Ramsay's *Political Discourses* (1838) asserted 'among the various forces which in the moral world are constantly at war with each other, some lead to Union, others to Disunion', in establishing his dichotomy of *central* and *local* powers.[46] Acts of local administrative union, as in national and international affairs, could be fraught with contention. The 'union' of the reformed English poor law in the 1830s was the source of enduring dread for the poor.[47] One satirical comment on the new system – an engraving entitled 'Poor Law Disunion', displays a couple being dragged apart to their separate wards by the poor law staff, their hands symbolically missing each other under the doorway marked 'The Union' (see Figure 0.2).[48]

The tendency to union or disunion, as already indicated, has ecclesiastical, theological and religious aspects. Dictionaries, including Samuel Johnson's, in defining the word 'union', provided a legal usage specifically related to (personal) union in religious bodies: 'a combining or consolidation of two churches in one which is done by the consent of the bishop the patron incumbent'.[49] There was also the creation or breakup of denominational unity (the deprecation of the Protestant Reformation by the Oxford Movement, for example, as more of a loss through disunion).[50] There was the forging of

Figure 0.2 Design derived from woodcut in *The Bude Light: A Social ... Skiterary Monthly Illuminator* (London: Cunningham, 1841), p. 145. Image courtesy of James Gregory.

ecumenical bodies such as that attempted under von Döllinger at Bonn in 1874–1875.[51] This was also an era which saw pioneering interfaith activity in which some spoke of the 'prospective religious union of the human family' and others anticipated a 'grand union of the world's religions'.[52] Solidarity might be expressed on interfaith lines through working together on social issues and developing friendships, as was the case for some Jewish and Christian women activists in late-nineteenth-century Britain.[53] Missionary work might be seen as promoting union of belief, but as the Anglican clergyman and poet Robert Hawker said, 'For God's sake, let us try to agree together at home, before we transplant our demoniacal dis-union to foreign lands'.[54]

Modern technology assisted transcontinental and global union through steam-powered land and maritime transport, telegraphy and transoceanic cables. The Leeds Parliamentary Reform Association gestured to modern science when fraternally greeting Daniel O'Connell and fellow Irish repealers in 1840: 'England and Ireland are now enabled almost to shake hands with each other; our steam inventions have cast a floating bridge across the Irish channel, which is traversed by hundreds and thousands of our respective peoples'.[55] But at the end of the century Leo Tolstoy scorned the millennium effected 'when all shall be united from one end of the world to the other', by telegraphy, telephony and balloons, because human nature would remain in disunion.[56]

Union encompassed conjunctions of interests and mind – material and spiritual connections. At the level of affective relations within the domestic sphere, there were acts of union and threats of disunion.[57] They might have wider implications for 'debates about marriage are not simply about private, intimate relationships; these controversies are ways of negotiating the meanings and values of the nation'.[58] Despite the fact that no state recognised the marriages of enslaved men and women as 'legal' or binding, such unions were of lasting importance to these couples and their families in the antebellum United States.[59] Eighteenth-century sermons on envy touched on the threat of disunion to family happiness.[60] Jeremy Bentham in discussing divorce in 'Principles of the Civil Code' argued that 'a principle of disunion among married persons introduces negligence and disorder'. John Stuart Mill used these terms in an unpublished essay on marriage referring to 'perpetual bickering and disunion'.[61] His partner Harriet Mill wrote of union and disunion of feelings and character in an essay on female enfranchisement in 1851.[62] Sarah Ellis's *The Wives of England*, a famous text published in 1843, spoke of 'discoveries made which have fully justified an entire disunion of the parties thus associated', in marriage. Radical periodicals discussed marriage law reforms under the title of disunion.[63] This is quite apart from the idea of gender difference as disunion (for example, 'intellectual disunion').[64] Women becoming enfranchised and expressing political opinions, it was feared, would disunite families.[65] Disunion also came into the family through in-laws damaging the 'loving patriarchal union', according to Dinah Craik's *Studies from Life* (1862).[66] The fear and threat of 'unhallowed disunion' in its ultimate large-scale expression of civil war between brothers was realised in the United States in the 1860s (see Figure 0.3).[67]

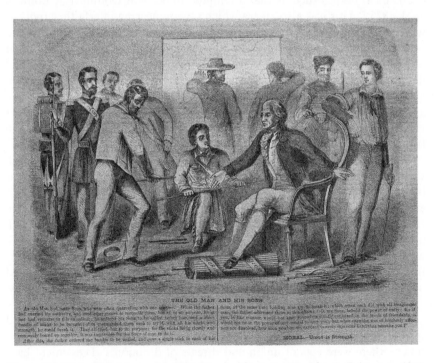

Figure 0.3 'The Old Man and His Sons', *Harper's Weekly*, 2 February 1861, p. 76. Image courtesy of James Gregory.

Union and disunion go together.[68] Some commentators, such as the mid-century author Edwin Paxton Hood, optimistically saw union and amalgamation in religion as the happy eventual fruit of sectarian divisions.[69] But nonconformist Protestants might generally be viewed as preferring their state of disunion.[70] Others, committed to the established church's stability, saw threats from external enemies and, like the Congregationalist minister Henry Rogers, detected 'fatal signs of disunion from within'.[71] Advocates of a non-denominational *national* education in the mid-Victorian period justified themselves by pointing to the disunion of religious bodies.[72] Commentators saw the progress of humanity, no less, at stake from the existence of union or disunion in Anglo-French relations: the émigré Ivan Golovin commenting in 1848: 'The progress of mankind depends upon the union of these two nations; and their disunion must be injurious to liberty'.[73] How union and disunion might be seen in racial terms is something to explore further: the essayist Charles Lamb's discussion of his own anti-Semitism, in the essay on 'Imperfect Sympathies', refers to 'so deadly a disunion'.[74]

In the scientific realm, amateurs and experts played with the idea of union in nature and chemistry (with its atomic and molecular unions, for example) and found analogies in human nature.[75] Psychology was turned to by the novelist Catherine Crowe in 1848 to explore states of disunion of body and spirit such as sleep, as a 'foretaste of its future destiny', the body would experience disunion from the spirit. A sense of disunion in the waking state was abnormal, 'hence it is that somnambulists and clairvoyantes are chiefly to be found amongst sickly women'.[76] The mathematician Royston Piggott told an audience of the Eastbourne Natural History Society in 1881, 'All organic matter is in one tremendous turmoil of union and disunion'.[77] The anti-Darwinian Samuel Butler provocatively described eating as 'a mode of love; it is an effort after a closer union; so we say we love roast beef ... the effort is after closer union and possession'.[78] Famously the philosopher Herbert Spencer sought to elaborate an evolutionary theory in which increasingly complex forms developed out of simple forms: arguably union was at its heart. In *Social Statics* (1851) he commented:

> as man has been, and is still, deficient in those feelings which, by dictating just conduct, prevent the perpetual antagonism of individuals and their consequent disunion, some artificial agency is required by which their union may be maintained. Only by the process of adaptation itself can be produced that character which makes social equilibrium spontaneous.[79]

The barrister and keen anthropologist George Harris, studying civilisation in what he thought was a scientific manner in 1861, cogitated on 'union', civilisation tending to promote it at a national level and globally: 'The complete accomplishment of civilization is indeed mainly dependent upon, and principally effected by this union and co-operation of its different Elements'.[80]

Social evolution was also invoked in terms of political unions, thus discussion of Anglo-Irish relations by the liberal activist Wordsworth Donisthorpe in 1894, referred to the argument 'urged against union or in favour of disunion ... that the two peoples in question are in different stages of social evolution'.[81]

In the political discourse of union and disunion Irish nationalists could find much to emphasise in the latter category, by way of explaining the continuation of British rule: 'Disunion among yourselves, was the cause of their prostration. *Disunion!* – in that obnoxious word, contained the history of Irelands wrongs', and 'Disunion it was that gave footing to that foreign power, and handed over the government of the country to its minions. Disunion has made impregnable the fortress of the enslaver'.[82] In the British context, it was Irish discourse in which the language of union and disunion was particularly fraught, take this passage from a letter by a Catholic priest, on O'Connellism, in 1847:

> Union is a mere instrument – in itself neither good nor evil, and just as powerful for evil as for good. Union is not truth, nor virtue, nor happiness; but truth and virtue tend, through union, as an instrument to happiness, which is the final end of man, and of all human machinations. This instrument, like all the other gifts of God or devices of men, may be used or abused. To speak of the value of union in the abstract is to speak nonsense. To speak of the evils of disunion is equally nonsensical. Truth and virtue are the kernel of all good; error and vice the origin of all misfortune. A union not centered in virtue is the shell of a blind nut. It is well to break it.[83]

Then there was this, Richard Doyle's comment on the philanthropy of the English side of the union with Ireland, during the Irish famine (see Figure 0.4).

Political memoirs made references to party divisions in terms of disunion.[84] When Irish Home Rule split the Liberal party, there was much coverage of British politics in terms of union and disunion in the late nineteenth century.[85]

Representing union and disunion in literature and art

Unions and disunions are commemorated: Independence Day being, after all, the 'anniversary of the disunion of the United States from England'.[86] Union was represented in physical form in monuments to dynastic, national and federal union: or so Laycock argued, 'The most remarkable illustrations of this aesthetic and constructive evolution of the idea of social unity have been erected by two free nations – namely, the British House of Parliament, and the Capitol at Washington'.[87] Parliament, through statuary, history painting, mosaic and heraldry, presented a united kingdom: the representation of the union, and the episodes of disunity caused by decorative schemes,

Figure 0.4 Richard Doyle, 'Union is Strength', *Punch*, 17 October 1846, p. 161. Image courtesy of the University of Plymouth, Rare Books Collection.

has been explored in detail recently by James Ford, who contributes a chapter to our book.[88] Beyond such imperial and republican architecture, union had artistic representation. In political projects of union, the mobilisation of poetry, prose and graphic propaganda occurred; extolling or vilifying the act of union with Ireland in 1800, for example.[89]

The origins of American Civil War iconography of disunion reside in the eighteenth-century visual rhetoric of the revolution. Lithographic and wood-engraved serpents or hydras of disunion or secession (strangled or clubbed by infant or adult Hercules) thematically originated in the famous image of the divided serpent with the motto 'JOIN, or DIE' of 1754 – and the variant 'UNITE or DIE' – to encourage the union of colonies against changing enemies.[90] Recent discussion of the photographic response to antebellum and Civil War politics has identified disjunction and an effort to construct permanence, through the new medium of daguerreotype photography.[91]

The representation of 'union' in trade-union banners, and commemorative medals, are manifestations of the attempt to celebrate and extol union materially and performatively.[92] In James Gregory's chapter in this collection, which studies the diplomatic ramifications of the English holiday visit to Paris organised in April 1849, several designs of commemorative medals struck in Paris, displaying the hands clasped in unity, are noted. The symbolic gesture of hands clasped or shaking can be traced through a wide range of nineteenth-century British, European and American artefacts from pledge cards for the late-Victorian Gospel Temperance Union, commemoration of the successful Atlantic telegraphic link ('The laying of the cable – John and Jonathan joining hands', as one cartoon depicted the event in 1858), the iconography of Marianne and Britannia for the Franco-British Exhibition of 1908 and the socialist Walter Crane's famous design for workers of the world uniting. Sometimes, when it was a matter of personal diplomacy, for instance, representing friendly intimacy need not involve bodily contact: thus a print (published internationally) commemorating the cordiality of Emperor Napoleon III and Victoria depicted the two royal couples sharing a box at the Paris Opera in 1855, with the legend '*Hail! happy union!*'[93]

One of our contributors, Margaret Marwick, looks to literary treatment of union and disunion in the context of the British nonconformist movement against the union of church and state. Union and disunion appeared in all sorts of novels, including romances of marital bliss imperilled and gained; examples where the maxim of 'union is strength' is invoked include the poet and prolific novelist Harriet Maria Gordon Smythies' *Courtship and Wedlock; or, Lovers and Husbands* in 1850.[94] Novels offered, to quote Smythies elsewhere, 'passionate pictures of the union of two hearts'.[95] The novelist, often working to support families after marital disunion or economic failure, might write with experience of the reality of domestic division. Catherine Crowe's eponymous heroine in *Linny Lockwood* (1854) observes, 'poverty would be sure to create disunion'.[96] In Charles Reade's *Hard Cash* (1863) appears the observation, 'disunion, a fast-growing plant, when men set it in the soil of the passions'.[97] In other cases, such as early nineteenth-century novels by Walter Scott and Sydney Owenson, the marriage union plot is a device to explore metaphorically, the 'union' of nations.[98] American writers would also comment on their political unions through novels and poetry.[99]

Conclusion

> What is ... more continually in our ears – continually exemplified most convincingly before our eyes than that old fable of the bundle of sticks, 'Union is Strength.' From the history of a nation to a game at chess, we wonderingly behold the magic power of that time-honoured dictum. Viewing the matter in a higher light it is strictly enjoined by our creed. How comes it, then, we are so loath to practise what in a spiritual and material sense we are all ready to admit is capable of yielding rich fruit? The cause is not far to seek. Jealousy, weakness, and all other imperfectness, wage a Titan war against faint and uncertain strivings.

So commented the author of an essay on 'co-operation' in the British feminist *Victoria Magazine* in 1868.[100] This introduction demonstrates how prevalent ideas of union and disunion (and efforts to realise and avoid these states) were in nineteenth-century culture through its survey of discourse and representation. Our contributors consider the disunion created through the politics of architectural sculpture, and literary treatments of current union or disunion (literary plots prominently involve the themes of disunion, reunion and union). They explore enterprises of popular diplomacy combined with commerce, attempting to create *entente cordiale* between historic enemies. From the local and familial to international relations, our authors demonstrate how fruitful the lens of union and disunion are to understanding the period in Anglo-American culture. Without overstating a 'transatlantic' culture in our period, it is worth remembering the keen American interest in the fate of the Irish under the British state's union, and the fascination with the United States' disunion in Britain (as well as internationally), to take merely the subject of political union. The American ambassador to Portugal published *Union, Disunion, and Reunion: A Letter to General Franklin Pierce, Ex-president of the United States* in London with the publisher Richard Bentley in 1862.[101]

Chronologically, the essays focus on the era before 1914, after which a new global conflict created new demands to realise the maxim 'union is strength', triggered new acts of disunion and reunion, and proliferated through old and new media, familiar tropes of unity and disunity.[102] Our topic of union and disunion, examined as a historical theme from the perspective of various nineteenth-century histories, local, national, and international, is novel. It is also timely. In Britain, with present-day concerns about Scottish independence and the repercussions of the vote for Brexit, it is natural to turn to history to seek understanding of disunitive tendencies.[103]

Notes

1 Also anniversary in 1807 of the Union with Scotland, see A. Murdoch, ed., *Scotland and the Union 1707–2007* (Edinburgh: Edinburgh University Press, 2008); A. Raffe, '1707, 2007, and the Unionist turn in Scottish history', *Historical Journal* 53:4 (2010), pp. 1071–1083.

2 H. Dunckley, *The Charter of the Nations: Or, Free Trade and Its Results. An Essay on the Recent Commercial Policy of the United Kingdom, to which the Council of the National Anti-corn Law League Awarded Their First Prize* (London: Cash, 1854), p. 28: 'Free Trade ... closes an era of disunion and distrust'.

3 See R.E. Lundgren, *Norway-Sweden: Union, Disunion, and Scandinavian Integration* (Princeton, NJ: Princeton University Press, 1959); T. Leiren, 'Catalysts to Disunion: Sigurd Ibsen and Ringeren, 1898–1899', *Scandinavian Studies* 71:3 (Fall 1999), pp. 297–310.

4 See Gabriele Rossetti's phrase, 'Italy, nourishing within its own bosom the germ of disunion', quoted in I.C. Wright, transl., *The Purgatorio of Dante: Translated* (London: Longman, Rees, Orme, Brown, Green and Longman, 1836), p. 353 (notes to Canto VI).

5 German unification could be heralded by Britons as a positive development, on racial grounds. Thus Andrew Paton, 'for no nation has suffered more from disunion ... Whatever ... gives real unity and solidity to Germany, must be viewed with satisfaction by the Briton', *Highlands and Islands of the Adriatic: Including Dalmatia, Croatia, and the Southern Provinces of the Austrian Empire* (London: Chapman and Hall, 1849), vol. 2, pp. 295–296.

6 On the *Zollverein*, see A. Green, 'Representing Germany? The Zollverein at the World Exhibitions, 1851–1862', *Journal of Modern History* 75:4 (2003), pp. 836–863 and C.H. Shiue, 'From Political Fragmentation towards a Customs Union: Border Effects of the German Zollverein, 1815 to 1855', *European Review of Economic History* 9:2 (2005) pp. 129–162.

7 See D. Keogh and K. Whelan, eds, *Acts of Union: The Causes, Contexts and Consequences of the Act of Union* (Dublin: Four Courts, 2001). On Latin currency union, see L.L. Einaudi, 'From the Franc to the "Europe": The Attempted Transformation of the Latin Monetary Union into a European Monetary Union, 1865–1873', *Economic History Review*, 53:2 (May 2000), pp. 284–308; M. Flandreau, 'The Economics and Politics of Monetary Unions: A Reassessment of the Latin Monetary Union, 1865–71', *Financial History Review* 7:1 (2000), pp. 25–44, J. Maloney, 'Britain's Single Currency Debate of the Late 1860s', *European Journal of The History of Economic Thought* 13:4 (2006), pp. 513–531, H.P. Willis, *A History of the Latin Monetary Union; a Study of International Monetary Action* (Chicago: Chicago University Press, 1901).

8 See A.L. Tucker, '"Newest Born of Nations": Southern Thought on European Nationalisms and the Creation of the Confederacy, 1820–1865' (unpublished doctoral thesis, University of South Carolina, 2014); N. Carter, *Britain, Ireland and the Italian Risorgimento* (Basingstoke: Palgrave Macmillan, 2015).

9 See E.A. Freeman on the Ottomans, *Historical Essays* (London: Macmillan, 1892), vol. 3, p. 420.

10 On Bacon's comment, see J. Spedding, et al., eds, *The Works of Francis Bacon* (London: Longmans, Green, Reader and Dyer, 1868), vol. 10, p. 236; A.H. Sayce, *Introduction to the Science of Language* (London: Kegan Paul, 1880), vol. 1, p. 218. The movement towards a universal language was propelled by desire to end human disunion, for example, R. Jones, *The Origin of Language and Nations* (London: Hughs, 1764), preface, [p. 1].

11 For critical comments on language, union and disunion, J.M. Ludlow, 'The "Idea" of Nationality: Savoy', *Macmillan's Magazine*, March 1860, pp. 354–363 [p. 354].

12 See coverage of discussion, in 'Anglo-American Union', *The Review of Reviews* (March 1896), p. 323; E. Anthony, 'Mr. Andrew Carnegie and the Re-Union of the English Speaking Race', *Westminster Review* 163:6 (June 1905), pp. 636–642.

13 See P. Galison and D.J. Stump, *The Disunity of Science: Boundaries, Contexts, and Power* (Stanford, CA: Stanford University Press, 1996); T.A. Graham, 'Conceptualizing the (Dis)unity of Science', *Philosophy of Science* 71:2 (April 2004),

pp. 133–155; J. Dupré, 'The Disunity of Science' *Mind* 92:367 (n.s., July 1983), pp. 321–346; H. Margenau, 'Foundations of the Unity of Science', *Philosophical Review* 50:4 (July 1941), pp. 431–439.

14 See the translation, A-L-G de Staël, *Germany*, ed. by O.W. Wright, 2 vols (New York, Derby and Jackson, 1859), vol. 2, p. 285. See G.J. Somsen, 'A History of Universalism: Conceptions of the Internationality of Science from the Enlightenment to the Cold War', *Minerva* 46:361 (September 2008); R.M. Mikulski, 'Anglo-American Networks and the Early Academic Profession, 1815–1861' (unpublished doctoral thesis, State University of New York at Buffalo, 2014).

15 C. Hall, 'The Rule of Difference: Gender, Class and Empire in the Making of the 1832 Reform Act', in *Gendered Nations: Nationalisms and Gender Order in the Long Nineteenth Century*, ed. by I. Blom, K. Hagemann and C. Hall (Oxford: Berg, 2000) p. 107.

16 D. Rabin, *Britain and Its Internal Others, 1750–1800: Under Rule of Law* (Manchester: Manchester University Press, 2017); see also C. Hall, K. McClelland, and J. Rendall, *Defining the Victorian Nation: Class, Race, Gender and the British Reform Act of 1867* (Cambridge: Cambridge University Press, 2000); C. Hall, *Civilising Subjects: Metropole and Colony in the English Imagination, 1830–1867* (Cambridge: Polity Press, 2002).

17 Sir Richard Temple argued, *Cosmopolitan Essays* (London: Chapman, 1886), p. 137: 'It is violent disunion among themselves that has caused the Indians to be a subject-nation for many centuries; they think, then, that it is the ultimate union among her sons, despite differences of opinion, which makes England the mistress'; C.T. Metcalfe, *The Life and Correspondence of Charles, Lord Metcalfe: From Unpublished Letters and Journals Preserved by Himself, His Family, and His Friends* (London: R. Bentley, 1854), vol. 1, p. 243, 'In the disunion of the Sikhs there were elements both of safety and of danger to the British'; H.M. Stanley, *How I Found Livingstone: Travels, Adventures and Discoveries in Central Africa*, 2nd edn (London: Sampson, Low, Marston, Low and Searle, 1872), p. 218, on the Wakimbu tribe, 'But here, as elsewhere, disunion makes them weak'.

18 'Union of Papists and Dissenters to Achieve the Disunion of Church and State', *Fraser's Magazine* 13, May 1836, p. 519.

19 'No Success Without Union', *Coventry Herald*, 5 November 1847.

20 On a world's temperance union, see comments pro and anti-, including caustic comment of John Dunlop, T. Beggs, *The Proceedings of the World's Temperance Convention: Held in London, Aug. 4th and Four Following Days, with the Papers Laid Before the Convention, Letters Read, Statistics and General Information Presented* (London: Gilpin, 1846), p. 45, 'There was a difference betwixt the word union – and the thing union. If begun it would contain within itself the elements of disunion'. The International Telegraph Union was formed in 1865. The Woman's Christian Temperance Union was established in 1875, and the Women's Social and Political Union was formed in 1903. On transatlantic labour see S. Parfitt, *Knights across the Atlantic: The Knights of Labor in Britain and Ireland* (Liverpool: Liverpool University Press, 2016).

21 M. Brown, 'Transatlantic Reformers: Politics, Gender and Prostitution in the British and American Women's Movements, 1830–1900' (unpublished doctoral thesis, University of London, 2016).

22 Thus, for example, in discussing absolute monarchy and the British polity, *Britannia Languens, or a Discourse of Trade: Shewing the Grounds and Reasons of the Increase and Decay of Land-Rents, National Wealth and Strength* (London: 1680): 'a great part of the transcendent Policy of this our Form of Government consists in the high Obligations and means of a Union' between prince and parliament.

23 See comment, in K.H. Digby, *Compitum, or the Meeting of the Ways at the Catholic Church* (London: Dolman, 1854) p. 592, on disunion and the afterlife; and on disunion and Christian dogma, see August Neander's work, translated by J.E. Ryland, *Lectures on the History of Christian Dogmas*, 2 vols (London: H.G. Bohn, 1858), vol. 1; and for expression in verse, C.H. Hitchings, 'Souls Disunion', *The Ladies' Companion*, 1 December 1851, p. 253. On death as disunion, see Thomas Browne's *Hydrotaphia* (1658), ch. 1.

24 In theology, take, for example, Isaac Watts's discussion, 'The Doctrine of Unions, is one of the most unknown and unsearchable Difficulties in natural Philosophy', in *The Glory of Christ as God-Man Display'd, in 3 Discourses. With an Appendix* (London: Oswald, 1746); and Thomas Flower's *The Doctrine of Union between Christ and the Believer: Being the Substance of Thirteen Sermons* (London: Ward, 1740). For Victorian usage, see J. Cox, *The Believer's Position and Prospects; or, Thoughts on Union to Christ* (London: Ward, 1856). For understanding of Jewish conceptions of disunion and union, see Joseph Caryll on Job, 'The reason which they give of it is this, because then was the first disunion, that made the first second that ever was; all before was one (*sub unissimo Deo*) under the One-most God. But to leave this fancy to the Jewish doctors, among many others of the like nature, there is somewhat in the notion itself, namely, that division and disunion are the evils of the creature, all natural disunions are the afflictions of natural things'. Quoted in *Things New and Old: Or, A Storehouse of Similes, Sentences, Allegories, Apophthegms, Adages, Apologues, Divine, Moral, Political, & c., with Their Several Applications. Collected and Observed from the Writings and Sayings of the Learned in All Ages to this Present* (London: Tegg, 1869), vol. 2, p. 217.

25 And 'disunion' has been applied to study of Machiavelli, see V. Kahn, 'Reduction and the Praise of Disunion in Machiavelli's "Discourses"', *Journal of Medieval and Renaissance Studies* 18:1 (1988), pp. 1–19.

26 R. Clarke, *A Sermon Preach'd Before the Honourable House of Commons, at St. Margaret's, Westminster, on Wednesday, Feb. 4, 1740–1* (London: E. Say, 1741), p. 13.

27 See R. Kersh, *Dreams of a More Perfect Union* (Ithaca, NY: Cornell University Press, 2001), p. 43.

28 Kersh, *Dreams of a more Perfect Union*, p. 26, referring to the parable of the shepherd's staff of union, from Zechariah 2. Kersh cites the work of D.H. Fischer, *Albion's Seed: Four British Folkways in America* (1989) on the 'importance of unity' to Puritan sermonic discourse into the eighteenth century, p. 26: the words of Edwards, *A Humble Attempt to Promote Explicit Agreement and Visible Union in God's People* (Boston, 1747) are quoted by Fischer at p. 190 of *Albion's Seed*.

29 By the by, William Hazlitt, 'Lecture 7', in W.C. Hazlitt, ed., *Lectures on the English Poets, and the English Comic Writers* (London: G. Bell, 1876), p. 175, contrasts Burns with William Wordsworth on the basis of the latter's 'total disunion and divorce of the faculties of the mind from those of the body'.

30 *Transactions of the Social Union. Formed for the Improvement of Civil Society* (London: T. Becket; J. Johnson; Debrett; T. Hookham; and White and Son, 1790), p. 4.

31 T. Laycock, *Mind and Brain: Or, the Correlations of Consciousness and Organisation; with Their Applications to Philosophy, Zoology, Physiology, Mental Pathology, and the Practice of Medicine* (Edinburgh: Sutherland and Knox, 1860), vol. 2, p. 125.

32 As the OED notes, of the usage of 'cement', quoting from Edward Irving, *Babylon* (1826) I. iii. 246 Faith is the cement of all domestic and social union.

33 'Christian Union', *Eclectic Review*, June 1845, pp. 664–684 [p. 664], reviewing Essays on Christian Union (London: Hamilton, Adams).
34 J. Morley, *On Compromise* (London: Chapman and Hall, 1874), p. 96. The work refers on several occasions to 'social union' in terms of the bonds of a society.
35 For example, 'The Social Disunion of the Nation', *The Spectator*, 5 November 1892, p. 641. See also the temperance and moral reformer, Joseph Livesey, 'The Disunion of Society, and the Means of Removing It', *The Moral Reformer* 2:10 (October 1832), pp. 293–298.
36 E. Carpenter, *Civilisation: Its Causes, and Cure and Other Essays* (London: Sonnenschein, 1889), p. 25.
37 The Albany 'Plan of Union' involving Benjamin Franklin, also drew on British concerns about the colonies' security in the 1750s: Timothy Shannon argues, 'the idea of colonial union owed as much to British officials as it did to colonial Americans', *Indians and Colonists at the Crossroads of Empire: The Albany Congress of 1754* (Ithaca, NY: Cornell University Press, 2002), pp. 55–56. References to 'union' in Franklin's writings, and among other leading American rebels are discussed in Kersh, *Dreams of a More Perfect Union*, p. 40, and see more broadly his analysis of union usage, 1764–1773 through newspapers to study 'Americans' propensity to express national sentiments in the language of union' (p. 39).
38 See E.R. Varon, *Disunion!: The Coming of the American Civil War, 1789–1859* (Chapel Hill: University of North Carolina Press, 2008), on the discourse of disunion.
39 C.J. Riethmüller, *Alexander Hamilton and His Contemporaries; or, The Rise of the American Constitution* (London: Bell & Daldy, 1864), pp. 123–124.
40 C. Mackay, *Life and Liberty in America: Or, Sketches of a Tour in the United...*, vol. 2, p. 184.
41 R.C. Pell, *Forward or Backward?* (New York: Miller, 1863), p. 4.
42 R. Cobden, 'The American Constitution at the Present Crisis. Causes of the Civil War in America. By J. Lothrop Motley Manwaring', *National Review*, October, 1861.
43 For example, Laycock, *Mind and Brain*, vol. 2, pp. 122–123.
44 For imperial-focussed discourse on union and disunion, see C.J. Rowe, *Bonds of Disunion; Or, English Misrule in the Colonies* (London: Longmans, Green, 1883) pp. 1–2: 'those political measures for the government of our Colonies which, while intended to weld the empire into one harmonious whole, whereof each part should derive its laws from a common centre, were, and under any circumstances would be, so many centrifugal forces tending to disunion between England and her Colonies. Every now and again we are regaled with some elaborated scheme of quasi-legislative union between Great Britain and her Colonies wherever situate'. See also, for review, *The Athenaeum* 2928 (8 December 1883), pp. 737–738.
45 From the vast historiography on British trade unions we note G.R. Boyer, 'What Did Unions Do in Nineteenth-Century Britain?' *Journal of Economic History* 48:2 (June 1988), pp. 319–332; E.F. Biagini, 'British Trade Unions and Popular Political Economy, 1860–1880', *Historical Journal* 30:4 (December 1987), pp. 811–840 and E.J. Hobsbawm, 'General Labour Unions in Britain, 1889–1914', *Economic History Review*, 1:2/3 (n.s., 1949), pp. 123–142. There is no space here, to discuss union and disunion as themes in radical British discourse, with its flourishing languages of union in relation to popular politics, organisations of trades, and in promoting new attempts to create societies outside conventional politics and economic relations; or the anti-radical critique of union.
46 G. Ramsay, *Political Discourses* (London: Adam and Charles Black, 1838), p. 301.

47 On the debates leading to the welfare reforms brought about by the New Poor Law (1834 4 & 5 Will. IV c. 76), see the multi-volume evidence of witnesses compiled in the 'Royal Commission of Inquiry into Administration and Practical Operation of Poor Laws', *Parliamentary Papers*, 1834, No. 44, Vols. 27–39, pp. 1–8323.

48 *The Bude Light: A Social ... Skiterary Monthly Illuminator* (London: Cunningham, 1841), p. 145.

49 *A Dictionary of the English Language* (London: Pickering, 1828), vol. 1.

50 'Bishop Jewel; His Character, Correspondence, and Apologetic Treatises', *The British Critic*, July 1841, p. 2: 'Too many of us speak as if we had gained more by the Reformation (that deplorable schism) in freedom, than we have lost by it in disunion'.

51 See *Report on the Proceedings at the Reunion Conference held at Bonn between the 10th and the 16th of August, 1875* (London: Pickering, 1876), including Dr P. Schaff's comments p. 79: 'We do not want an absorptive union or a dead uniformity, but a living unity in liberty, and liberty in unity'. See T.L. Strange, *The Sources and Development of Christianity* (London: Trübner, 1875), pp. ix–x 'if even the semblance of union was to be secured, it could only be by the parties engaged casting a cloak of charity over their diverging opinions'.

52 See *World's Congress of Religions* (Boston, MA: Arena, 1893), J. Gmeiner, 'Primitive and Prospective Religious Union of the Human Family', which hoped in the 'comparatively near future' for this 'union of mankind' to be 'fitly crowned by religious unity' (p. 182); the other quotation, p. 304, is from Kinza Ringem, Hirai of Japan.

53 A. Summers, *Christian and Jewish Women in Britain, 1880–1940: Living with Difference* (Basingstoke: Palgrave Macmillan, 2017).

54 F.G. Lee, *Memorials of the Late Rev. Robert Stephen Hawker, M. A.: Sometime Vicar of Morwenstow, in the Diocese of Exeter* (London: Chatto and Windus, 1876) p. 151.

55 *Dublin Monitor*, 26 November 1840.

56 L. Tolstoy (C. Garnett, transl.) *'The Kingdom of God Is within You', Christianity Not as a Mystic Religion but as a New Theory of Life* (New York: Cassell, 1894), p. 341.

57 J.-J. Rousseau's *Emile*, Book 5 refers to 'disunion of hearts', let all possible calamities be accumulated on two affectionate and congenial spirits, they will find more true happiness in weeping together than they would have found in all the riches of the world, poisoned by the disunion of heart (qu'ils n'en auroient dans toutes les fortunes de la terre, empoisonnées par la désunion des cœurs'), the translation here being T.L. Peacock's. See his novel *Melincourt* (London: Printed for T. Hookham, Jun. and Co, 1817), p. 171.

58 L.J. Harris, *State of the Marital Union: Rhetoric, Identity, and Nineteenth-Century Marriage Controversies* (Waco, TX: Baylor University Press, 2014), p. 129.

59 E. West, *Chains of Love: Slave Couples in Antebellum South Carolina* (Urbana: University of Illinois Press, 2004).

60 Sermon 17, 'Of Envy and Contention', *Sermons, Chiefly Intended to Promote Faith, Hope, and Charity. By Vicesimus Knox, D.D* (Dublin: Printed by John Ershaw, 1792), p. 365.

61 J.S. Mill, 'On Marriage, 1832–33?', in *The Collected Works of John Stuart Mill*, vol. 21 *Essays on Equality, Law, and Education*, ed. by J.M. Robson (Toronto: University of Toronto Press, 1984), pp. 37–49 [p. 47].

62 J. Bentham, *Introduction to the Study of The Works of Jeremy Bentham* (Edinburgh: W. Tait, 1843) vol. 1, p. 354; [H. Mill], 'Enfranchisement of Women'*Westminster and Foreign Quarterly Review* 55 (July 1851), pp. 289–311.

63 'Family Disunion', *Leader and Saturday Analyst* 9:453 (27 November 1858), p. 1290.

64 See J.M. Allan, *The Intellectual Severance of Men and Women* (London: T.C. Newby, 1860), p. 6.

65 On these and the mobilisation of other complaints against women's greater freedoms, see S. Crozier-De Rosa, *Shame and the Anti-Feminist Backlash: Britain, Ireland and Australia 1890–1920* (New York: Routledge, 2018).

66 'The Enfranchisement of Female Freeholders and Householders', *Journal of Social Science* 1 (1866), p. 615; D.M. Craik, *Studies from Life* (London: Hurst and Blackett, 1862), p. 257.

67 The phrase is from Jackson's proclamation regarding nullification, 10 December 1833.

68 See from Hegel's *Logic*, 'We must know that the Progressus is the alternation of the union and of the disunion of the two moments; and, again, we must know that the union and disunion are themselves inseparable' J.H. Stirling, *The Secret of Hegel: Being the Hegelian System in Origin, Principle, Form, and Matter: In Two Volumes* (London: Longman, Green, Longman, Roberts and Green, 1865), vol. 2, pp. 153–154.

69 E.P. Hood, *The Age and Its Architects: Ten Chapters on the English People in Relation to the Times* (London: Gilpin, 1850), p. 423.

70 This sentiment is suggested as being in decline, in C.J. Shebbeare's *The Greek Theory of the State and the Nonconformist Conscience: A Socialistic Defence of Some Ancient Institutions* (London: Methuen, 1895), p. 63.

71 'Recent Developments of Tractarianism', reprinted in H. Rogers, *Essays, Selected from Contributions to the Edinburgh Review* (London: Longman, Brown, Green and Longmans, 1855), vol. 1, p. 152.

72 R. Cobden, *Speeches on Questions of Public Policy. Vol. 2 (War, Peace, and Reform)* (London: T. Fisher, Unwin, 1870, p. 603, from House of Commons debate, 22 May 1851.

73 I. Golovine, *The Russian Sketch-Book*, 2 vols (London: T.C. Newby, 1848), vol. 1, p. 64.

74 C. Lamb, *Elia. The Last Essays of Elia*, 4 vols (London: Moxon, 1855), vol. 3, p. 92.

75 See, for instance, the repetitious treatment of union in James Hinton's self-published *Selections from Manuscripts*, vol. 1 (London: 1856), including: union of absolute law and liberty (p. 535), and 'polar' unions.

76 C. Crowe, *The Night Side of Nature, Or, Ghosts and Ghost Seers,* 2 vols (London: T.C. Newby, 1849), vol. 1, pp. 170–171.

77 *Eastbourne Gazette*, 26 January 1881.

78 S. Butler, *Luck, or Cunning as the Main Means of Organic Modification?: An Attempt to Throw Additional Light upon the Late Mr. Charles Darwin's Theory of Natural Selection* (London: Trübner, 1887).

79 H. Spencer, *Social Statics: Or, the Conditions Essential to Human Happiness Specified, and the First of Them Developed* (London: J. Chapman, 1851), p. 282.

80 G. Harris, *Civilization Considered as a Science, in Relation to Its Essence, Its Elements, and Its End* (London: Bell and Daldy, 1861).

81 W. Donisthorpe, *Individualism: A System of Politics* (New York: Macmillan, 1894), p. 15.

82 *Tipperary Free Press*, 1 October 1831; *Kilkenny Journal*, 4 December 1847.

83 *Newry Telegraph*, 9 January 1847. See also the references to 'disunion' in John Denvir's *The Irish in Britain: From the Earliest Times to the Fall and Death of Parnell* (London: Kegan Paul, Trench, Trübner, 1894).

84 E. Herries, *Memoir of the Public Life of the Right Hon. John Charles Herries in the Reigns of George III., George IV., William IV. and Victoria* (London: J. Murray, 1880), vol. 2.

85   For example, 'Union and Disunion', *Saturday Review of Politics, Literature, Science and Art* 62:1610 (4 September 1886), pp. 310–311.

86   The comment is Kinahan Cornwallis's, *The New El Dorado: Or, British Columbia* (London: T.C. Newby, 1858), p. 308.

87   Laycock, *Mind and Brain*, vol. 2, p. 127.

88   See J.E.H. Ford, 'The Art of Union and Disunion in the Houses of Parliament, 1834–1928' (unpublished doctoral thesis, University of Nottingham, 2016).

89   Thus the Royal Academician's James Barry's design, in the British Museum collection, 1868, 0612.2142, and such ephemera as 'The Union Song', a print by Peltro William Tonkins (1801), and also his 'Union Wreath' of the same year. Decorated fans presented the 'United Sisters (Ashton and Hadwen); the Repeal movement would stimulate such graphic comments as the cartoonist George Cruikshank's 'The Queen and the Union', with O'Connell poised above the two female personifications, arms joined in amity, ready to hack them apart with the axe of repeal (1843). *Inter alia*, an old meaning of 'union' was harmony in colour and design.

90   L.C. Olson, *Benjamin Franklin's Vision of American Community: A Study in Rhetorical Iconology* (Columbia: University of South Carolina Press, 2004), ch.3. See, for instance, the Currier and Ives lithograph showing the apotheosis of George Washington, 'The Spirit of The Union' (1860), 'The Great Disunion Serpent', reproduced in A.B. Maurice and F.T. Cooper, *The History of the Nineteenth Century in Caricature* (New York: Dodd, Mead, 1904), p. 158; and 'Young America Rising At The Ballot Box And Strangling The Serpents Disunion And Secession' *Harper's Weekly*, 1 September 1860; and J.M. Nevin's Two Engravings, 'The Spirits Abroad – The Spirit of Union' and 'The Spirits Abroad – The Spirit of Disunion', *Harper's Weekly*, 28 July 1860.

91   See J.R. Stilgoe, 'Disjunction, Disunion, Daguerreotype' in his *Landscape and Images* (Charlottesville: University of Virginia Press, 2005).

92   See A. Ravenhill-Johnson, *The Art and Ideology of the Trade Union Emblem, 1850–1925* (London: Anthem, 2013), p. 32, on the common trade-union symbol of the clasped hands. For earlier gloss on the fable of the rods or fasces, another motif of union, see *Fables of Aesop and Other Eminent Mythologisto with Morals and Reflecions by Roger L'Estronge* (London: Sare, 1692), p. 62.

93   Lithograph by M. Alophe, *Hail! Happy Union! The State Visit to the Royal Italian Opera, on Thursday, April 19th, 1855* (Paris and New York: Goupil et Cie, 1855), British Museum, 1982, U.2062.

94   *Courtship and Wedlock* (London: T.C. Newby, 1850).

95   *A Warning to Wives: Or, The Platonic Lover, by the Author of 'Cousin Geoffrey'* (London: T.C. Newby, 1847), vol. 2, p. 27.

96   C. Crewe, *Linny Lockwood. A Novel*, 2 vols (London: Routledge, 1854), vol. 2, p. 39.

97   C. Reade, *Hard Cash, a Matter-of-Fact Romance* (London: Chatto and Windus, 1888), p. 98.

98   D. Wallace, '"Two Nations at War Within It": Marriage as Metaphor in Margiad Evans's *Country Dance* (1932)', in *Rediscovering Margiad Evans: Marginality, Gender and Illness*, ed. by K. Bohata and K. Gramich (Cardiff: University of Wales Press, 2013), pp. 24–38, citing Scott's *Waverley* (we should also include *Redgauntlet*) and Owenson's *The Wild Irish Girl*. See also 'The Jacobite, the Marriage Plot, and the End of Scottish History' in M.M. Martin, *Mighty Scot, The: Nation, Gender, and the Nineteenth-Century Mystique of Scottish Masculinity* (Albany: State University of New York Press, 2009). The point is also made in M. Campbell, *Irish Poetry under the Union, 1801–1924* (Cambridge University Press, 2014), p. 15. For British poetry on union and reunion, P.M. Ball, *The Heart's Events: The Victorian Poetry of Relationships* (London: The Athlone Press, 1976).

99 For *Uncle Tom's Cabin* and *The Sword and the Distaff* as comment on the national union, see P. Okker, 'Serial Politics in William Gilmore Simm's *Woodcraft*', in *Periodical Literature in Nineteenth-Century America*, ed. by K.M. Price and S. Belasco Smith (Charlottesville, VA: University of Virginia Press, 1995), p. 162; on 'romance of reunion' see K. Keely, 'Marriage Plots and National reunion: The Trope of Romantic Reconciliation in Postbellum Literature', *Mississippi Quarterly* 51 (1998), pp. 621–648. See H. Levine, 'Union and Disunion in "Song of Myself"', *American Literature* 59:4 (December 1987), pp. 570–589.

100 'Co-operation', *Victoria Magazine*, May 1868, pp. 50–56 [p. 50].

101 J.L. O'Sullivan, *Union, Disunion, and Reunion: A Letter to General Franklin Pierce, Ex-president of the United States* (London: R. Bentley, 1862). For British views, see J.J. Barnes and P.P. Barnes, *The American Civil War Through British Eyes Dispatches from British Diplomats: November 1860–April 1862* (Kent, Ohio: Kent State University Press, 2003); B.E. Kinser, *The American Civil War in the Shaping of British Democracy* (London: Routledge, 2011).

102 For example, Senia Pašeta has provided an excellent and nuanced analysis of continuity and change in the attitudes of Irish women nationalists from the turn of the century up to the end of the Great War: see S. Pašeta, *Irish Nationalist Women, 1900–1918* (Cambridge: Cambridge University Press, 2013).

103 See L. Colley, *Acts of Union and Acts of Disunion: What Has Held the UK Together – and What Is Dividing It?* (London: Profile Books, 2014); A.I. Macinnes, *Union and Empire: The Making of the United Kingdom in 1707* (Cambridge: Cambridge University Press, 2007), L. Colley, *Britons: Forging the Nation 1707–1837* (New Haven: Yale University Press, 1992); R. Saunders, *Yes to Europe! The 1975 Referendum and Seventies Britain* (Cambridge: Cambridge University Press, 2018).

Bibliography

'Anglo-American Union', *The Review of Reviews*, March 1896, p. 323.

'Bishop Jewel; His Character, Correspondence, and Apologetic Treatises', *The British Critic*, July 1841, p. 2.

'Christian Union', *Eclectic Review*, June 1845, pp. 664–684.

'Family Disunion', *Leader and Saturday Analyst* 9:453 (27 November 1858), p. 1290.

'Royal Commission of Inquiry into Administration and Practical Operation of Poor Laws', *Parliamentary Papers*, 1834, no. 44, vols. 27–39.

'The Enfranchisement of Female Freeholders and Householders', *Journal of Social Science* 1 (1866), p. 615.

'The Social Disunion of the Nation', *The Spectator*, 5 November 1892, p. 641.

'Union and Disunion', *Saturday Review of Politics, Literature, Science and Art* 62:1610 (4 September 1886), pp. 310–311.

A Dictionary of the English Language (London: Pickering, 1828), vol. 1.

A Warning to Wives: Or, The Platonic Lover, by the Author of 'Cousin Geoffrey' (London: T.C. Newby, 1847), vol. 2.

Allan, J.M. *The Intellectual Severance of Men and Women* (London: T.C. Newby, 1860).

Alophe, M. *Hail! Happy Union! The State Visit to the Royal Italian Opera, on Thursday, April 19th, 1855* (Paris and New York: Goupil et Cie, 1855).

Anon. *Britannia Languens, or a Discourse of Trade: Shewing the Grounds and Reasons of the Increase and Decay of Land-Rents, National Wealth and Strength* (London: Printed for Tho. Dring and Sam. Crouch, 1680).

Anon. 'Co-operation', *Victoria Magazine*, May 1868, pp. 50–56.

Anon. 'No Success without Union', *Coventry Herald*, 5 November 1847.

Anon. 'Union of Papists and Dissenters to Achieve the Disunion of Church and State', *Fraser's Magazine* 13, May 1836, p. 519.

Anthony, E. 'Mr. Andrew Carnegie and the Re-Union of the English Speaking Race', *Westminster Review* 163:6 (June 1905), pp. 636–642.

Ball, P.M. *The Heart's Events: The Victorian Poetry of Relationships* (London: The Athlone Press, 1976).

Barnes, J.J. and P.P. Barnes, *The American Civil War through British Eyes Dispatches from British Diplomats: November 1860–April 1862* (Kent, OH: Kent State University Press, 2003).

Beggs, T. *The Proceedings of the World's Temperance Convention: Held in London, Aug. 4th and Four Following Days, with the Papers Laid Before the Convention, Letters Read, Statistics and General Information Presented* (London: Gilpin, 1846).

Bentham, J. *Introduction to The Study of The Works of Jeremy Bentham* (Edinburgh: Tait, 1843), vol. 1.

Biagini, E.F. 'British Trade Unions and Popular Political Economy, 1860–1880', *Historical Journal* 30:4 (December 1987), pp. 811–840.

Boyer, B.R. 'What Did Unions Do in Nineteenth-Century Britain?' *Journal of Economic History* 48:2 (June 1988), pp. 319–332.

Brown, M. 'Transatlantic Reformers: Politics, Gender and Prostitution in the British and American Women's Movements, 1830–1900' (unpublished doctoral thesis, University of London, 2016).

Browne, T. *Hydrotaphia*, ch. 1.

Butler, S. *Luck, or Cunning as the Main Means of Organic Modification?: An Attempt to Throw Additional Light upon the Late Mr. Charles Darwin's Theory of Natural Selection* (London: Trübner, 1887).

Campbell, M. *Irish Poetry under the Union, 1801–1924* (Cambridge: Cambridge University Press, 2014).

Carpenter, E. *Civilisation: Its Causes, and Cure and Other Essays* (London: Sonnenschein, 1889).

Carter, N. *Britain, Ireland and the Italian Risorgimento* (Basingstoke: Palgrave Macmillan, 2015).

Clarke, R. *A Sermon Preach'd Before the Honourable House of Commons, at St. Margaret's, Westminster, on Wednesday, Feb. 4, 1740–1* (London: E. Say, 1741).

Cobden, R. 'The American Constitution at the Present Crisis. Causes of the Civil War in America. By J. Lothrop Motley Manwaring', *National Review*, October, 1861.

Cobden, R. *Speeches on Questions of Public Policy. Vol. 2 (War, Peace, and Reform)* (London: T. Fisher, Unwin, 1870).

Colley, L. *Acts of Union and Acts of Disunion: What Has Held the UK Together – and What Is Dividing It?* (London: Profile Books, 2014).

Colley, L. *Britons: Forging the Nation 1707–1837* (New Haven, CT: Yale University Press, 1992).

Cornwallis, K. *The New El Dorado: Or, British Columbia* (London: T.C. Newby, 1858).

Courtship and Wedlock (London: T.C. Newby, 1850).

Cox, J. *The Believer's Position and Prospects; or, Thoughts on Union to Christ* (London: Ward, 1856).

Craik, D.M. *Studies from Life* (London: Hurst and Blackett, 1862).

Crewe, C. *Linny Lockwood. A Novel,* 2 vols (London: Routledge, 1854), vol. 2.

Crowe, C. *The Night Side of Nature, Or, Ghosts and Ghost Seers,* 2 vols (London: T.C. Newby, 1849), vol. 1.

Crozier-De Rosa, S. *Shame and the Anti-Feminist Backlash: Britain, Ireland and Australia 1890–1920* (New York: Routledge, 2018).

Denvir, J. *The Irish in Britain: From the Earliest Times to the Fall and Death of Parnell* (London: Kegan Paul, Trench, Trübner, 1894).

Digby, K.H. *Compitum, or the Meeting of the Ways at the Catholic Church* (London: Dolman, 1854).

Donisthorpe, W. *Individualism: A System of Politics* (New York: Macmillan, 1894), p. 15.

Dublin Monitor, 26 November 1840.

Dunckley, H. *The Charter of the Nations: Or, Free Trade and Its Results. An Essay on the Recent Commercial Policy of the United Kingdom, to which the Council of the National Anti-corn Law League Awarded Their First Prize* (London: Cash, 1854).

Dupré, J. 'The Disunity of Science' *Mind* 92:367 (n.s., July 1983), pp. 321–346.

Eastbourne Gazette, 26 January 1881.

Einaudi, L.L. 'From the Franc to the "Europe": The Attempted Transformation of the Latin Monetary Union into a European Monetary Union, 1865–1873', *Economic History Review,* 53:2 (May 2000), pp. 284–308.

Flandreau, M. 'The Economics and Politics of Monetary Unions: A Reassessment of the Latin Monetary Union, 1865–71', *Financial History Review* 7:1 (2000), pp. 25–44.

Flower, T. *The Doctrine of Union between Christ and the Believer: Being the Substance of Thirteen Sermons* (London: Ward, 1740).

Ford, J. 'The Art of Union and Disunion in the Houses of Parliament, 1834–1928' (unpublished doctoral thesis, University of Nottingham, 2016).

Freeman, E.A. *Historical Essays* (London: Macmillan, 1892), vol. 3.

Galison, P. and D.J. Stump, *The Disunity of Science: Boundaries, Contexts, and Power* (Stanford, CA: Stanford University Press, 1996).

Golovine, I. *The Russian Sketch-Book,* 2 vols (London: T.C. Newby, 1848), vol. 1.

Graham, T.A. 'Conceptualizing the (Dis)unity of Science', *Philosophy of Science* 71:2 (April 2004), pp. 133–155.

Green, A. 'Representing Germany? The Zollverein at the World Exhibitions, 1851–1862', *Journal of Modern History* 75:4 (2003), pp. 836–863.

Hall, C. *Civilising Subjects: Metropole and Colony in the English Imagination, 1830–1867* (Cambridge: Polity Press, 2002).

Hall, C. 'The Rule of Difference: Gender, Class and Empire in the Making of the 1832 Reform Act', in *Gendered Nations: Nationalisms and Gender Order in the Long Nineteenth Century,* ed. by I. Blom, K. Hagemann, and C. Hall (Oxford: Berg, 2000), pp. 107–137.

Hall, C., K. McClelland, and J. Rendall, *Defining the Victorian Nation: Class, Race, Gender and the British Reform Act of 1867* (Cambridge: Cambridge University Press, 2000).

Harris, G. *Civilization Considered as a Science, in Relation to Its Essence, Its Elements, and Its End* (London: Bell and Daldy, 1861).

Harris, L.J. *State of the Marital Union: Rhetoric, Identity, and Nineteenth-Century Marriage Controversies* (Waco, TX: Baylor University Press, 2014).

Hazlitt, W.C. ed., *Lectures on the English Poets, and the English Comic Writers* (London: G. Bell, 1876).

Herries, E. *Memoir of the Public Life of the Right Hon. John Charles Herries in the Reigns of George III., George IV., William IV. and Victoria* (London: J. Murray, 1880), vol. 2.

Hinton, J. *Selections from Manuscripts*, vol. 1 (London: 1856).

Hitchings, C.H. 'Souls Disunion', *The Ladies' Companion*, 1 December 1851, p. 253.

Hobsbawm, E.J. 'General Labour Unions in Britain, 1889–1914', *Economic History Review*, 1:2/3 (n.s., 1949), pp. 123–142.

Hood, E.P. *The Age and Its Architects: Ten Chapters on the English People in Relation to the Times* (London: Gilpin, 1850).

Jones, R. *The Origin of Language and Nations* (London: Hughs, 1764).

Kahn, V. 'Reduction and the Praise of Disunion in Machiavelli's "Discourses"', *Journal of Medieval and Renaissance Studies* 18:1 (1988), pp. 1–19.

Keely, K. 'Marriage Plots and National reunion: The Trope of Romantic Reconciliation in Postbellum Literature', *Mississippi Quarterly* 51 (1998), pp. 621–648.

Keogh, D. and K. Whelan, eds, *Acts of Union: The Causes, Contexts and Consequences of the Act of Union* (Dublin: Four Courts, 2001).

Kersh, R. *Dreams of a More Perfect Union* (Ithaca, NY: Cornell University Press, 2001).

Kilkenny Journal, 4 December 1847.

Kinser, B.E. *The American Civil War in the Shaping of British Democracy* (London: Routledge, 2011).

Knox, V. *Sermons, Chiefly Intended to Promote Faith, Hope, and Charity. By Vicesimus Knox, D.D* (Dublin: Printed by John Ershaw, 1792).

Lamb, C. *Elia. The Last Essays of Elia*, 4 vols (London: Moxon, 1855), vol. 3.

Laycock, T. *Mind and Brain: Or, the Correlations of Consciousness and Organisation; with Their Applications to Philosophy, Zoology, Physiology, Mental Pathology, and the Practice of Medicine* (Edinburgh: Sutherland and Knox, 1860), vol. 2.

Lee, F.G. *Memorials of the Late Rev. Robert Stephen Hawker, M. A.: Sometime Vicar of Morwenstow, in the Diocese of Exeter* (London: Chatto and Windus, 1876).

Leiren, T. 'Catalysts to Disunion: Sigurd Ibsen and Ringeren, 1898–1899', *Scandinavian Studies* 71:3 (Fall 1999), pp. 297–310.

L'Estrange, R. *Fables of Aesop and Other Eminent Mythologisto with Morals and Reflecions* (London: Sare, 1692).

Levine, H. 'Union and Disunion in "Song of Myself"', *American Literature* 59:4 (December 1987), pp. 570–589.

Livesey, J. 'The Disunion of Society, and the Means of Removing It', *The Moral Reformer* 2:10 (October 1832), pp. 293–298.

Ludlow, J.M. 'The "Idea" of Nationality: Savoy', *Macmillan's Magazine*, March 1860, pp. 354–363.

Lundgren, R.E. *Norway-Sweden: Union, Disunion, and Scandinavian Integration* (Princeton, NJ: Princeton University Press, 1959).

Macinnes, A.I. *Union and Empire: The Making of the United Kingdom in 1707* (Cambridge: Cambridge University Press, 2007).

Mackay, C. *Life and Liberty in America: Or, Sketches of a Tour in the United States and Canada in 1857-8*, vol. 2. (New York: Harper and Brothers, 1859).

Maloney, J. 'Britain's Single Currency Debate of the Late 1860s', *European Journal of The History of Economic Thought* 13:4 (2006), pp. 513–531.

Margenau, H. 'Foundations of the Unity of Science', *Philosophical Review* 50:4 (July 1941), pp. 431–439.

Martin, M.M. *Mighty Scot, The: Nation, Gender, and the Nineteenth-Century Mystique of Scottish Masculinity* (Albany: State University of New York Press, 2009).

Maurice, A.B. and F.T. Cooper, *The History of the Nineteenth Century in Caricature* (New York: Dodd, Mead, 1904).

Metcalfe, C.T. *The Life and Correspondence of Charles, Lord Metcalfe: From Unpublished Letters and Journals Preserved by Himself, His Family, and His Friends* (London: R. Bentley, 1854), vol. 1.

Mikulski, R.M. 'Anglo-American Networks and the Early Academic Profession, 1815–1861' (unpublished doctoral thesis, State University of New York at Buffalo, 2014).

[Mill, H.], 'Enfranchisement of Women', *Westminster and Foreign Quarterly Review* 55 (July 1851), pp. 289–311.

Mill, J.S. 'On Marriage, 1832–33?', in *The Collected Works of John Stuart Mill*, vol. 21 *Essays on Equality, Law, and Education*, ed. by J.M. Robson (Toronto: University of Toronto Press, 1984), pp. 37–49.

Morley, J. *On Compromise* (London: Chapman and Hall, 1874).

Murdoch, A. ed., *Scotland and the Union 1707–2007* (Edinburgh: Edinburgh University Press, 2008).

Newry Telegraph, 9 January 1847.

Okker, P. 'Serial Politics in William Gilmore Simm's *Woodcraft*', in *Periodical Literature in Nineteenth-Century America*, ed. by K.M. Price and S. Belasco Smith (Charlottesville: University of Virginia Press, 1995).

Olson, L.C. *Benjamin Franklin's Vision of American Community: A Study in Rhetorical Iconology* (Columbia: University of South Carolina Press, 2004), ch. 3.

Oxford English Dictionary.

Parfitt, S. *Knights across the Atlantic: The Knights of Labor in Britain and Ireland* (Liverpool: Liverpool University Press, 2016).

Pašeta, S. *Irish Nationalist Women, 1900–1918* (Cambridge: Cambridge University Press, 2013).

Paton, A. *Highlands and Islands of the Adriatic: Including Dalmatia, Croatia, and the Southern Provinces of the Austrian Empire* (London: Chapman and Hall, 1849), vol. 2.

Peacock, T.L. *Melincourt* (London: Printed for T. Hookham, Jun. and Co, 1817).

Pell, R.C. *Forward or Backward?* (New York: Miller, 1863).

Rabin, D. *Britain and Its Internal Others, 1750–1800: Under Rule of Law* (Manchester: Manchester University Press, 2017).

Raffe, A. '1707, 2007, and the Unionist Turn in Scottish History', *Historical Journal* 53:4 (2010), pp. 1071–1083.

Ramsay, G. *Political Discourses* (London: Adam and Charles Black, 1838).

Ravenhill-Johnson, A. *The Art and Ideology of the Trade Union Emblem, 1850–1925* (London: Anthem, 2013).

Reade, C. *Hard Cash, a Matter-of-Fact Romance* (London: Chatto and Windus, 1888).

Report on the Proceedings at the Reunion Conference held at Bonn between the 10th and the 16th of August, 1875 (London: Pickering, 1876).

Riethmüller, C.J. *Alexander Hamilton and His Contemporaries; or, The Rise of the American Constitution* (London: Bell & Daldy, 1864).

Rogers, H. *Essays, Selected from Contributions to the Edinburgh Review* (London: Longman, Brown, Green and Longmans, 1855), vol. 1.

Rowe, C.J. *Bonds of Disunion; Or, English Misrule in the Colonies* (London: Longmans, Green, 1883).

Ryland, J.E. *Lectures on the History of Christian Dogmas,* 2 vols (London: H.G. Bohn, 1858), vol. 1.

Saunders, R. *Yes to Europe! The 1975 Referendum and Seventies Britain* (Cambridge: Cambridge University Press, 2018).

Sayce, A.H. *Introduction to the Science of Language* (London: Kegan Paul, 1880), vol. 1.

Shannon, T. *Indians and Colonists at the Crossroads of Empire: The Albany Congress of 1754* (Ithaca, NY: Cornell University Press, 2002).

Shebbeare, C.J. *The Greek Theory of the State and the Nonconformist Conscience: A Socialistic Defence of Some Ancient Institutions* (London: Methuen, 1895).

Shiue, C.H. 'From Political Fragmentation towards a Customs Union: Border Effects of the German Zollverein, 1815 to 1855', *European Review of Economic History* 9:2 (2005), pp. 129–162.

Somsen, G.J. 'A History of Universalism: Conceptions of the Internationality of Science from the Enlightenment to the Cold War', *Minerva*, 46 (September 2008), p. 361.

Spedding, J. et al., eds., *The Works of Francis Bacon,* Vol. 10 (London: Longmans, Green, Reader and Dyer, 1868).

Spencer, H. *Social Statics: Or, the Conditions Essential to Human Happiness Specified, and the First of Them Developed* (London: J. Chapman, 1851).

Staël, A-L-G de. *Germany,* ed. by O.W. Wright, 2 vols (New York, Derby and Jackson, 1859), vol. 2.

Stanley, H.M. *How I Found Livingstone: Travels, Adventures and Discoveries in Central Africa,* 2nd edn (London: Sampson, Low, Marston, Low and Searle, 1872).

Stilgoe, J.R. *Landscape and Images* (Charlottesville: University of Virginia Press, 2005).

Stirling, J.H. *The Secret of Hegel: Being the Hegelian System in Origin, Principle, Form, and Matter: In Two Volumes* (London: Longman, Green, Longman, Roberts and Green, 1865), vol. 2.

Strange, T.L. *The Sources and Development of Christianity* (London: Trübner, 1875).

Summers, A. *Christian and Jewish Women in Britain, 1880–1940: Living with Difference* (Basingstoke: Palgrave Macmillan, 2017).

Temple, R. *Cosmopolitan Essays* (London: Chapman, 1886).

The Athenaeum 2928 (8 December 1883), pp. 737–738.

The Bude Light: A Social ... Skiterary Monthly Illuminator (London: Cunningham, 1841).

Things New and Old: Or, A Storehouse of Similes, Sentences, Allegories, Apophthegms, Adages, Apologues, Divine, Moral, Political, &c., with Their Several Applications. Collected and Observed from the Writings and Sayings of the Learned in All Ages to this Present (London: Tegg, 1869), vol. 2.

Tipperary Free Press, 1 October 1831.

Tolstoy, L. (C. Garnett, transl.) *'The Kingdom of God Is within You,' Christianity Not as a Mystic Religion but as a New Theory of Life* (New York: Cassell, 1894).

Tonkins, P.W. 'The Union Song' (1801).

Tonkins, P.W. 'Union Wreath' (1801).

Transactions of the Social Union. Formed for the Improvement of Civil Society (London: T. Becket; J. Johnson; Debrett; T. Hookham; and White and Son, 1790).

Tucker, A.L. '"Newest Born of Nations": Southern Thought on European Nationalisms and the Creation of the Confederacy, 1820–1865' (unpublished doctoral thesis, University of South Carolina, 2014).

Union, Disunion, and Reunion: A Letter to General Franklin Pierce, Ex-president of the United States (London: R. Bentley, 1862).

Varon, E.R. *Disunion!: The Coming of the American Civil War, 1789–1859* (Chapel Hill: University of North Carolina Press, 2008).

Wallace, D. '"Two Nations at War within It": Marriage as Metaphor in Margiad Evans's *Country Dance* (1932)', in *Rediscovering Margiad Evans: Marginality, Gender and Illness*, ed. by K. Bohata and K. Gramich (Cardiff: University of Wales Press, 2013), pp. 24–38.

Watts, I. *The Glory of Christ as God-Man Display'd, in 3 Discourses. With an Appendix* (London: Oswald, 1746).

West, E. *Chains of Love: Slave Couples in Antebellum South Carolina* (Urbana: University of Illinois Press, 2004).

Willis, H.P. *A History of the Latin Monetary Union; a Study of International Monetary Action* (Chicago: Chicago University Press, 1901).

World's Congress of Religions (Boston, MA: Arena, 1893).

Wright, I.C. transl., *The Purgatorio of Dante: Translated* (London: Longman, Rees, Orme, Brown, Green and Longman, 1836).

Part I

Representing union and disunion in art

1 To 'purchase union thus cheaply'

The controversial statue of an Irish Archbishop in the United Kingdom's Houses of Parliament

James E.H. Ford

High on the walls of the House of Lords Chamber stand statues of eighteen of the barons and prelates who sealed Magna Carta (Figure 1.1). Among them is the figure of Henry de Loundres, Archbishop of Dublin between 1213 and his death 1228 (Figure 1.2). Designed by the sculptor John Evan Thomas, the statue was installed above the sovereign's throne at the south end of the Chamber in 1852. Cast in copper and finished to appear like bronze, it depicts the thirteenth-century archbishop in his vestments, a bible in his right hand and a crosier in his left. Easily overlooked due to the overwhelming decorative ornament in Charles Barry and Augustus Welby Pugin's interior, it is perhaps hard to imagine that this unassuming Victorian sculpture was once the subject of heated public debate and no small amount of controversy. This controversy did not revolve around the completed statue, but took place seven years prior to its installation when, in late 1845, de Loundres was excluded from the planned Magna Carta statue scheme. This caused a storm of indignation and protest in Ireland, with nationalists such as Daniel O'Connell and the writers of the *Nation* newspaper quick to attack the royal commission responsible for the Houses of Parliament's decoration. The decision also drew condemnation from Irish unionists, in particular the poet Samuel Ferguson. In what today would be derided as a U-turn, the Fine Arts Commission ultimately conceded, commissioning the statue of de Loundres in 1847. Not all of the Commissioners agreed with this concession, however, with Sir Robert Harry Inglis MP lamenting that they should have to 'purchase union thus cheaply'.

Given the profile of the protagonists, it is perhaps surprising that the controversy surrounding the Magna Carta statue scheme has gone largely unnoticed, both in wider histories of Irish events in the period and more focussed studies of the individuals involved.[1] Furthermore, although accounts of the decoration of the Houses of Parliament have noted that the plan for the statues was altered, art historians have been unaware of the precise details and debates that lay behind the alteration.[2] In providing a detailed account of this forgotten controversy, this chapter argues that the reaction in Ireland, specifically that of Ferguson, alerted the Fine Arts Commission

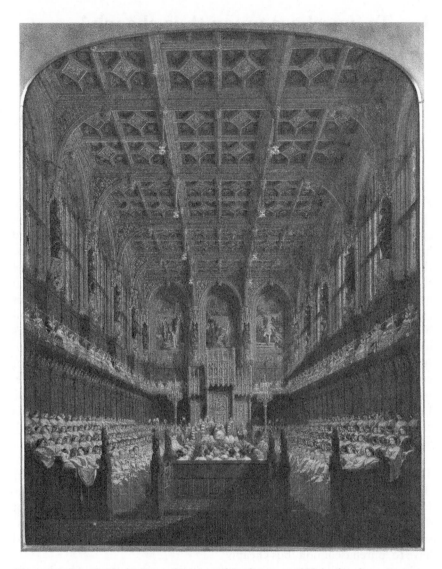

Figure 1.1 Joseph Nash, *State Opening of Parliament, 1857*, bodycolour on paper, 1858. Photo: Parliamentary Art Collection.

to the potential disunion that the task to decorate the Houses of Parliament could engender, particularly on the other side of the Irish Sea. The result was that, alongside the eventual decision to include the Archbishop of Dublin in the Lords Chamber, decorative schemes planned subsequently by the Commission would attempt to create an inclusive version of the United Kingdom's history; an art of union that addressed not only English themes, but Scottish, Welsh and, crucially, Irish subjects too.

Figure 1.2 Statue of Henry de Loundres, Archbishop of Dublin, by John Evan
Thomas, 1852. Photo: James E.H. Ford.

The Fine Arts Commission

The famous Victorian edifice known as the Houses of Parliament owes its
existence to a fire that destroyed most of Parliament's former home on 16
October 1834. Designed by Charles Barry, the new Palace of Westminster, to
give the building its official name, was one of the largest and most significant
architectural projects in nineteenth-century Britain. The schemes to decorate the building, both externally and internally, were equally ambitious.

During the main building period between 1840 and the 1860s, these included a wealth of architectural embellishments and decorative detail overseen by Barry, with the assistance of Pugin, and mural and sculptural programmes under the control of the Fine Arts Commission.

Formed in 1841 under the chairmanship of the young Prince Albert, and with the influential artist and arts administrator Charles Lock Eastlake as its secretary, the Fine Arts Commission eventually counted leading statesmen, historians and intellectuals among its two dozen or so members. The Commission's aim was to use the decoration of the new Parliament buildings 'for the purpose of promoting and encouraging the Fine Arts in [the] United Kingdom'.[3] The early years of the Commission were occupied with investigating materials and techniques suitable for use in such an important project, and with staging large and extremely popular prize exhibitions to stimulate art in the United Kingdom and identify potential artists for employment. By 1844 the Commission was ready to tackle the task of deciding specific subjects for the decorative schemes, beginning with sculpture. The appointment to the Commission of Thomas Babington Macaulay and Philip Henry Stanhope, Viscount Mahon on 4 May 1844 proved central to this.[4] On joining the Commission, these two eminent historians were immediately placed on a new subcommittee, chaired by Mahon, which undertook a number of important tasks. Principal among these were drawing up 'a general list of distinguished persons of the United Kingdom, to whose memory statues might with propriety be erected in or adjoining the New Houses of Parliament' and determining the individuals to be commemorated with statues in the Lords Chamber.[5]

Although Mahon's subcommittee was not set up until 1844, the Commission as a whole had briefly discussed statues for the Lords Chamber as early as 1843, where it resolved that they should be of the sovereigns of England cast in bronze.[6] At a meeting of Mahon's subcommittee on 14 March 1845, however, a resolution was passed to place statues of celebrated peers in the Lords Chamber instead of sovereigns.[7] The following day, Macaulay wrote to Mahon with suggestions.[8] These comprised of Peers of the Blood Royal, Lords Spiritual and Lords Temporal. Macaulay explained:

> I have introduced all the noblemen who have governed England as protectors during a minority, and this I think is rather an advantage. It is also an advantage, I think, that the list includes the lineal ancestors of the two first Dukes, Norfolk and Somerset, of the premier Marquess, Winchester, and of the first Earl who signs the roll as an Earl, Lord Shrewsbury. It includes also the ancestors of one of the noblest Scottish families. No Irish names occur to me. For as to Strongbow and De Burgh, the mention of their names would be offensive to one Irish colleague.[9]

The last two sentences show Macaulay's awareness of the need to include figures that relate to the different nations, or at least kingdoms, of the United Kingdom. The reference to two early Anglo-Norman conquerors of Ireland also indicates his awareness of the potential of the Commission's choice of subjects to upset national sensitivities. In this instance, this appears only to extend to other Commissioners and not to the peoples of the United Kingdom as a whole, with Thomas Wyse, the only Irish member, being the 'one Irish colleague' to whom Macaulay referred. Despite Macaulay's assumption, it is, however, unlikely that Wyse would have found the choices offensive as his family descended from an old Anglo-Norman family who had been given land by Strongbow (Richard de Clare, 2nd Earl of Pembroke) for assisting in his Irish campaigns in the 1160s.[10] Nevertheless, given his Scottish background, Macaulay appears to have been more aware of the national sensitivities of the Celtic fringe nations than most of the other Commissioners. It is also notable that at this time he was writing his seminal *History of England* which, despite its name, gives consideration to the histories of Scotland, Wales and Ireland.

The belief in the need to include the other nations soon disappeared from the plan for the statues in the Lords Chamber. At the suggestion of Prince Albert, the subcommittee instead developed a scheme to fill the eighteen niches with figures of the barons and prelates who enforced Magna Carta. The list of figures was outlined in a report submitted to the Commission dated 15 May 1845.[11] In the report, the subcommittee noted how the 'very narrow size of the niches, and their gothic form' limited its choice 'to characters drawn from the feudal age, and, as usual with effigies of that period, presenting little or no variety of attitude'.[12] Referring to a plan to install stained glass windows depicting British sovereigns, it further explained that:

> the difference of character as laymen, or as prelates, would afford a picturesque variety of attire, and that the historical analogy would be most suitably attained by placing side by side in the same House of the Legislature, in windows or in niches, the successive holders of Sovereign power, and the first founders of constitutional freedom.[13]

At a meeting of the Commission on 16 May 1845, Prince Albert requested that an explanation of the grounds for choosing the names be supplied by the subcommittee.[14] As the country's leading medievalist this task fell to Hallam, who submitted the answer in the form of a letter addressed to Eastlake, dated 17 May 1845.[15] In the letter, Hallam explained that there were far more individuals involved in Magna Carta than eighteen, and the most senior of those by rank were not necessarily the most important in terms of obtaining the charter. The subcommittee therefore decided to choose eighteen names that 'appeared most worthy of being commemorated on this occasion'.[16] One by one, Hallam provided explanations for their inclusion. Having discussed Stephen Langton, the Archbishop of Canterbury, Hallam explained the presence of the other prelate on the list, William, Bishop of London:

> The next in station is the Archbishop of Dublin. But, as he did not hold an English see, it seemed more desirable to select William, Bishop of

London, whose see is next in dignity among those who were present and whose name may be found in history.[17]

The rest of the Commissioners accepted Hallam's reasoning, apparently having no inkling that what they presumably took as a perfectly rational argument for the exclusion of the Archbishop of Dublin would cause consternation and outrage in Ireland.[18]

The art of disunion

The Commission published the results of the subcommittee's deliberations in a report in mid-October 1845. Subsequently, the details of the report were circulated either wholly or in part in newspapers throughout the United Kingdom, appearing in London papers such as the *Times* on 16 October and the *Freeman's Journal* in Dublin the following day.[19] The first sign of potential trouble came in the *Times*'s assessment. While supporting the idea of placing the Magna Carta statues in the Lords Chamber, the writer warned:

> The exclusion of the Archbishop of Dublin from among the prelates, and the substitution of William Bishop of London, may perhaps be taken hold of as a grievance by the Irish agitators, who will declare that Ireland has not her fair share of stone representatives in the new Houses of Parliament.[20]

The mocking tone of the *Times*'s prediction was consistent with its general position regarding Ireland and those who called for repeal of the 1800 Acts of Union, particularly the repeal movement's lionised leader, Daniel O'Connell MP, who in 1840 founded the Repeal Association, a mass political movement whose campaigning set the Irish political agenda during the 1840s.[21] However, the writer also shows awareness of the potentially controversial nature of the decisions the Commission was making, something the Commissioners themselves evidently lacked.

Four days later the *Times* was proved right. At the first of a number of Repeal Association meetings where O'Connell attacked the Commission's report, he derided the exclusion of the Archbishop of Dublin. Drawing laughter from the crowd, he focussed on Hallam's explanation and described why the Archbishop had been overlooked:

> He was only an Irish bishop, and, consequently, had no right to have a statue! They accord the distinction to an English bishop [William, Bishop of London], merely because he was an Englishman – they refused it to an Irish bishop merely because he was an Irishman, and yet there are people (heaven help their sense!) who say the countries are *united* and virtually the same.[22]

O'Connell also attacked other elements of the Commission's report, which he characterised as a 'curious lubrication ... curious in its omissions, and yet more curious for the names that are inserted in it'.[23] One figure included on the list of 'distinguished persons' came in for particular attack: Oliver Cromwell, who for many Irish Catholics was the single most hated figure connected with English / British rule.[24]

The *Nation* newspaper, mouthpiece of the pro-repeal Young Ireland movement, also initially focussed on the list of distinguished persons, particularly the small number of Irishmen that had been put forward for 'Imperial fame'. This was despite the fact, the paper noted, that the list was meant to represent 'distinguished persons of the *United Kingdom,* of which [...] this island purports, for the present to form a part'.[25] The *Nation* put this lack of Irish representation partly down to the makeup of the subcommittee, which it noted consisted of five Englishmen, one 'half Scotchman' (Macaulay) and one Irishman (Wyse).[26] On the subject of the Archbishop of Dublin, the *Nation* echoed O'Connell's sentiments, highlighting the crucial phrase 'as he did not hold an English see' for particular criticism, and sardonically agreeing that the Bishop of London was 'clearly more desirable – an English Bishop before an Irish Archbishop'.[27]

Although these initial instances of complaint by Irish nationalists about the exclusion of Henry de Loundres are important, they took place alongside the complaints about the 'list of distinguished persons' and were, in that sense, not unique. The debate entered a new phase, however, when the lawyer, poet and prominent Irish unionist Samuel Ferguson joined the fray. In the November 1845 volume of the Tory *Dublin University Magazine,* Ferguson published an open letter to Henry Hallam.[28] Over six pages, he laid out a series of arguments to refute Hallam's conclusion and persuade him to reinstate the Archbishop of Dublin. Ferguson began by expressing his regret that:

> another seeming slight to the people of this part of the United Kingdom should be added to those pernicious distinctions (as unfounded generally as they are invidious), which have so long excited dissention and bitterness between the two most numerous and powerful sections of her majesty's subjects. The evil of such contempt, real or seeming, is greatly enhanced by the eminence in rank and reputation of those at whose hands it is experienced.[29]

Ferguson evidently struggled to reconcile the event and the other slights he alludes to with his unionism. Noting his hopes that the decision was the result of 'some technical mistake', he wrote that he would only believe the alternative 'with extreme and painful reluctance'.[30] Setting out this alternative, he argued:

> that, in this postponement of an Irish to an English prelate, by reason only of the locality of the see of the former, a portion of the United

Kingdom has been vilipended by a committee, whose duty it was to consult the proper pride and just national recollections of all those whose representatives are to assemble in the new Houses of Parliament.[31]

As Eve Patten has shown, for Ferguson the 1840s marked a period of increasing disaffection with British rule.[32] Though Patten does not discuss the Henry de Loundres issue, Ferguson's complaint should be seen as part of what she describes as a 'decade of insecurity and flux' regarding his support of the Union.[33] During this period, he also became close to some of the Young Irelanders, particularly fellow lawyer and poet Thomas Davis, who co-founded the *Nation* and was a leading contributor. While Ferguson did not support the political end to which they worked, in Davis and the *Nation* he found like-minded cultural nationalists who seemed to promise an inclusive Irish national identity that Ferguson could subscribe to with pride in the face of Anglo-British caricature and ignorance.[34]

Seeing the political capital that could be made from Ferguson's intervention in the de Loundres controversy, the *Nation* produced a second, more detailed assessment of the issue.[35] Praising Ferguson for setting out his case 'in a most scholarly way', the article repeated and expanded upon his arguments.[36] However, the *Nation* deviated from Ferguson's opinion in one crucial respect that illustrates the differences between their positions on the Union. Unlike Ferguson, the paper was keen to emphasise that it felt no outrage at the exclusion of the Archbishop of Dublin from the Houses of Parliament. Justifying why so much space had been given to this 'comparatively unimportant subject', the paper claimed that it was not:

> because we care one fig that injustice has been done [...] but because we are delighted to find, in a gentleman of such great ability, and, at the same time, such marked Conservative politics as Mr Ferguson is known to possess, so thoroughly national a spirit as breaks forth in every line of his letter.[37]

Ferguson's letter marked a turning point in the controversy that the *Times* had not predicted. The open criticism of the Commission from an influential member of the Protestant Ascendancy hinted that disaffection in Ireland might become more widespread than the existing nationalist agitation, which already posed the greatest threat to the United Kingdom since it had come into existence in 1801. Its importance was indicated when Hallam penned a reply to Ferguson that was published at the historian's request in the December issue of the *Dublin University Magazine*.[38] Recognising Ferguson's complaint, Hallam expressed his regret about the situation:

> It would give me very great pain, as I am sure would be felt also by every member of the commission to which I have the honour to belong, to be supposed capable of casting the least slight on the Irish nation, or on eminent men of past times, in whose glory their country is interested.[39]

After attempting to explain his thinking behind what he termed 'the un-lucky question about the Archbishop of Dublin', Hallam acknowledged that, taking into account the distinguished character of the prelate, his role in Magna Carta, and 'considering also still more the wishes which many, in common with yourself, probably entertain', it would give him 'great pleas-ure' to see de Loundres installed in his niche.[40]

Hallam's conciliatory note was tempered, however, when he drew a dis-tinction between those 'in common' with Ferguson and the nationalist complainants. Presumably in a reference to the article published only six days previously in the *Nation*, Hallam described how he could not under-stand 'why those whose chief business it has been to represent the con-nection of Ireland with the English crown as one of mere oppression and bondage, should pretend to care about the admission or exclusion of an Anglo-Norman prelate'. However, 'the case is very different', he continued, 'with the truly loyal Irish' such as Ferguson.[41]

Unsurprisingly, these comments drew a vitriolic response in the pages of the *Nation*.[42] In answer to Hallam, the paper asserted its lack of aware-ness that those who opposed the Union 'ever did care, or pretend to care, about the admission or exclusion of the Archbishop of Dublin'. The *Nation* accepted that Hallam 'would feel pain to be supposed capable of casting a slight upon the Irish nation', but highlighted the accidental nature of the insult as being part of the problem. Returning once again to Hallam's in-itial reasoning, the author stated that 'it was the plain unconsciousness of a wish to offend, the instinctive, unintentional insolence of the committee, and the naïf simplicity' of the reason given to exclude the Archbishop that led the *Nation* to notice the matter at all. Presumably as a result of Hallam's attempt to drive a wedge between Ferguson and the Young Irelanders, the *Nation* also distanced itself from Ferguson, stating: 'if Mr Ferguson and his clients, the "truly loyal Irish," imagine that the country has gained anything by the discussion, we heartily wish them joy'. Evidently concerned that by commenting on the decoration of the Houses of Parliament they had inad-vertently validated the institution it embodied, the *Nation* pledged not to involve itself in such debates again.[43]

A further notable voice who joined the debate at this point was Henry Grattan Jnr, a repeal MP and the son of Henry Grattan Snr, who had played a leading role in Ireland increasing its legislative independence in 1782 and was one of the foremost opponents of the 1800 Acts of Union. Speaking at a meeting of the Repeal Association, Grattan Jnr noted that Hallam had questioned why the Irish should interfere in the statues to be placed in the new Houses of Parliament when they were repealers.[44] In an important de-velopment that linked the controversy to specific contemporary events in Ireland, Grattan Jnr argued that Irish nationalists were no less loyal to the Crown than unionists, but that they sought 'restitution of their rights, for something else besides the reports of commissioners were necessary when the people were dying in ditches and starving'.[45] This was, of course, a reference to the Great Famine that had begun to grip parts of Ireland and which would lead, largely through British inaction, to the deaths of around one-eighth of the island's population.

To 'purchase union thus cheaply'

At a meeting of the Commission in early 1846, a resolution was passed, at the suggestion of Hallam, to substitute the Archbishop of Dublin for the Bishop of London.[46] No reason was given for this alteration, which would have received unanimous support were it not for Robert Harry Inglis MP, a member of the original subcommittee that drew up the Magna Carta scheme. To register his dissent, Inglis submitted a written explanation that made a number of reasoned historical arguments to justify why the original plan should stand.[47] His account of the controversy not only makes his view plain, but also indicates something of the Commission's reasoning behind its change of heart. Summarising the case against which he is arguing, Inglis wrote:

> It is said [...] that de Londres' introduction, however tardily, would even now give pleasure, and that when there is so easy a mode of removing jealousy and anger, and of substituting a kindly and grateful feeling, the members of the Committee ought at once to abandon their own previous recommendations in such a matter and to yield to such a wish, and to purchase union thus cheaply.[48]

While, for Inglis, the inclusion of the Archbishop of Dublin may have been a cheap means of preventing disaffection in Ireland, the other Commissioners evidently believed that it was a necessary diplomatic move to prevent further disunion. As Hallam had earlier made clear, however, this appeasement was not aimed at the likes of O'Connell and the *Nation*. Had opposition only come from nationalist quarters, as the *Times* initially expected, it seems unlikely that any attention would have been paid to their complaints. However, the very public involvement of a prominent Irish unionist in the debate had made the stakes markedly higher. With the allegiance of the 'truly loyal Irish', such as Ferguson, necessary for the Union's continuation, it was their 'jealously and anger' that the Commission was attempting to replace with 'a kindly and grateful feeling'. Nationalists, by comparison, were considered unworthy of such treatment.

The Commission's change of heart over de Loundres successfully placated Ferguson on the issue. Writing to his mother from Paris three months after Hallam agreed to the substitution, he noted he had visited the tomb of Lawrence O'Toole at Eu in Normandy in order to examine the costume so 'that we may know how to dress his successor in the See of Dublin, Archbishop de Londres, for whom, you probably have heard, I have obtained a niche in the new House of Lords'.[49] In the same letter, he described Hallam as having had 'the manliness to acknowledge that he had been wrong'.[50]

In her biography of her husband, Lady Ferguson wrote that this 'was a triumph of which Ferguson was proud, the more so that Sir Robert Peel, in an autograph letter, had stated that there were "great difficulties in the way of carrying the suggestion into effect"'.[51] However, the U-turn cannot be said to have purchased Ferguson's undying support for the Union, at least not in the short term. The poet's disillusionment with British rule continued to grow, as his resentment at the slights of which he had earlier spoken turned to indignation at the government response to the Great Famine. Ferguson even briefly flirted with repeal, becoming in 1848 a founder member of the Protestant Repeal Association. Even then, though, he did not oppose the Union in principle, just the way that it operated in practice. His agitation for repeal ended after only a few months, largely as a result of the failed Young Ireland Rebellion of 1848 and its aftermath.[52] Subsequently, his support for the Union returned and he became so strongly associated with unionism that his brief period as a repealer was almost entirely forgotten.[53]

The art of Union

In addition to the U-Turn over Henry de Loundres, the 1845 controversy had a more lasting impact on the Commission's approach to the decoration of Parliament when, in 1846, it fully focussed its attention on painted schemes for the building. In the midst of the Henry de Loundres controversy in late 1845, Prince Albert began drafting a memorandum suggesting subjects for specific locations.[54] Following comments by Sir Robert Peel, a final version was laid before the Commission and read by Albert at a meeting on 6 February 1846.[55] Albert described the task of selecting topics for paintings as 'the most difficult subject perhaps, which this Commission has to consider'.[56] Though he explained the subjects chosen should be 'the chief events of British History', Albert's room-by-room plan is notable for the fact that it includes no events from the pre-Union history of Scotland, Ireland or Wales.

However, Albert's subjects were not set in stone, and Mahon took the chair of a new subcommittee tasked with advancing towards a finalised list of subjects for paintings. This subcommittee first met on 1 May 1846 when, at the suggestion of Hallam, it resolved that 'a selection of certain conspicuous events in British history should be made, to be the subjects of paintings by native artists'. The committee concluded their meeting by agreeing to Sir Robert Harry Inglis's proposal that each member be invited to submit a list of subjects selected either from Albert's paper or from the general range of British history, keeping in mind the historic importance of the subjects and their suitability for reproduction in painting.[57] The lists drawn up by Inglis, Mahon and Hallam survive.[58] Inglis chose solely English subjects, as did Mahon. Hallam, however, is the only one of the three that made any attempt to include scenes from the histories of the United Kingdom's nations other than England. Of the fifteen subjects he suggested, the final three relate to Scotland and Ireland. One, 'the Battle of Culloden', concerns the final confrontation of the 1745 Jacobite rebellion. Another, 'Columba surrounded by the monks of Iona', links Scotland and Ireland through the Irish missionary monk Saint Columba. However, it is Hallam's third suggestion that is particularly important. While each of the other fourteen events is specifically titled, the fifteenth merely reads: 'Any conspicuous event in early Irish history'. This conscious inclusion of an Irish scene was almost certainly a further conciliatory gesture resulting from the Archbishop of Dublin furore. Yet despite Hallam's pre-eminence as a historian, his imprecise, tentative description hints at his unease about proposing a suitable subject, no doubt born of his earlier experience.

In 1847 the Commission published a report outlining the final subjects for wall paintings throughout the building.[59] This built on Hallam's suggestions by including, alongside a majority of English subjects, Scottish, Welsh and Irish scenes. Notably, no adverse comment came from unionist quarters including Ferguson, while, with the *Nation* keeping its word not to get involved and O'Connell's death that year, nationalists were equally silent. As with many of the planned decorative schemes, the Scottish, Welsh and Irish scenes remained unrealised after the winding up of the Commission following Prince Albert's death in 1861. The subjects exist, therefore, only as titles with unfulfilled potential. Among them are scenes from the lives of figures such as the heroic Scottish King of the Wars of Independence, Robert Bruce, and the first English Prince of Wales, Edward of Caernarvon, as well as 'events from early Irish history': the death of the High King of Ireland Brian Boru and the marriage of Strongbow and Aoife MacMurrough, daughter of the King of Leinster. Encapsulating this diversity of national subjects, the Commission planned to 'illustrate the component parts of the United Kingdom' by installing in Central Lobby, at the very centre of the building, four large mosaics depicting St George for England, St Patrick for Ireland, St Andrew for Scotland and St David for Wales.[60] Like the planned paintings, the Central Lobby mosaics remained unrealised during the Commission's lifetime. However, unlike the paintings, subsequent generations did complete them.[61] Installed between 1870 and 1924, they dominate the heart of the United Kingdom's legislature and are the only concrete manifestation of the Commission's attempt to deploy art to promote union, an attempt partly born of the disunion sowed in 1845 by the exclusion of Henry de Loundres from the planned statues for the House of Lords Chamber.

Notes

1 Brief references are found in M.C. Ferguson, *Samuel Ferguson in the Ireland of his Day* (London: Blackwood, 1892), pp. 112, 167 and A. Deering, *Sir Samuel Ferguson, Poet and Antiquarian* (Philadelphia: University of Pennsylvania, 1931), p. 64.

2 For example, see T.S.R. Boase, 'The Decoration of the New Palace of Westminster', *Journal of the Warburg and Courtauld Institutes* 17:3 (1954), pp. 319–358 (p. 340) and R.J.B. Walker, *Catalogue of Paintings, Drawings, Sculpture and Engravings in the Palace of Westminster*, 4 vols (typescript, 1988; copies available in the Parliamentary Archives, the London Library, and the libraries of the

National Portrait Gallery, London, and Courtauld Institute of Art, London), vol. 4, pt. 4, pp. 53, 121–125.

3 *First Report of the Commissioners on the Fine Arts*, HC 412 (1842), 5.

4 'Warrant Appointing Additional Commissioners', *Third Report of the Commissioners on the Fine Arts*, HC 585 (1844), pp. 5–6.

5 *Fourth Report of the Commissioners on the Fine Arts*, Appendix 1, p. 9: 'Report of Committee, with list of distinguished persons to whose memory statues might be erected', 11 March 1845.

6 'FAC Minutes', 12 April 1843, Fine Arts Commission 1841–1844, Royal Archives, Windsor (RA) VIC/MAIN/F/29/31. Material from the Royal Archives is cited with the permission of Her Majesty Queen Elizabeth II.

7 'FAC Minutes', 14 March 1845, Fine Arts Commission 1845–1850, RA VIC/MAIN/F/30/2.

8 Thomas Babington Macaulay to Viscount Mahon, 15 March 1845, Stanhope Papers, Kent Archive and Local History Service, Maidstone (KALHS) U1590/C348/7/1, U1590/C348/7/2. Material from the Stanhope Papers is quoted by kind permission of the Board of Trustees of the Chevening Estate.

9 KALHS U1590/C348/7/1, U1590/C348/7/2.

10 J.J. Auchmuty, *Sir Thomas Wyse 1791–1862: The Life and Career of an Educator and Diplomat* (London: P.S. King, 1939), p. 189.

11 'Report of Committee respecting selection of Persons whose effigies might be placed in the Niches of the House of Lords', 15 May 1845, *Fourth Report*, Appendix 2, pp. 10–11.

12 *Fourth Report*, Appendix 2, p. 10.

13 *Fourth Report*, Appendix 2, p. 10.

14 *Fourth Report*, Appendix 2, p. 11.

15 *Fourth Report*, Appendix 3, 'Letter from Mr Hallam', pp. 11–12.

16 *Fourth Report*, Appendix 3, p. 11.

17 *Fourth Report*, Appendix 3, pp. 11–12.

18 The Commission resolved to adopt the subcommittee's report and Hallam's explanatory letter in early June 1845. See 'FAC Minutes', 6 June 1845, RA VIC/MAIN/F/30/13.

19 'London, Thursday, October 16, 1845', *The Times*, 16 October 1845, p. 5; 'Statues in the Houses of Parliament', *Freeman's Journal*, 17 October 1845, p. 4.

20 *The Times*, 16 October 1845, p. 5.

21 M. de Nie, *The Great Irish Famine and British Public Opinion* (Madison: University of Wisconsin Press, 1995), pp. 98–99, 112, 138.

22 'Conciliation Hall', *Freeman's Journal*, 21 October 1845, p. 3.

23 Quoted in *Freeman's Journal*, 21 October 1845, p. 3.

24 For a discussion of this element of the Irish response to the 1845 report, see J.E.H. Ford, 'The Art of Union and Disunion in the Houses of Parliament, 1834–1928' (unpublished doctoral thesis, University of Nottingham, 2016), ch. 3.

25 'One Hundred and Twenty-One Distinguished Persons. Report of the Fine Arts Committee', *Nation*, 25 October 1845, p. 9 (original emphasis).

26 *Nation*, 25 October 1845, p. 9.

27 *Nation*, 25 October 1845, p. 9.

28 Samuel Ferguson, 'Letter to Mr Hallam: Henri de Londres', *Dublin University Magazine*, November 1845, pp. 628–634.

29 Ferguson, 'Letter to Mr Hallam', p. 628.

30 Ferguson, 'Letter to Mr Hallam', p. 629.

31 Ferguson, 'Letter to Mr Hallam', p. 629.

32 E. Patten, *Samuel Ferguson and the Culture of Nineteenth-Century Ireland* (Dublin: Four Courts Press, 2004), pp. 99–130.

33 Patten, *Samuel Ferguson*, p. 99.
34 Patten, *Samuel Ferguson*, p. 99.
35 'Mr. Ferguson's Letter', *Nation*, 1 November 1845, p. 12.
36 *Nation*, 1 November 1845, p. 12.
37 *Nation*, 1 November 1845, p. 12.
38 Henry Hallam, 'Letter from Henry Hallam Esq', *Dublin University Magazine*, December 1845, pp. 728–729.
39 Hallam, 'Letter from Henry Hallam Esq', p. 728.
40 Hallam, 'Letter from Henry Hallam Esq', p. 728.
41 Hallam, 'Letter from Henry Hallam Esq', p. 728.
42 *Nation*, 6 December 1845, p. 10.
43 *Nation*, 6 December 1845, p. 10.
44 *Nation*, 20 December 1845, p. 3.
45 *Nation*, 20 December 1845, p. 3.
46 *Seventh Report of the Commissioners on the Fine Arts*, HC 862 (1847), Appendix 2.1, 'Alteration in the selection, before made, of personages whose Effigies might be placed in the House of Lords', p. 16. As a result of the resolution being published, this is the only aspect of the controversy that has been widely known. For example, see Boase, p. 340.
47 *Seventh Report*, Appendix 2.2, 'Statement by Sir Robert H. Inglis, explaining his reasons for not agreeing as to the expediency of such alteration', p. 16.
48 *Seventh Report*, Appendix 2.2, p. 16.
49 Quoted in Ferguson, *Samuel Ferguson*, pp. 166–167. There is no evidence to support Ferguson's claim that he had a role in the statue's design.
50 Quoted in Ferguson, *Samuel Ferguson*, p. 167.
51 Quoted in Ferguson, *Samuel Ferguson*, p. 112.
52 Patten, *Samuel Ferguson*, p. 125.
53 Patten, *Samuel Ferguson*, pp. 11, 128–129.
54 Albert, untitled draft memorandum on subjects for paintings in the new Houses of Parliament, n.d. (c. November 1845), RA VIC/MAIN/F/30/32.
55 Sir Robert Peel to Albert, 21 November 1845, RA VIC/MAIN/F/30/33 and 34. Albert, 'Memorandum (Private)', n.d. (c. 6 February 1846), KALHS U1590/O170.
56 Albert, 'Memorandum (Private)', KALHS U1590/O170.
57 'Minutes of a Committee of the FAC', 1 May 1846, KALHS U1590/O170.
58 All three are untitled but dated 8 May 1846, KALHS U1590/O170.
59 *Seventh Report*, Appendix 1, 'Report of the Committee appointed to select subjects in Painting and Sculpture, with a view to the future decoration of the Palace of Westminster', pp. 9–15.
60 *Seventh Report*, Appendix 1, p. 10. A full examination of the 1847 schemes through the prism of the Union is given in Ford, 'The Art of Union and Disunion', ch. 4.
61 For a detailed history of the mosaics, see Ford, 'The Art of Union and Disunion', ch. 6.

Bibliography

Auchmuty, J.J. *Sir Thomas Wyse 1791–1862: The Life and Career of an Educator and Diplomat* (London: P.S. King, 1939).

Boase, T.S.R. 'The Decoration of the New Palace of Westminster', *Journal of the Warburg and Courtauld Institutes* 17:3 (1954), pp. 319–358.

'Conciliation Hall', *Freeman's Journal*, 21 October 1845, p. 3.

De Nie, M. *The Great Irish Famine and British Public Opinion* (Madison: University of Wisconsin Press, 1995).

Deering, A. *Sir Samuel Ferguson, Poet and Antiquarian* (Philadelphia: University of Pennsylvania, 1931).

Ferguson, M.C. *Samuel Ferguson in the Ireland of His Day* (London: Blackwood, 1892).

Fifth Report of the Commission on the Fine Arts, HC 685 (1846).

First Report of the Commissioners on the Fine Arts, HC 412 (1842).

Ford, J.E.H. 'The Art of Union and Disunion in the Houses of Parliament, 1834–1928' (unpublished doctoral thesis, University of Nottingham, 2016).

Fourth Report of the Commissioners on the Fine Arts, HC 671 (1845).

Hallam, H. 'Letter from Henry Hallam Esq', *Dublin University Magazine*, December 1845, pp. 728–729.

'London, Thursday, October 16, 1845', *The Times*, 16 October 1845, p. 5.

'Mr. Ferguson's Letter', *Nation*, 1 November 1845, p. 12.

Patten, E. *Samuel Ferguson and the Culture of Nineteenth-Century Ireland* (Dublin: Four Courts Press, 2004).

'One Hundred and Twenty-One Distinguished Persons. Report of the Fine Arts Committee', *Nation*, 25 October 1845, p. 9.

Ferguson, S. 'Letter to Mr Hallam: Henri de Londres', *Dublin University Magazine*, November 1845, pp. 628–634.

Kent Archive and Local History Service, Maidstone. The Stanhope Papers, U1590.

Royal Archives, Windsor. Minutes of the Fine Art Commission, 1841–1844. VIC/MAIN/F/29/31.

Royal Archives, Windsor. Minutes of the Fine Arts Commission 1845–1850. VIC/MAIN/F/30/2.

Second Report of the Commissioners on the Fine Arts, HC 499 (1843).

Seventh Report of the Commissioners on the Fine Arts, HC 862 (1847).

Sixth Report of the Commission on the Fine Arts, HC 749 (1846).

'Statues in the Houses of Parliament', *Freeman's Journal*, 17 October 1845, p. 4.

Third Report of the Commissioners on the Fine Arts, HC 585 (1844).

Walker, R.J.B. *Catalogue of Paintings, Drawings, Sculpture and Engravings in the Palace of Westminster*, 4 vols (typescript, 1988; copies available in the Parliamentary Archives, the London Library, and the libraries of the National Portrait Gallery, London, and Courtauld Institute of Art, London).

2 Leave or remain? Antidisestablishmentarianism in Margaret Oliphant's *Salem Chapel*

Margaret Markwick

Introduction: union and disunion in nineteenth-century English Christianity

In 1847, the bishop of Exeter, Henry Phillpotts, always a stickler for orthodoxy and never one to shirk controversy,[1] declined to install George Gorham as vicar of Brampford Speke. Gorham was known as an adversarial evangelical; while vicar of St Just with Penwith in Cornwall, he had advertised for a curate 'free from Tractarian error', to Phillpotts' fury. In seeking to deny Gorham his transfer to the Devon living, bishop Phillpotts declared that his views on baptismal renewal were unsound. Gorham appealed to the ecclesiastical Court of Arches.

This dispute gripped the nation. If the decision went against Gorham, evangelicals from the Church of England would be up in arms. Equally, if Gorham won his case, this might prompt even more Anglo-Catholics to cross to Rome, and it was only two years earlier that John Newman had made that crossing, taking with him many of his acolytes. During the four years that it took the court to reach its decision, over fifty books were published about baptismal regeneration, that is, whether baptism alone was sufficient to ensure the remission of sin (a literal interpretation of the words of the prayer book), or whether you also needed to live a clean and godly life to enter the gates of heaven.[2] These fifty books were about a subject that many twenty-first-century readers might think arcane and obscure. For the Victorians, it was another important and relevant debate, alongside apostolic succession, prayerbook rubric, and the disestablishment of the Church of England. For them, these religious debates mattered, and one indication of this is the degree to which these discussions became themes in the popular fiction of the time. Thus, Charlotte Yonge's novels are grounded in Tractarian thinking; Charles Kingsley wrote novels advancing 'muscular Christianity'; the Trollopes, Anthony and Fanny, wrote novels discrediting low-church evangelicals; Disraeli's *Lothair* is staunchly anti-Catholic; while Hesba Stretton's forte was the Christian Socialist tale.[3] And in Margaret Oliphant's *Salem Chapel*, we have a nuanced defence of an Established Church. Anthony Trollope's *Phineas Redux*, written soon after the disestablishment of the

Church of Ireland, features an imagined bill to disestablish the Church of England. As the debate progresses, it becomes a trope for probity in politics. We might seek in vain for such literary finesse in Oliphant's fiction, but what we regularly find is engagement with the ecclesiastical issues of the day. For while there is little depth to her study of dissenting creed and Anglican theology, Oliphant, like so many of her contemporaries, filters the debates and their shifts over time till they become embedded in her fiction.

When Martin Luther nailed his ninety-five theses to the church door in 1517, he lit a flame of dissent against the Roman church that spread through Europe. It is important to distinguish this from Henry VIII's declaration that the English Catholic Church was to be independent of the See of Rome. The Anglican Church remained, and still remains, a Catholic and apostolic church. Its protestant aspect only began to emerge in Edward VI's reign, re-affirmed by Elizabeth as she rolled back Mary's attempts to re-unite the Anglican Church with Rome. In the upheavals of the 1670s, to reinforce the Anglican nature of the State, Parliament had passed the Test and Corporation Acts, which confined public office to communicating members of the Church of England. These were hugely discriminatory, and their effects were only partly assuaged by annual Acts of Indemnity which enabled non-conformist local mayors and Members of Parliament legally to take office. There was a constant rumbling of calls for the disestablishment of the Church of England.[4]

The Test and Corporation Acts were finally repealed in 1828, and followed by the hotly contested Roman Catholic Relief Act in 1829.[5] But far from these moves dampening down the debate, it raged more fiercely than ever when the bishops in the House of Lords two years later voted down the first Reform Bill, in 1831. Riots and rampage ensued, bishops' palaces were sacked, the clergy were attacked in the street and effigies of bishops were burnt on Guy Fawkes night. Although a second reading was passed, enough bishops and archbishops voted for an amendment which emasculated the Bill. The first Reform Act finally passed into law in 1832, with no bishops dissenting.[6]

But outrage continued, with attacks on bishops' stipends, their pluralities, and the abuse of residency. All this contributed to significant introspection on the part of the clergy of the Church of England. One group from Oxford University, and centred on Oriel College, set about re-stating the principles of the Church of England as a Catholic and Apostolic Church, in pamphlets known as Tracts. Clergy who supported these tracts were called 'Tractarians' and 'of the Oxford movement', and 'Puseyites', after Edward Bouverie Pusey, a leading member of the group. Not all the tracts were contentious, but they all called for greater attention to be paid to the rubric of the 1662 *Book of Common Prayer*; several addressed apostolic succession, and five examined baptism and baptismal renewal. Criticism of the tracts came largely from the evangelical wing of the Church of England, clergymen who sided with George Gorham and his view of baptismal regeneration.

Straddling the middle ground was the Broad Church movement, arguing that the strength of Anglicanism was its capacity to embrace both ends of the spectrum.

The context for Margaret Oliphant's *Salem Chapel* (1862–1863)

It is impossible to overestimate how these arguments dominated the day-to-day lives of ordinary people. Magazines proliferated, reflecting every nuance of religious taste and belief. The Evangelicals had *Good Words, Leisure Hour, Gospel* and *General Baptists*. The dissenting factions, including the temperance movement, had *Working Men's Friend, Cottage Gardener, Family Friend* and *Family Tutor*. *The Christian World*, edited by Emma Jane Worboise, a prolific writer of improving fiction, promoted the religious sensation novel.[7] *Blackwood's Edinburgh Magazine*, first published in 1817, was a Scottish Tory journal which promoted literature and fiction. The owners, John and William Blackwood, met the young novelist Margaret Oliphant in 1851, when she was in Edinburgh visiting her relatives. On her return home, she wrote to her new friends, asking them to publish her third novel, *Katy Stewart*, another Scottish tale, in their magazine.

Oliphant (1828–1897) is one of that amazing generation of driven Victorian women like Catherine Gore, Fanny Trollope and Mrs Humphry Ward, who rescued their family finances with their pen, maintaining the show of the 'angel in the house' by day, while writing furiously into the night to provide the bread and butter.[8] Oliphant's early work supplemented her husband's precarious income as an artist in stained glass, and provided some material security when she was first married. In 1859 she found herself a widow with two small children and pregnant with a third, with an inheritance of debt from her husband. She settled in Windsor and sent her two young sons to Eton. When her widowed brother lost his health, she opened her home to him, his son – who joined her sons at Eton – and his two daughters. Her brother's son Frank grew into an intelligent hard-working young man, who died soon after taking up a prestigious post in India. Her own daughter, her ewe-lamb, died when she was ten. Her two sons squandered their talents and died in their early thirties. She herself died three years after her second son.[9]

She financed her life-style partly through the patronage of John Blackwood, the publisher, who took much of her writing for his magazine. The breadth of her output is prodigious; biography, sacred and secular, travel, book reviews, short stories, critical analysis (particularly of French literature), ghost stories and novels (nearly a hundred), historical, domestic and sensation. Never a polemicist, she turned her hand to whatever would be sure to sell. By the end of her life she had worn a hole in her finger.[10]

The *Carlingford Chronicles* was one of her most successful and profitable ventures. Her first, *The Rector* explores the concept of the priesthood as a calling. Is ministering to the sick and the dying an integral part of that calling, and what bearing do ecclesiastic enthusiasms have on the cure of souls? A very low-church rector of long-standing dies, and the living is given to a middle-aged Fellow of All Souls. He finds himself unequal to the task of providing spiritual comfort to his flock, and in less than a year he retreats back to his ivory tower. His incompetence as a parish priest is in stark relief to the perpetual curate's devotion to the poor, for Frank Wentworth, a Tractarian ritualist, has successfully established a mission church down by the canal among the bargemen, a very contemporaneous theme. As the 1850s progressed, the Tractarians were particularly successful in establishing new churches in the densely populated inner cities where, as the special 1851 religious census so tellingly showed, there were too few clergy and too few churches to serve the ever-expanding population.[11] It was felt that the working classes, being less literate, would be attracted by Tractarian symbolism in the celebration of faith.[12] *The Rector* shows Oliphant engaging sympathetically with the many shades of Anglican belief and practice. *The Doctor's Family* is a much more secular tale, but there are still ecclesiastical interjections readily understood by her readership. 'Handsome young coxcomb, with all his Puseyitical pretences!' the eponymous doctor mutters to himself of Frank Wentworth, the perpetual curate. Tractarians were identifiable by their dress. They wore waistcoats that buttoned up to the neck, and full-length cassocks, rather than the more serviceable knee-length one favoured by the Broad Church, and frequently disregarded entirely by the most evangelical.[13] All this is implied in 'coxcomb' before the reinforcement of 'Puseyitical'.

Salem Chapel, published in 1863, is the third of the series, and Oliphant's most successful novel.[14] Its success earned her £1,500 for her next Carlingford novel, *The Perpetual Curate*, her highest payment ever. It is a hybrid novel. Its primary plot is a classic Oliphant domestic tale of a dissenting congregation's relationship with their minister, a young man chosen by them on the strength of his preaching, and expected by them to preach sermons to their taste. This is executed with great wit and sharp observation, much of it class-ridden. Within this tale is a prototype of the sensation genre, with all the requisite ingredients – an attempt at a bigamous marriage, a seemingly fallen woman looking for redemption, a kidnapping, a failed murder, and a conclusion that beggars belief. In 1862, Oliphant wrote a lengthy article for *Blackwood's Magazine* attacking the craze for sensation novels. She admired *The Woman in White*, which she critiqued at length, but was scathing about all the other attempts to chill and curdle the reader's blood, singling out *Great Expectations*, published in 1860–1861, and Mrs Henry Wood's *East Lynne*, also 1861, for particular opprobrium.[15] Nevertheless, she was a writer with a living to earn and a lifestyle to support.

Salem Chapel is set in the recent past, and we can hypothesise that it is probably set in the late 1840s, since the chapel's new minister is fresh out of Homerton, a non-conformist college which moved to New College, London, in 1851 when Homerton became a teacher-training institution. It is also set late enough in the 1840s for trains to run regularly from Carlingford to London, and for Vincent to be able to travel to Northumberland in a day. There are two bookshops in Carlingford. One has an extensive array of publications from the Religious Tract Society, and the other a full range of editions of *The Christian Year*, thus one that targets an evangelical audience seeking improving tales, and one catering for the high-church market, with John Keble's immensely popular series of devotional poems. These are indicators which would have been readily accessible to the reading public. Literate Victorians were attuned to picking up such metonymic nuances, just as they would 'read' the implications of 'coxcomb' and 'Puseyitical', mentioned above. However, while there is a wealth of metonomy about the Anglican Church, there is little figuration about dissent. Oliphant says in 1856 to John Blackwood, 'I don't like English dissent, though I am a Free Church woman[...]I like the English Establishment a great deal better than the English sectarians'.[16]

The main plot of *Salem Chapel* is straightforward enough. Arthur Vincent, the son of a dissenting minister, intelligent, well educated and newly graduated from Homerton College, is chosen by the congregation of Salem Chapel to be their new minister, on the strength of his preaching skills. His flock is made up of small tradespeople just beginning to feel the benefits of improved prosperity; they can afford to educate their daughters, and one has a son at theological college. His preaching begins to fill the pews each Sunday, and he gives a course of lectures on why the Church of England should be disestablished, which fills the local Music Hall six Thursday nights running. Vincent begins to dream of making converts in the staunchly Church of England Grange Lane, where the quality live. But much as Vincent decries the priesthood of an established church, 'These men had joined God and Mammon – they were in the pay of the State', his assurance begins to crack.[17] He has met Lady Western, the leading lady of the local gentry, and is utterly smitten. He mistakes her kindness for intimacy, and is overjoyed to be invited to supper. His flock is aghast and constantly remind him it is they who pay his wages; they are paying for someone who will come to their tea-meetings, preach sermons they choose, not someone who apes gentry ways. Torn between his dissenting beliefs and his wish to be his own man, he begins to recognise the stronger position of Frank Wentworth, the Tractarian perpetual curate of St Roque's, who concerns himself only with 'his prayer book and the poor', who owes his priesting to a bishop, not to his congregation.[18] In the end he resigns his position and makes his living as a writer, founding 'a new organ of public opinion', the *Philosophical Review*.[19]

Intertwined with this story is a melodrama with all the plot ingredients that Oliphant so ridiculed in her essay on sensation fiction. It concerns a newcomer to Carlingford, Mrs Hilyard, an occasional member of the congregation of Salem Chapel. She is a woman of mystery, living in poverty, supporting herself as a seamstress, doing the coarsest sewing, but visited by the gentry, the Lady Western who puts Vincent's heart into such a flutter.

Mrs Hilyard has a beautiful young daughter, Alice, who tragically still has the mind of a child, 'a girl that has grown up an idiot',[20] and who currently lives away with a governess. She asks Vincent to help her protect her daughter from her husband, who wishes to marry Alice to some rich old man, if only he could find her hiding-place. Will his mother and sister, who live at some distance, harbour her? Meanwhile, his sister, Susan, is planning to marry a man known as Mr Fordham, newly arrived in their neighbourhood, who seemingly has no relations to vouch for him. In a plot twist worthy of any devised by Mary Braddon or Mrs Henry Wood, Susan Vincent's fiancé is none other than Mrs Hilyard's husband, either planning a bigamous marriage or worse, or seeing her as bait in a trap to catch his daughter.[21] Mrs Vincent receives an anonymous letter warning her of Mr Fordham's duplicity, and hurries to Carlingford to seek her son's advice. While she is away, Fordham kidnaps his daughter and Susan. Vincent abandons his followers to scour the length and breadth of England in his search for them, often missing them by minutes. He finally tracks them to Dover, to discover that the villainous Fordham has been shot in the head, and his sister, the prime suspect, is nowhere to be found. She eventually arrives at Carlingford delirious and comatose with shock. The would-be bigamist does not die, and swears an affidavit that Susan Vincent is not his attacker. The agents of the police leave Carlingford in search of their true quarry. Alice, constantly asking for her Susan, reappears at her bedside. Susan immediately wakes from her coma to do the task she undertook, to protect Alice. She and Alice and her mother go abroad for two or three years, and return to live with Vincent in London. In this space of time, his sister has grown into a Juno of a woman, with a commanding presence, and Alice is now a delightful young lady in full possession of her wits. The hint at the end is that Vincent may marry Alice, a plot resolution which may be testing too far the willing suspension of disbelief.[22]

There is a marked contrast of tone in the telling of the two stories. Scenes set in Salem Chapel and its congregation are a balance of hyperbole and bathos, Vincent's aspiration to convince the quality of Carlingford of the superiority of dissent, with the reality of tea-meetings with the decidedly down-market congregation of Salem Chapel. 'Cheerful folks and no display', says Mrs Pigeon, decked out in gaudy silks and finery; while Lady Western's invitation to supper is 'Circe's cup'.[23] At the tea-meeting, Phoebe Tozer, nubile daughter of the butterman, pink and plump, 'dispensed the fragrant lymph'.[24] Aitches are universally dropped, except by Phoebe, who has been sent to school to learn better ways.[25] Whenever the Tozers' door opened, 'the odours of the bacon and the cheese from the shop came in like a musty shadow of the boiled ham and sausage within'.[26]

The sensation plot unfurls in a miasma of melodrama, 'that dark and secret ocean of life'.[27] Initially it is Susan's unprotected exposure to the wicked ways of the world that preoccupy Vincent; his journey to track down Mr Fordham 'might be life or death for Susan'.[28] 'Was she, indeed, really a bride, with nothing but truth and sweet honour in the contract which bound her, or was she the sport of a villanous pastime that would break her heart?'[29] The astute reader fathoms that Mrs Hilyard's husband, he of the 'vile hands' is indeed the enigmatic Fordham when Vincent, telegraphing his sister about the imminent arrival of Alice and governess, glimpses his quarry on the train just leaving Carlingford.[30] This plot twist is only confronted by Vincent, his mother and Mrs Hilyard five chapters later. 'We have both thrust our children into the lion's mouth ... Go, poor woman, and save your child if you can, and so will I'.[31] At one point in his mad chase round the English countryside, he misses Fordham by seconds as, yet again, a train carries away his quarry. 'Now it was gone into the black night, into the chill space, carrying a hundred innocent souls and light hearts, and among them, deadly crime and vengeance, the doomed man and his executioner', since Mrs Hilyard is on the same train.[32]

Passages of purple prose such as this are interleaved with scenes back at Salem Chapel, to great comic effect: 'You was intimated to begin that course on the miracles, Mr Vincent, if you'll excuse *me*, on Sunday' says Mr Tozer.[33] And always the constant refrain, 'If a minister ain't a servant, we pays him his salary at the least, and expects him to please us', a strategy which highlights the competition between the two plots, as they jostle for position front of stage.[34] Indeed, there are points where the playing out of the mechanicals' argument with their minister assumes a melodramatic air that competes with the sensation plot, as the dissenting congregation's meeting to air their dissenting views about their minister's priorities, and Vincent's impassioned and impromptu speech on the meaning of 'love one another', threaten to invade and outdo the theatrical territory of the sensation plot. As the two devices collide, it becomes difficult to discern which plot is parodying the other. Does the manufactured sensation of the second plot ape the drama played out at Salem Chapel to determine if the 'He who pays the piper calls the tune' is God, or a committee of grocers? Or does Oliphant's framing of the Salem Chapel saga in bathos critique the secular and profane sensation plots that abounded in the 1860s? For just as, seemingly, in order to keep his post, Arthur Vincent must give his congregation what they want, not what he feels called to give them, so the demands of the reading public press Oliphant to write what they want, which is not necessarily what she would like to do. These competing demands are explored by Elisabeth Jay where she quotes Leslie Stephen. She had 'sold her brain, her very admirable brain, prostituted her culture and enslaved her intellectual liberty in order that she might earn her living and educate her children'.[35]

Intervening at all turns of both plots is Vincent's mother, a widow of small stature, but greater presence, who valiantly tries to keep rampant speculation rooted in reality as she battles to protect her family's reputation. She has lived the balancing act of a dissenting minister's bounden duty to his congregation. She has walked that tightrope between intimacy and aloofness. She tries hard to impart this knowledge to Vincent, knowing it is as important to engage with the church cleaners as to put in an appearance at the tea-meetings. It is Mrs Vincent who makes the impassioned plea to the butterman not to push Vincent into resigning his position, 'he will throw it all up, as so many talented young men in our connection do nowadays'.[36] This strikes home, 'The widow's Parthian arrow had gone straight to the butterman's heart'.[37] Tozer, the butterman, if Vincent could only lower himself to notice it, is in reality, Vincent's greatest ally. He does recognise Vincent's outstanding talents. He responds in a practical way, by standing bail for £200 when the policeman is insisting on staying in the house till Susan comes out of her coma so he can arrest her. As it is, Vincent's sensibilities are constantly offended by the smell of ham and butter which pervades the whole house. For the Tozers, it's the odour of prosperity. To Vincent it's the ever-present reminder of their lowly status, of a piece with dropping their aitches, and angling him as a 'catch' for their daughter. But Tozer is a man of honest good sense, and when Mrs Vincent speaks to him about how many young men from the 'connexion' kick against the constraints, and leave, he recognises the truth in what is happening to young Vincent. He takes on the rest of the flock valiantly, and while he is successful in helping them understand their good fortune in having a minister of Vincent's superior understanding, it is not enough to sway Vincent. He preaches a final powerful sermon about the love of God, and our duty to love one another, and resigns. It is not loss of faith on Vincent's part which drives him to this. It is the recognition that he cannot have two masters.

> I am one of those who have boasted in my day that I received my title to ordination from no bishop, from no temporal provision, from no traditional church, but from the hands of the people . . . I resign to your hands your pulpit, which you have erected with your money, and hold as your property. I cannot hold it as your vassal . . . I am either your servant, responsible to you, or God's servant, responsible to Him – which is it? I cannot tell, but no man can serve two masters, as you know.[38]

While he insists on refuting apostolic succession, 'I received my ordination from no bishop', and in spite of his successful evening lectures on the ills of an established church, Vincent does have Anglican leanings. 'He was almost as particular as the Rev. Mr Wentworth of St Roque's about the cut of his coat and the precision of his costume, and decidedly preferred the word clergyman to the word minister'.[39] In fact, we learn very little about Vincent's dissenting theology. He seems to have little taste for evangelising. He certainly does not try to offer Mrs Hilyard spiritual comfort. Apart from despising ritual and believing that the riches of the Church of England are an obstacle to holiness, comparing the Archbishop of Canterbury unfavourably to Paul the tent-maker,[40] the nearest he comes to professing a Christian belief is his address to his congregation before his final sermon, where he proclaims that 'love one another' means standing shoulder to shoulder with each other, standing side by side, in loyalty and support. It is a powerful address, and he walks out of the assembly 'with a sense of freedom, and a thrill of new power and vigour in his heart'.[41]

The Perpetual Curate (1864)

Oliphant was well-versed in the heart-raising effects of a fine preaching style. The previous year she had published a biography of Edward Irving, a Scottish divine who also filled halls and churches with his fine preaching. He too was brought down low by the cavilling of Scottish Presbyterians but went on to found the millenarianist Holy Catholic Apostolic Church. She had been brought up in the Scottish Free Church. One of the advantages for her parents of the move from Scotland to Liverpool when she was ten was the existence of a nearby Free Church Chapel. In her autobiography she writes:

> As a matter of fact, I know nothing about chapels, but took the senti-ment and a few details from our old church in Liverpool, which was Free Church of Scotland, and where there were a few grocers and other such good folk whose ways with the minister were wonderful to behold.[42]

As early as 1855, Blackwood's asked her to write a response to F.D. Maurice's *The Patriarchs and Lawgivers of the Old Testament.* In her article, she took Maurice to task over complicating the stories of the Old Testament.[43] In a voice at time cynical, sometimes world-weary, often using hyperbole and bathos, she dismissed Maurice's arguments as irrelevant to the common man. It was well received by Blackwood's, who afterwards regularly called on her to write on religious topics: 'Religion in Common Life' (1856),[44] 'Reli-gious Memoirs' (1858), and 'Edward Irving' (1858, an early encapsulation of her later *Life of Edward Irving*).[45] Towards the end of her life they published her 'Fancies of a Believer' (1895).[46] For Blackwood's at any rate, her grasp of the popular vein of religious thinking, was bankable.

She wrote most of the *Chronicles of Carlingford* between 1863 and 1866, with *Phoebe, Junior* as a last trumpet in 1876, and current religious issues percolate through all of them. She introduces themes of church patronage. Is it right that an Oxford College, remote from Carlingford life and its needs, should be free to appoint a scholar like Mr Proctor to be rector, when there is a crying need for ministry in the poor working-class district down by the canal? To be sure, the perpetual curate of St Roque's does an outstanding job with the working man, but is it fair that he is paid £40 p.a. and augments this from his none-too-great personal income while the rector has a com-fortable living? What *are* the hallmarks of Christianity? Is dissent in its way more corrupt, when congregations are so lacking in Christian charity?

While there are few mentions of Frank Wentworth in *Salem Chapel*, his story threads in and out of the *Carlingford Chronicles*, until he becomes the primary subject in *The Perpetual Curate*. Perpetual curacies had been in existence since the dissolution of the monasteries, and in the nineteenth century, with increasing urbanisation and population migration, many churches found themselves unable to serve the larger populations, with their concentrations of urban labouring poor. In some cases, new churches were built, but more often chapels of easement were built in existing parishes, with permanent curates appointed, often on very poor stipends. This is Frank Wentworth's situation; he is the perpetual curate of St Roque's, a chapel of easement, built in the 1840s, designed by Gilbert Scott, a perfect example of Gothic revival.[47] He is staunchly Tractarian, 'as near Rome as a strong and lofty connection of the really superior catholicity of the Anglican Church would permit him to be' and intones the services, decorates his altar, has a surpliced choir and lighted candles.[48] With the compliance of the old rector, he has established a mission church down by the canal, to serve the bargemen. He has erected a tin chapel and is respected and admired by these labourers. He has recruited two parishioners, the Misses Woodhouse, to be Sisters of Mercy, visiting the poor and sick in their grey cloaks.[49] This is all of a piece with the principles of early Tractarians. Edward Pewsey had a great calling to establish urban missions towards the un-churched working poor, and had himself endowed a church in Leeds, St Saviour's, to promote his ideals.[50]

In *The Perpetual Curate* (1864), Mr Vincent has come and gone from Salem Chapel, Mr Procter has retreated to his sanctuary at All Souls, we are waiting for Mr Morgan to succeed him as rector, and Frank Wentworth is still the perpetual curate of St Roque's, on £40 a year, and still hopelessly in love with Lucy Woodhouse. It is a story of small-town gossip and intrigue. A rather silly seventeen-year-old girl has run away, a mystery man has been taken in by our perpetual curate, an elderly man dies intestate, with no adequate provision for his daughters, the new rector takes exception to the sterling work Frank Wentworth is doing with the bargemen in the poorest district of the town, and the Wentworths, long-established gentry with a fine estate at some distance from Carlingford, are having all the problems common to such families: a ne'er-do-well heir, under-achieving sons who must be sent to the colonies, a squire in poor health worrying about how to provide for a wife and a large number of offspring and a clergyman son (not Frank!) agonising about crossing to Rome. Woven into this are some fine debates about the nature of apostolic succession (if a clergyman of the Church of England perverts to Rome, does he cease to be a priest?), the function of ritual in the *Book of Common Prayer* (are candles on altars and intoned services uncanonical?) and the true essence of the practice of Christian belief (if Frank, by good deeds, can persuade a bargeman to reform his ways and bring his six children for baptism, does his preference for a surpliced choir make him less of a Christian?). Like the question of baptismal renewal, these were all issues that were being hotly contested, and Oliphant knows her audience would be up-to-date with the arguments. On page 233, for instance, as Frank ponders, with some amusement, on the sermon possibilities of sibling competition, 'that virtuous uninteresting elder brother', and the brothers of the prodigal son, he imagines what 'Dr Cumming, or the minister of Salem Chapel' might have made of it. Dr Cumming was a Presbyterian minister with a powerful preaching style. Like Edward Irving, he took a dwindling congregation in London, and boosted membership from 90 to 900. He wrote over 150 books, was virulently anti-Catholic, and apocalyptic in his view of the current world.[51]

Phoebe, Junior (1876)

By the time Oliphant wrote *Phoebe, Junior* in 1876, much of the ecclesiastical debate had moved on and, with it, the clerical scene in Carlingford. Twenty years later, Frank Wentworth, the newly appointed rector at the end of *The Perpetual Curate*, is gone.[52] Grange Lane is falling into genteel decline. Mr Tozer, the butterman and his wife now live in Lady Western's old house. Mr Beecham (Arthur Vincent's successor as minister to Salem Chapel), has married Phoebe Tozer. He has learnt not to drop his aitches, and is now the minister of a thriving, forward-looking non-conformist chapel near Regents Park in London, and a man of liberal view, 'Depend on it, my dear sir ... the Establishment is not such an unmitigated evil as some people consider it', though Phoebe, who in *Salem Chapel* 'understood pretty well about her h's, and did not use the double negative', has lapses and calls her husband 'Henery'.[53] They have a twenty-year-old daughter Phoebe junior, a well-educated young woman of independent view, who goes to Carlingford to look after her grandmother who has been ill. The Reverend Mr May, another high-church man, is now the perpetual curate, but has a stipend of more than £300 a year. He is a widower, prone to debt, has a newly ordained son who befriends the latest young minister at Salem Chapel. True to form, this minister, Harold Northcote, has made a public address in Carlingford, attacking the extravagances of the Church of England in general, and the well-paid chaplaincy recently accepted by young Reginald May in particular. Reginald shows no animosity and offers him friendship in true Christian spirit. His humility in doing the pastoral duties for the rector, 'Since I have been here [. . .] in this sinecure as you call it [. . .] I have been everybody's curate. If the others have too much work, and I too little, my duty is clear, don't you think?', strikes Northcote to his heart, and he accepts his hand of friendship.[54] Reginald's father enjoys informed debate and welcomes Northcote to his home and his table (where he duly falls in love with Ursula, the eldest daughter). Northcote recognises the true Christian spirit in this:

> A stranger, belonging to an obscure class, I had no claim upon them except that I had done what ought to have closed their house against me. And you know how they have interpreted that. They have shown me what the Bible means.[55]

The Salem Chapel flock are as aghast as ever at their minister's cosying up to the priesthood. As Mrs Pigeon, the arch stirrer in Vincent's day, says,

'If ever there was an iniquity on this earth, it is a State Church, and all the argufying in the world won't put that out of me'.[56]

But there is a dark side to Mr May's life. Deeply in debt, he has forged Mr Tozer's signature on a bill, and the day of reckoning comes. Tozer is bent on justice, but Mr May suffers a fit and is clearly too ill to face up to what he has done. Phoebe Junior comes to the rescue. She recognises what Mr May has done; she purloins the forged bill from her grandfather, talks to all the aggrieved parties, persuades Northcote to settle the bill and burns it before Mr May's own eyes. Phoebe Junior is a classic Oliphant heroine, a woman of agency, in a world where many of the men are ineffectual.

The moral equivocation around Mr May's criminal activities and the manner of his escaping justice are balanced against Christian love in the May household, and the bickering judgementalism of the dissenters. As Phoebe says, 'Who has been kind to me in Carlingford except the Mays? Nobody. Who has asked me to go to their house and share everything? None of your Salem people, grandpapa'.[57] This mirrors precisely Harold Northcote's Carlingford experience. When Ursula accepts him, he withdraws from his ministerial calling, recognising, as Phoebe did, that the dissenting congregation have, as Vincent so eloquently preached, a very blinkered interpretation of 'Be sure that you love one another'. He gives up the Liberation Society, that great organ of dissent, 'coming to see that Disestablishment was not a panacea for national evils any more than other things'.[58]

Conclusion: Anglican and other crises of faith in the English novel after Oliphant

Oliphant's presentation of Protestant dissenters like Beecham and Northcote modifying their view of the Established Church reflects the progressively changing nature of ecclesiastical debate. The heat left the disestablishment controversy in 1868 when that great source of irritation among dissenters, the church rate, was abolished.[59] By the time Oliphant wrote *Phoebe, Junior* in 1876, disestablishment arguments were less about the disabilities of dissenters and more about the future of the Church of England in an increasingly secular society. For while Charlotte Yonge and Emma Jane Worboise, for instance, never faltered in their mission to present their own interpretations of Christian belief in their fictions, there was a groundswell of change. David Strauss' *Life of Jesus*, translated by George Eliot and published in 1846, opened up debate about the historical Jesus and the Messianic Christ. The progressive revelations of natural science also fuelled re-evaluation of accepted truths. Charles Lyell's *Principles of Geology* (1830–1833) challenged people's belief in the literal account of creation found in Genesis and underpinned the even greater controversy of Charles Darwin's *On the Origin of Species*, in 1859. These advancements in scientific understanding did not in themselves undermine the Established Church. As Chadwick points out, 'The most eminent English geologists were not only Christian, but clergymen, not only clergymen, but devout'.[60] However, they shifted the expressions of religious thought in the popular novel, as the doubts formed by new thinking creep into plot formation. William Hale White's *The Autobiography of Mark Rutherford* (1881) typifies this shift, and paves the way for that great novel of doubt, Mrs Humphry Ward's *Robert Elsmere* (1888), described by John Sutherland as 'Probably the best-selling "quality novel" of the century'.[61] Elsmere is a Church of England clergyman whose faith is sorely tested by rationalist debate, and who gives up his comfortable living to lead the life of a missionary among the poor of East London. He sets up a movement, the New Christian Brotherhood, propounding Christian belief as a metaphor rather than taking the Bible as a literal truth. He dies young, of overwork and tuberculosis.

By the beginning of the twentieth century, religion as a theme in the popular novel had somewhat faded. Two world wars and attempts to make sense of world events saw some re-awakening. Evelyn Waugh's *Brideshead Revisited* (1945)[62] is perhaps the best known, for its nostalgic reflections on the certainties of Roman Catholic faith and on an England ruled by its aristocracy. Barbara Pym's sardonic tales of life in Anglican backwaters have a loyal and discerning following,[63] while Susan Howatch's immensely popular *Starbridge* series (1987–1994) explores the development of Anglican doctrine through the twentieth century.[64] While they are like a triumphal shout that the genre is not dead, it is unlikely that the expression of religious belief will ever match its apogee of the Victorian age. As Jay points out:

> Throughout the Victorian period [. . .] it was assumed that a man's religious life was so emotionally bound up with his social existence and behaviour that to ignore it was to sacrifice a major insight into the influences forming a man's character [. . .] religion was native to the novel's sphere.[65]

It was part of Oliphant's genius to recognise and exploit this.

Notes

1 Owen Chadwick is the prime authority on the history of the Church of England, and I draw widely on his accounts in vol. 1 of his two-volume *The Victorian Church* (London: Adam and Charles Black, 1970). For Phillpott's attack on the soundness of bishop Hampden's doctrine, for instance, see pp. 237–250.

2 Chadwick, *Victorian Church*, pp. 250–271.

3 There are some notable explorations of the Victorian religious novel: see V. Cunningham, *Everywhere Spoken Against: Dissent in the Victorian Novel* (Oxford: Clarendon Press, 1975); E. Jay, *The Religion of the Heart: Anglican Evangelicalism and the Nineteenth Century Novel* (Oxford: Clarendon Press, 1979); and the unmissable M. Maison, *Search your Soul, Eustace* (London: Sheed and Ward, 1962).

4 Treatments of dissent in England lead inexorably back to Luther and developments in Europe, often via John Bunyan. Many of the commentators cited in this

essay make this journey, but for more explicit exploration, see C. Hill, *Puritanism and Revolution* (Harmondsworth: Penguin, 1986) and J.C.D. Clark, *English Society 1660 – 1832: Religion, Ideology and Politics During the Ancien Regime*, 2nd edn (Cambridge: Cambridge University Press, 2000).

5 Chadwick, *Victorian Church*, pp. 7–17.
6 Chadwick, *Victorian Church*, pp. 24–47.
7 R.D. Altick, *The English Common Reader*, 2nd edn (Columbus: Ohio State University Press, 1998), pp. 348–364.
8 Coventry Patmore's immensely popular long poem, *The Angel in the House* (London: John W Parker, 1858) sold 250,000 copies in his lifetime. Patmore's 'angel' devotes her life to supporting her husband, ministering to the children and running the household as a model of domestic economy.
9 E. Jay, *Mrs Oliphant: 'A Fiction to Herself': A Literary Life* (Oxford: Clarendon Press, 1995), pp. 11–24.
10 V. Colby and R.A. Colby, *The Equivocal Virtue: Mrs Oliphant and the Victorian Literary Market Place* (Hamden, CT: Archon, 1966), p. viii.
11 In 1851, alongside the regular census, a census of religious attendance was conducted the following Sunday. See D. M Thompson, 'The Religious Census of 1851', in *The Census and Social Structure*, ed. by R. Lawton (London: Cass, 1978), pp. 241–288.
12 See R. Strong, 'The Oxford Movement and Missions', in *The Oxford Handbook of the Oxford Movement*, ed. by S.J. Brown, P. Nockles, and J. Pereiro (Oxford: Oxford University Press, 2017), p. 486.
13 *The Doctor's Family*, p. 99. See J. Mayo, *A History of Ecclesiastical Dress* (London: Batsford, 1984), ch. 8.
14 Jay, *Mrs Oliphant: 'A Fiction to Herself'*, p. 288.
15 'Sensation Novels', *Blackwood's Edinburgh Magazine* 91:559 (May 1862), pp. 564–584.
16 Jay, *Mrs Oliphant: A Fiction to Herself*, p. 147.
17 M. Oliphant, *Salem Chapel* (1863; London: Virago, 1986), p. 77. Full details of the modern editions of Oliphant's other works cited here are in the bibliography.
18 Oliphant, *Salem Chapel*, p. 94.
19 Oliphant, *Salem Chapel*, p. 457.
20 Oliphant, *Salem Chapel*. p. 253.
21 The whole novel does pulsate with unnarrated sexual exploitation, as Winifred Hughes puts it, 'the unbeatable combination of sin and sentiment'. See W. Hughes, *The Maniac in the Cellar: Sensation Novels of the 1860s* (Princeton, NJ: Princeton University Press, 1981), p. 112.
22 The concept of a dormant mind being restored to full intelligence is further explored in *Innocent*, serialised in *The Graphic*, 1873.
23 Oliphant, *Salem Chapel*, p. 19; p. 69.
24 Oliphant, *Salem Chapel*, p. 98.
25 Oliphant, *Salem Chapel*, p. 10.
26 Oliphant, *Salem Chapel*, p. 40.
27 Oliphant, *Salem Chapel*, p. 114.
28 Oliphant, *Salem Chapel*, p. 133.
29 Oliphant, *Salem Chapel*, p. 136.
30 Oliphant, *Salem Chapel*, p. 106.
31 Oliphant, *Salem Chapel*, p. 160.
32 Oliphant, *Salem Chapel*, pp. 227–228.
33 Oliphant, *Salem Chapel*, p. 169.
34 Oliphant, *Salem Chapel*, p. 174.
35 Jay, *Mrs Oliphant: 'A Fiction to Herself'*, pp. 290–292.
36 Oliphant, *Salem Chapel*, p. 364.

37 Oliphant, *Salem Chapel*, p. 365.
38 Oliphant, *Salem Chapel*, p. 453.
39 Oliphant, *Salem Chapel*, p. 4.
40 Oliphant, *Salem Chapel*, p. 77.
41 Oliphant, *Salem Chapel*, p. 454.
42 M. Oliphant, *Autobiography and Letters of Mrs Margaret Oliphant*, ed. by Mrs Harry Coghill, 1899 (Leicester: Leicester University Press, 1974), p. 84.
43 'Modern Light Literature-Theology' *Blackwood's Edinburgh Magazine* 78:477 (July 1855), pp. 72–86.
44 'Religious Memoirs', *Blackwood's Edinburgh Magazine* 83:512 (June 1858), pp. 703–718.
45 'Edward Irving', *Blackwood's Edinburgh Magazine* 84:517 (November 1858), pp. 567–585.
46 'Fancies of a Believer', *Blackwood's Magazine* 157:952 (February 1895), pp. 237–255.
47 M. Oliphant, *The Perpetual Curate* (1864; London: Virago, 1987), p. 8. Gilbert Scott designed the Albert memorial and many of the government buildings in Whitehall.
48 Oliphant, *Perpetual Curate*, p. 3.
49 For an interesting account on the development of women's roles in the Tractarian movement see C.E. Herringer, 'The Revival of Religious Life: The Sisterhoods', in *The Oxford Handbook of the Oxford Movement*, ed. by S.J. Brown, P. Nockles, and J. Pereiro (Oxford: Oxford University Press, 2017), pp. 387–397.
50 Strong, 'The Oxford Movement and Missions', p. 485.
51 See biographical entry in *Dictionary of National Biography*, ed. by L. Stephen and S. Lee, vol. 5, p. 297.
52 Oliphant, *Phoebe, Junior*, p. 211.
53 Oliphant, *Phoebe, Junior*, p. 2, p. 7, Oliphant, *Salem Chapel*, p. 10.
54 Oliphant, *Phoebe, Junior*, p. 197.
55 Oliphant, *Phoebe, Junior*, p. 243.
56 Oliphant, *Phoebe, Junior*, p. 229.
57 Oliphant, *Phoebe, Junior*, p. 296.
58 Oliphant, *Phoebe, Junior*, p. 340.
59 Chadwick, *Victorian Church*, pp. 142–158.
60 Chadwick, *Victorian Church*, p. 559.
61 J. Sutherland, *The Longman Companion to Victorian Fiction* (Harlow: Longman, 1990), p. 539.
62 E. Waugh, *Brideshead Revisited* (1945; London: Chapman and Hall, 1960).
63 For instance, B. Pym, *Some Tame Gazelle* (1959; London: Panther Books, 1984).
64 Susan Howatch's six *Starbridge* novels were all published between 1987 and 1995 by Collins and HarperCollins. See variously S. Howatch, *Glittering Images* (London: Collins, 1987); S. Howatch, *Glamorous Powers* (London: Collins, 1988); S. Howatch, *Ultimate Prizes* (London: Collins, 1989); S. Howatch, *Scandalous Risks* (London: Collins, 1990); S. Howatch, *Mystical Paths* (London: HarperCollins, 1992); S. Howatch, *Absolute Truths* (London: HarperCollins, 1995).
65 Jay, *The Religion of the Heart*, p. 2.

Bibliography

Altick, R.D. *The English Common Reader*, 2nd edn (Columbus: Ohio State University Press, 1998).

Chadwick, O. *The Victorian Church*, 2 vols (London: Adam and Charles Black, 1966), vol. 1.

Clark, J.C.D. *English Society 1660–1832: Religion, Ideology and Politics During the Ancien Regime*, 2nd edn (Cambridge: Cambridge University Press, 2000).

Colby, V. and R.A. Colby, *The Equivocal Virtue: Mrs Oliphant and the Victorian Literary Market Place* (Hamden, CT: Archon, 1966).

Cunningham, V. *Everywhere Spoken Against: Dissent in the Victorian Novel* (Oxford: Clarendon Press, 1975).

Darwin, C. *On the Origin of Species* (1859; Oxford: Oxford University Press, 1996).

Disraeli, B. *Lothair* (1870; London: Peter Davies, 1927).

Herring, G. 'Devotional and Liturgical Renewal: Ritualism and Protestant Reaction', in *The Oxford Handbook of the Oxford Movement*, ed. by S.J. Brown, P. Nockles, and J. Pereiro (Oxford: Oxford University Press, 2017), pp. 398–409.

Herringer, C.E. 'The Revival of Religious Life: The Sisterhoods', in *The Oxford Handbook of the Oxford Movement*, ed. by S.J. Brown, P. Nockles, and J. Pereiro (Oxford: Oxford University Press, 2017), pp. 387–397.

Hill, C. *Puritanism and Revolution* (Harmondsworth: Penguin, 1986).

Howatch, S. *Absolute Truths* (London: HarperCollins, 1995).

Howatch, S. *Glamorous Powers* (London: Collins, 1988).

Howatch, S. *Glittering Images* (London: Collins, 1987).

Howatch, S. *Mystical Paths* (London: HarperCollins, 1992).

Howatch, S. *Scandalous Risks* (London: Collins, 1990).

Howatch, S. *Ultimate Prizes* (London: Collins, 1989).

Hughes, W. *The Maniac in the Cellar: Sensation Novels of the 1860s* (Princeton, NJ: Princeton University Press, 1981).

Jay, E. *Mrs Oliphant: 'A Fiction to Herself': A Literary Life* (Oxford: Clarendon Press, 1995).

Jay, E. *The Religion of the Heart: Anglican Evangelicalism in the Nineteenth Century Novel* (Oxford: Clarendon Press, 1979).

Keble, J. *The Christian Year: Thoughts in Verse for the Sundays and Holydays throughout the Year* (1827; Oxford: Collingwood, 1832).

Lyell, C. *Principles of Geology* (1830–1833; Chicago: University of Chicago Press, 1991).

Maurice, F.D. *The Patriarchs and Lawgivers of the Old Testament* (London: Macmillan, 1855).

Mayo, J. *A History of Ecclesiastical Dress* (London: Batsford, 1984).

Oliphant, M. *Autobiography and Letters of Mrs Margaret Oliphant*, ed. by Mrs Harry Coghill (1899; Leicester: Leicester University Press, 1974).

Oliphant, M. 'Edward Irving', *Blackwood's Edinburgh Magazine* 84:517 (November 1858), pp. 567–585.

Oliphant, M. 'Fancies of a Believer', *Blackwood's Magazine* 157:952 (February 1895), pp. 237–255.

Oliphant, M. *Katy Stewart: A true story* (Edinburgh: Blackwoods, 1853).

Oliphant, M. *The Life of Edward Irving* (London: Hurst and Blackwell, 1862).

Oliphant, M. *Miss Marjoribanks* (1866; London: Virago, 1988).

Oliphant, M. *Phoebe, Junior* (1876; London: Virago, 1989).

Oliphant, M. *The Perpetual Curate* (1864; London: Virago, 1987).

Oliphant, M. *The Rector and The Doctor's Family* (1863; London: Virago, 1986).

Oliphant, M. 'Religion in Common Life', *Blackwood's Edinburgh Magazine* 79:484 (February 1856), pp. 243–246.

Oliphant, M. 'Religious Memoirs', *Blackwood's Edinburgh Magazine* 83:512 (June 1858), pp. 703–718.

Oliphant, M. *Salem Chapel* (1863; London: Virago, 1986).

Oliphant, M. 'Sensation Novels', *Blackwood's Edinburgh Magazine* 91:559 (May 1862), pp. 564–584.

Maison, M. *Search your Soul, Eustace* (London: Sheed and Ward, 1962).

Pym, B. *Some Tame Gazelle* (1959; London: Panther, 1984).

Stephen, L. and S. Lee, eds, *Dictionary of National Biography* (Oxford: Oxford University Press, 1921–1922).

Strauss, D. *The Life of Jesus, Critically Examined* (1836; transl. George Eliot 1846; London: S.C.M. Press, 1973).

Strong, R. 'The Oxford Movement and Missions', in *The Oxford Handbook of the Oxford Movement*, ed. by S.J. Brown, P. Nockles, and J. Pereiro (Oxford: Oxford University Press, 2017), pp. 483–499.

Sutherland, J. *The Longman Companion to Victorian Fiction* (Harlow: Longman, 1990).

Thompson, D.M. 'The Religious Census of 1851', in *The Census and Social Structure*, ed. by R. Lawton (London: Cass, 1978), pp. 241–288.

Trollope, A. *Phineas Redux* (1873; Oxford: Oxford University Press, 1991).

Ward, M. *Robert Elsmere* (1888; Oxford: Oxford University Press, 1987).

Waugh, E. *Brideshead Revisited* (1945; London: Chapman and Hall, 1960).

White, W.H. *Autobiography of Mark Rutherford* (1881; London: Unwin, 1892).

Part II
Union and disunion in Europe

3 Popular efforts to forge union

The English visit to Paris in April 1849

James Gregory

Introduction

In the Paris Museum collection a crude white-metal medal bears the legend, 'Visite rendue par les Français à Londres, septembre 1848; et par les Anglais à Paris, avril 1849', one of several medal designs (see Figure 3.1) commemorating an amicable episode in Anglo-French relations in the aftermath of continental revolution.[1] British and French newspapers reported and depicted these efforts to promote 'fraternal union' from the welcome to several hundred Englishmen and their wives at Boulogne to such entertainments as a banquet given by the National Guard to the 'deputation' in Paris. The French response was extraordinary for what was an unofficial excursion of ordinary Englishmen (and women) to the Second Republic.

This chapter examines the event's significance through treatment in newspapers, in the satirical press, accounts such as the pamphlet by John Bill of Farley Hall, Staffordshire (1795–1853), the anonymous *What I saw in Paris during Easter 1849* and commentary from the political elite.[2] The excursion offers a bourgeois or popular diplomatic aspect to the *entente cordiale* (a term current in the early 1840s) following tension over such incidents

Figure 3.1 Medal commemorating the return visit of the English to Paris, April 1849. Author's collection.

as the Spanish Marriages controversy (1846) and before the much-studied Anglo-French accord of 1904.[3]

The return visit to Paris alarmed British critics because of its irregular constitution. For *The Times* it was

> an accidental assemblage of individuals of the middle class from London and other large towns of England, without any official character or pretensions, who have availed themselves of a short holyday to visit a city to which they conceived themselves, in sort, to have been bidden.[4]

Yet '[n]one better than the tradesmen of England can assure the shopkeepers of Paris of the benefits of peace', *The Times* conceded. Where *The Times* was scornful others were more welcoming, but similarly equated the National Guard of 'master tradesmen and journeymen' with the English middle classes.[5] 'It is to the pleasant interchange of the middle classes of countries one with another', commented the *Norwich Mercury*, 'that the world shall get chiefly over the hostile prejudices'.[6] A year before, English weavers, iron-workers and other workers had faced violence in the revolution's aftermath, in northern France.[7]

Background: October 1848–February 1849

The visit to France was presented as a reaction to the National Guards' visits to London in September and October 1848 when they were welcomed to 'public establishments' and Mansion House, the latter commemorated by medals.[8] *Punch's* 'Mes Impressions de Voyage. By a Garde Nationale in London', which accompanied a cut, 'French National Guards in London', observed, 'the National Guard has been the best diplomatists that one country ever sent to another'.[9] Ideas about reciprocating were stimulated: in December *The Satirist* reported the Northumbrian and Newcastle Yeomanry planned a 'return visit to France', consisting of 'butchers, bakers, barbers, and host of other shopkeepers ... it would be more appropriate to designate the loyal corps a "Trades Union"'.[10]

The figurehead for the actual 'deputation' in Easter 1849 was a Middlesex magistrate and vice-president of the West London Literary and Scientific Institution, Francis Lloyd (1803–1875), who had been a Warwickshire JP and High Bailiff of Birmingham.[11] With Quaker lineage, he was partner in the banking firm of Taylor and Lloyds, until malpractice in 1839 forced his resignation.[12] A Francophile, Lloyd reportedly established a bank in Paris.[13] In 1842 *Bentley's Miscellany* published Lloyd's 'A Visit to the Bank of France', which boasted of his friendship with one of the bank's directors. A projected essay series on French politicians began with a study of the opposition politician in the July Monarchy's Chamber of Deputies, Odilon Barrot.[14] Further essays were reprinted in his anonymous *Pilferings from the Paris and Dover Postbag* (1842), dedicated to the ambassador to France, Lord Cowley.[15]

In 1840 Lloyd attempted to ease tensions over France's middle-eastern policy through a pamphlet that (he claimed) 'soften[ed] much of the asperity and bitterness felt and expressed at the time'. He was thanked by 'almost all the great party leaders', including members of the Chambers of Peers and Deputies who had been critical of England.[16] His correspondents included the president of the Council of Ministers, Marshal Soult (Soult, when he had attended the queen's coronation as special ambassador, was invited to Birmingham by a deputation that included Lloyd, in 1838[17]). Controversy ensued when Soult's confidential letter was leaked to the French press, triggering a declaration of his political creed. Lloyd claimed not to have intended the letter to be public when he shared it with ambassador Granville, Baron Rothschild and other English acquaintances.[18] Lloyd's efforts in 1840 were ignored in the British press coverage of April 1849.

Lloyd's several essays on travels in northern France included one printing a speech given as the sole Englishman at a banquet of the *garde nationale* in the autumn of 1848. In French he told them, 'without order there is no liberty, and to ensure order and liberty in Europe, these two great nations, France and England, must be friends'.[19] He believed that

> were every Englishman to use opportunities that present themselves, favourable to the growth of friendly feelings between our two countries, instead of fomenting national prejudices, chances of war would be rendered as remote as the most Utopian member of the Peace Congress could desire.

Lloyd was in Paris in January and February 1849, then at the London Guildhall when the French *charge d'affaires* in the presence of guests that included Lord Palmerston, eulogised England as the land of liberty.[20]

To promote the return visit of Britons an 'International English and French Association' was advertised in February.[21] The *Morning Post* noted 'an enormous placard' with details about the return visit, visible in the street.[22] The *Post* commented on its parliamentary sponsors, a group of 'young and new-born M.P.s who will be immortalised in the *Charivari*, and to whose exertions we shall in all probability be indebted for a new and enlarged edition of *Les Anglais pour rire*'. The five Liberal MPs were the geographer James Wyld (1812–1887), MP for Bodmin; the ship-owner, carrier and textile manufacturer Humphrey Brown, MP for Tewkesbury (*c.*1803–1860); the antislavery agitator George Thompson (1804–1878), MP for Tower Hamlets; the former linen draper and supporter of the Anti-Corn Law League, John Williams, MP for Macclesfield (died 1855) and Brodie Willcox (1786–1862), MP for Southampton and co-founder of the P & O Stream Navigation Company.

The prospectus began: 'We dine together – we, France and England, in a family sense – you, France, dine with me to-day, and I, England, claim your hospitality tomorrow'. A visit of the citizenship must include the 'simply competent', beside the rich, and thus 'some commercial considerations – for those who find it really necessary to put business into the pocket of pleasure'. Commercial travellers and other businessmen could capitalise on the conviviality: 'I go as an item in the general nationality ... and it may so happen that I may bring home with me the spring fashions of the young republic'.[23]

Punch found the pamphlet odd, 'verbs ... in a state of frightful disagreement with their nominative cases, and antecedents are running wildly about in vague pursuit of their missing relatives'.[24] The association's claim to provisional registration was raised by the Conservative MP for Bridport, Alexander Baillie Cochrane in the Commons on 22 February 1849, as its proceedings involved the 'dignity and character of the House of Commons', prompting an unedifying debate on the subject. Cochrane asked Home Secretary George Cornwell Lewis if it was a hoax and the Speaker objected to Cochrane putting a question to individual members and speaking on a question unconnected to public business.[25] The *Globe*'s critical account of the MPs' involvement in this 'mountebank, catchpenny concern' appeared on 24 February. It referred to an advertisement with their names 'paraded for the last ten days on a great blue van up and down Piccadilly and Regent street', and saw it as an attempt by the MPs to garner signs of consequence such as dining with the French President.[26] The satirical *Puppet-Show* and *Punch* unsubtly referred to the debtor status of some of the MPs (Boulogne being famously the resort of English debtors).[27]

The company scheme fell through even though some press reports would describe the visit as under its auspices.[28] A notice appeared in the press a month later, informing the public that it would be managed by Joseph Crisp who had made a reputation as the contractor for excursion trips to and from Liverpool, Manchester, Bath, Bristol, London and Paris.[29] Crisp's scheme for an Easter holiday was promoted in the London and provincial newspapers.[30] The public was told that 'the French government have in the most friendly and liberal spirit offered every facility for the gratification and accommodation of the visitors'. There would be a 'committee of surveillance', of respectable individuals, issuing free pass cards for the excursionists' admission to exhibitions in Paris and the neighbourhood, including the palace of Versailles.[31] Not all were confident about the outcome. *Bell's Life in London* contrasted the National Guards with the English who were attracted by the trip's cheapness but lacked the Frenchmen's bond of 'interest and discipline'. This was dangerous since they might make mistakes 'neither creditable to themselves nor to their country'. The remedy would be 'bands with certain recognised heads' and regulations. If not, they would be 'a horde of ill-regulated wanderers, lose time, money, and character'.[32] With the prejudice of a Paris correspondent, the *Morning Post* in early March referred to thousands of 'cocktail cockneys' enjoying the 'intellectuality of a refined civilisation', for £5.[33]

In the event only 250 made up the excursion because of fears that it would be too crowded or a hoax.[34] Joining Lloyd in April was the former Sheriff of London and future MP, the railway financier and entrepreneur Robert Kennard (1800–1870). Others on the 'committee' included Philip Nind (*c*.1814–1866), proprietor of the famous Sablonierre Hotel in Leicester Square who conversed with the French politicians for the deputation.[35]

The itinerary and social composition of the 'Return Party'

The visit was well planned. Crisp organised medals for the excursionists to wear, with the union jack at the centre of rosettes, small brass designs 'bearing for a device two hands clasped, as emblematic of the happy union between the two countries', with the inscription 'Union is strength'.[36] The first-class tickets provided by Crisp were five guineas for a week with bed and breakfast. One party left on 4 April and returned on 12 April, a second set off on 7 April and returned on 14 April. The first group was fêted on its arrival at Boulogne on the steam-packets *Queen of the French* and *Queen of the Belgians*. Passing through an archway emblazoned 'To the Fraternal Union of England and France', The Quaker Asenath Nicholson claimed that 'tears fell from many a manly eye'.[37] In her recollection, the English were ashamed of the contrast between their general Francophobia, and the noble response of the French, with their bouquets and ceremonies, 'candidly acknowledge[ing] that their object in that excursion was wholly their own curiosity'.[38]

Travelling by rail and stopping to be welcomed at Amiens where half an hour's refreshment was timetabled, the party arrived in the capital for eight days; 'every place of curiosity' was available. A soirée honoured them on 10 April at the famous Hôtel des Princes, 179 Rue Richelieu (where Crisp based the organisation's headquarters). They were greeted with apparent enthusiasm by working-class Parisians.[39] At an entertainment hosted by the Prefect of the Seine at the Hôtel de Ville, 11 April, 'God Save the Queen' and 'Rule Britannia' were played. The National Guard hosted a select dinner for a small group of the Englishmen picked by Lloyd, at Salle Valentino in the Rue St Honore, at which the President of the Peace Society, the anticlerical republican Francisque Bouvet, delivered a speech (see Figure 3.2). There was a similar welcome on the party's return on 12 April via Boulogne where the theatre was decorated with English and French symbols and mottoes such as 'Union' and 'Fraternity'. The Sous-Prefet was joined by red-dressed fisherwomen to present the mingling of classes in the republic in Nicholson's account.

The *Morning Post* called the excursionists leaving Folkestone on 5 April a 'motley pack', whose members brought business cards to distribute among the National Guards and servants.[40] The *Illustrated London News*'s engravings of the deputation on 7 April (in the accompanying text uncertainly estimated that there were 'nearly 300' or 'nearly 2000' visitors) depicted bourgeois

Figure 3.2 Caricature by Gustave Doré, *Journal Pour Rire*, 21 April 1849, reprinted as
'The Grand International punch-bowl' in G. Doré, *Two Hundred Sketches*
(London: Warne, 1867), p. 63. Courtesy of the University of Plymouth.

Britons clutching portmanteaux and umbrellas at Boulogne (see Figure 3.3).[41]
Members staying at the Hôtel Meurice included a London merchant and
watchmaker, two country surgeons, two Wiltshire gentlemen, and – from one
Midland town – two ironmongers, a bookseller, tailor and innkeeper.[42]

Figure 3.3 'The Return Visit to Paris', *Illustrated London News*, 7 April 1849, p. 294. Author's collection.

The 'monster' visit was promoted outside London: the 'provinces … invited to join in the good work of perfecting the friendly understanding which is daily growing stronger between the two countries'.[43] Newspapers carried accounts from returning townsmen: the *Worcestershire Chronicle* compared the scale of the Hotel de Ville's reception room with 'our Corn-market Hall'.[44]

The *Reading Mercury* endorsed the metropolitan papers' accuracy 'as some of our own townsmen form part of this social expedition'.[45]

After the event, it was said that two who had made fools of themselves on the excursion had been 'professional men'.[46] The *Morning Post* sarcastically observed that Lloyd set himself up 'as a sort of ambassador from Great Britain to the French grocers, tailors and hairdressers, who made a descent upon London last summer'.[47] The British excursionists were 'evidently artizans of the humblest description, and people who get their living by le petit commerce, doing a very small amount of business, if their appearance afforded any just indication of their prosperity'.[48] As to Lloyd, he donned the 'uniform of the Warwickshire yeomanry, and thus accoutred his French and English admirers suppose him to be invested with the military glories of the Duke, Radetzky, Windischgraetz, and Soult'. For the *Post*'s correspondent, Lloyd was a 'good humoured martinet' keeping some semblance of discipline in his 'travelling menagerie'.

The Spectator belittled the affair as an 'International Pleasure Party and Picnic Association', and contrasted the French visit in 1848 with something 'got up to promote passenger-traffic and other commercial dealings'.[49] The rumour that members of the party had their cards to hand out at the Hotel de Ville soirée was probably true. One hyperbolic advertisement for Moses and Son, tailors, clothiers and hatters of Bradford and London, spoke of the visit, where 'I was myself, in propria persona', and claimed that a participant in Moses's outfit had been sketched, and the clothes then copied by Parisian tailors, hatters and bootmakers, with the words 'À La Moses' appearing in displays.[50] John Taylor Sinnett in the mass-market *London Journal* told readers, 'skilful handicraftsmen', *should* take part in future visits. He emphasised the commercial benefits for 'honest and laborious industrials', from this 'large social intercourse'.[51] Other commentators feared the damage to national pride by an event 'jobbed' by an agent.[52] In future more care should be taken to represent the 'real character of England', since some in the party had confirmed the prejudices about the British passion for 'beer, black-strap [alcohol with molasses], and strong punch'.[53]

The political and satirical response in France and Britain

> The French and the English may have different interests, which may sometimes even become hostile, but they know that they have a great common interest – that of liberty, of civilisation, of humanity, and that such interest can only be safe by their union.[54]

So the *Journal des Débats litterraires et politiques* commented on the English party which arrived at a dramatic moment for the republic whose president after 10 December 1848 was Louis-Napoleon Bonaparte.[55] The *Journal des Débats* was relieved at this point that Paris was in a fit state, using the homely analogy of receiving visitors in 'the midst of a removal', and reflecting on the 'elasticity' with which the Champs Elysée and boulevards returned to populousness. *The Times*, endorsing Londoners's reluctance to join the excursion *en masse* in early April, referred to the 'smiling face of the volcano'.[56] One excursionist's report noted 'fewer marks of the affairs of February and June than you would expect to find'.[57] There would soon be disruption. The Assemblée Nationale based in the eighteenth-century Palais Bourbon voted to intervene against the Roman Republic in the papal lands (a force was sent to Civita Vecchia later in the month).[58]

The French newspapers reported the English party's presence and reception.[59] *L'Illustration* (modelled on the *Illustrated London News*) included splendid engravings from the English arrival at Boulogne onwards; with humorous cuts by Charles-Marie de Sarcus, aka 'Quillenbois', on an Englishman's actions in Paris, including sporting the *kepi* to signify the entente cordiale and ogling ladies in the park.[60] The paper published an engraving of the 'raout' to the English at the Hôtel des Princes, commented on the Parisian reception of the English, and contrasted their appearance with the prevailing caricature of Englishmen. As one English paper had predicted, the episode was ripe for satire, and the front page of Philipon's *Journal Pour Rire* was an article illustrated by Gustave Doré, Edmond Morin and others, entitled 'Les Anglais à Paris – Entente Cordiale Anglo-Francaise' (see Figure 3.4).

Alphonse Balleydier, historian of the republican guard, also published an account in *Visite rendue par l'Angleterre à la France*.[61] The poet-statesman Alphonse Lamartine's *Le Conseiller du peuple* quoted Lloyd's speech, and

Figure 3.4 The reception at Boulogne lampooned by Gustave Doré, *Journal Pour Rire*, 21 April 1849, reprinted as 'The First Glass of Champagne' in *Two Hundred Sketches*, p. 61. Courtesy of the University of Plymouth.

commented that the republic was the first to give the world the spectacle of these visits of people to people, true ambassadors of peace and international fraternity. Fraternal toasts and amiable speeches were congresses and treaties, and more sincere or alive than official diplomacy. Paris had put her heart, soul and enthusiasm into the hospitality (Lamartine was presented with an eloquent address from members of party who were inhabitants of Westminster).[62]

According to John Bill, from the very beginning the French government's involvement was apparent: 'the gratifying intelligence was communicated to us that the Government had sent down orders to the authorities to shew us every attention', and dispense with the checking of luggage at Boulogne. The Prefect of the Seine, Jean Jacques Berger, informed Lloyd that they would show 'how much they desire to strengthen the ties of friendship between the two countries'.[63] Crisp's card gained admission to the Chamber of Deputies and a section of the gallery was given over to the English party.[64] The Governor of Les Invalides granted access to the tomb of Napoleon and members of the party were shown round by Jerome Bonaparte, cousin of the Prince President. The Minister of Public Works facilitated free admission to all the sights and at the Opéra there was a special performance. By contrast, *The Times* reported that when the English first arrived Berger had no official notification and the ambassador, Lord Normanby, lacked instructions. No decision could be taken by the colonels of the *gardes nationaux* without instructions and notice, and the Municipal Council had not met: 'difficult circumstances', therefore, led Berger to seek advice from Normanby and Léon Faucher, Minister of the Interior.[65] After Lloyd and Nind met with him, Normanby expressed 'his satisfaction at our friendly visit to the French capital'. The elegant diplomat attended the fête at the Hôtel de Ville 'in a plain black suit, and wearing the ribband and star of the Bath'.[66]

In the British parliament further criticism of the visit appeared. Baillie Cochrane returned to it in the context of a motion from Richard Cobden on international arbitration, 12 June 1849. Cochrane saw the same arguments enunciated by the Peace Society and during Crisp and Lloyd's excursion, that 'there was so much good feeling manifested by the French party that he was almost persuaded that England and France were united by land'.[67] Another point of controversy was the eccentric Whig peer and former Lord Chancellor Henry Brougham (1778–1868) whose detractors associated him with the amusing scheme (as they saw it). They tracked this, from his alleged rudeness to the excursionists on the Boulogne steam-packet, through to the Hôtel Meurice in Paris, where he was spotted by John Bill.[68] Brougham's hostility to the venture appeared in an anecdote going the rounds of Parisian society.[69] Brougham was over wintering in Cannes when the July Monarchy fell, and sought to stand as candidate for Var when the Provisional Government called a National Assembly. Correspondence on this affair created embarrassment when revealed in April 1848.[70] The satirical *Puppet-Show* gave currency to gossip that Crisp engaged Brougham as 'speechmaker – interpreter – and valet-de-place to the excursionists'.[71]

The daily English-language newspaper *Galignani*, readers were told, was instructed to correct the impression he had led the party.[72] A cheeky cartoon appeared in *Punch* on 21 April 1849 (see Figure 3.5).[73]

The Whig peer raised the matter in the Lords in May, hoping that, for the sake of Anglo-French peace 'all intercourse by public bodies between them would in future cease, and that the only communication between them would be carried on by the two Governments'.[74] But this followed laughter caused by the Marquis of Londonderry ribbing him for travelling with the recent English visitors. 'There was not the slightest foundation for such assertion', Brougham said.[75] The excursionist John Bill's account, published in 1850, detected envy given the peer's 'morbid appetite for notoriety'.[76] The press picked up his animus, the English-language *Boulogne Gazette* castigating his 'fit of envious jealousy'.[77] The *Principality*, a Welsh paper, explained the elite's suspicions: for when people fraternised the diplomat's occupation would be gone, 'then mutual prejudices will be softened down, then mutual interests will be better understood – rulers will not find it so easy to carry on the game of war'.[78]

Coverage in influential national press organs was commented on by *The Era*, seeing *The Times* as typically condescending while *Punch* was 'at heart of and for the people', and therefore merciful.[79] *The Times*, noting the 'honest

Figure 3.5 John Leech, 'Landing of Lord Brougham and the English at Boulogne', *Punch*, 21 April 1849, p. 158. Courtesy of the University of Plymouth.

fidelity' of the pictorial records, worried about further excursionists.[80] The leader on 18 May feared such excursions were 'anything but productive of mutual amity and goodwill': with decency and propriety not safeguarded by the mere ability to pay 3*l* 10*s*. How would members of a 'bacchanalian excursion party' of the 'lowest and least instructed classes' react to the Parisian mob?[81] The ultimate lesson of the Paris excursion for *The Times* was an appreciation of 'the security and stability of property and government' at home.[82]

Punch varied from the good humoured to the biting, identifying the backers as debtors seeking Boulogne refuge and lampooning Brougham's egotism.[83] Its rival, *Puppet-Show*, noted the projected association and presented a 'before and after' account of excursionists transformed from suetty and carpet-bag-carrying John Bulls to suave, monocled, moustachioed and cigarette-smoking cosmopolitans.[84] In 'France and England' it showed a democratic and socialist waiter asking why it was possible that the young Englishman, 'on a cheap visit to Paris', was vote-less (the second republic inaugurated universal manhood suffrage) and asked, if the good time was not coming, if he had no talent for barricades, to which the reply was 'No; in that case, I believe the best plan would be – "To wait a little longer."'[85]

The excursion was satirised in the *New Monthly Magazine* in May 1849.[86] Lloyd became Green of Peckham, naively subsidising the excursion, being undercut by the wily 'Mr Crispin' and hiring a yeomanry-cavalry dress from 'Mr Nathan, in Tichborne Street, Piccadilly', with 'a fancy medal and a pair of black moustaches'. The story incorporated details of the excursion including the *Illustrated London News*'s engraving in April 1849. Green identified 'the portrait of the bald-headed old gentleman in spectacles (an eminent greengrocer in the Haymarket)'. It was augmented by quotations from one of his carpet-bagged battalion, Mr Toby, with his 'extremely greasy pocket-book, nearly filled with market transactions' who preferred visiting the abattoirs to the National Assembly. The excursionists, it was claimed, included an escaped lunatic 'from the neighbourhood of the Regent's Park'. The story ends, in Green's complacent and naïve account, with the striking of a 'very handsome medal' by the French government, bearing Green's portrait between a cap of liberty and two hands clasped –with the simple inscription, 'A | JOLLY GREEN, | LA FRANCE RECONNAISSANTE. | 1er Avril, 1849'. The joke is, of course, on him, when he comments that he 'cannot exactly understand why the period of our visit has been antedated'.

Lloyd – unsympathetic to 'the communists, ultra republican and journalist-led Parisian multitude', had said in early 1849, 'At no time could an Englishman traverse Europe with prouder step than at this moment'.[87] *The Times*, seeing the British polity 'vaccinated' against the events of 1848, noted, 'we can now disport ourselves in the very focus of contagion … some scores of the good citizens of London who on this day last were marshalled with swords and staves to the terror of alien propagandists', were now in Paris.[88] Radical responses to the episode included the Chartist *Northern Star*'s reprinting of a note, but little else on the affair.[89] Passmore Edwards in the progressive *People's Journal* deprecated the scheme as a private speculation and noted the 'undeserved notoriety' given to 'certain individuals', but saw in it the 'genius of peace' before which militarism would fail. The event, if 'comparatively insignificant ... at first sight', was 'a fact which will never be effaced from the memories of France and England'.[90]

The Era ended its commentary by identifying the visitors as a 'sample of the stable population of Great Britain – those who make "the pressure from without"', having also asked, 'who were the few who originated the Corn-law League?'[91] The *Globe* linked the strange language of the association prospectus with the praise for the radical Richard Cobden 'at a banquet of Genoese or Venetian Free-Traders'.[92] Wishing to promote international peace, Cobden did see the excursion as a positive sign.[93] Before the Congrès des amis de la paix universelle met in Paris in August 1849, here was an attempt at union of a decidedly pragmatic, mixed and low key nature.[94] The radical MP William Ewart's address at the congress minimised diplomatic unions as 'unions of paper': 'Unions such as these among the people themselves are unions of the heart. These will be unions of strength. These will be unions of duration'.[95]

The American Elihu Burritt, a member of the Peace Congress Committee of London active in pressing for arbitration instead of war, linked the National Guards' visits in the autumn of 1848 with the formation of a peace society in Paris.[96] He noted in February 1849, 'the law of kindness exercised upon these National Guards does not terminate with the result of a mere entertainment in Paris, to which they will invite the municipal authorities of the towns they visited'.[97] Burritt pointed to the development of international communication already in 1847, 'very beautiful and interesting' correspondence and visits by communities, 'for the first time in the history of nations'.[98] The large towns of England had sent friendly letters to their French counterparts.[99] It was a 'new kind of popular diplomacy between the peoples'.[100]

Communications and transport technology harmonised relations. One newspaper saw in the enterprising Joseph Crisp the 'gradual progress of steam-communication among the nations of the world' bringing about a slow growth in the friendship of nations.[101] *The Times*, anxious about the impact of travel outside individuals or small parties, correctly emphasised that this was designed to put money in the pockets of the 'steamboat and railway' speculators.[102] The *British Quarterly Review* would recall, 'Cheap excursion trains ... brought hundreds of Parisian National Guardsmen to these shores, and safely delivered thousands of English excursionists in Paris, whom we could well spare in exchange'.[103]

Conclusion

The 'English party, including no known names' as the *Illustrated London News* described it, constituted a 'little episode in international history'.[104] *Punch* had predicted damage to Anglo-French relations through the 'folly, twaddle and something more', mixed up in the association's scheme.[105] Later the magazine attributed the 'growing evil' of mustachios on the British upper lip to the cheap excursion.[106] The Paris correspondent of *The Times* had a different assessment: enthusiasm was such that it was 'fortunate they have so soon left, as no one knows to what extent it might have been carried'.[107]

Lloyd claimed his motivation was 'to show how greatly England desired the well-being and tranquillity of France'.[108] We lack the accounts of most of those who participated under Crisp's guidance, who had cautioned his party to 'always ... shew an accommodating disposition, and a desire to oblige ... although you do not approve of all the customs you find'. The event was a success for Crisp. He sold commemorative medals struck at the Paris mint at the British and Foreign Excursion office (gold copies were presented to the queen, President of the French Republic and others[109]), and organised excursions to Paris on Whitsun in 1849, and to the Paris Exposition, Ghent and Brussels, the Rhine, and South of France through the summer and autumn of 1849.[110] The *Literary Gazette* in 1850 carried an advertisement for the 'anniversary of the Grand and Unprecedented Reception given to Mr Crisp's Easter Party of 1849', where 'many English of Distinction and Officers of the Fr[ench] National Guard will be present'.[111]

The *London Journal* prophesied that 5 April would 'long be remembered ... let it be entered in all our tablets and private journals'.[112] *The Times* thought that Michelet ought to note the playing of 'Rule Britannia' by the *gardes nationales* for the English visitors, should he write a history of the 'third French revolution'.[113] Samuel Neil's handbook of modern history in 1857 briefly noted that 'The National Guard of Paris give a grand banquet to the English visitors at Paris, April 15'. More expansively, the *Histoire populaire contemporaine de la France* in 1864 recorded it with the engraving of the Boulogne deputation from *L'Illustration* as a curious episode that diverted Parisians from the political world. Modern histories of the entente cordiale ignore it.[114] This brief study allows us to see the temporary interest in the 'Five Pound' Paris trip as fraternal union or realisation of amity by the British and French press, and by the British and French authorities.[115]

Notes

1 Possibly by Lewis Jonat, see *The Times*, 14 April 1849, p. 5; *Derby Mercury* 18 April 1849; a Paris correspondent, *The Times*, 16 April, refers to 'an English artist named Jones'. On the medal, see Musée Carnavalet collection: http://parismuseescollections.paris.fr/fr/musee-carnavalet/oeuvres/visite-rendue-par-lesfrancais-a-londres-septembre-1848-et-par-les-anglais#infos-principales (accessed 14 February 2017). For Valentin Borrel's design with Queen Victoria's profile and the inscription on the reverse, see http://parismuseescollections.paris.fr/fr/musee-carnavalet/oeuvres/visite-des-nationaux-anglais-aux-gardes-nationaux-parisiens-avril-1849#infos-secondaires-detail (accessed 16 April 2019). On the visit in 1848, see the work listed in *Catalogue de l'histoire de France* (Paris: Firmin Didot, 1861), vol. 7, p. 392 as *La XIe Légion a Londres; par un caporal des radis de la banlieue*. This visit had medallic commemoration, see *Banbury Guardian*, 1 March 1849.

2 'J.B. Esq.' *The English Party's Excursion to Paris, in Easter Week 1849: To Which Is Added, a Trip to America, Etc. Etc. Etc* (London: Longman, 1850); 'One of the Excursionists', *What I Saw in Paris during Easter 1849. Forming a Complete Guide for the English Excursionist to the Sights of Paris* (London: Macdonald, 1849).

3 Antoine Capet noted, in A. Capet, ed., *Britain, France and the Entente Cordiale Since 1904* (Basingstoke: Palgrave Macmillan, 2006), p. 2, over sixty works studying the entente cordiale are listed by the Royal Historical Society bibliography, dating back to 1916. For high-political British perspective, see D. Brown, 'Palmerston and Anglo-French Relations, 1846 – 1865', in *Anglo-French Relations since the Late Eighteenth Century*, ed. by G. Stone and T.G. Otte (2008; London: Routledge, 2013), which notes the 'era of growing extra-parliamentary influence, even on foreign policy-making' (pp. 45–46).

4 *The Times*, 16 April 1849, p. 4.

5 *The Era*, 22 April 1849.

6 *Norwich Mercury*, 14 April 1849.

7 F. Bensimon, 'British Workers in France, 1815 – 1848', *Past & Present* 213:1 (2011), pp. 147–189, reproducing 'A Specimen of French "Fraternité" – English Labourers Driven out of France', *Punch*, 11 March 1848, p. 120.

8 *Illustrated London News*, 7 April 1849.

9 'Mes Impressions de Voyage. By a Garde Nationale in London,' *Punch*, 4 November 1848, p. 193 and 'French National Guards in London', p. 194.

10 *The Satirist*, 16 December 1848, p. 545.

11 *Address of Francis Lloyd, Esq., (Vice-President) to the West London Literary, Scientific, and Mechanics' Institution, Manor House, King's Road, Chelsea, at the close of the first lecture session terminating May 21, 1847* (London: B.D. Cousins, 1847).

12 On his Quaker background, see H. Lloyd, *The Quaker Lloyds in the Industrial Revolution* (1975; Abingdon: Routledge, 2006), p. 268. Lloyd, p. 268 states this resignation was due to perjured witnesses, but *The Legal Guide*, 14 September 1839, pp. 313–314, shows Lloyd's involvement with a pretended widow who was his mistress.

13 Reported in *Coventry Herald*, 15 January 1841.

14 'Shadowings of French Politicians,' *St James's Magazine* January 1842, pp. 107–112; reviewed in *Morning Advertiser*, 8 January 1842.

15 First published as *The Paris Estafette; Or, Pilferings from the Paris and Dover Post-Bag ... Embellished with Portraits and Wood Cuts* (London: Biggs [1842]), I cite *Pilferings from the Paris and Dover Postbag* (London: Routledge, 1843), pp. 68–86.

16 *Pilferings from the Paris and Dover Postbag*, p. 169, see also p. 132.

17 *Staffordshire Advertiser*, 28 July 1838; *Mechanics' Magazine*, 4 August 1838, pp. 301–302; *The Spectator*, 28 July 1838. Lloyd's pamphlet was *Adresse d'un Anglais à la Nation Française. Discours adressé à un cercle de députés français, par M. Lloyd, pendant nombre d'années banquier et magistrat en Angleterre, après un dîner qui lui a été offert ainsi qu'à plusieurs de ses compatriotes à Paris, le 3 novembre 1840* (Paris: Delaunay, 1840). See *Annales du parlement français, session 1841. Du 5 novembre 1840 au 25 Juin 1841* (Paris: Firmin Didot, 1841), vol. 3, p. 244: 3 December 1840, M. Bechard, referring to a letter of 27 November in *Le Moniteur*, and Soult's reply; London *Evening Standard*, 5 December 1849; *Worcestershire Chronicle*, 9 December 1840, translation of Soult's letter.

18 *Pilferings*, pp. 169–170.

19 'The "Grande Fete De La Fraternite" of The National Guard, And Inauguration of The Port of Caen,' *Metropolitan Magazine* 54:214 (February 1849), pp. 161–175 (my translation, p. 174).

20 'The "Grande Fete De La Fraternite" of the National Guard', p. 175.

21 *London Evening Standard*, 15 February 1849.

22 *Morning Post*, 19 February 1849.

23 The prospectus does not survive, but its introduction was quoted by Baillie Cochrane in the Commons, see *Parliamentary Debates*, 3rd series, vol. 102, House of Commons, 22 February 1849, cols. 1098 – 1100, and in the press, e.g. *The Spectator*, 24 February 1849, p. 171.

24 *Punch*, 3 March 1849, p. 93.

25 *The Times*, 23 February 1849, p. 3; *Parliamentary Debates*, 3rd series, vol. 102, House of Commons, 22 February 1849, col.1100.

26 *Globe*, 24 February 1849.

27 *The Puppet-Show*, 3 (1849), p. 88.

28 For example, *Essex Standard*, 13 April 1849.

29 *Freeman's Journal*, 12 March 1849.

30 *The Athenaeum*, 24 March 1849 and 31 March 1849; *The Satirist; or, the True Censor of the Times*, 24 March 1849; p. 133; *Oxford Journal*, 10 March 1849; *Birmingham Journal*, 10 March 1849; *London Evening Standard*, 8 March 1849.

31 *Kentish Gazette*, 27 March 1849.

32 *Bell's Life in London*, 25 February 1849.

33 *Morning Post*, 8 March 1849.

34 Bill, *The English Party's Excursion to Paris*, p. 10.

35 On Nind's hotels, P. Cunningham's *Handbook to Modern London* (London: Murray, 1851), p. xxxii.

36 Bill, *The English Party's Excursion to Paris*, p. 104.

37 A. Nicholson, *Loose Papers; Or, Facts Gathered During Eight Years' Residence in Ireland, Scotland, England, France, and Germany* (New York: Anti-Slavery Office, 1853), p. 206.

38 Nicholson, *Loose Papers*, p. 207.

39 *Globe*, 14 April 1849, reprinting from *The Times*.

40 *Morning Post*, April 1849.

41 *Illustrated London News*, 7 April 1849; *Globe*, 10 April 1849; 'The English Visit to Paris', *The Satirist*, 14 April 1849.

42 *English Party's Excursion to Paris*, p. 30 (Bill's visit to the Assembly is reprinted at p. 58).

43 *Birmingham Journal*, 17 February 1849; *Oxford Journal*, 17 February 1849.

44 *Worcestershire Chronicle*, 18 April 1849.

45 *Reading Mercury*, 14 April 1849.

46 *The Era*, 22 April 1849.

47 *Morning Post*, 9 April 1849. The five hundred are described as Londoners: 'Railway Excursion to Paris', *Wolverhampton Chronicle*, 18 April 1849.

48 *Morning Post*, 14 April 1849.

49 *The Spectator*, 14 April 1849.

50 *Bradford Observer*, 26 April 1849; *Leeds Intelligencer*, 28 April 1849.

51 *London Journal*, 28 April 1849, p. 120. On Sinnett, see A. King, *The London Journal 1845–83: Periodicals, Production, and Gender* (Aldershot: Ashgate, 2004), p. 70. On Anglo-French connections through immigration by British workers see Bensimon, 'British Workers in France'. Bensimon notes connections in the Chartist era but cautions against overestimating internationalism.

52 *Inverness Courier*, 19 April 1849.

53 *Nottingham Review*, 20 April 1849.

54 *The Times*, 17 April 1849, p. 8, translating *Journals des Débats* of 14 April 1849.

55 See C. Guyver, *The Second French Republic 1848–1852: A Political Reinterpretation* (London: Palgrave Macmillan, 2016).

56 *The Times*, 10 April 1849, p. 4.

57 *Worcestershire Chronicle*, 18 April 1849.

58 *What I Saw in Paris during Easter 1849*, p. 49, states that 'two galleries, immediately in front of the President and the tribune, were set apart for the use of the English Visitors'.

59 I have used the Bibliothèque Nationale's *Gallica* database, but not extensively studied the French-language press, e.g. regional titles such as *Le National Boulonnais*, which began 3 March 1849. Bill, *The English Party's Excursion to Paris*, pp. 136–137, quotes the enthusiastic English-language *Boulogne Gazette*, 17 April 1849.

60 *L'Illustration, Journal Universel*, 14 April 1849, p. 101.

61 A. Balleydier, *Visite rendue par l'Angleterre à la France, ou Une semaine à Paris pendant les vacances de Pâques* (London: Office of Des Chemins de fer et Navigations, 1849). In introductory letters, p. xv, Pierre-Jean de Béranger's lines from 'La Sainte Alliance des Peuples' were quoted: 'Peuples, formez une sainte alliance, | Et donnez – vous la main!' (p. xv). Verse was delivered by Napoleon Theil (1808 – 1878), in *Seize mois de commandement dans la garde nationale parisienne* (Paris: Thunot, 1849), pp. 23–25 from a poem in *la Patrie*.

62 'Deuxième Partie: Almanach Politique', *Le Conseiller du Peuple* (1849), pp. 78–81. On address and Lamartine's reply, *The Economist*, 14 April 1849, p. 412.

63 Letter dated 31 March 1849, reprinted *Glasgow Herald*, 9 April 1849.

64 Bill, *The English Party's Excursion to Paris*, p. 60.

65 *The Times*, 9 April 1849, p. 4.

66 As reported in newspapers and reprinted in *What I Saw in Paris*, p. 5; p. 7. The 'Raout des Anglais' features in C. Merruau, *Souvenirs de l'hôtel de ville de Paris. 1848-1852* (Paris: Plon, 1875), p. 327.

67 *Parliamentary Debates*, 3rd series, vol. 106, House of Commons, 12 June 1849, col. 69.

68 Bill, *The English Party's Excursion to Paris*, p. 31.

69 *The Times*, 2nd morning edition 13 April, reprinted in *Evening Mail*, 13 April 1849.

70 J. Campbell, *Lives of Lord Lyndhurst and Lord Brougham* (London: Murray, 1869), vol. 8, pp. 550–556.

71 *Puppet-Show*, vol. 3 (1849), p. 162; also *Morning Chronicle*, 9 April 1849 on this rumour.

72 *Norwich Mercury*, 14 April 1849.

73 *Punch*, 21 April 1849, p. 158.

74 *Parliamentary Debates*, 3rd series, vol. 105, House of Lords, 25 May 1849, cols. 969–972. See T.H. Ford, *Chancellor Brougham and His World: A Biography* (Chichester: Rose, 1995).

75 *Globe*, 15 May 1849.

76 Bill, *The English Party's Excursion to Paris*, p. 112.

77 *Kentish Gazette*, 3 July 1849.

78 *The Principality*, 18 May 1849.

79 *The Era*, 22 April 1849.

80 *The Times*, 10 April 1848, p. 4.

81 *The Times*, 18 May 1849, p. 5.

82 *The Times*, 10 April 1849, p. 4.

83 'Grand Interlittoral Visit between Chelsea and Battersea', *Punch*, 3 March 1849, p. 93; 'Small Shot Fired by a Five-Pounder; Or, What I Saw in France during My Recent Excursion', *Punch*, April 1849, p. 183; 'Shameful Hoax!!! The "International Visit" Turns Out to Be a Meeting of Creditors!!!' *Punch*, 21 April 1849, p. 163; 'England's Return Visit to France (From Lord Brougham, Punch's own Reporter)', *Punch*, 14 April 1849, p. 148.

84 *Puppet-Show*, vol. 3 (1849), p. 88; *Puppet-Show*, vol. 3 (1849), p. 159. Crisp recommended travellers carry luggage in this form: Bill, *The English Party's Excursion to Paris*, p. 4.

85 *Puppet-Show*, vol. 3 (1849), p. 243. See also, 'Lord Brougham's French Oration', *Puppet-Show*, vol. 3 (1849), p. 162 and 'The International Visit,' p. 163.

86 'Mr Jolly Green's Account of the Great Paris Excursion', in the *New Monthly Magazine*, May 1849, pp. 84–99.

87 'The Grande Fête de la Fraternité,' pp. 171–172.

88 *The Times*, 10 April 1849, p. 4.

89 *Northern Star*, 24 March 1849.

90 J.P. Edwards, 'The English in Paris', *People's Journal* 7 (January–June 1849), pp. 250–252.

91 *The Era*, 22 April 1849.

92 *Globe*, 24 February 1849.

93 Letter to Joseph Sturge, 16 April 1849, reprinted in A. Howe, ed., *The Letters of Richard Cobden II: 1848–1853* (Oxford: Oxford University Press, 2010), p. 130. See A. Howe, 'Reforging Britons: Richard Cobden and France', in *La France et l'Angleterre au XIXe siècle: échanges, représentations, comparaisons*, ed. by S. Aprile and F. Bensimon (Paris: Créaphis, 2006) pp. 89–104.

94 *Congrès des amis de la paix universelle réuni à Paris en 1849: compte-rendu, séances, résolutions adoptées, discours* [etc.] (Brussels: Lesigne, 1849).

95 *Report of the Proceedings of the Second General Peace Congress Held in Paris on the 22nd, 23rd and 24th of August, 1849* (London: Gilpin, 1849), p. 49.

96 Josselin, a young French magistrate, appeared on the platform of a Peace meeting in Exeter Hall, 31 October 1848, in National Guard uniform: *British Review*, November 1851, p. 6. See *Report of the Proceedings of the Second General Peace Congress Held in Paris*, p. 2: 'friendly excursion visits between large parties of the French National Guards and of individuals from this country, tended much to predispose the French people in favour of the Peace Movement'.

97 *Aberdeen Press and Journal*, 21 February 1849.

98 E. Burritt, 'People-Diplomacy: Or, the Mission of Friendly International Addresses between England and France', reprinted in *Thoughts and Things at Home and Abroad* (Boston, MA: Phillips, Sampson, 1854), pp. 329–333.

99 *Banffshire Journal*, 20 February 1849.

100 M. Ceadel, *The Origins of War Prevention: The British Peace Movement and International Relations, 1730–1854* (Oxford: Clarendon Press, 1996); M.J. Turner, *Independent Radicalism in Early Victorian Britain* (Westport, CT: Praeger, 2004), p. 147 on the Peace Congress Committee after the international peace congress in Brussels in September 1848. On Sturge's 'people diplomacy', A. Tyrell, *Joseph Sturge and the Moral Radical Party in Early Victorian Britain* (London: Croom Helm, 1987), ch. 13.

101 *Morning Chronicle*, 29 May 1849; *Norwich Mercury*, 14 April 1849 saw the demise of stately diplomacy's demise through 'steam and railways ... iron-hearted reformer'.

102 *The Times*, 18 May 1849, p. 5.

103 'Paris in 1855', *British Quarterly Review* 22:44 (1 October 1855), pp. 428–455 [p. 430].

104 *Illustrated London News*, 21 April 1849.

105 *Punch*, 3 March 1849, p. 93.

106 *Punch*, 9 June 1849, p. 219.

107 *The Times*, 16 April 1849, p. 6.

108 *Kentish Gazette*, 3 July 1849.

109 *Bell's Weekly Messenger*, 12 May 1849.

110 For example, *The Examiner*, 6 October 1849. By 1850 he had organised ten excursions to Paris, *Manchester Courier*, 11 May 1850. See D.M. Williams and J. Armstrong, 'Steam Shipping and the Beginnings of Overseas Tourism: British Travel to North-Western Europe, 1820 – 1850', *Journal of European Economic History* 35:1 (2006), pp. 125–148.
111 *Literary Gazette*, 23 March 1850, p. 222.
112 *London Journal*, 28 April 1849, pp. 119–120 [p. 119].
113 *The Times*, 16 April 1849, p. 4.
114 *Histoire populaire contemporaine de la France* (Paris: Hachette et Cie, 1864), vol. 1, pp. 161–162. But in the context of the Great War, *L'Instantané. Supplement Illustré de la Revue Hebdomadaire* 20 July 1918, see reproduction of the medal, and C. Claro's article, pp. 405–407.
115 The phrase is from *Visite rendue*, p. 7.

Bibliography

'Deuxième Partie: Almanach Politique', *Le Conseiller du Peuple* (1849), pp. 78–81.
'England's Return Visit to France. (From Lord Brougham, Punch's own Reporter', *Punch*, 14 April 1849, p. 148.
'French National Guards in London', *Punch*, 4 November 1848, p. 194.
'Grand Interlittoral Visit between Chelsea and Battersea', *Punch*, 3 March 1849, p. 93.
'Lord Brougham's French Oration, *Puppet-Show*, vol. 3 (1849), p. 162.
'Mes Impressions de Voyage. By a Garde Nationale in London,' *Punch*, 4 November 1848, p. 193.
'Mr Jolly Green's Account of the Great Paris Excursion', *New Monthly Magazine*, May 1849, pp. 84–99.
'Paris in 1855', *British Quarterly Review* 22:44 (1 October 1855), pp. 428–455.
'Shameful Hoax!!! The "International Visit" Turns Out to Be a Meeting of Creditors!!!' *Punch*, 21 April 1849, p. 163.
'Small Shot Fired by a Five-Pounder; Or, What I Saw in France during My Recent Excursion', *Punch*, April 1849, p. 183.
'The English Visit to Paris', *The Satirist*, 14 April 1849.
'The International Visit,' *Puppet-Show*, vol. 3 (1849), p. 163.
Aberdeen Press and Journal, 21 February 1849.
Annales du parlement français, session 1841. Du 5 novembre 1840 au 25 Juin 1841 (Paris: Firmin Didot, 1841), vol. 3.
Anon., *Congrès des amis de la paix universelle réuni à Paris en 1849: compte-rendu, séances, résolutions adoptées, discours* [etc.] (Brussels: Lesigne, 1849).
Anon., *What I Saw in Paris during Easter 1849. Forming a Complete Guide for the English Excursionist to the Sights of Paris... By One of the Excursionists* (London: R. Macdonald, 1850).
Balleydier, A. *Visite rendue par l'Angleterre à la France, ou Une semaine à Paris pendant les vacances de Pâques* (London: Office of Des Chemins de fer et Navigations, 1849).
Banbury Guardian, 1 March 1849.
Banffshire Journal, 20 February 1849.
Bell's Life in London, 25 February, 4 March 1849.
Bell's Weekly Messenger, 12 May 1849.
Bensimon, F. 'British Workers in France, 1815–1848', *Past & Present* 213:1 (2011), pp. 147–189.

Bill, J. *The English Party's Excursion to Paris, in Easter Week 1849. To Which Is Added, a Trip to America, Etc., Etc., Etc.,* (London: Longman, 1850).

Birmingham Journal, 17 February, 10 March 1849.

Bradford Observer, 26 April 1849.

British Review, November 1851, p. 6.

Brown, D. 'Palmerston and Anglo-French Relations, 1846–1865', in *Anglo-French Relations since the Late Eighteenth Century*, ed. by G. Stone and T.G. Otte (2008; London: Routledge, 2013) pp. 41–58.

Burritt, E. *Thoughts and Things at Home and Abroad* (Boston, MA: Phillips, Sampson, 1854).

Campbell, J. *Lives of Lord Lyndhurst and Lord Brougham* (London: Murray, 1869), vol. 8.

Capet, A. ed., *Britain, France and the Entente Cordiale since 1904* (Basingstoke: Palgrave Macmillan, 2006).

Catalogue de l'histoire de France (Paris: Firmin Didot, 1861), vol. 7.

Ceadel, M. *The Origins of War Prevention: The British Peace Movement and International Relations, 1730–1854* (Oxford: Clarendon Press, 1996).

Coventry Herald, 15 January 1841.

Cunningham, P. *Handbook to Modern London* (London: Murray, 1851).

Derby Mercury, 18 April 1849.

Doré, G. *Two Hundred Sketches* (London: Warne, 1867).

Edwards, J.P. 'The English in Paris', *People's Journal* 7 (January–June 1849), pp. 250–252.

Essex Standard, 13 April 1849.

Evening Mail, 13 April 1849.

Evening Standard, 5 December 1849.

Ford, T.H. *Chancellor Brougham and His World: A Biography* (Chichester: Rose, 1995).

Freeman's Journal, 12 March 1849.

Glasgow Herald, 9 April 1849.

Globe, 24 February, 10 April, 14 April, 15 May 1849.

Guyver, C. *The Second French Republic 1848–1852: A Political Reinterpretation* (London: Palgrave Macmillan, 2016).

Histoire populaire contemporaine de la France (Paris: Hachette et Cie, 1864), vol. 1.

Howe, A. 'Reforging Britons: Richard Cobden and France', in *La France et l'Angleterre au XIXe siècle: échanges, représentations, comparaisons*, ed. by S. Aprile and F. Bensimon (Paris: Créaphis, 2006), pp. 89–104.

Howe, A. *The Letters of Richard Cobden II: 1848–1853* (Oxford: Oxford University Press, 2010).

Illustrated London News, 7 April, 21 April 1849.

Inverness Courier, 19 April 1849.

Journals des Débats litterraires et politiques (Paris), 14 April 1849.

Kentish Gazette, 27 March, 3 July 1849.

King, A. *The London Journal 1845–83: Periodicals, Production, and Gender* (Aldershot: Ashgate, 2004).

L'Illustration, Journal Universel, 14 April 1849.

L'Instantané. Supplement Illustré de la Revue Hebdomadaire, 20 July 1918.

Leech, J. 'Landing of Lord Brougham and the English at Boulogne,' *Punch*, 21 April 1849, p. 158.

Leeds Intelligencer, 28 April 1849.

Literary Gazette, 23 March 1850.

Lloyd, F. 'Shadowings of French Politicians,' *St James's Magazine* January 1842, pp. 107–112.

Lloyd, F. 'The "Grande Fete De La Fraternite" of The National Guard, And Inauguration of The Port Of Caen,' *Metropolitan Magazine* 54:214, February 1849, pp. 161–175.

Lloyd, F. 'The Bank of England v. the Country bankers,' *Metropolitan Magazine*, August 1833, pp. 285–289.

Lloyd, F. *Address of Francis Lloyd, Esq., (Vice-President) to the West London Literary, Scientific, and Mechanics' Institution, Manor House, King's Road, Chelsea, at the close of the first lecture session terminating May 21, 1847* (London: B.D. Cousins, 1847).

Lloyd, F. *Adresse d'un Anglais a la Nation Française. Discours adressé à un cercle de députés français, par M. Lloyd, pendant nombre d'années banquier et magistrat en Angleterre, après un dîner qui lui a été offert ainsi qu'à plusieurs de ses compatriotes à Paris, le 3 novembre 1840* (Paris: Delaunay, 1840).

Lloyd, F. *Pilferings from the Paris and Dover Postbag* (London: Routledge, 1843).

Lloyd, H. *The Quaker Lloyds in the Industrial Revolution* (1975; Abingdon: Routledge, 2006).

London Evening Standard, 15 February, 8 March 1849.

Manchester Courier, 11 May 1850.

Mechanics' Magazine, 4 August 1838.

Medal, April 1849, http://parismuseescollections.paris.fr/fr/musee-carnavalet/oeuvres/visite-rendue-par-lesfrancais-a-londres-septembre-1848-et-par-les-anglais#infos-principales (accessed 14 February 2017).

Medal, April 1849, designer Valentin Borrel, http://parismuseescollections.paris.fr/fr/musee-carnavalet/oeuvres/visite-des-nationaux-anglais-aux-gardes-nationaux-parisiens-avril-1849#infos-secondaires-detail (accessed 16 April 2019).

Merruau, C. *Souvenirs de l'hôtel de ville de Paris. 1848–1852* (Paris: Plon, 1875).

Morning Advertiser, 8 January 1842.

Morning Chronicle, 9 April, 29 May 1849.

Morning Post, 19 February, 8 March, 9 April, 14 April 1849.

Musée Carnavalet collection.

Nicholson, A. *Loose Papers; Or, Facts Gathered During Eight Years' Residence in Ireland, Scotland, England, France, and Germany* (New York: Anti-Slavery Office, 1853).

Northern Star, 24 March 1849.

Norwich Mercury, 14 April 1849.

Nottingham Review, 20 April 1849.

Oxford Journal, 17 February, 10 March 1849.

Parliamentary Debates, 3rd series, vol. 102, House of Commons, 22 February 1849, cols.1098–1099.

Parliamentary Debates, 3rd series, vol. 105, House of Lords, 25 May 1849, cols.969–972.

Parliamentary Debates, 3rd series, vol. 106, House of Commons, 12 June 1849, col.69.

Punch, 9 June 1849.

Reading Mercury, 14 April 1849.

Report of the Proceedings of the Second General Peace Congress Held in Paris on the 22nd, 23rd and 24th of August, 1849 (London: Gilpin, 1849).

Sinnett, J.T. 'England's Return Visit to France', *London Journal*, 28 April 1849, pp. 119–120.

Staffordshire Advertiser, 28 July 1838.

The Athenaeum, 24 March, 31 March.

The Economist, 14 April 1849.

The Era, 22 April 1849.

The Examiner, 6 October 1849.

The Legal Guide, 14 September 1839, pp. 313–314.

The Principality, 18 May 1849.

The Puppet-Show, vol. 3 (1849), p. 88.

The Satirist; or, the True Censor of the Times, 16 December 1848; 24 March 1849.

The Spectator, 28 July 1838; 24 February, 14 April 1849.

The Times, 23 February, 9 April, 10 April, 14 April, 16 April, 17 April, 18 May 1849.

Theil, N. *Seize mois de commandement dans la garde nationale parisienne* (Paris: Thunot, 1849).

Turner, M.J. *Independent Radicalism in Early Victorian Britain* (Westport, CT: Praeger, 2004).

Tyrell, A. *Joseph Sturge and the Moral Radical Party in Early Victorian Britain* (London: Croom Helm, 1987).

Williams, D.M. and J. Armstrong, 'Steam Shipping and the Beginnings of Overseas Tourism: British Travel to North-Western Europe, 1820–1850', *Journal of European Economic History* 35:1 (2006), pp. 125–148.

Wolverhampton Chronicle, 18 April 1849.

Worcestershire Chronicle, 9 December 1840, 18 April 1849.

4 Rose Blaze de Bury and the 'unfeminine' German and European politics of disunity

Rachel Egloff

Introduction

> It is daily more and more affirmed, that in England we care nothing for
> what passes upon the Continent; that the more grave events become,
> the more we seem to find a sort of proud pleasure in announcing to the
> world our satisfaction at our own ignorance, and our utter indifference
> to whatever may happen to our neighbours.[1]

This passage, which has a strong contemporary resonance, was written by
the nineteenth-century author Baroness Rose Blaze de Bury in *Germania:
Its Courts, Camps and People* (hereafter referred to as *Germania*) published
in two volumes in 1850. In this work, she discussed German political affairs,
in particular questions of cultural and political unity and disunity among
German-speaking areas and adjacent territories. Blaze de Bury wrote
Germania for a British audience, with the intention of enlightening the
'ignorant' and 'indifferent' British.[2] In so doing, she also addressed cultural
disunity between Britain and continental Europe. Furthermore, as a female
writer on a subject, European politics, which was viewed as 'unfeminine',
Blaze de Bury had to overcome a perceived disunity between her gender and
the seeming 'masculine' content of her work. Reviews of *Germania* picked
up on this seeming disjointedness between authorship and content.[3] Some
reviewers underlined her perceived 'masculine' style which was described as
'graphic', 'startling' and 'fearless'.[4] *The Standard* was more explicit: giving
'the fair authoress [...] full credit for extensive reading, for sound critical
judgment, and for a delicate taste; but we were not at all prepared for the
masculine vigour, the bold excursiveness, and the graphic power'.[5]

This chapter focusses on Blaze de Bury's *Germania* and examines Blaze
de Bury's ideas on increased political unity within the German-speaking
world as well as between Germany and Britain. It also considers how some
nineteenth-century women writers tried to unite their female authorship
with their perceived 'masculine' content and style – using Blaze de Bury
as a case study.[6] Two brief introductory sections provide a biographical
introduction to the little-known author and a historical contextualisation
of disunity in nineteenth-century Britain, the German-speaking world and

between the two. I then study *Germania* closely by focussing on the paradoxes of historical-literary writing and witness-reporting, demonstrating how Blaze de Bury tried to claim authority and credibility as a writer on German and Anglo-German culture and politics.[7]

Baroness Rose Blaze de Bury's biography

Mary Pauline Rose Stuart was born in Scotland, apparently in 1813, but little is known about her childhood and early adult life.[8] Widespread rumours that she was the illegitimate daughter of Henry Brougham, Scottish-born liberal statesman, Lord Chancellor, and co-founder of the *Edinburgh Review* and University College London, shroud her birth in mystery.[9] She married the French musicologist and diplomat Henri Blaze de Bury and published five novels, travel writing, memoirs, and over forty journal and newspaper articles in English, French and German.[10] She travelled through Europe and had the ears of high-ranking political decision-makers right up until her death in 1894. She was alleged to have acted as an agent for Whig politician Lord John Russell in Vienna.[11] Her contemporary Julius Fröbel provided the following description of her:

> Of Madam Blaze de Bury I must say that she is one of the most remarkable characters I have met during my lifetime. [...] Alongside her very unusual aptitude for initiating and executing great interests in the areas of politics and high finance, she did not lack literary talent. [...] the fervour of this woman did not merely vent itself in words but I saw an expression on the lady's face that alarmed me. She said: 'One finds it inexplicable how a lady can come to passionately pursue politics – but passion is personal! – for a true woman everything is personal!'[12]

Fröbel documented Blaze de Bury's frustration at the seeming incompatibility between being a woman writer and being fascinated by politics. Traditional analyses of nineteenth-century politics have assigned women a peripheral role.[13] However, the current discussion has moved on to examine the 'nature and extent of their political worlds'.[14] The increased inclusion of women in current studies of nineteenth-century politics is in part due to a broadening of the definition of politics and political culture. In 1845 the *Morning Chronicle* wrote that:

> on the one hand, the active participation of women in political agitation and debate is, generally speaking, decidedly undesirable; that, on the other hand, there are, from time to time, certain public questions of a quasi-political character on which the expression of female opinion and feeling is both natural and graceful – are safe truisms.[15]

It appears that the paper was starting to consider a broadening of the definition of 'political' when talking about 'quasi-political' questions. The article suggested that there might be different kinds or areas of involvement in politics, by using masculinised and feminised language, namely, by contrasting political 'agitation and debate' reserved for men, and political 'opinion and feeling' allowed for women. The writer added that female political feeling was 'natural and graceful' and suggested a physical underpinning to the alleged weaker sex's political role. Although the *Morning Chronicle* considered female participation possible in a broad definition of politics, it retained a discriminatory distinction between the sexes' varying approaches to politics. Blaze de Bury, like many nineteenth-century women, participated in politics in an intellectual context through literary activity.[16] However, what distinguished Blaze de Bury from other politically active women was the area she was passionate about: 'hard' international European politics.[17]

As well as being a regular Channel-crosser, Blaze de Bury travelled to the German-speaking world from her home in Paris many times between 1848 and 1871. Her political agency was enmeshed with her dealings in the finance sector as 'a major shareholder in the Anglo-Austrian Bank'.[18] For example, in connection with 'a railway enterprise', in which she did not invest her own means but spent wealthy gentlemen's capital who had got themselves 'into her clutches'.[19] Following her travels and first-hand political advocacy she published the political commentary and travel report *Germania*. Addressing a British readership, she described her vision of the German-speaking world as '[u]nion, but not unity, [...] a state, formed of several states united together but not making *one*'.[20]

Great Britain and German-speaking continental Europe

In the mid-nineteenth century, when Blaze de Bury travelled to the German-speaking world, there was no German nation-state. Though the twentieth century has taught us to think of the world in terms of national entities, this was less so for the Victorians, who 'still functioned within prenational, dynastic dimensions'.[21] Moreover, the terms 'German' and 'Germanic' were used synonymously, which suggests a less nationalistic outlook.[22] The Holy Roman Empire of over five hundred independent states ended with the abdication of Emperor Francis II in 1806.[23] In 1818 a Prussian *Zollverein* (customs union) was created and gradually expanded throughout Germany.[24] By 1848, a federal Diet in Frankfurt served as a quasi-federal institution for the loosely bound Confederation of 39 states, but there was 'no German government, administration, or [...] army'.[25] The Frankfurt Diet was followed by a new *Vorparlament* (pre-parliament), and the Frankfurt parliament, but Germany (i.e. the re-unified state we know today) did not exist.[26] Two years after the end of the Holy Roman Empire, the empire of Austria was founded. In 1815 the *Deutscher Bund* (German Confederation) was under the presidency of Austria. The Austrian empire included non-German-speaking territories, and in 1867 the *Österreichisch-Ungarischer Ausgleich* (Austrio-Hungarian Compromise) brought about a personal union (i.e. dual sovereignty) between Austria and the kingdom of Hungary under Franz Joseph I.[27] His rule spanned various Slavic communities, parts of northern Italy and Romanian groups. By the mid-nineteenth century Prussia and Austria were the leading powers in the German-speaking world, which led to two possible forms of future 'German' unity: a *Kleindeutsche Lösung* (Germany without Austria) or a *Grossdeutsche Lösung* (Germany with Austria).[28] This dualism was partly resolved in 1866 with the *Augustbündnis* (Alliance of August) followed by the *Norddeutscherbund* (North German Confederation Treaty) a year later.[29] After France's defeat by Prussia and her allies in 1871 the political unification of German territories came about as a *Kleindeutsche Lösung*.[30] This marked the foundation of the German state and the clear separation of it from Austria and her empire.

British cultural identities were also not clear-cut. After the personal union of the crowns of Scotland and England in 1603 when James VI of Scotland became James I of England and Ireland, it took a further hundred years before acts of union constitutionally united Scotland and England as one kingdom of Great Britain.[31] In 1801 Ireland was joined with Great Britain, forming the United Kingdom of Great Britain and Ireland.[32] Wales had been annexed with England in the Tudor state, through legislation in 1535–1542.[33] During Blaze de Bury's lifetime Great Britain meant England, Scotland and Wales. However, like in the German-speaking world, increasing political unity did not necessarily entail cultural unity. In discussing nineteenth-century Britishness, Chris Williams has argued, 'one is inevitably faced with the problem of demarcating it from a sense of "Englishness". For Englishness was at the core of Britishness, even if it was not synonymous with it'.[34] It was common for 'Englishness', 'English' or 'England' to be used where 'Britishness', 'British' or 'Britain' were meant.[35]

Consequently, in the nineteenth century, both Britain and the German-speaking world had to contend with political and cultural forms of unity and disunity. They also had to consider how they stood in relation to one another and in relation to European-wide power structures.[36] Germany and Austria (including her Empire) were viewed very differently. The Austrian Empire was looked upon with suspicion and branded as an illiberal despotic European relic.[37] However, the part of the German-speaking world that interested Victorians most, was where present-day Germany is.[38] Blaze de Bury's aim was to investigate why this was, despite the fact that Austria, not Germany, was 'by her position, formed to be the natural ally of Great Britain', and though Britain and Austria were 'capable of completing each other in almost every respect', Austria was, 'of all continental countries, the most unpopular in Great Britain'.[39] Enthusiasm for Germany and animadversion towards the Austrian Empire was a fairly recent phenomenon in Britain. Some have argued that in Britain there was little interest in the German-speaking world before the nineteenth century because of difficulties of travel, the level of literacy (particularly of German), high costs of printing (particularly of niche subjects pertaining to Germany) in Britain, and also due to the idea that the Thirty Years' War had destroyed German culture and thought.[40] Certain key events explain the extensive interest of the Victorians in Germany, ranging from the Protestant reformation, the Hanoverian accession, and a shared philosophical rejection of the Enlightenment in the late eighteenth century.[41] These movements undoubtedly influenced Britain and sowed the seed for the great Victorian interest in Germany. However, notwithstanding this religious, literary, and cultural interest, German politics remained nebulous in British perceptions. It was this blind-spot which Blaze de Bury was concerned with. She advocated increased political understanding and cultural differentiation in Britain's perceptions of the German-speaking world.

Uniting a female signature with 'unfeminine' politics of disunity

Having briefly navigated relations of disunity in Germany, Britain, and between the two, I now consider two questions regarding Blaze de Bury's work. First, how she presented her ideas for increased political unity within the German-speaking world as well as with Britain, and second, how she tried to unite her writing as a woman – which was not masked behind a nom de plume or concealed by anonymity – with a perceived 'masculine' political content and style. Blaze de Bury claimed authority and credibility as a writer on perceived 'masculine' inter-German and Anglo-German 'hard' politics. Her political views are briefly laid out before presenting some of her strategies for uniting her female pen and 'masculine' topics. These strategies included claiming authority by continuing in a long line of historical-literary political writing and also by presenting herself as a travelling witness of every-day politics.

In 'The Austrian Empire in 1862', in the *North British Review*, Blaze de Bury observed that there was

> the possibility of unity of administration, or rather of co-operation in each separate part of the State with the other parts of it, so as to arrive at a just division of general political rights and duties, without trenching upon the particular obligations and privileges of each nationality.[42]

In doing so, she noted her appreciation for increased political-administrative unity, which did not, however, need to be all-encompassing. Retaining difference and individuality did not exclude cooperation. A decade earlier in *Germania*, Blaze de Bury had already highlighted the dual issue of augmented German unity and disunity. She criticised that '[i]nstead of trying to solve Bousset's problem of "unity in variety", the present governors of Austria have, like their French prototypes, become worshippers of uniformity'.[43] She further laid out how disunity affected non-German-speaking areas under Austrian rule. She feared that the current 'policy tends to count but one – the Austrian or Germanic element' – and suspected that 'much harm may come, if the present rulers of Austria do not considerably modify their system of Germanic supremacy of the Slavonic tribes'.[44]

To convey these political insights, Blaze de Bury instrumentalised literary and historical writing. In an age when the divide between literature and works of history had not yet been sharpened by the professional history developing in German universities, Blaze de Bury continued a long tradition of inter-weaving history and literature in her discussion of politics.[45] By doing this, she strengthened her authority as a political commentator. She claimed that Germany did experience some political unity under the emperor Henry IV:

> These were the times, too, of Germany's *political* unity, of her greatness, of her glory [...]. And I doubt whether, in the year of grace 1106, the an-tipathy between the different races was much stronger than it is in the present year, 1850.[46]

She also quoted Tacitus' *Germania* as an epigraph of her own book.[47] Al-though Tacitus hinted at similarities and contrasts between the German tribes and Rome he, unlike Blaze de Bury, steered clear of a direct com-parison. In the above quote from 'The Austrian Empire in 1862' Blaze de Bury described how 'the first years of the sixteenth century' demonstrate, 'the possibility of unity of administration [...] without trenching upon the particular obligations and privileges of each nationality'.[48] Blaze de Bury was referring to the emperor Maximilian I, who reigned from 1508 to 1519 and recognised the need for reform and a quasi-democratic parliamentary foundation (*Reichsregiment* and *Reichskammergericht*) to maintain unity in his Empire.[49] However, in the same paragraph Blaze de Bury also mentioned Friedrich Schiller's *Wallenstein* (1800) – a fictionalisation of the life of the warrior Albrecht Wallenstein (von Waldstein) who fought for the Habsburg emperor during the Thirty Years' War and 'attempted to put Austria's practical power on a level with her traditional power'.[50] In this way, she used a historical-literary inter-genre style of political writing. Likewise, in *Germania*, Blaze de Bury proposed that the customs in the town Eferding were reminiscent of the *Niebelungen Lied*.[51] She also described how in Vienna the actor Johann Nestroy (1801–1862) 'hazards political epigrams' about cur-rent affairs by reciting lines from Schiller and Johann Goethe among oth-ers.[52] Blaze de Bury's historical-literary writing demonstrated that she was knowledgeable and competent, that she followed in a long, male-dominated tradition of political writing, and that she was therefore a credible narrator.

Blaze de Bury's goal was to strengthen political and financial links be-tween Britain and Austria, to counterweigh growing Prussian supremacy and to keep Russia and France 'in check'.[53] Her overarching ambition was to increase cultural understanding in Britain about the tension between unity and disunity within Germany but also between Germany and Britain. Blaze de Bury used various textual strategies to achieve these aims. For example, in *Germania*, by using a first-person narration, she could address the reader as the writer of the book (mostly referred to as 'we') as well as the traveller (or witness) of her story (mostly referred to as 'I'). She therefore created a method of validating her own opinions and doubly vilifying those of characters she met on the road whom she allowed to speak in direct discourse. In this way, Blaze de Bury underlined her abstract political observations with every-day life examples – as witnessed by her. The concept of giving witness testimony in literature is seemingly fraught with internal contradiction. Testimony assumes the accuracy of rendering one's experiences, whereas 'literariness (traditionally understood as a group of stylistic and fictionalizing values) seems to disqualify the truthfulness of such message'.[54] In *Germania*, Blaze de Bury worked with this paradox of reporting the truth yet packaging it into a literary form. For example, she described her experiences when reaching Cologne. Upon her arrival at the inn, she stayed in the main bar area so that she could observe the locals.[55] She reported how a group of local men were talking about horses.

'No later than last Wednesday, I did what I tell you; I jumped upon my horse, which is a good fifteen hands high, without stirrups, and that before Bassermann; you may ask him.' 'Bassermann!' echoed the whole party, in tones of unutterable contempt, 'he's a Bavarian!' As if that quality entirely precluded the possibility of his judging of anything, unless it might be beer. [...] Oh! dreams of united Germany![56]

Through her first-person narration Blaze de Bury put herself in the position, not only of a political commentator, but also in the position of an eye witness of local German affairs for her British reader. In so doing, she highlighted political and cultural disunity in German-speaking and adjacent territories as well as addressed cultural misunderstanding between these areas. At the same time, she described herself as witnessing local political deliberations in a male-dominated setting which was based on (stereotypically German) horses and beer – neither of which were perceived to be particularly lady-like.[57] The combination of Blaze de Bury's witness reports about German (dis-)unity and the descriptions of her presence in a 'masculine' environment narrowed the gulf between her gender and her book's perceived 'masculine' political content.

Nineteenth-century diplomacy was dominated by 'social politics' and was therefore, albeit informally, accessible for women.[58] Blaze de Bury had access to diplomatic and other political circles in the German-speaking world. By describing her physical presence in this male-dominated environment she further cemented her authority. In a flashback, she described her time spent in Cologne in September 1842 where the king of Prussia Friedrich Wilhelm IV (1795–1861) was being celebrated at a banquet. As a witness, Blaze de Bury reported that the Austrian archduke Johann (1782–1859) was present at these festivities and had been gifted the sixteenth Prussian infantry corps. She recorded the archduke's reaction after receiving the gift:

> The Emperor, my master, sent me hither. The gift of a regiment from your Majesty, has caused me deep delight, for I have thereby become a member of an army, which has done great things, and which stood unshaken in the hour of need! Together we then fought the great fight of freedom victoriously. So long as Prussia and Austria, and the other lands of Germany are united, so long shall we remain unshaken in our force, as the granite rocks of our own mountains.[59]

Blaze de Bury argued that these were the facts, as witnessed by her, and that the press and certain political parties had later twisted the Archduke Johann's words to advocate an all-inclusive German unity and the eradication of cultural difference. Blaze de Bury explained that

> [u]nion, but not unity, [...] a state, formed of several states united together but not making *one* [...] this was a possibility up to a certain point, and this it was of which the toast proposed by the Archduke was intended to convey an idea.[60]

With the advantage of greater hindsight and archival research, the renowned historian Heinrich von Treitschke, in *Deutsche Geschichte* (1879–1894), agreed that the Archduke's words had been misconstrued by the press. He quoted the same words Blaze de Bury had recollected and added:

> The newspapers assured that he had said: 'No Austria, no Prussia anymore! One single Germany up and down, one single Germany firm like its mountains!' In nations that are trembling toward a big decision, the forces of myth formation preside with enigmatic strength; They now threw themselves upon the Austrian, and made him a popular [vernacular] hero.[61]

In this instance at least, as a witness, Blaze de Bury was correct in her assessment of the contemporary mood and press. She genuinely had a point to prove about an important political occurrence and statement which were contended at the time she was writing. By describing her physical presence in a man's world and by positioning herself as the credible eye witness, Blaze de Bury not only described the German debate on political unity and disunity, but also further assimilated her gender with the 'masculine' environment.

Blaze de Bury also made use of her position as a witness of current affairs to elaborate on Anglo-German disunity. She did so by juxtaposing herself with another British traveller. She differentiated between herself as an example of cultural harmony, and the British gentleman as an example of cultural disunity. The British gentleman traveller was visibly uncomfortable among

Germans. Blaze de Bury found that 'there was something inexpressibly amusing in the struggle that was evidently dividing this inward man'.[62] This 'Harley Street' gentleman was 'established before the stove, a pair of glasses fixed upon his nose, and the "Times" in his hand, wherein he was studying the London news, by way, I presume, of initiating himself into what was going on in Germany'.[63] By introducing this Harley Street gentleman, Blaze de Bury furthered her credibility in the eye of the British reader as she proved her familiarity with British behaviour and culture. She also discomfortingly pointed a finger at her readers suggesting that some of them might be as ignorant and uncomfortable about Germany as the Harley Street gentleman was portrayed to be. The fact that the traveller was described as wearing glasses highlighted his intense focus on the only noticeably English item in the room – *The Times* – and his blurred peripheral vision and understanding of everything German around him.

Blaze de Bury thought that the British felt superior towards continental Europe and that this sentiment was unjustified.[64] Once again, making use of her double voice (I and we), she declared that

> if you recognise 'nationality' as the right which a country has to be possessed and governed only by national rulers, it is true that Austria may lose Lombardy, but I do not see what then is to protect or justify France in keeping Alsatia, or ourselves in preserving anything beyond our three-Island kingdoms – *ex encore*! this must depend upon the good pleasure of the Welsh, the Irish, and the Scotch, who may take it into their heads to object to the Normanno-Saxon sway.[65]

To illustrate this, she addressed the attitude of the British towards the Austrians. She reported meeting a British man and his daughters at St. Pölten. She called him Mr Smith, though he really 'rejoices in a far more aristocratic name'.[66] According to Blaze de Bury: 'They did not speak the language; they did not know the people; but they hated them cordially, called them barbarians, and thought it was a right and proper thing so to do'.[67] Blaze de Bury let Mr Smith report his part of their conversation in his own patronising words:

> 'Now Madame' said Mr. Smith, [...] like a man who is preparing to beat you dispassionately, to convince you by strong reasoning, to be cool-headed and clear, statesmanlike, [...] 'I am a High Tory [...] I think I may say, Queen Victoria, God bless her! Has no better subject than I am! [I] find the cruelty of these Austrians in Italy [...] the most revolting occurrence of modern history'.[68]

Smith continued at some length about how proud he was to be British and superior, and how barbaric and inhumane the Austrians were. Blaze de Bury, unamused by Smith's opinions and attitude, applied Edmund Burke's words to him: were they driven out of the country this day 'nothing would remain to tell that it had been possessed, during the inglorious period of their dominion, by anything better than the ourang-outang or the tiger!'[69] Smith, supposing that the statement referred to the Austrians in Italy, was quick to heartily agree and express his admiration.[70] Blaze de Bury then revealed that Burke had said these words during a speech on Fox's East India Bill in 1783, and that

> the dominion alluded to theirein [sic] [...] is our dominion in India! – the dominion of the magnanimous, and liberty-loving, and humane Britons, whom you, Mr. Smith, are – chiefly on account of these great qualities – so proud of calling your compatriots.[71]

Blaze de Bury concluded that '[n]either Mr. Smith nor the young ladies knew precisely what to reply [...] and they were grateful to the [...] courier for telling them the carriage was ready'.[72] In this passage Blaze de Bury highlighted the similarities between British and Austrian policies abroad yet also the perceived differences and animosity between them. However, to make a convincing argument about European disunity to a British gentleman, she chose to ventriloquise Burke and, in that sense, just as she had quoted Archduke Johann and Tacitus, spoke through a man, to drive home her own political agenda.

Similarly to the before mentioned reviews, the *Morning Post*'s reviewer remarked on her unusual 'masculine' traits, focussed on her 'unfeminine' ones. They wrote that:

> [T]he baroness possesses, through her influential connections, very peculiar facilities for acquiring exclusive information on the topics treated of, and is reported to have been on the most friendly terms with almost all the illustrious characters male and female, whom the events of the last two years have brought into European celebrity. [...]. The baroness is also understood to have penetrated into provinces and localities rarely visited by tourists, and still glowing with the embers of civil war [...].[73]

Commenting on Blaze de Bury's role as a first-hand witness of her reports, these remarks could be seen as reflecting – intentionally or not – on Blaze de Bury's sex and character. The 'peculiar facilities' for information gathering sound uncannily like an allusion to pillow talk and the description of her 'penetration' into 'provinces and localities rarely visited' and still 'glowing' superimposes 'masculine' sexual drive and character. Reviewers' elaborations about her unusual 'masculine' and 'unfeminine' traits highlight the confusion and tension the seeming disunity between being a woman and writing about 'hard' European politics caused.

This chapter provided an insight into Blaze de Bury's ideas for increased political unity within the nineteenth-century German-speaking world as well as between Germany and Britain. It further demonstrated how, as a nineteenth-century woman writer, she tried to unite her female penmanship and signature with her perceived 'masculine' political content and style of *Germania*. The examples presented in this chapter, which illustrate Blaze de Bury's instrumentalisation of historical-literary and witness-report writing, have demonstrated how she claimed authority and credibility as a writer on Anglo-German culture and politics. However, though *Germania* was, on the whole, received in a positive light by reviewers, their surprise at the signature-content, 'female-masculine' gender combination casts doubt on whether Blaze de Bury's strategies were entirely successful. To borrow Blaze de Bury's own terminology, it seems that to the nineteenth-century reviewer, the contents of *Germania: Its Courts, Camps and People* and its author represented: 'Union, but not unity', a book formed of two perceived genders joined together but nevertheless not quite making *one*.

Notes

1 R. Blaze de Bury, *Germania: Its Courts, Camps, and People*, 2 vols (London: Colburn, 1850), vol. 1, p. ix.
2 Blaze de Bury, *Germania* 1, p. ix. Blaze de Bury used 'English' to refer to the British. See L. Colley, *Britons: Forging the Nation 1707–1837*, 2nd edn (New Haven, CT: Yale University Press, 2005), pp. xiii, xv.
3 On the reception of *Germania* see R. Egloff, 'The Study of the Life and Works of Blaze de Bury: A Counter-Narrative of Women's Involvement in Nineteenth-Century European Transcultural Politics' (unpublished doctoral thesis, Oxford Brookes University, 2019). Some of the research for this chapter stems from this larger PhD project.
4 [Anon.], 'Mr. Colburn's New Publications', *Athenaeum*, 7 September 1850, p. 960; [Anon.], 'Literature', *Standard*, 21 August 1850, p. 3; [Anon.], 'Literature', *Morning Post*, 24 August 1850, p. 6.
5 [Anon.], *Standard*, 21 August 1850, p. 3.
6 This chapter's usage of the terms masculine, feminine and unfeminine refers to mid-nineteenth-century perceptions thereof.
7 The terms German and Germany refer to German-speaking parts of Europe pre-1871.
8 Rose was her preferred first name. Her first name has been spelled Mary or Marie and her surname Stuart or Stewart. See J. Voisine, 'La Baronne Blaze de Bury (1813(?)–1894) et son role litteraire', *Thesis* (Paris: Faculté des lettres de Paris, 1955), p. 10.
9 R. Egloff, 'Blaze de Bury, Marie Pauline Rose (1813–1894)', in *The Companion to Victorian Popular Fiction*, ed. by K. Morrison (Jefferson, NC: McFarland, 2018), p. 29; R. Egloff, 'Blaze de Bury, Marie Pauline Rose (1813–1894)', in *Encyclopedia of Victorian Women Writers*, ed. by L. Scholl (London: Palgrave, forthcoming 2019). For more about Brougham see Henry Brougham (posthumous), *The Life and Times of Henry Lord Brougham: Written by Himself*, 3 vols (Edinburgh: William Blackwood and Sons, 1871).
10 [Anon.], 'Marriages', *Spectator*, 26 October 1844, p. 1016.
11 J. Fröbel, *Ein Lebenslauf, Erinnerungen und Bekenntinsse*, 2 vols (Stuttgart: J. G. Gottaschen Buchhandlung, 1891), vol. 2, pp. 205, 209.

12 Original: Von Madame Blaze de Bury muss ich sagen, dass Sie eine der merk-würdigsten Persönlichkeiten ist, welche ich während meines Lebens kennen gelernt habe. [...] Neben ihrer ganz ungewöhnlichen Befähigung zur Anregung und Betreibung großer Interessen im Gebiete der Politik und haute finance [fehlte es ihr] auch nicht an literarischen Talenten. [...] die Leidenschaft des Weibes machte sich nicht bloss in Worten Luft und ich habe an der Frau einen Gesichtsausdruck gesehen, der mich erschreckt hat, - sagte sie: 'Man findet es unerklärlich, wie eine Frau dazu kommt, mit Leidenschaft Politik zu treiben; aber die Leidenschaft ist persönlich!–Bei einer rechten Frau ist alles persönlich!' (own translation). Fröbel, *Ein Lebenslauf*, vol. 2, pp. 93–94.

13 See, for example, E. Showalter, *A Literature of Their Own: British Women Novelists from Brontë to Lessing* (Princeton, NJ: Princeton University Press, 1977), pp. 28–29.

14 S.M. Richardson, *The Political Worlds of Women: Gender and Politics in Nineteenth Century Britain* (Oxford: Routledge, 2013), p. 1.

15 [Anon.], *Morning Chronicle*, 8 April 1845.

16 Sarah Richardson posits that some political arenas 'were exclusively masculine'. Women tended to be involved in every-day politics centred around the home. Richardson, pp. 9, 14. A current study that attempts to undo this perception is G. Sluga and C. James, eds, *Women, Diplomacy and International Politics since 1500* (Abingdon: Routledge, 2016).

17 Joseph Nye's late twentieth-century definitions of 'hard' and 'soft' power were developed by Liz Sperling and Charlotte Bretherton who considered 'hard' politics the discussion of 'mainstream' issues driven by men, and 'soft' political topics that appeal to women. J. Nye, *Bound to Lead: The Changing Nature of American Power* (New York: Basic Books, 1990); L. Sperling and C. Bretherton, 'Women's Policy Networks and the European Union', *Women's Studies International Forum*, 19 (1996), pp. 303–313.

18 S.W. Murray, *Liberal Diplomacy and German Unification: The Early Career of Robert Morier* (Westport, CT: Praeger, 2000), pp. 172–173, 78.

19 Murray, *Liberal Diplomacy*; also J. Eibner, *Our Natural Ally: The Times and the Austrian Empire, 1841–1867* (forthcoming).

20 Blaze de Bury, *Germania*, vol. 1, p. 10.

21 J. Davis, *The Victorians and Germany* (Bern: Peter Lang, 2007), p. 20.

22 M. Oergel, 'The Redeeming Teuton: Nineteenth-Century Notions of the "Germanic" in England and Germany', in *Imagining Nations*, ed. by G. Cubitt (Manchester: Manchester University Press, 1998), pp. 75–91 (p. 81).

23 See, for example, B. Stollberg-Rilinger, *Das Heilige Römische Reich Deutscher Nation: Vom Ende des Mittelalters bis 1806* (Munich: C. H. Beck, 2013); and B. Stollberg-Rilinger, *The Holy Roman Empire: A Short History* (Princeton, NJ: Princeton University Press, 2018).

24 The *Zollverein* officially came into force in 1834. It entailed the unprecedented full economic union of independent states without mandating a political union or federation. Austria was not part of the *Zollverein*. See C.H. Shiue, 'From Political Fragmentation Towards a Customs Union: Border Effects of the German Zollverein, 1815–1855', *European Review of Economic History* 9:2 (2005), pp. 129–162.

25 J.A.S. Grenville, *Europe Reshaped, 1848–1878* (Glasgow: Fontana, 1976), p. 56. Prussia, for example, held Polish territory and the Habsburgs ruled over Hungarian and other domains. Prussia and Austria dominated the Confederation but each of them, in their own right, held territories that did not form a part of the Confederation. Even after 1871, when Germany was unified and became a clearly defined entity, the usage of the term Germany was still not clear-cut. There were (and still are) significant German-speaking territories outside of the newly united Germany, for example, in Austria and Switzerland.

26 See, for example, J.J. Sheehan, *German History 1770–1866* (Oxford: Clarendon Press, 1989), pp. 672–729; M. Kotulla, *Deutsche Verfassungsgeschichte: Vom Alten Reich bis Weimar (1495–1934)* (Berlin: Springer, 2008), pp. 423–424.

27 J. Andrássy, *Ungarns Ausgleich mit Österreich vom Jahre 1867* (1897; Paterborn: Europäischer Geschichtsverlag, 2011); D. Brodbeck, *Defining Deutschtum: Political Ideology, German Identity, and Music-Critical Discourse in Liberal Vienna* (Oxford: Oxford University Press, 2014), p. 7.

28 See, for example, T. Nipperdey, *Deutsche Geschichte 1800–1866: Bürgerwelt und starker Staat* (München: C. H. Beck, 1994), pp. 674–804.

29 M. Kotulla, 'Norddeutscher Bund', in *Deutsche Verfassungsgeschichte: Vom Alten Reich bis Weimar (1495–1934)* (Berlin: Springer, 2008), pp. 487–510.

30 For more on the nineteenth-century unification of Germany see A. Stiles and A. Farmer, *The Unification of Germany 1815–90*, 2nd edn (London: Hodder & Stoughton, 2001); or J. Whaley, *Germany and the Holy Roman Empire: Maximilian I to the Peace of Westphalia: 1490–1648* (Oxford: Oxford University Press, 2012).

31 See, for example, A. Macinnes, *Union and Empire: The Making of the United Kingdom in 1707* (Cambridge: Cambridge University Press, 2007); or Colley, *Britons: Forging the Nation 170 –1837*.

32 L. Colley, *Acts of Union Acts of Disunion: What Has Held the UK Together - And What Is Dividing It?* (London: Profile Books, 2014), pp. 95–106.

33 C. Williams, 'The Anglicisation of Wales', in *English in Wales: Diversity, Conflict, and Change*, ed. by N. Coupland (Clevedon: Multilingual Matters, 1990), pp. 19–47.

34 C. Williams, 'British Identities', in *A Companion to Nineteenth-Century Britain*, ed. by C. Williams (Malden, MA: Blackwell, 2004), p. 546.

35 Colley, *Britons: Forging the Nation 1707–1837*, pp. xiii, xv.

36 For more on Anglo-German relations see, for example, A. Epple, 'A Strained Relationship: Epistemology and Historiography in Eighteenth- and Nineteenth-Century Germany and Britain', in S. Berger and C. Lorenz, eds, *Nationalizing of the Past: Historians as Nation Builders in Modern Europe* (London: Palgrave Macmillan, 2015), pp. 86–106; H.R. Klienberger, *The Novel in England and Germany: A Comparative Study* (London: Oswald Wolff, 1981); B. Korte, 'From Picturesque to Political: Transcultural Perspectives on Germany in Victorian Popular Periodicals, 1850 to 1875', *German Life and Letters* 68:3 (15 June 2015), pp. 356–369; or F.L. Muller, *Britain and the German Question: Perceptions of Nationalism and Political Reform, 1830–1863* (Basingstoke: Palgrave, 2001).

37 This was mainly due to the perception of Klemens von Metternich's policies. See S. Hamish, ed., *Enlightened Absolutism: Reform and Reformers in Later Eighteenth-Century Europe* (Basingstoke: Palgrave, 1990); or A. Sked, 'Explaining the Habsburg Empire, 1830–1890', in *Themes in Modern European History 1830–1890*, ed. by B. Waller (London: Routledge, 2002), pp. 123–158.

38 Davis, *The Victorians and Germany*, p. 9.

39 Blaze de Bury, 'The Austrian Empire in 1862', p. 285.

40 See, for example, G. Davis, *German Thought and Culture in England 1700–1770* (Chapel Hill: University of North Carolina Press, 1969), pp. 1–7.

41 See, for example, Davis, *The Victorians and Germany*, pp. 25, 27, 33; or Terry Pinkard, *German Philosophy 1760–1860: The Legacy of Idealism* (Cambridge: Cambridge University Press, 2002), p. 11.

42 Blaze de Bury, 'The Austrian Empire in 1862', pp. 188–189.

43 Jacques Bénigne Bossuet (1627–1704) was a French historian and theologian, who pondered the question of unity in variety among the Christian sects – in particular Catholicism's ability to achieve unity. Blaze de Bury, *Germania*, vol. 2, p. 173.

44 Blaze de Bury, *Germania*, vol. 2, pp. 174–175.

45 For example, the so-called first modern historian of ancient Rome, Edward Gibbon, epitomises this tradition. He was praised for his objectivity and unusually great use of primary sources, which would influence a new methodological way of writing history. However, at the same time, his *History of the Decline and Fall of the Roman Empire* (1776–1789) would not be as well understood and as pleasurably read were it not for his literary irony, sumptuous prose style and unscientific aphorisms.

46 Blaze de Bury, *Germania*, vol. 1, pp. 26–27.

47 Tacitus, *Agricola and Germania* (Oxford: Oxford University Press, 1999). See also A. Gudeman, 'The Sources of the Germania of Tacitus', in *Transactions and Proceedings of the American Philological Association* (Baltimore, IL: Johns Hopkins University, 1990), pp. 93–111.

48 Blaze de Bury, 'The Austrian Empire in 1862', pp. 288–289.

49 The *Reichskammergericht* (Imperial Chamber Court) became one of the highest judicial institutions in the Holy Roman Empire. Unlike the *Reichskammergericht*, the *Reichsregiment* (imperial government) was a unified democratic forum among the Princes of the Holy Roman Empire in Nüremberg. It failed shortly after its creation but was reformed again in 1521. Whaley, *Germany and the Holy Roman Empire*, pp. 32–33.

50 Blaze de Bury, 'The Austrian Empire in 1862', p. 289; K.-M. Guth, ed., *Friedrich Schiller: Wallenstein. Vollständige Ausgabe der Trilogie: Wallensteins Lager / Die Piccolomini / Wallensteins Tod* (1800; Berlin: Hofenberg, 2016).

51 Blaze de Bury, *Germania*, vol. 2, p. 48.

52 Blaze de Bury, *Germania*, vol. 2, pp. 112–113.

53 Blaze de Bury, 'The Austrian Empire in 1862', p. 286.

54 M. Delaperrière, 'Testimony as a Literary Problem', in *Nonfiction, Reportage and Testimony*, ed. by M. Skotnicka (Warsaw: Institute of Literary Research Polish Academy of Sciences, 2014), pp. 42–54 (p. 42).

55 In 1815 Cologne (now in North Rhine-Westphalia) had been assimilated into the kingdom of Prussia during the Congress of Vienna.

56 Blaze de Bury, *Germania*, vol. 1, pp. 6–7.

57 For more on nineteenth-century symbolism of the horse and its gender dynamics see G. Dorré, *Victorian Fiction and the Cult of the Horse* (Aldershot: Ashgate, 2006).

58 E. Chalus, 'Elite Women, Social Politics and the Political Worlds of Late Eighteenth-Century England', *Historical Journal* 43:3 (2000), pp. 669–697.

59 Original: 'Der Kaiser mein Herr, hat mich hergesandt in dieses Lager. Dass Eure Königliche Majestät mir ein Regiment zu verleihen geruht, ist mir eine große Freude gewesen; denn ich bin dadurch Mitglied eines Heeres geworden, welches in der Zeit der Noth unerschütterlich dagestanden und Großes geleistet hat. Vereint haben wir damals den großen Freiheitskampf siegreich bestanden. So lange Preußen und Oesterreich, so lange das übrige Deutschland, so weit die deutsche Zunge klingt, einig sind, werden wir unerschütterlich dastehen, wie die Felsen unserer Berge' (own translation). Blaze de Bury, *Germania*, vol. 1, p. 10.

60 Blaze de Bury, *Germania*, vol. 1, p. 10.

61 Original: '[D]ie Zeitungen versicherten, er hätte gesagt: "Kein Österreich, kein Preußen mehr! Ein einig Deutschland hoch und her, ein einig Deutschland fest wie Seine Berge!" In Nationen die einer großen Entscheidung entgegenzittern, walten die Kräfte der Mythenbildung mit rätselhafter Stärke' (own translation). H. Von Treitschke, *Deutsche Geschichte im Neunzehnten Jahrhundert*, 5 vols (1927; Paterborn: Europäischer Geschichtsverlag, 2015), vol. 5, p. 172.

62 Blaze de Bury, *Germania*, vol. 1, pp. 6–7.

63 Blaze de Bury, *Germania*, vol. 1, pp. 6–7.

64 Blaze de Bury, *Germania*, vol. 1, p. ix.

65 Blaze de Bury, *Germania*, vol. 2, pp. 345–347.
66 Blaze de Bury, *Germania*, vol. 2, p. 79.
67 Blaze de Bury, *Germania*, vol. 2, p. 79.
68 Blaze de Bury, *Germania*, vol. 2, p. 85.
69 Blaze de Bury, *Germania*, vol. 2, p. 84.
70 After the Congress of Vienna, Austria controlled parts of northern Italy, which led to the three wars of Italian Independence between 1848 and 1866. See F. J. Coppa, *The Origins of the Italian Wars of Independence* (1992; Abingdon: Routledge, 2013).
71 Blaze de Bury, *Germania*, vol. 2, p. 86.
72 Blaze de Bury, *Germania*, vol. 2, p. 86.
73 [Anon.], 'The Sovereigns and Courts of Europe', *Morning Post*, 24 July 1850, p. 8; [Anon.], *Standard*, 26 July 1850, p. 1.

Bibliography

Andrássy, J. *Ungarns Ausgleich mit Österreich vom Jahre 1867* (1897; Paterborn: Europäischer Geschichtsverlag, 2001).

[Anon.], 'Literature', *Morning Post*, 24 August 1850, p. 6.

———, 'Literature', *Standard*, 21 August 1850, p. 3.

———, 'Marriages', *Spectator*, 26 October 1844, p. 1016.

———, *Morning Chronicle*, 8 April 1845.

———, 'Mr. Colburn's New Publications', *Athenaeum*, 7 September 1850, p. 960.

———, 'The Sovereigns and Courts of Europe', *Morning Post,* 24 July 1850, p. 8.

———, *Standard*, 26 July 1850.

Blaze de Bury, R. 'The Austrian Empire in 1862', *North British Review* 37 (November 1862), pp. 285–322.

———, *Germania: Its Courts, Camps, and People*, 2 vols (London: Colburn, 1850).

Brodbeck, D. *Defining Deutschtum: Political Ideology, German Identity, and Music-Critical Discourse in Liberal Vienna* (Oxford: Oxford University Press, 2014).

Brougham, H. *The Life and Times of Henry Lord Brougham: Written by Himself*, 3 vols (Edinburgh: William Blackwood and Sons, 1871).

Chalus, E. 'Elite Women, Social Politics and the Political Worlds of Late Eighteenth-Century England', *Historical Journal* 43:3 (2000), pp. 669–697.

Colley, L. *Britons: Forging the Nation 1707–1837*, 2nd edn (New Haven, CT: Yale University Press, 2005).

———, *Acts of Union Acts of Disunion: What Has Held the UK Together – And What Is Dividing It?* (London: Profile Books, 2014).

Coppa, F.J. *The Origins of the Italian Wars of Independence* (Abingdon: Routledge, 2013).

Davis, G. *German Thought and Culture in England 1700–1770* (Chapel Hill: University of North Carolina Press, 1969).

Davis, J. *The Victorians and Germany* (Bern: Peter Lang, 2007).

Delaperrière, M. 'Testimony as a Literary Problem', in *Nonfiction, Reportage and Testimony*, ed. by M. Skotnicka (Warsaw: Institute of Literary Research Polish Academy of Sciences, 2014), pp. 42–54.

Dorré, G. *Victorian Fiction and the Cult of the Horse* (Aldershot: Ashgate, 2006).

Egloff, R. 'Blaze de Bury, Marie Pauline Rose (1813–1894)', in *The Companion to Victorian Popular Fiction*, ed. by K. Morrison (Jefferson, NC: McFarland, 2018), p. 29.

————, 'Blaze de Bury, Marie Pauline Rose (1813–1894)', in *Encyclopedia of Victorian Women Writers*, ed. by L. Scholl (London: Palgrave Macmillan, forthcoming 2019).

————, 'The Study of the Life and Works of Blaze de Bury: A Counter-Narrative of Women's Involvement in Nineteenth-Century European Transcultural Politics' (unpublished doctoral thesis, Oxford Brookes University, 2019).

Eibner, J. *Our Natural Ally: The Times and the Austrian Empire, 1841–1867* (forthcoming).

Epple, A. 'A Strained Relationship: Epistemology and Historiography in Eighteenth- and Nineteenth-Century Germany and Britain', in *Nationalizing of the Past: Historians as Nation Builders in Modern Europe*, ed. by S. Berger and C. Lorenz, (London: Palgrave Macmillan, 2015), pp. 86–106.

Fröbel, J. *Ein Lebenslauf, Erinnerungen und Bekenntinsse*, 2 vols (Stuttgart: J. G. Gottaschen Buchhandlung, 1891).

Grenville, J.A.S. *Europe Reshaped, 1848–1878* (Glasgow: Fontana, 1976).

Gudeman, A. 'The Sources of the Germania of Tacitus', in *Transactions and Proceedings of the American Philological Association* (Baltimore, IL: Johns Hopkins University, 1990), pp. 93–111.

Guth, K.-M. ed., *Friedrich Schiller: Wallenstein. Vollständige Ausgabe der Trilogie: Wallensteins Lager / Die Piccolomini / Wallensteins Tod* (1800; Berlin: Hofenberg, 2016).

Hamish, S. ed., *Enlightened Absolutism: Reform and Reformers in Later Eighteenth-Century Europe* (Basingstoke: Palgrave, 1990).

Klienberger, H.R. *The Novel in England and Germany: A Comparative Study* (London: Oswald Wolff, 1981).

Korte, B. 'From Picturesque to Political: Transcultural Perspectives on Germany in Victorian Popular Periodicals, 1850 to 1875', *German Life and Letters* 68 (15 June 2015), pp. 356–369.

Kotulla, M. *Deutsche Verfassungsgeschichte: Vom Alten Reich bis Weimar (1495–1934)* (Berlin: Springer, 2008).

Macinnes, A. *Union and Empire: The Making of the United Kingdom in 1707* (Cambridge: Cambridge University Press, 2007).

Muller, F.L. *Britain and the German Question: Perceptions of Nationalism and Political Reform, 1830–1863* (Basingstoke: Palgrave Macmillan, 2001).

Murray, S.W. *Liberal Diplomacy and German Unification: The Early Career of Robert Morier* (Westport, CT: Praeger, 2000).

Nipperdey, T. *Deutsche Geschichte 1800–1866: Bürgerwelt und starker Staat* (Munich: C. H. Beck, 1994).

Nye, J. *Bound to Lead: The Changing Nature of American Power* (New York: Basic Books, 1990).

Oergel, M. 'The Redeeming Teuton: Nineteenth-Century Notions of the "Germanic" in England and Germany', in *Imagining Nations*, ed. by G. Cubitt (Manchester: Manchester University Press, 1998), pp. 75–91.

Pinkard, T. *German Philosophy 1760–1860: The Legacy of Idealism* (Cambridge: Cambridge University Press, 2002).

Richardson, S.M. *The Political Worlds of Women: Gender and Politics in Nineteenth Century Britain* (Oxford: Routledge, 2013).

Sheehan, J.J. *German History 1770–1866* (Oxford: Clarendon Press, 1989).

Shiue, C. 'From Political Fragmentation towards a Customs Union: Border Effects of the German Zollverein, 1815–1855', *European Review of Economic History* 9:2 (2005), pp. 129–162.

Showalter, E. *A Literature of Their Own: British Women Novelists from Brontë to Lessing* (Princeton, NJ: Princeton University Press, 1977).

Sked, A. 'Explaining the Habsburg Empire, 1830–1890', in *Themes in Modern European History 1830–1890*, ed. by Bruce Waller (London: Routledge, 2002), pp. 123–158.

Sluga, G. and C. James, eds, *Women, Diplomacy and International Politics since 1500* (Abingdon: Routledge, 2016).

Sperling, L., and C. Bretherton, 'Women's Policy Networks and the European Union', *Women's Studies International Forum* 19 (1996), pp. 303–313.

Stiles, A. and A. Farmer, *The Unification of Germany 1815 – 90*, 2nd edn (London: Hodder & Stoughton, 2001).

Stollberg-Rilinger, B. *Das Heilige Römische Reich Deutscher Nation: Vom Ende des Mittelalters bis 1806* (Munich: C. H. Beck, 2013).

———, *The Holy Roman Empire: A Short History* (Princeton, NJ: Princeton University Press, 2018).

Tacitus, *Agricola and Germania*, ed. by Anthony Birley (Oxford: Oxford University Press, 1999).

Voisine, J. 'La Baronne Blaze de Bury (1813(?) – 1894) et son role litteraire', *Thesis* (Paris: Faculté des lettres de Paris, 1955).

Von Treitschke, H. *Deutsche Geschichte im Neunzehnten Jahrhundert.* 5 vols (1927; Paterborn: Europäischer Geschichtsverlag, 2015).

Whaley, J. *Germany and the Holy Roman Empire: Maximilian I to the Peace of Westphalia: 1490–1648* (Oxford: Oxford University Press, 2012).

Williams, C. 'The Anglicisation of Wales', in *English in Wales: Diversity, Conflict, and Change*, ed. by Nikolas Coupland (Clevedon: Multilingual Matters, 1990), pp. 19–47.

———, 'British Identities', in *A Companion to Nineteenth-Century Britain,* ed. by C. Williams (Malden, MA: Blackwell, 2004), pp. 534–552.

Part III

The politics of union and disunion in Great Britain

5   Scottish political leadership and Anglo-Scottish union in the long nineteenth century

Gordon Pentland

Introduction

Few could doubt that both unions of various description and leadership are contemporary obsessions. Historians of Scottish politics have, of course, long been interested in the first of these in the shape of the Anglo-Scottish union of 1707, its causes, course and consequences. Recent decades have witnessed a far more nuanced and variegated history of that union and of the various unionisms and nationalisms (the plural form is important here) that held it as a central point of reference.[1]

This effort has gone some way to address a wider problem: the poverty of explicitly *political* history within postwar Scottish historical studies. Michael Fry (himself, significantly, an excellent political historian, but one sitting somewhat outside of the academic profession) lamented this a long time ago.[2] The thinness of Scotland's political history (especially, but not only, for the nineteenth century) has been compounded by its unevenness. Historians have sought out 'progressive' themes (liberalism or radicalism) or otherwise been on the hunt for nationalism. The casualties from this unbalanced historiography should be obvious. Much more ink, for example, has been spilt on the National Association for the Vindication of Scottish Rights (NAVSR) – a small, short-lived and cranky protest movement – than on the Conservative Party in nineteenth-century Scotland.[3]

An additional absence here is any study of specifically Scottish political leadership. This is a theme well represented within British political historiography as a whole, perhaps most notably in the well-known Anglophone appetite for political biography. More recently, existing ways of approaching political leadership within history have been cross-fertilised by insights from politics disciplines, anthropology and elsewhere.[4] As a theme within Scottish historiography leadership is almost entirely absent. The Scottish tradition of political biography is thin and underdeveloped, and there is a comparative absence of work on political 'elites', upon whom any study of leadership must necessarily focus.

This chapter is a limited effort to bring together these two themes. It aims to examine and compare how three Scottish political leaders – Henry

Dundas, Francis Jeffrey and Lord Rosebery – articulated visions of the Anglo-Scottish union (and almost necessarily the British-Irish union) as part of their public lives. In that sense it aligns with a fruitful body of work on the English/British context, which has re-examined elites and their publics and more especially their rhetorical presence, on the premise that 'in an important sense, politicians are what they speak and publish'.[5] The emphasis on a small group of case studies allows for a more adequate treatment of political languages in Scotland. It further allows us to move beyond the rather artificial distinction between 'unionist' and 'nationalist' positions without falling back from these upon awkward hybrids such as 'unionist-nationalism'.

Henry Dundas, first Viscount Melville (1742–1811)

Of the three case studies presented here, Dundas continues to be the most controversial. In a pale Caledonian imitation of the Rhodes Must Fall movement, in 2016 an activist glued a plaque to the imposing monument to Dundas in Edinburgh's New Town:

> Henry Dundas, 1st Viscount Melville
> 'THE GREAT TYRANT'
> 1742–1811
> As de-facto ruler of Scotland, he brutally crushed rebellious demands for democracy.
> As Home Secretary, he succeeded in delaying the abolition of slavery.
> He remains the last person in Britain to have been impeached for embezzlement of public funds.
> May we remember who looks down on us.[6]

Eighteenth-century Britons would have required no reminders. Across his active parliamentary career from his appointment as Lord Advocate in Lord North's government in 1775 through to his impeachment in 1805, Dundas was among the most caricatured politicians of the age in what was a 'golden age' of visual satire. Certainly he fell behind the now very familiar images of George III, Pitt, Fox and Burke: but he was ahead of the rest, very recognisably a public figure.[7] These prints embraced the full spectrum of political imagery: from straightforward satires on power and overbearing ambition with Dundas as a colossus (as Walpole had been represented and Gladstone would be); to meanly personal attacks on both his (and Pitt's) fondness for the bottle.[8] Nonetheless, certain commonalities run across them.

One was Dundas's Scottishness. Dundas's political star rose in the aftermath of the concentrated episodes of anti-Scottishness that had met the short-lived administration of the Earl of Bute. Some of the obloquy attached to 'Bute' and to 'Scotch politics' was necessarily also directed at Dundas. The second constant was Dundas's consuming interest in and pursuit of place and power. Frequently both of these themes were inter-linked in the prints. One of the sources of Dundas's power and reputation completed the picture in one of those images that was well known to con-temporaries. Gillray's 'Wha wants me' depicted Dundas in a Scots bon-net, throwing his commodious tartan plaid around the diminutive figure of his political boss, William Pitt the Younger.[9] His attachment to Pitt was central to Dundas's rise and was a portable source of support across the remainder of his career.

As a Scot holding not only the Lord Advocate's post but also a series of high-profile ministries carrying much wider responsibilities (Treasurer of the Navy, President of the Board of Control, Home Secretary, Secretary at War, First Lord of the Admiralty) he has been presented as an interesting test case of the degree to which the union of 1707 had been 'completed' ap-proaching the end of the century. Dundas has usually been characterised as a 'fixer' or a 'manager', certainly in the Scottish context where his electoral ascendancy was almost complete. This, however, underplays his considera-ble public role, albeit a role with a much more limited audience than would become standard in the nineteenth century. Dundas was a prominent and powerful orator at a time when the parliamentary speaking was both more closely and widely reported and was becoming more politically important than it had been.[10]

This ability to speak – as it was for other non-aristocratic aspirants to office – was important for Dundas. He had made a name for himself within Scotland with legal defences, of course, but also political speeches, such as one addressing the issue of reform of the county franchise.[11] Those numerous diary accounts, which have provided fuel for biographies of Dundas, paid close attention to his parliamentary speech and to Dundas as a powerful speaker. Following his more famous account of Dundas's Scotticisms, Nathaniel Wraxall was one contemporary who roundly praised his speeches:

> His voice, strong, clear, and sonorous, enabled him to surmount the noise of a popular assembly, and almost to enforce attention at mo-ments of the greatest clamour or impatience. Far from shunning the post of danger, he always seemed to court it; and was never deterred from stepping forward to the assistance of Ministers by the violence of Opposition, by the unpopularity of the measure to be defended, or by the difficulty of the attempt. His speeches, able, animated, and ar-gumentative, were delivered without hesitation, and unembarrassed by any timidity. If they displayed no ornaments of style and no beauties of composition, it was impossible to accuse them of any deficiency in ster-ling sense or in solid ability. He was the most powerful auxiliary whom Lord North could boast of in the Lower House.[12]

Dundas spoke often and at length. In responding to questions around re-form and to other areas of policy in Scotland, and in later spearheading the ministry's approach to union with Ireland, it's possible to build a composite picture of Dundas's public vision of union.

One plausible interpretation is that in his person, actions and accomplish-ments Dundas strove for and represented the completion of the 1707 union. Nowhere was this more apparent than in his speech on forfeited estates in August 1784.[13] Coming hot on the heels of the extraordinary period of consti-tutional instability that accompanied the younger Pitt's first ministry – during which Dundas claimed to have been striving for another kind of union alto-gether, a union of competing parties and factions – the measure was presented as consensual and conciliatory. Wraxall remembered it as 'one of the most en-larged and liberal, as well as wise and conciliating measures … I never remem-ber to have seen the house more unanimous on any point'.[14] It also appears to have been one of only two of Dundas's speeches ever to be anthologised in primer books of oratory.[15]

The measure was one that sought to close the book on the recent Scottish past and in particular the Jacobite rising of 1745–1746: 'It was then judged necessary, in order to strike a terror into that part of the na-tion, that its inhabitants should be put under a kind of proscription, and thereby disqualified from serving the State in any capacity'. It was the context provided by imperial expansion, and the Seven Years' War, that provided Scots highlanders with a means of overcoming this proscription. Here Dundas had the added benefit of being able to court his young po-litical ally Pitt, by eulogising his father 'a man above the level of illib-eral and injudicious prejudices' who (Dundas quoted from Pitt directly) 'sought only for merit … and [I] found it in the mountains of the North'. For Dundas, the proscribed highlanders had worked off their debt 'and with their blood they purchased glory to themselves, and victory to Great Britain'. This vision of completing the union was broadened out. Because there should be no 'premium for rebellion', the excess value of the land should be put to other ends, more especially a canal linking the Forth and the Clyde: a means of lifting Scotland economically and a measure 'of the greatest utility to the three kingdoms'.[16]

Dundas's speech was on Scotland, but in its background was the question of Ireland, as would be the case with all three case studies in this chapter. In the 1780s ongoing discussions around legislative independence and trade arrange-ments prompted political leaders to question and clarify the Anglo-Scottish un-ion. It was a very similar cocktail fifteen years later in Dundas's more famous and most widely circulated speech – on union with Ireland.[17] The speech was based in part on the researches of an academic auxiliary, John Bruce, erst-while professor of logic at Edinburgh university. Bruce's historical research in his *Report on the Events and Circumstances Which Produced the Union of the Kingdoms of England and Scotland* provided a rhetorical blueprint for Dundas.[18]

Isaac Cruikshank literally caricatured Dundas's position in 'An Irish Union!'
The print had Dundas reading from a folio *History of Scotland* to a sceptical
Irishman in the process of being wed to a bewildered John Bull:

> I'll read ye a little aboot the same Business in my ain country – you
> will find how many made the siller frae that time to this – depend upon
> it Paddy ye will be much happier - and mair independent than ever.[19]

As far as Dundas was concerned, the print was not far off the mark. His
speech highlighted the long-term commercial benefits of union for Scotland
and its central role within a wider imperial vision. While Ireland waited
to accrue its union dividend in economic terms, it could contribute, as the
Scots had done, by providing manpower for imperial defence.

If Alvin Jackson is undoubtedly correct that, looked at as a whole, the
Irish union was 'a deal, rather than an ideal', it was also underpinned by
this more visionary language on the part of leaders such as Dundas.[20] But
there were, of course, tensions within this view of union, which become
clearer when we look across Dundas's career as a whole. For example, his
treatment of questions around the Church of Scotland or around Scots law
foreshadowed the sort of 'strict constructionist' unionism that was common
in the nineteenth century and which shared a distinct resemblance to many
features normally associated with nationalism.[21] On the latter, for example,
on a celebrated motion to enquire into criminal law in 1794 (really an effort
to protest a high profile series of sedition trials):

> [He] conceived it his duty to enter his solemn protest as a Represent-
> ative of the People of Scotland, against any alteration taking place in
> the jurisprudence of that country ... nor could he agree to destroy, at
> one blow all those rules and modes of procedure which were expressly
> reserved by the Articles of Union.[22]

There's a line from this argument – what might reasonably be seen as a
variety of legal nationalism – through to the more famous critique of union
embodied in Walter Scott's *Malachi Malagrowther* letters of the 1820s and
to the NAVSR (Figure 5.1).

The following year, however, having made these claims as to the inviola-
bility of the union settlement, his treatment of the powers of Parliament in
defending the suspension of habeas corpus in 1795 placed no limits around
its abilities: 'There was no part of that sacred system handed down to us by
our ancestors that was not subject to revisal'.[23] Dundas was confronting
some of the dilemmas and articulating arguments that would characterise
unionist politics over subsequent centuries. There was a vision of union that
could be powerfully communicated – but it was mutable, pragmatic and not
always consistent.

Figure 5.1 John Kay, 'Patent for a Knighthood', an etching lampooning Henry
Dundas in 1794. Image courtesy of James Gregory.

Francis Jeffrey (1773–1850)

That a popular view of Dundas as some kind of despotic villain could de-
velop in the nineteenth century was partly down to the hatchet job done by
Francis Jeffrey, but even more persistently by his close collaborator (and
Dundas's own nephew) Henry Cockburn. Radicals of the 1790s certainly
communicated an unflattering portrait of Dundas to posterity, but nowhere
was it more systematically and enduringly developed than in the writings of
Cockburn. In his semi-autobiographical *Memorials of His Time* and *Journal*
and in his polemical collection of Scottish sedition trials (which gave pride
of place to the trials of the 1790s), he painted an unflattering portrait of his
uncle:

Henry Dundas, an Edinburgh man, and well calculated by talent and manner to make despotism popular, was the absolute dictator of Scotland, and had the means of rewarding submission, and of suppressing opposition, beyond what were ever exercised in modern times by one person, in any portion of the empire ... we had no free political institutions whatever.[24]

This was part of a wider victim-history developed by the Scottish Whigs as a group of political 'outs'. By painting this bleak picture of a feudal and absolutist Scotland, they highlighted and magnified their own achievements: establishing the *Edinburgh Review* as an organ for free discussion; reviving and spearheading calls for institutional reform within Scotland; and presiding over the apotheosis of these efforts in the package of reform measures that began with electoral reform in 1832.[25]

Francis Jeffrey – another lawyer – was at the centre of these developments and according to Cockburn 'above all, there was Jeffrey, in brilliancy the star of the whole party'.[26] Jeffrey (see Figure 5.2) is not often thought of as

Figure 5.2 'The Late Lord Jeffrey', *Illustrated London News*, 2 February 1850, p. 76. Image courtesy of James Gregory.

a *political* leader at all and in general he has been of much more interest to literary scholars for his role within modern literary criticism. As the vanguard of Whig efforts to shape and control reform movements in the 1810s and 1820s, however, and as Lord Advocate in Early Grey's government with responsibility for the Reform Bill (Scotland), he begs to be treated seriously as a politician, even if he was a slightly reluctant one.

Certainly from his journalism in the *Edinburgh Review* and from some of his political speeches we can discern a certain vision of Anglo-Scottish union. At the base of the Whig critique of Scottish institutions lay an Enlightenment inheritance that has been termed an 'Anglo-British patriotism'.[27] This involved a tendency to regard not only the shape of Scotland's pre-union historical development, but also what remained of its distinctive political and legal institutions, as fundamentally illiberal. The purpose of politics was to rid Scotland of these unwelcome survivals and bring it within the bounds of the English constitution.

In levelling a good deal of their criticism at 'corrupt' or 'feudal' Scots institutions Jeffrey and his collaborators have thus been seen as Anglicizers, intent on the completion of an imperfect union. The route to this was assimilation with English norms.[28] There is much to be said for that view of the Scottish Whigs. It was underlined by Jeffrey's one inheritance from his Oxford education, an affected English accent delivered with a kind of nasal whine. The programmatic statements of political economy or oppositional journalism, however, should be taken as no more than one source – albeit a significant one – for how Scottish Whig politicians thought about and engaged with the union.

In practice, Jeffrey's position was much more ambiguous and complex. So, for example, in one of those activities that established him as a leader of Scottish Whiggery – defending men accused of political crimes – it is straightforward to identify statements which seem to draw Jeffrey towards the kind of legal nationalism espoused by Dundas in 1794.[29] It was most notable in the treason trials of 1820, which, because of the assimilation of Scottish and English treason laws in 1708, foregrounded some of the ambiguities of the union. Jeffrey's objection was to the appearance of an English lawyer, Serjeant Hullock, for the prosecution:

> This is a tribunal for the trial of Scotch crimes ... it is a tribunal to administer the Scottish law only. That it resembles the law of England is no argument at all: with respect to Scotchmen it is nothing but the Scotch law; it is as much the Scotch law, as all British statutes extending to Scotland are Scotch law ... We have nothing, in short, to do with the law of England here.[30]

Read alongside much of the existing historiography, that sounds like a Tory statement that puts Jeffrey in the same camp as his apparent *bêtes noires*, Dundas, Scott and others, defending the immutability of Scotland's legal institutions as the principal means of maintaining national distinctiveness. Indeed, the Tory sheriff-depute of Stirlingshire, Ronald McDonald, passed Jeffrey a note encouraging him to challenge Hullock to a duel, for which McDonald would act as second.[31]

A similarly nuanced engagement with the union was apparent during that moment when Jeffrey was most clearly a Scottish political leader, when he had to act as the key Scottish member of the ministry seeking the passage of the Reform Acts between 1830 and 1832. He faced arguments – similar in tone to many of Dundas's from the 1790s – that Scotland's constitution either forbade the kinds of reforms being canvassed or, more frequently, that Scotland's existing economic prosperity was a stark warning against tinkering with those arrangements that had produced it. In those arguments union provided the prop and rationale for a defence of a very limited vision of the political nation and those entitled to belong to it.[32]

In the face of those kinds of argument, Jeffrey deployed a number of responses. There is, of course, evidence for the sort of assimilationist outlook outlined above. At points, Jeffrey could junk the whole of Scotland's pre-union history as containing nothing relevant for understanding political liberty: 'the theatre of atrocious crime – of cruel religious and civil wars, and of every horror that could barbarize a nation'.[33] At a couple of moments, Jeffrey certainly did concede that England had a longer history and richer heritage of liberty than did Scotland. He could also endorse the view that in England political reform could be seen as 'restoration', whereas in Scotland, political institutions and practices had to be devised from scratch.

More often the contrast he sought to draw was not necessarily with England. Jeffrey was much more likely to speak (and write) in more abstract terms of social development as a whole, rather than regarding one individual national experience as an infallible guide to the future. Jeffrey, deploying the wide-angle lenses of conjectural history, looked much further to make the general point that 'liberty was the daughter, not the mother of riches'.[34] In short, the job for politicians was to fit their political institutions to the current state of commercial society. The biggest mistake was for politicians to oppose reform with the goal of maintaining commercial growth. What was true for discussions of legal reform was true for political reform: modernisation as a goal was far more important than assimilation.

Where the former could be achieved by the latter, Jeffrey was perfectly content. Sensitivity to Scottish difference, however, and a concern that distinctive solutions may be required around central aspects of reform – efforts to identify and enfranchise a 'respectable' middle-class constituency or to design an adequate electoral machinery for Scotland – ran throughout his tenure as Lord Advocate. Placed into the day-to-day workings of government, the requirement to identify areas of Scottish distinctiveness and to legislate for or protect these comes across as a pressing issue. In the context of the reform crisis such considerations emerged around issues like the provision of additional parliamentary seats, which became a complex point of contest between different 'national' claims. Jeffrey waited for 'English nationality' to abate, was fearful of O'Connell's ability to leverage Irish claims, and disdainful of concessions to 'the cheese-eating, goaty Principality of Wales'.[35]

Behind some of his crankier statements lay a more general dissatisfaction with the practical operation of government within the union-state. Jeffrey's experiences highlighted a familiar set of issues that were by no means restricted to any 'party' position across the nineteenth century but demonstrate how the operation of governing institutions shaped leaders' perceptions of the union. In November 1831, Jeffrey complained: 'Government will not take the trouble to understand anything merely Scotch'.[36] For the union to work smoothly required some mechanism for consideration and legislation on areas where Scotland's experience was distinctive. This could come with a powerful cabinet minister who either was a Scot, or was interested enough in Scotland. For decades after Dundas's death, however, that was a comparatively rare occurrence and so 'Scotch business' was managed in a pretty ad hoc kind of a way.

Without any such mechanism, much of Jeffrey's time was spent lobbying the cabinet to indicate that it simply could not extend measures that had been deemed fit for England to the Scottish context. It should go without saying, this hardly fits the image of a dogmatic assimilationist. In seeking to lobby effectively, there were considerable efforts to mobilise Scottish opinion – to provide backing for the arguments Jeffrey was making to an intransigent cabinet. So his cultivation of newspapers and efforts to constitute a distinctly 'Scottish' public opinion – were partly to back government at a moment of crisis, but also to keep it honest on the Scottish aspects of the question.

Jeffrey, as a leader, came from a very different political perspective to Dundas, but there are numerous similarities between their public statements on the union. He also provides insight into how this outlook could be shaped by practical experience of the mechanisms of government, in Jeffrey's case as he navigated a difficult transition identified by Cockburn: 'to be no longer the easy critic of measures but their responsible conductor'.[37] Jeffrey and Cockburn renewed calls for a Scottish Secretary – or at the very least a responsible 'Scotch minister' – partly because of dissatisfaction with that situation.

Archibald Primrose, fifth Earl of Rosebery (1847–1929)

The individual who, more than any other, argued for and secured the eventual appointment of a Scottish Secretary in 1885 affords a final case study. Lord Rosebery is perhaps most remembered as a close friend of Gladstone, stage manager of the Midlothian campaign, figurehead of Liberal imperialism and a kind of brilliant failure who based his career on refusing office or resigning at the drop of a hat (see Figure 5.3). His prominence as a

Figure 5.3 Lord Rosebery. Engraving from photograph by George Jerrard *c.*1896.
Image courtesy of James Gregory.

speaker, politician and fabulously wealthy member of society made him a
figure within the British world at a moment when the association between
politics and celebrity became especially strong. The longevity and immen-
sity of his reputation in Scotland stood in contrast to his more seasonal
fame elsewhere. Various epithets – 'The Diogenes of Dalmeny' or 'The Un-
crowned King of Scotland' – indicated his place in the public imagination
north of the border, where autobiographies very frequently mention both
him and the mesmerising and transformative experience of seeing and hearing him speak. That reputation was not only based on his connection with
Gladstone, which saw the pair sometimes styled as 'the father and son of the
Scottish people'.[38] It was also based on his careful cultivation of political
power in Scotland.[39]

Weber famously based his account of charismatic leadership partly on
Gladstone's achievement and his 'victory over the notables'.[40] Clearly Rosebery was a different fish from Gladstone. Gladstone (however implausibly)

could transcend his privileged background to become, in A.J.P. Taylor's memorable phrase, 'Sir Robert Peel and Fergus O'Connor rolled into one – an explosive combination'.[41] Rosebery – whose entire political career was shaped by his early ascent to his earldom – was more in the tradition of the gentleman leader.[42] In speaking to and persuading audiences, though, there are many passages which suggest an effect similar to that of Gladstone's, especially in Scotland. J.M. Barrie's pen portrait is one such: 'Once when Lord R was firing an Edinburgh audience to the delirium point, an old man in the hall shouted out, "I dinna hear a word he says, but it's grand, it's grand!"'[43]

His concern with the union was there from what was his first public speech of note, delivered to the Edinburgh Philosophical Society in 1871. As we might expect from someone who was a Macaulay afficionado from his youth, Rosebery's historical vision of union departed little from the kind of overall dynamic with which both Jeffrey (and indeed Dundas) had been comfortable. In that opening speech, he sought to explain how Edinburgh 'known for centuries as the uncouth and rugged home of an almost savage poverty' had become 'one of the greatest intellectual centres of the world' – and his answer: 'the indirect cause of this phenomenon was undoubtedly the Act of union between England and Scotland'.[44] It is easy enough to find similar treatments from across his rhetorical career. Speaking, importantly, on the theme of Scottish history in his inaugural address at Aberdeen university, for example, the imagery was even more striking:

> from the time of the corporate union, when, thank God, she ceased to have a history, this little rugged country made an advance in prosperity resembling the progress of some state in Western America, with free institutions planted on a virgin soil.[45]

The very topic of that inaugural – Scottish History – reveals another facet of his character in his deep and committed interest in Scottish culture and history. While he shared something of that quality of Gladstone's of being able to appear in different guises in different parts of the United Kingdom, no one could doubt Rosebery's genuine patriotism when it came to Scotland.

With the high profile of the Midlothian campaign in 1879, Rosebery's challenge was how to convert that enthusiasm and popularity into political power (while maintaining the aristocratic pretence that he wasn't really interested in power). In practical political terms, much of the most important part of his political career was driven by the need to address a problem he raised in his Edinburgh University rectorial address:

> it is difficult in some circumstances to unite with perfect compatibility the feeling for the nationality with loyalty to the centre. There is no such difficulty in Scotland. But the question is interesting how far the separate nationality may be asserted without danger to the common bond.[46]

In the range of possible junior offices dangled in front of him in Gladstone's second ministry, it was the question of Scottish administration that drove him. Rosebery's early concern – and arguably his principal legislative achievement – was to inaugurate that process of administrative devolution that so shaped the union in the twentieth century. He began in earnest in a speech in the House of Lords in 1881, when he paraphrased Disraeli to complain: 'the people of Scotland, at the present moment, are mumbling the dry bones of political neglect, and munching the remainder biscuit of Irish legislation'.[47]

As that phrase encapsulates, the motive force behind Rosebery's campaign came from a number of points, none of which was entirely new in the 1880s. First, the conduct of Scottish affairs was a longstanding complaint, stretching back to at least Jeffrey's time. A Whig motion in 1804 had highlighted the anomaly of the Lord Advocate's schizophrenic role as a legal officer and a 'Scotch minister'. It had been periodically raised thereafter including in a motion from Lord Fife in 1881, during which Rosebery lamented: 'The government of a country by the legal profession is almost unexampled in the world'.[48]

Second, the upshot of these imperfect arrangements was stagnation in Scottish affairs at a moment where the efficiency of Parliament was widely discussed and legislated on.[49] This had been given recent exposure by the ministry's shelving of measures that were intensely discussed in Scotland, but which fell victim to an overburdened Parliament. This constant theme of the neglect of Scottish affairs very seriously soured relations between Rosebery and Gladstone at points, most notably in the winter of 1882:

> That you have been too busy to attend to Scottish business arrangements I can readily believe. But that is exactly where the mischief lies. No minister of importance has the time to look after Scottish matters ... I serve a country which is the backbone of our party, but which is never recognised. I and those whom I have consulted feel that it is necessary to make a stand on its behalf.[50]

Finally, Ireland was again the stimulus to think through the workings of the Anglo-Scottish union. More urgent Irish business crowded out Scottish initiatives and Rosebery pointed persistently to how Ireland's 'assertion of the separate nationality', however unconstitutional it might be, delivered results in legislative terms. Perhaps the most celebrated sulky statement on this was to Edward Hamilton after another rebuff from Gladstone:

> Justice for Ireland means everything done for her, even to the payment of the natives' debts. Justice to Scotland means insulting neglect. I leave for Scotland next week with the view of blowing up a prison or shooting a policemen.[51]

In navigating these obstacles, Rosebery summed up the characteristic dilemma of Scottish political leadership:

> for me there is no middle term of usefulness between that of absolute independence and cabinet office. As absolutely independent, I hold a position in Scotland, of which I do not think so highly as others may, but one which I greatly cherish. As a cabinet minister, I should hold a position in Great Britain which it is an honour to covet. But by accepting office outside the cabinet, I lose both.[52]

It might be argued, of course, that in Rosebery's case the question of Scottish administration was instrumental: the union and its defective machinery was a lever to prise open the cabinet and achieve the kind of influence he usually affected not really to want. Placed alongside his enduring interest in local government (including his high profile stint on London County Council), in issues around Irish Home Rule (including a fascination with Charles Stuart Parnell), and in Scottish cultural life, such an interpretation seems unsustainable.

There was no position of sufficient political clout into which leadership of Scottish opinion could effectively translate. It has been a biographical convention to compare Rosebery to Pitt, to whom Rosebery was related through his mother and whose biography he wrote. But Dundas provides an equally plausible comparison. Rosebery may have believed that while 'Dundas did a great deal of good for Scotland ... the principles of his government were wholly bad', but the rich web of Scottish, British and imperial patriotisms in which Rosebery was immersed (and between which he made no hard-and-fast distinctions) along with the concern to secure Scotland's interests at the very highest level are notable.[53] This was a flexible framework within which to operate and it needed to be in the increasingly fraught Liberal politics of the 1880s and 1890s.

Conclusion

What do these three tentative case studies reveal about the relationship between political leadership and the union in Scotland? Despite the very different political pedigrees and outlooks of all three men and the very different contexts in which they operated substantial commonalities are present across a century. Not least the structural constraints and opportunities that conditioned experiences of Scottish political leadership remained broadly similar across the 'long nineteenth century'. How different leaders navigated these and engaged with the union reveal a number of other similarities.

The first will not surprise anyone. Politicians were capable of inconsistency. Positions held when speaking on the union often could not be reconciled with other statements about, for example, the nature of parliamentary sovereignty. A focus on leadership provides a useful way of exploring the flexibility of the union's use within political rhetoric. The second is that we can partly explain these tensions and inconsistencies, not only from the nature of the union itself, but also against the backdrop of Colin Kidd's confection of 'banal unionism'.[54] For these leaders, as for the political cultures within which they worked, the union was simply part of the wallpaper. Most of the time, it was there but it did not matter, and so could be discussed in a very broad and frequently quite careless way. The third is that, the Anglo-Scottish union was only very rarely, if ever, discussed individually. Debates around Ireland were most frequently the context in which Scots forced to think about and articulate their visions of union.

The final conclusion is that for none of these leaders are binary notions of 'unionist' or 'nationalist' politics especially useful. Arguably they are not of much use now and they work even less effectively in considering the nineteenth century. At certain times the sort of dilemma that has characterised contemporary Scottish politics – Iain McLean put it well for the postwar Labour Party, 'Scottish Labour politicians have had to resolve the tensions between their Scottishness and their Labourness' – could emerge, but these were rare.[55] Instead Scottish political leadership and how practising politicians approached the union, provides a window onto the elusive hybrid middle ground of Scottish political culture.

Notes

1 The scholarship is too large to summarise here, but for influential examples see G. Morton, *Unionist-nationalism: Governing Urban Scotland, 1830–1860* (East Linton: Tuckwell, 1999); C. Kidd, *Union and Unionisms: Political Thought in Scotland, 1500–2000* (Cambridge: Cambridge University Press, 2008); A. Jackson, *The Two Unions: Ireland, Scotland, and the Survival of the United Kingdom, 1707–2007* (Oxford: Oxford University Press, 2012); J. Mitchell, *The Scottish Question* (Oxford: Oxford University Press, 2014).
2 M. Fry, 'The Whig Interpretation of Scottish History', in *The Manufacture of Scottish History*, ed. by I.L. Donnachie and C.A. Whatley (Edinburgh: Polygon, 1992), pp. 72–89. A more recent appraisal of Scottish political history is E. Cameron, 'The Political Histories of Modern Scotland', *Scottish Affairs* 85 (2013), pp. 1–28.
3 Though see the recent doctoral thesis of another contributor to this volume, G. Hutchison, 'Origins of the Scottish Conservative Party, 1832–1868' (unpublished doctoral thesis, University of Edinburgh, 2018).
4 For recent overviews see *Oxford Handbook of Political Leadership*, ed. by R.A.W. Rhodes and P.T. Hart (Oxford: Oxford University Press, 2014); A. Brown, *The Myth of the Strong Leader: Political Leadership in the Modern Age* (London: Bodley Head, 2014).
5 P. Williamson, *Stanley Baldwin: Conservative Leadership and National Values* (Cambridge: Cambridge University Press, 1999), p. 15.
6 A. Ramsay, 'Why, Thanks to Alex Salmond, I'm Honouring Our Tyrants in Edinburgh', *Commonspace*, 10 May 2016. www.commonspace.scot/articles/3984/adam-ramsay-why-thanks-alex-salmond-im-honouring-our-tyrants-edinburgh (accessed 12 June 2017); 'Edinburgh Ready to face up to Dark Past of Henry Dundas', *The Herald*, 14 August 2018.

7 The best biography is M. Fry, *The Dundas Despotism* (Edinburgh: Edinburgh University Press, 1992). For the prints see G. Pentland, '"We Speak for the Ready": Images of Scots in Political Prints, 1707–1832', *Scottish Historical Review* 90 (2011), pp. 64–95.

8 'DUN-SHAW' and 'God Save the King – in a Bumper, or – an Evening Scene, Three Times a Week at Wimbleton [sic]', in *Catalogue of Personal and Political Satires Preserved in the Department of Prints and Drawings in the British Museum*, ed. by F.G. Stephens and M.D. George, 11 vols (London: British Museum, 1870–1954), nos 7281, 8651.

9 Pentland, '"We Speak for the Ready"', pp. 84–90.

10 C. Reid, *Imprison'd Wranglers: The Rhetorical Culture of the House of Commons, 1760–1800* (Oxford: Oxford University Press, 2012).

11 *Caledonian Mercury*, 14 October 1775.

12 *The Historical and the Posthumous Memoirs of Sir Nathaniel Wraxall, 1772–1784*, ed. H.B. Wheatley, 5 vols (London: Bickers, 1884), vol. 1, pp. 426–427.

13 *Parliamentary Register*, 2 August 1784, pp. 320–326.

14 *Memoirs of Sir Nathaniel Wraxall*, vol. 4, p. 1.

15 J. Mossop, *Elegant Orations, Ancient and Modern, for the Use of Schools* (London: G. Kearsley, 1788), pp. 17–22.

16 *Parliamentary Register*, 2 August 1784, pp. 320–322.

17 *Parliamentary Register*, 7 February 1799, pp. 705–731. A version of the speech went through multiple editions as *Substance of the Speech of the right hon. Henry Dundas, in the House of Commons, Thursday, Feb. 7, 1799, on the Legislative Union with Ireland* (London: J. Wright, 1799).

18 A. Murdoch, 'Henry Dundas, Scotland and the Union with Ireland, 1792–1801', in *Scotland in the Age of the French Revolution*, ed. B. Harris (Edinburgh: John Donald, 2005), pp. 135–139.

19 'An Irish Union!', in *Catalogue of Personal and Political Satires*, ed. Stephens and George, no. 9344.

20 Jackson, *Two Unions*, p. 99.

21 Kidd, *Union and Unionisms*, p. 6.

22 *Parliamentary Register*, 25 March 1794, p. 650.

23 *Parliamentary Register*, 17 November 1795, p. 227.

24 H. Cockburn, *Memorials of His Time* (Edinburgh: Adam and Charles Black, 1856), p. 88; H. Cockburn, *Examination of the Trials for Sedition Which Have Hitherto Occurred in Scotland*, 2 vols (Edinburgh: David Douglas, 1888).

25 See J. Clive, *Scotch Reviewers: The Edinburgh Review, 1802–1815* (London: Faber & Faber, 1957); G. Pentland, *Radicalism, Reform, and National Identity, 1820–1833* (Woodbridge: Boydell & Brewer, 2008); T. Orme, 'The Scottish Whig Party, c.1801–1820' (unpublished doctoral thesis, University of Edinburgh, 2013).

26 Cockburn, *Memorials*, 261. See also H. Cockburn, *Life of Lord Jeffrey, with a Selection from His Correspondence*, 2 vols (Edinburgh: Adam and Charles Black, 1852).

27 C. Kidd, 'North Britishness and the Nature of Eighteenth-century British Patriotisms', *Historical Journal* 39 (1996), pp. 361–382.

28 Fry, 'Whig Interpretation'; Jackson, *Two Unions*, pp. 239–241.

29 See G. Pentland, 'State Trials, Whig Lawyers and the Press in Early Nineteenth-century Scotland', in *Political Trials in an Age of Revolutions: Britain and the North Atlantic*, ed. by M.T. Davis, E. Macleod, and G. Pentland (Cham: Palgrave Macmillan, 2019), pp. 213–236.

30 C.J. Green, *Trials for High Treason, in Scotland, under a Special Commission, held at Stirling, Glasgow, Dumbarton, Paisley, and Ayr, in the Year 1820*, 3 vols (Edinburgh: Manners and Millar, 1825), vol. 1, p. 92.

31 P. Mackenzie, *Old Reminiscences of Glasgow and the West of Scotland*, 2 vols, 3rd edn (Glasgow: James P. Forrester, 1890), vol. 1, p. 155.
32 For these debates see G. Pentland, 'The Debate on Scottish Parliamentary Reform, 1830–2', *Scottish Historical Review* 85 (2006), pp. 102–132.
33 *Parliamentary Debates*, 3rd series, VIII, 63.
34 *Parliamentary Debates*, 3rd series, III, 61.
35 National Library of Scotland, Adv. MSS, 9.1.8, f. 77, Francis Jeffrey to Henry Cockburn, 5 September 1831.
36 National Library of Scotland, Adv. MSS, 9.1.8, f. 92, Jeffrey to Cockburn, 1 November 1831.
37 National Library of Scotland, Adv. MSS, 9.1.8, f. 1, 'Preface' by Cockburn, n.d.
38 Gavin Ogilvy [J.M.Barrie], *An Edinburgh Eleven* (London: *British Weekly* Office, 1889), p. 12.
39 The best biographies on the Scottish and the wider contexts respectively are R. Akroyd, 'Lord Rosebery and Scottish Nationalism, 1868–1896' (unpublished doctoral thesis, University of Edinburgh, 1996); R.R. James, *Rosebery: A Biography of Archibald Philip, Fifth Earl of Rosebery* (London: Weidenfeld & Nicolson, 1963).
40 E.F. Biagini, *Liberty, Retrenchment and Reform: Popular Liberalism in the Age of Gladstone, 1860–1880* (Cambridge: Cambridge University Press, 1992), ch. 7. For a useful broad discussion of charisma and leadership in this period see H. te Velde, 'Charismatic Leadership, c.1870–1914: A Comparative European Perspective', in *Making Reputations: Power, Persuasion and the Individual in Modern British Politics*, ed. by J. Gottlieb and R. Toye (London: I. B. Tauris, 2005), pp. 42–55, 203–206.
41 Cited in Biagini, *Liberty, Retrenchment and Reform*, p. 380.
42 J. Belchem and J. Epstein, 'The Nineteenth-century Gentleman Leader Revisited', *Social History* 22 (1997), pp. 164–193.
43 [Barrie], *Edinburgh Eleven*, p. 12.
44 *The Union of England and Scotland. An Inaugural Address delivered at the opening of the Session of the Edinburgh Philosophical Institution, 1871–72 by Lord Rosebery* (Edinburgh, Edmonston and Douglas, 1871), p. 2.
45 *Rectorial Address delivered before the students of Aberdeen University, in the Music Hall at Aberdeen, Nov. 5, 1880 by Lord Rosebery* (Edinburgh, David Douglas, 1880), p. 16.
46 *A Rectorial Address delivered before the students at the University of Edinburgh Nov. 4, 1882. By Lord Rosebery* (Edinburgh: David Douglas, 1882), p. 7.
47 James, *Rosebery*, pp. 120–121.
48 Akroyd, 'Lord Rosebery', p. 222.
49 Ryan A. Vieira, *Time and Politics: Parliament and the Culture of Modernity in Nineteenth-century Britain and the British World* (Oxford: Oxford University Press, 2015).
50 British Library, Gladstone Papers, Add MS 44288, f. 126, Rosebery to Gladstone, 16 December 1882.
51 British Library, Hamilton Papers, Add MS 48612, f. 12, Rosebery to Hamilton, n.d. [MS note 'before 9 Dec. 1882'].
52 British Library, Glasdstone Papers, Add MS 44228, ff. 176–177, Rosebery to Gladstone, 30 July 1883.
53 Cited in Akroyd, 'Lord Rosebery', p. 212.
54 Kidd, *Union and Unionisms*, pp. 10–13.
55 I. McLean, 'Scottish Labour and British Politics', in *The Scottish Labour Party: History, Institutions and Ideas*, ed. by G. Hassan (Edinburgh: Edinburgh University Press, 2005), p. 148.

Bibliography

Akroyd, R. 'Lord Rosebery and Scottish Nationalism, 1868–1896' (unpublished doctoral thesis, University of Edinburgh, 1996).

Belchem, J. and J. Epstein, 'The Nineteenth-century Gentleman Leader Revisited', *Social History* 22 (1997), pp. 164–193.

Biagini, E.F. *Liberty, Retrenchment and Reform: Popular Liberalism in the Age of Gladstone, 1860–1880* (Cambridge: Cambridge University Press, 1992).

British Library, Gladstone Papers, Add MS 44288, f. 126, Rosebery to Gladstone, 16 December 1882.

British Library, Gladstone Papers, Add MS 44228, ff. 176–177, Rosebery to Gladstone, 30 July 1883.

British Library, Hamilton Papers, Add MS 48612, f. 12, Rosebery to Hamilton, n.d. [MS note 'before 9 Dec. 1882].

Brown, A. *The Myth of the Strong Leader: Political Leadership in the Modern Age* (London: Bodley Head, 2014).

Caledonian Mercury, 14 October 1775.

Cameron, E. 'The Political Histories of Modern Scotland', *Scottish Affairs* 85 (2013), pp. 1–28.

Clive, J. *Scotch Reviewers: The Edinburgh Review, 1802–1815* (London: Faber & Faber, 1957).

Cockburn, H. *Examination of the Trials for Sedition Which Have Hitherto Occurred in Scotland*, 2 vols (Edinburgh: David Douglas, 1888).

Cockburn, H. *Life of Lord Jeffrey, with a Selection from His Correspondence*, 2 vols (Edinburgh: Adam and Charles Black, 1852).

Cockburn, H. *Memorials of His Time* (Edinburgh: Adam and Charles Black, 1856).

Dundas, H. *Substance of the Speech of the Right Hon. Henry Dundas, in the House of Commons, Thursday, Feb. 7, 1799, on the Legislative Union with Ireland* (London: J. Wright, 1799).

'DUN-SHAW' and 'God Save the King – in a Bumper, or – an Evening Scene, Three Times a Week at Wimbleton [sic]', in *Catalogue of Personal and Political Satires Preserved in the Department of Prints and Drawings in the British Museum*, ed. by F.G. Stephens and M.D. George, 11 vols (London: British Museum, 1870–1954), nos 7281, 8651.

Fry, M. *The Dundas Despotism* (Edinburgh: Edinburgh University Press, 1992).

Fry, M. 'The Whig Interpretation of Scottish History', in *The Manufacture of Scottish History*, ed. by I.L. Donnachie and C.A. Whatley (Edinburgh: Polygon, 1992), pp. 72–89.

Green, C.J. *Trials for High Treason, in Scotland, under a Special Commission, held at Stirling, Glasgow, Dumbarton, Paisley, and Ayr, in the Year 1820*, 3 vols (Edinburgh: Manners and Millar, 1825), vol. 1.

Hutchison, G. 'Origins of the Scottish Conservative Party, 1832–1868' (unpublished doctoral thesis, University of Edinburgh, 2018).

Jackson, A. *The Two Unions: Ireland, Scotland, and the Survival of the United Kingdom, 1707–2007* (Oxford: Oxford University Press, 2012).

James, R.R. *Rosebery: A Biography of Archibald Philip, Fifth Earl of Rosebery* (London: Weidenfeld & Nicolson, 1963).

Kidd, C. 'North Britishness and the Nature of Eighteenth-century British Patriotisms', *Historical Journal*, 39 (1996), pp. 361–382.

Kidd, C. *Union and Unionisms: Political Thought in Scotland, 1500–2000* (Cambridge: Cambridge University Press, 2008).

Mackenzie, P. *Old Reminiscences of Glasgow and the West of Scotland*, 2 vols, 3rd edn (Glasgow: James P. Forrester, 1890), vol. 1.

McLean, I. 'Scottish Labour and British Politics', in *The Scottish Labour Party: History, Institutions and Ideas*, ed. by G. Hassan (Edinburgh: Edinburgh University Press, 2005).

Mitchell, J. *The Scottish Question* (Oxford: Oxford University Press, 2014).

Morton, G. *Unionist-Nationalism: Governing Urban Scotland, 1830–1860* (East Linton: Tuckwell, 1999).

Mossop, J. *Elegant Orations, Ancient and Modern, for the Use of Schools* (London: G. Kearsley, 1788).

Murdoch, A. 'Henry Dundas, Scotland and the Union with Ireland, 1792–1801', in *Scotland in the Age of the French Revolution*, ed. by B. Harris (Edinburgh: John Donald, 2005), pp. 135–139.

National Library of Scotland, Adv. MSS, 9.1.8, f. 1, 'Preface' by Cockburn, n.d.

National Library of Scotland, Adv. MSS, 9.1.8, f. 77, Francis Jeffrey to Henry Cockburn, 5 September 1831.

National Library of Scotland, Adv. MSS, 9.1.8, f. 92, Jeffrey to Cockburn, 1 November 1831.

'Ogilvy, Gavin' [J.M. Barrie], *An Edinburgh Eleven* (London: *British Weekly* Office, 1889).

Orme, T. 'The Scottish Whig Party, c.1801–1820' (unpublished doctoral thesis, University of Edinburgh, 2013).

Oxford Handbook of Political Leadership, ed. by R.A.W. Rhodes and P. T Hart (Oxford: Oxford University Press, 2014).

Parliamentary Debates, 3rd series, III, 61.

Parliamentary Debates, 3rd series, VIII, 63.

Parliamentary Register, 17 November 1795, p. 227.

Parliamentary Register, 2 August 1784, pp. 320–322.

Parliamentary Register, 2 August 1784, pp. 320–326.

Parliamentary Register, 25 March 1794, p. 650.

Parliamentary Register, 7 February 1799, pp. 705–731.

Pentland, G. 'The Debate on Scottish Parliamentary Reform, 1830–2', *Scottish Historical Review* 85 (2006), pp. 102–132.

Pentland, G. *Radicalism, Reform, and National Identity, 1820–1833* (Woodbridge: Boydell & Brewer, 2008).

Pentland, G. 'State Trials, Whig Lawyers and the Press in Early Nineteenth-century Scotland', in *Political Trials in an Age of Revolutions: Britain and the North Atlantic*, ed. by M.T. Davis, E. Macleod, and G. Pentland (Cham: Palgrave Macmillan, 2019), pp. 213–236.

Pentland, G. '"We Speak for the Ready": Images of Scots in Political Prints, 1707–1832', *Scottish Historical Review* 90 (2011), pp. 64–95.

Primrose, A. *A Rectorial Address Delivered Before the Students at the University of Edinburgh Nov. 4, 1882. By Lord Rosebery* (Edinburgh: David Douglas, 1882).

Primrose, A. *A Rectorial Address Delivered Before the Students of Aberdeen University, in the Music Hall at Aberdeen, Nov. 5, 1880 by Lord Rosebery* (Edinburgh: David Douglas, 1880).

Primrose, A. *The Union of England and Scotland. An Inaugural Address Delivered at the Opening of the Session of the Edinburgh Philosophical Institution, 1871–72 by Lord Rosebery* (Edinburgh: Edmonston and Douglas, 1871).

Ramsay, A. 'Edinburgh Ready to face up to Dark Past of Henry Dundas', *The Herald*, 14 August 2018.

Ramsay, A. 'Why, Thanks to Alex Salmond, I'm Honouring Our Tyrants in Edinburgh, *Commonspace*, 10 May 2016. www.commonspace.scot/articles/3984/ adam-ramsay-why-thanks-alex-salmond-im-honouring-our-tyrants-edinburgh (accessed 12 June 2017).

Reid, C. *Imprison'd Wranglers: The Rhetorical Culture of the House of Commons, 1760–1800* (Oxford: Oxford University Press, 2012).

te Velde, H. 'Charismatic Leadership, c.1870–1914: A Comparative European Perspective', in *Making Reputations: Power, Persuasion and the Individual in Modern British Politics*, ed. by J. Gottlieb and R. Toye (London: I. B. Tauris, 2005).

The Historical and the Posthumous Memoirs of Sir Nathaniel Wraxall, 1772–1784, ed. H.B. Wheatley, 5 vols (London: Bickers, 1884), vols. 1, 5.

Vieira, R.A. *Time and Politics: Parliament and the Culture of Modernity in Nineteenth-century Britain and the British World* (Oxford: Oxford University Press, 2015).

Williamson, P. *Stanley Baldwin: Conservative Leadership and National Values* (Cambridge: Cambridge University Press, 1999).

6　An 'illegal Union of Lawyers, and Writers, and Political Baronets'

The Conservative party and Scottish governance, 1832–1868

Gary D. Hutchison

Introduction

In the 1830s, a radical broadsheet described the then-Conservative administration of Scotland as an 'illegal Union of Lawyers, and Writers, and Political Baronets'.[1] In fact, Scottish governance was anything but united. This chapter explores how partisan politics affected the character of Scotland's governance within the mid-nineteenth-century Union.[2] It asserts that the Conservative party played a role in rendering modes of governance variable and uncertain.[3] First, the party's role in governing Scotland through the office of Lord Advocate, the Faculty of Advocates and on a local level will be examined.[4] This illustrates the ways in which inter- (and, more significantly, intra-) party struggles made the office of Lord Advocate one of fluctuating importance and influence. Following on from this, the ways in which the UK party leadership influenced Scottish affairs will be discussed.[5] Rather than a relationship defined by top-down headquarters imposition, governing Scotland, in fact, involved negotiation and compromise between central and peripheral party branches. Finally, the ways in which this set of circumstances fostered an innovative Conservative attitude to Scotland's place within the Union will be explored. This will uncover how the party originally came to embrace its longstanding commitment to administrative devolution.[6] It will argue that influential elements within the Conservative party had a long pedigree of support for Scottish administrative devolution in various forms. This suggests that its later role in supporting successful bipartisan efforts in this direction should not be overlooked.

Central and local Scottish governance: 1832–1868

The Lord Advocate was, in a formal sense, merely an advisor to the Home Secretary.[7] In practice, however, the post-holder was the *de facto* Minister for Scotland at Westminster and head of governance within Scotland. They generally possessed a substantial amount of autonomy, in addition to their legal duties as Scotland's premier law officer. Given Sir Robert Peel's long periods in office, Conservative Lord Advocates effectively ran Scotland for much of the early post-1832 period. After 1847, however, the short-lived nature of Derbyite Conservative governments, combined with broader changes taking place within Scottish civil society, increasingly restricted the party's formal and informal influence over Scotland's governance.

The post of Lord Advocate was an inescapably political one, as was that of the Lord Advocate's deputy, the Solicitor-General. The Conservative George Patton was chosen for this latter position in 1859, for instance, largely because he had donated substantial sums to the party, and had spent years actively promoting the party's interests in his native Perthshire.[8] Patton triumphed because he was a 'most useful and active Conservative'.[9] Though the opinions of prominent Scottish Conservatives held significant weight when choosing the senior Scottish law officers, the ultimate decision rested with the Westminster leadership, and in every case a clearly partisan figure was chosen.

This primacy did not prevent the Scottish branch of the party from coming into frequent conflict with the UK Conservative apparatus. A lawyer-dominated faction within the Scottish party, headed initially by the Scottish judge Sir John Hope, was most influential before 1832 and immediately after it. Hope was, in fact, the 'political baronet' referred to in the radical broadsheet. In 1834, however, a conflict which flared up over Scottish legal appointments presaged the shift in party power from the faction of Edinburgh lawyers to a patchwork of Scottish county magnates. The appointment of Sir William Rae as Lord Advocate was uncontroversial, given his good working relationship with Peel and longstanding service as Lord Advocate in the Liverpool, Canningite and Wellington-Peel Ministries.[10] The appointment of relatively junior lawyer Duncan McNeill (see Figure 6.1) as Solicitor-General, however, split opinion in the Scottish party, as some had expected that another, more senior Advocate would be appointed. One partisan stalwart thought that the 'party is sorely annoyed and disappointed by the recent law appointments here'.[11]

This discontent eventually became known to new Scottish party leader, the Duke of Buccleuch (see Figure 6.2). He, in turn, informed Peel of the discontent, adding that many thought McNeill's surprise appointment by Peel had been a result of Hope's plotting: 'the cry arose "that the old jobbing system was revived and that none but those favoured by a Hope or a Dundas would get office in reward"'.[12] This was a reference to the area of lesser legal appointments, such as County Sheriffs and minor judicial posts, which had previously been in the gift of Hope and Robert Dundas.[13] Though Hope hadn't actually had anything to do with the appointment, these widespread assumptions illustrate that Hope's clique was disliked both within the Faculty of Advocates and by the wider public.[14] Eventually, Buccleuch decided to personally intervene to cool tensions. His decisive role in this matter is a clear indication that Hope was being marginalised even by his fellow lawyers, and that Buccleuch's star was in the ascendant, shifting the interconnected forces of party, legal and governmental influence from Edinburgh

Figure 6.1 Lord Colonsay (Duncan McNeill) from 'Modern Athenians. No. 39' by
Benjamin W. Crombie, originally published 1848. Image courtesy of
James Gregory.

lawyers to county magnates.[15] As such, the union of lawyers and the political baronet was broken, replaced by the political duke and allied aristocrats.

The Conservative party played a prominent role in the workings of the
wider Faculty of Advocates, but it is also true that the Faculty itself played

Figure 6.2 The fifth duke of Buccleuch, a carte de visite portrait by William and
Daniel Downey. Image courtesy of James Gregory.

a prominent role in the party's, and the country's workings. While Scottish
public opinion, parliamentary representatives, and leading politicians were
predominantly Liberal, especially after 1847, the composition of the judiciary and faculty did not reflect this: 'There will be no great difficulty in finding fit persons to be selected for promotion to the Bench; it is curious that

with the exception of Rutherford late Lord Advocate, every Advocate of eminence is Conservative'.[16] Many middling Conservative Lord Advocates proved to be far better members of the senior judiciary than political animals. Duncan McNeill served as Lord Justice General and Lord President of the Court of Session between 1852 and 1867, while John Inglis served as Lord President of the Court of Session from then until 1891, and was described by Omond as 'the central figure in the legal world of Scotland'.[17]

This Conservative judicial predominance had a significant impact on the course of Scottish history. Indeed, because common law was an important element of the Scottish legal firmament throughout the period, much of the everyday regulation of Scottish society was undertaken by the courts, rather than parliament.[18] The party's influence was essentially negative, insofar as it had a disproportionate ability to thwart political reforms, or was exercised in the courts, which were ostensibly separate from the arena of public and popular politics. For these reasons, the Conservatives' impact on Scotland in the mid-nineteenth century more broadly has been somewhat overlooked in subsequent scholarly work.

The notable talent of Scottish Conservative lawyers did, however, hinder the party's ability to source and retain adequate Lords Advocate. The loss of Conservative Lord Advocates to the Scottish judicial bench was a constant problem throughout the period. Scottish Conservative lawyer Archibald Campbell Swinton summed up the drawbacks of the position neatly: put off by the 'brief tenure of office which any Conservative Crown Counsel is likely to have', even those who did seek the office were eventually 'seduced ... to claim the softer cushion of the bench'.[19]

Quite apart from the arduous and uncertain nature of the job, potential Conservative Lord Advocates also had the additional insecurity of their electoral base to consider. It was expected that Lord Advocates should hold a seat in parliament, which could throw up considerable difficulties when the policy decisions related to the post clashed with the necessities of electioneering. Some Lord Advocates had represented English constituencies before 1832, though this was recognised as less than ideal. In order to placate constituents on the Isle of Bute in 1841, Sir William Rae was forced to repudiate the religious policy of his own government. He defended himself to Sir John Hope, writing that he was obliged to 'sail as near to the wind as possible', by expressing vague misgivings about an official position which he himself had played a prominent role in formulating.[20] Given that Bute was the closest that the party had to an ultra-safe nomination seat in Scotland, this highlights that Conservative Lord Advocates were perennially hampered by the electoral requirements of the job.

Between 1832 and 1868, however, a new unofficial convention was formed, as Scottish Lord Advocates were increasingly expected to sit for Scottish constituencies. This underlines that even the seemingly stable attributes of the post of Lord Advocate were subject to subtle change over time. Between 1832 and 1868, Lord Advocates of all parties sat for Scottish constituencies, with only two (Conservative) exceptions. Ultimately though, this was also a big problem for the Conservative party, as they had few Scottish seats to spare.

These factors contributed to the generally underwhelming quality of Conservative Lord Advocates. Duncan McNeill was the last Conservative Lord Advocate to enjoy a lengthy tenure; subsequent Lord Advocates only served during the brief periods when the party was in office. No subsequent Conservative Lord Advocate up to 1868 (excepting the final post holder) lasted more than ten months in the position. Though there were a great many capable Conservative lawyers, almost none of them wanted the job because of the electoral hurdle. It was important for a Lord Advocate to hold a Scottish seat, yet a near-impossible task to find one willing to return a Conservative (and a carpetbagger Conservative at that) to Westminster. For instance, Lord Advocate John Inglis stood for Orkney in 1852 but was very narrowly defeated. He then contested the County Antrim constituency of Lisburn at a by-election, but lost by a mere three votes. A Scottish Lord Advocate seeking election for an Irish constituency was highly unusual.[21] During his second stint in office in 1858, Inglis was forced to sit for the English borough of Stamford. Inglis's break with convention prompted his successor David Mure to unsuccessfully request in 1859 that 'a quiet Borough in England [be] found for him' – he was eventually returned as member for Bute.[22]

These issues continued to dog the Scottish party up to and beyond 1868, as Mure's successor ran into similar trouble. George Patton was elected for the notoriously venal English seat of Bridgwater in an 1866 by-election, defeating the Liberal candidate Walter Bagehot, who was then Editor of the *Economist*.[23] He was obliged to contest the seat again soon after, this time unsuccessfully – likely because he hadn't distributed enough bribe money to the local electors on his second contest.[24] This didn't stop him being investigated for the bribes he had issued. The Conservative party thus started the period in Scottish governance with internal squabbles, and ended it with electoral scandal.

Many of the institutions which governed Scotland straddled the line between formal and informal, were firmly embedded in civil society, and were created locally rather than imposed from on high. Even in the burghs, though political power was held by the predominantly Liberal middle-class elite, this was not hegemonic. Conservatives did, in fact, sit on Town Councils in places such as Edinburgh and Glasgow throughout the period, despite their party being marginalised at a parliamentary level. It seems unlikely that they had no influence at all over the operation of local governance because, as Lindsay Paterson has observed, 'The Scottish middle class was too mundanely practical to allow ideological disputes to stand in the way of getting things done'.[25]

In the counties, local governance was generally less dominated by Liberals, local electors being subject to the same conditions which motivated the return of Conservative parliamentary candidates in rural areas. Moreover, the peculiar position of the legal profession in Scottish society again operated in the party's favour. The Sheriff of each county was the chief local representative of the state, involved in practically all facets of governmental affairs within their jurisdiction (though this was only true to a lesser extent in the burghs and larger cities). The appointment of Sheriffs and Sheriff-Substitutes was made by the Lord Advocate, with local elites enjoying some input in this process.[26] Though they were a slightly less politicised group of officials than the Lord Advocate and Solicitor-General, Sheriffs were frequently party stalwarts. Their affiliations bled into the execution of their duties, most prominently in political terms with regard to their rulings when presiding over electoral Registration Courts.

The party's in-built advantage was considerable; first, having spent a great deal of time in office before 1832 and up to 1847, Conservative Lord Advocates were able to manoeuvre sympathetic candidates into these open-ended posts; many of them served for decades. Second, with the majority of the bar (from which Sheriffs were chosen) being Conservative in inclination, this hobbled the efforts of Liberals to redress the balance during their own periods in office. Even after 1847, when the Conservatives were seldom in power at Westminster, the occasional appointment of Conservative party stalwarts was managed, such as the appointment of William Edmonstoune Aytoun as Sheriff of Orkney in 1852. Tory lawyer Archibald Alison (see Figure 6.3) had refused the Scottish

Figure 6.3 'The Late Sir Archibald Alison, Bart'. *Illustrated London News*, 15 June 1867, p. 605. Image courtesy of James Gregory.

Solicitor-Generalship in 1834 leaving the field open for Duncan McNeill, eschewing a national position in favour of becoming Sheriff of Lanarkshire.[27] This turned out to be a shrewd move; Peel's government was short-lived, whereas Alison was able to continue to wield influence during the long periods when his party was excluded from office, up to his death in 1867.[28] The influence of Sheriffs could reach into the cities, and their actions take on national significance – Alison's jurisdiction, for instance, included the city of Glasgow. In addition to dealing with cases affecting Scotland's largest city, Glasgow Sheriff Court evolved into the *de facto* chief commercial court of Scotland. As such, this ostensibly local position in fact afforded Alison significant national influence. Sheriffs, moreover, were always present on the parochially based Poor Law Boards which, from 1845, increasingly administered social welfare on a local level in Scotland.[29]

While the national Poor Law Board of Supervision was dominated by liberals, and many local boards by the liberally inclined middle classes and the clergy, their influence was not all-encompassing. The success of the board system resulted in it being duplicated many times to administer other areas, and new authorities were also given to existing boards. These local and national boards were composed mainly of Sheriffs, lawyers, members of other prominent professions and the aristocracy. Their duties were diverse and grew as legislation accumulated. They were, among other things, responsible for the Poor Law, lunatic asylums, prisons, borstals, housing regulation and property valuation.[30]

It is notable that the national Board of Supervision, arguably the most important, was required to contain the Sheriffs of three counties from different Scottish regions.[31] Moreover, Scottish aristocrats were still a significant presence on such bodies, the vast majority of whom were passively Conservative, or active members of the Conservative party. Indeed, the initial commission on the Scottish Poor Law had been chaired by Lord Melville, who had retired as the Conservative manager of Scotland in 1832. Moreover, the first Supervisory Board to be appointed contained several Conservatives, and John McNeill, the Conservative Lord Advocate's brother, acted as Chairman of that body until 1868.[32] Though no definitive evidence of McNeill's political beliefs is readily available, his worldview was characterised by a mix of moderate conservatism and whiggism.[33]

Overall, the appointment of Lord Advocates exposed a great deal of disunity within the Conservative party, and in the wider group who assisted the Lord Advocate in governing Scotland on a day-to-day basis. Further, their difficulties in relation to contesting Scottish and English seats illustrates that the conventions of the post were subject to informal constitutional change, this being spurred or stymied by partisan necessities. The Lord Advocate was torn between Edinburgh and London in more ways than one. Moreover, the Scottish Conservative party had a strong presence, and a marked effect, on Scottish governance at national and local levels, though this declined as their periods in office became more intermittent.

Nevertheless, they continued to exert some influence, though in a less visible or formal fashion. Conservatives exerted influence using a number of positions and institutions, including through the offices of Lord Advocate and Solicitor-General, and as members of national supervisory boards. At a local level, members of local boards also included a significant proportion of Conservative party members or supporters. Thus, every level of Scottish society was at least partly shaped by the Conservative party, and conservatism more generally.

Westminster Conservatives and Scotland, 1832–1868

While much power over governance was granted by the central state to Scottish and local levels, party input on Scottish governance from Westminster was by no means non-existent. Indeed, the highly integrated nature of Scottish governance within the Union meant that Westminster played a conspicuous role in its management. Yet, it remains the case that seemingly static institutional structures were dependent on day-to-day political and partisan circumstances. The nature and extent of this involvement in governance was often determined by who was involved. These were most often party figures whose positions were dependent on which faction was in power. As such, Westminster's role in Scottish governance waxed and waned. The Westminster Conservative party's role in this area was significant; during the early part of the period, the partisan governance of Scotland was deeply influenced by intimate Westminster involvement in Scottish affairs.

The party in Westminster was, if anything, more concerned with Scottish matters than their Liberal opponents, despite (or perhaps because of) that faction's electoral ascendancy north of the border. After 1847, long periods in opposition, combined with lacklustre Lord Advocates, resulted in less intervention, but more innovation from Westminster party figures. Their efforts, while of mixed effectiveness, constitute evidence of continued central interest in Scottish affairs and a willingness to pioneer different approaches. Home Secretaries, despite their nominal dominion over Scotland's governance, did not take a close interest in Scottish affairs – the Liberal Lord Palmerston was perhaps the Home Secretary most famously indifferent to Scottish matters.[34]

Sir James Graham was, however, the most prominent exception to this rule, serving as Home Secretary between 1841 and 1846. He was involved in the Scottish Conservative party's electoral business in the 1830s, particularly in western Scotland, and was elected Lord Rector of Glasgow University in succession to Peel.[35] Like his predecessors and successors at the Home Office, Graham had no wish to directly administer Scotland from Whitehall; he instead asked Buccleuch to undertake some activity related to Scottish affairs, for instance, because affairs were 'better arranged by a Cabinet minister on the spot, than by letters'.[36] Similarly, he complained to his Lord Advocate that 'we could do more by two hours of conversation than by writing volumes'.[37] Though figures such as Buccleuch, Hope, the Lord Advocate and the Solicitor-General met in Scotland to transact Scottish business, these meetings were themselves held at Graham's behest.[38] Despite this delegation to party figures on the ground, Graham was a strongly influential figure in Scottish governance, in addition to his electoral interests. As well as organising Scottish meetings in his absence, he also summoned the Scottish law officers to attend on him at his estate near Carlisle to discuss Scottish affairs.[39]

In organising the initial Poor Law Boards, he also kept partisan considerations in mind; both Peel and Graham consulted with Rae over the political composition of the Board of Supervision, to ensure that there would not be 'too strong an infusion of our political friends', but at the same time seeking to appoint non-Conservatives who were 'not offensive; constantly resident, and versed in country affairs', such as Lord Dunfermline, who was considered 'a Whig, but not violent in his political animosities'.[40] The appointment of those who supervised the new Scottish Poor Law apparatus, though ostensibly bipartisan, was not completely so. The party ensured that the board was as Conservative (or, failing that, as moderately whiggish) as possible.

This active involvement in Scotland's business occasionally led to conflict between the Scottish and UK wings of the party, such as when Graham's appointment of an acquaintance as Sheriff Clerk of Edinburghshire drew the ire of Buccleuch. Graham conceded that the unilateral appointment could be regarded as 'a breach of the respect due to you [Buccleuch]'.[41] Graham played a prominent part in governmental business north of the border, but it was necessary for him to do so on the basis of local advice, and in consultation with native party figures.

Prominent Conservative figure Lord Aberdeen also had a significant input on Scottish legislative and governmental affairs.[42] Even before his brief period acting as head of the Scottish party during Buccleuch's extended trip to the continent in 1838, he had also agreed to 'attend to Scotch Bills which have been brought from the House of Commons'.[43] Aberdeen was concerned about this area, concurring with Hope's sentiments that 'we ought to take some means to secure Scotch business in the House of Lords, its due share of attention'.[44] His input on Scottish issues, most notably the proposed reforms related to the Church of Scotland, was substantial – William Gladstone thought that 'the opinion which will have by far the greatest weight in determining the course of the Conservative leaders and party upon this matter, will be Lord Aberdeen's: after him I think Graham's, Clerk's, and Rae's'.[45] This descending list rather neatly sums up the hierarchy of party influence, though only for the Church Question, and only at that precise moment in time.[46] More broadly, the prevailing pattern was one of mixed competencies and competing spheres. This was underlined by Hope's influence over Aberdeen despite his controversial standing with the party and wider nation; he and Aberdeen exchanged hundreds of letters on the Church Question.[47]

Before 1847, the extent of central party involvement was further complicated by the position of Peel himself. He was a frequent visitor to Scotland,
and had a fairly deep knowledge of the country, going so far as to tell
Aberdeen that 'there is no one, hold Scotchmen, who feels a stronger attachment to that country than I do'.[48] Indeed, having been Home Secretary
for a great deal of the 1820s, he was well informed on the often-confusing
structure of Scottish politics.[49] It was likely this interest and background
which led him to involve himself deeply in complex and highly local party
issues such as the dissemination of Scottish patronage in the counties. Even
minor figures such as Scottish constituency agents appealed directly to him
for favour when moving south.[50]

Going in the other direction, Buccleuch was also a major conduit through
which applications for patronage themselves reached Peel.[51] More general
intelligence from Scotland, on the other hand, reached Peel from a wide
variety of sources, including contacts acquired during the famous banquet
held in his honour when he was elected as Lord Rector of Glasgow University. He corresponded, for instance, with the Lord Provost of Glasgow and
Conservative Chief Agent for Glasgow Robert Lamond, chiefly on how various Scottish and British issues were affecting popular opinion and electoral
prospects in the city.[52]

More broadly, the party's treatment of Scotland during the Peel years
contradicts the widely held perception, exacerbated by the handling of
the Church crisis, that it neglected Scottish business – three significant
Scottish bills were shepherded through parliament in 1845 alone, and Peel's
government of 1841–1846 contained four Scottish ministers.[53] The role of
Westminster figures in the Scottish party during the Peel era was significant, embracing both the governmental and electoral. This role, however,
was very far from autocratic; senior party members were more than willing
to take advice from all levels of the Scottish party, and to devolve responsibility where appropriate.

Given their long periods out of office after 1847, and the gradual decay of
the Scottish Conservative party in electoral terms, it might be expected that
links between senior Westminster figures and Scottish governance would be
diminished. Though this is true to some extent, the Earl of Derby, leader of
the Protectionist and later Conservative party after the Corn Law split, in fact
dispensed Scottish patronage himself while heading Conservative governments, in those relatively rare instances when he was in a position to do so.[54]

In contrast to Peel's more technocratic and aristocratic bent, Derby was
careful to cultivate intellectual and literary Scottish Conservatives, having
gone out of his way to procure a cadetship for the nephew of James Blackwood,
of the publishing family behind *Blackwood's Edinburgh Magazine*.[55] His
decisions in this regard were very astute given the limited means at his dis-
posal, and were evidence of a fairly good knowledge of the situation north of
the border – or, at least, a willingness to listen to the more perceptive Scots
Tory voices. For instance, Lord Eglinton, the leading Scottish Tory after

Buccleuch's withdrawal from politics, beseeched Derby not to 'lose sight of Alison and Aytoun, who have done so much service'.[56] Eglinton himself was a skilled manager of patronage, having been notably successful in dispensing it in another national context while serving as Lord Lieutenant for Ireland.[57] William Aytoun, the Conservative poet, was duly appointed Sheriff of Orkney and Shetland.[58] Archibald Alison, the best-selling Conservative historian and influential Sheriff of Lanarkshire, was made a baronet. The knowledge and skill of Derby was particularly evident here, as Alison, though a highly capable lawyer and very deserving of favour, held extremely authoritarian views. By giving him an honour instead of a judgeship, Derby had 'made one man extremely happy ... at the same time left it open to yourself perhaps to appoint a more efficient judge'.[59] This all indicates that Derby was very well aware of Scottish political currents, and moreover, was able to navigate the murky waters with skill.

He was also careful to reach out to Peelites in Scotland. Though his 1852 ministry did not attract many Peelites, Inverness-shire MP Henry Baillie did agree to become joint Secretary of the Board of Control.[60] His relative generosity may have hastened the reconciliation of many Scottish Peelites (at least within the Faculty of Advocates) with the Conservative party, as by the time Lord Aberdeen had left office in 1855 they had seen little reward for their loyalty to the peer.

By the later 1860s though, Derby's Scottish contacts had largely dried up through death, electoral defeat and other forms of attrition. In his 1858–1859 ministry, Derby had made Henry Lennox a Junior (Scottish) Lord of the Treasury. Lennox was the younger brother of the then-future sixth Duke of Richmond and Gordon, and sat for Chichester, where his family had significant electoral influence. There had, in fact, been rumbles of discontent in the Scottish party that such a figure with a loosened connection to Scotland was taking partial charge of Scottish business.[61] After the resignation of Lennox, the role was held by Peter Blackburn, and then by Sir Graham Graham-Montgomery in the next Derby ministry – though both sat for Scottish seats, they were effective nonentities. Indeed, it is notable that not a single Scottish Conservative MP served in a full cabinet post during the entire period between 1832 and 1868, though many peers did do so.

It was perhaps the electorally precarious nature of his Lord Advocates which prompted Derby to offer Buccleuch's son, Henry Douglas-Scott-Montagu, then resident in Hampshire and MP for his father's pocket-county of Selkirkshire, the position of *de facto* Minister for Scotland in the Commons. Montagu, however, thought himself 'unequal to take charge of and conduct Scotch business in the House', chiefly because he 'has lived but very little in Scotland, and never had the opportunity of taking any part in the ordinary county and country business'.[62] By the very end of the period, well-connected Conservatives who actually resided within Scotland were thin on the ground; this had the effect of loosening institutional and personal ties between Scotland and the party leadership in London. The autonomy of

Scottish party figures in carrying out day-to-day governance in the legal profession and interconnected Supervisory and local Boards thus increased essentially by default.

Scottish administrative devolution and the Conservatives, 1832–1859

Throughout the period, there were complaints from many quarters about the inconvenience of having Lord Advocates sitting for English seats, or who were unable to get into parliament altogether. Many used these issues to press for the creation of a Secretary of State for Scotland.[63] The various legal and political duties performed by the Lord Advocate in both Edinburgh and London made the position increasingly unworkable. The post's roles, if correctly carried out, involved helping to manage Scottish MPs in parliament, shepherding Scottish legislation through the House, governing Scotland from Edinburgh when parliament was not in session (and often when it was), and carrying out the myriad and onerous duties of Scotland premier law officer. It was primarily for these reasons that the Conservative party, somewhat counter-intuitively, became the primary advocates of territorial constitutional reform, in the shape of administrative devolution.

Even before 1832, Lord Melville, when *de facto* Scottish party manager, had unsuccessfully lobbied Peel for the creation of a Scottish Secretary and Scottish Office in the 1820s. He had suggested that the post be roughly similar to that of Chief Secretary for Ireland, sitting in the Commons, except that it would be politically expedient to ensure that the office-holder was a Scot (this was not true of the Irish Secretary – Melville, and Peel himself, had held this post).[64] At this time though, the unreformed electoral system meant that the Tory party had a stranglehold on the vast majority of Scottish Commons seats. By the 1850s, when successive Conservative Lord Advocates had proven themselves increasingly unsatisfactory, the central party under Derby was more open than Peel had been to innovative proposals which would have substantially altered Scotland's place in the Union. This was long before the creation of the Scottish Secretaryship in 1885. They were thus more open to reform than were the Liberals at this time, though this may be partly because the Liberals had a very competent and dedicated Lord Advocate in James Moncreiff, who served four lengthy terms between 1851 and 1869. He was an effective lawyer, legislator, administrator and Commons speaker, and ably carried out the onerous duties of the office for twenty years. By contrast, his Liberal predecessor, Andrew Rutherford, had been unable to handle the strain of such duties.[65]

In the 1850s, Derby showed his willingness to reorient Scotland's administrative position within the Union in the field of overlapping legal structures. He did so by solving the problem of Scotland's exclusion from the House of Lords judicial appeals process. At Select Committee hearings in 1856, opinions given by the Scottish judiciary were split, though Duncan McNeill favoured appointing a Scottish lawyer to the tribunal as a life peer. Nothing was done until 1866, when McNeill wrote a lengthy letter to Derby suggesting that he retire from the Scottish bench, in order to take up a seat in the Lords. Crucially, he suggested that he could be 'useful not only in the matter of Scotch appeals but also in reference to other Scotch business'.[66] Though McNeill was too old in the event to be of much use in either legal or party business, Derby did appoint him to a peerage in 1867. This constituted a clever, if only partially successful, composite attempt to resolve a longstanding legal anomaly, alleviate the shortage of senior Scottish party figures at Westminster, and reorient Scottish governance away from the Lord Advocate.

By far the most concrete evidence of a willingness to embrace reform, however, originates in the late 1850s. During the Conservative party's short-lived 1858–1859 administration, Derby had seriously considered constituting the Lord High Commissioner to the General Assembly of the Church of Scotland as 'a rival Official Agent, the minister for Scotland in the House of Lords, [and] a member of the Cabinet'.[67] Intended in a large measure to supersede the role played by the Lord Advocate, the plan was, however, unfeasible. Apart from anything else, many Scots were no longer members of the Established Church, and would not have accepted the combination of a semi-religious office with political mastery of the country. The original idea had been presented to Derby by Eglinton – who had previously been one of the prime movers behind the National Association for the Vindication of Scottish Rights (NAVSR).[68] In addition to being head of the Scottish party, he had also twice served as Irish Lord Lieutenant. It is notable that Eglinton wanted the position to be held by a wealthy peer who would go about it with a great deal of pomp and ceremony. While Melville's earlier proposal had been based on the Irish Secretaryship which he himself had held, Eglinton explicitly advocated the institution of a role much closer in resemblance to that of the Irish Lord Lieutenant – an office which he had occupied for much of the 1850s. Conveniently, this would also have solved the thorny problem of an electoral base – while the party had few Scottish MPs, the vast majority of the Scottish peerage was Tory.

The 1858–1859 ministry was, however, short-lived, and by the time Derby was back in office, Eglinton had passed away. With parliamentary reform dominating the agenda, territorial reform for Scotland was not a priority.[69] It is notable, however, that Disraeli's *Press* had expressed its approval of Eglinton and the NAVSR's advocacy for a Scottish Secretary.[70] Moreover, while Lord Rosebery and the Liberal party deserve the majority of the immediate credit for the eventually successful campaign for a Scottish Secretary in 1885, its supporters were not exclusively Liberal.[71] Indeed, the measure itself was passed under the auspices of a caretaker Conservative ministry, and some Liberals had been distinctly opposed to administrative devolution in the 1850s.[72] Though administrative devolution did not come to pass for another thirty years, its longer-term origins owe much to the Conservative party.

Conclusion

Scottish governance involved a confusing and constantly evolving jumble of institutions and figures across local, Scottish and British levels.[73] Even the post of Lord Advocate, arguably the single most stable element in this mix, was subject to change, which was inextricably connected to partisan considerations. Beneath this, overlapping legal, civic and voluntary institutions were closely connected to the ebb and flow of party politics.

In the elite sphere, far from neglecting Scotland, prominent Westminster Conservatives were closely involved in Scottish politics. Figures including Graham and Peel were well versed in Scottish particularities, often more so than their Liberal counterparts. Further, the assumption that the party's interest in Scotland declined after 1847 is flawed, as Derby and others showed a strong interest in Scotland. The deteriorating state of the party within Scotland itself encouraged them to innovate, in exploring new avenues of communication and administrative reform. In this area, they can be credited with keeping the idea of administrative devolution alive during an extended period in the middle of the century, a period which boasted very few advocates of territorial constitutional change for Scotland. Scotland's position in the mid-Victorian Union was superficially stable, but beneath the surface its role was constantly contested, negotiated and redefined. This state of flux had a marked and significant effect on the Conservative party, on Scottish society and on the evolution of the Union itself.

Notes

1 National Records of Scotland [henceforth NRS], MS Buccleuch, GD224/582/2/14. Printed letter from 'East Lothian Elector', c. 1834–35.
2 The most comprehensive existing work on Scottish politics more generally is I.G.C. Hutchison, *A Political History of Scotland 1832–1924: Parties, Elections, Issues* (Edinburgh: John Donald, 1986). Other monographs which touch on Scotland's governance in relation to partisan considerations include, most prominently, M. Fry, *Patronage and Principle: A Political History of Modern Scotland* (Aberdeen: Aberdeen University Press, 1987); M. Dyer, *Men of Property and Intelligence: The Scottish Electoral System Prior to 1884* (Aberdeen: Scottish Cultural Press, 1996).
3 With the exception of partial treatments in more general works, the mid-Victorian Scottish Conservative party remains an understudied area. The only extant scholarly works focus on specific facets of the party in restricted periods. See G.F. Millar, 'The Conservative Split in the Scottish Counties, 1846–1857', *Scottish Historical Review* 80:1 (2001), pp. 221–250; J.I. Brash, *Papers on Scottish Electoral Politics, 1832–1854* (Edinburgh: T. and A. Constable, 1974); J.I. Brash, 'The Conservatives in the Haddington District of Burghs, 1832–52', *Transactions of the East Lothian Antiquarian and Field Naturalists' Society* 11 (n.s. 1968), pp. 37–70.
4 No single work which examines Scotland's governance and administration in-depth during this period exists, but different facets, including county government, the working of the reformed Scottish Poor Law, and the character of Lord Advocates, have been explored. See A. Whetstone, *Scottish County Government*

in the Eighteenth and Nineteenth Centuries (Edinburgh: John Donald, 1981); I. Levitt, *Government and Social Conditions in Scotland, 1845–1919* (Edinburgh: Blackwood, Pillans & Wilson, 1988); G.W.T. Omond, *The Lord Advocates of Scotland. Second Series, 1834–1880* (London: Andrew Melrose, 1914).

5 Useful works on the UK party in this period include N. Gash, 'The Organization of the Conservative Party, 1832–1846, Part II: The Electoral Organization', *Parliamentary History* 2 (1983), pp. 131–152; 'The Organization of the Conservative Party, 1832–1846, Part I: The Parliamentary Organization', *Parliamentary History* 1 (1982), pp. 137–159; *Politics in the Age of Peel: A Study in the Technique of Parliamentary Representation, 1830–1850* (London: Longmans, Green, 1953); R. Blake, *The Conservative Party from Peel to Major* (London: Heinemann, 1997).

6 For the development of this in a broader context, see J. Mitchell, *Governing Scotland: The Invention of Administrative Devolution* (London: Palgrave Macmillan, 2003).

7 L. Paterson, *The Autonomy of Modern Scotland* (Edinburgh: Edinburgh University Press, 1994), p. 47.

8 Liverpool Record Office [henceforth LRO], MS Derby, 920 DER (14)/13/7/10. Lord Mansfield to Earl of Derby, 10 April 1859.

9 LRO, MS Derby, 920 DER (14)/164/17b/10. [?] Smith to Duke of Buccleuch, [April 1859].

10 M. Fry, 'Rae, Sir William, third baronet (1769–1842)', in *Oxford Dictionary of National Biography*, www.oxforddnb.com/view/article/23005 (accessed 23 February 2017).

11 NRS, MS Lothian, GD40/9/326/3. Colonel Macdonald to Lord Lothian, 4 January 1835.

12 NRS, MS Buccleuch, GD224/1031/5/7–9. Buccleuch to Sir Robert Peel, 12 January 1835.

13 Robert Dundas, 2nd Viscount Melville, had originally taken over as de facto Scottish manager from his father, Henry Dundas, and retired from politics in 1832. See Michael Fry, *The Dundas Despotism* (Edinburgh: John Donald, 1992).

14 NRS, MS Drummond of Hawthornden, GD230/580/18. Buccleuch to Sir Francis Drummond, 1 June 1835.

15 NRS, MS Buccleuch, GD224/1031/5/7–9. Buccleuch to Peel, 12 January 1835; MS Buccleuch, GD224/1031/4/18–19. Drummond to Buccleuch, 30 December 1834.

16 British Library [henceforth BL], MS Peel, 40517, fos 14–16. Buccleuch to Peel, 14 October 1842.

17 Omond, *The Lord Advocates of Scotland*, pp. 219–222.

18 Paterson, *The Autonomy of Modern Scotland*, p. 50.

19 National Library of Scotland [henceforth NLS], MS Makgill, GD82/472/5. Archibald Campbell Swinton to George Makgill, 25 February 1867.

20 BL, MS Aberdeen, 43205, fos 134–135. Sir William Rae to Sir John Hope, 11 July 1841.

21 Omond, *The Lord Advocates of Scotland*, p. 209.

22 Somerset Heritage Centre, MS Hylton, DD\HY/24/16/179. Duke of Montrose to Jolliffe, 11 April 1859.

23 F.W.S. Craig, *British Parliamentary Election Results, 1832–1885* (London: Macmillan, 1977), p. 61.

24 Bagehot had recently completed his seminal work, *The English Constitution*, which posited a distinction between 'dignified' and 'efficient' parts of the constitution. Given Bagehot's respectable vote-share, it seems very likely that he also engaged in widespread bribery and other corrupt practices; such activities sit uneasily with his forthright denunciation of corrupt practices in his writings. See W. Bagehot, *The English Constitution* (Oxford: Oxford University Press, 1945), pp. 130–131.

25 Paterson, *The Autonomy of Modern Scotland*, pp. 71, 54, 57.

26 Paterson, *The Autonomy of Modern Scotland*, p. 54.

27 BL, MS Peel, 40339, fo. 322. Peel to Rae, 19 December 1834; BL, MS Peel, 40339, fos 332–333. Henry Home Drummond to Rae, 21 December 1834.

28 For the underlying (and evolving) ideology which informed the exertion of this influence, see M. Michie, *An Enlightenment Tory in Victorian Scotland: The Career of Sir Archibald Alison* (East Linton: Tuckwell Press, 1997).

29 Paterson, *The Autonomy of Modern Scotland*, p. 54.

30 Paterson, *The Autonomy of Modern Scotland*, pp. 47–55.

31 G. Morton, *Unionist Nationalism: Governing Urban Scotland, 1830–1860* (East Linton: Tuckwell Press, 1999), p. 31.

32 Omond, *The Lord Advocates of Scotland*, pp. 140, 144.

33 Levitt, *Government and Social Conditions in Scotland*, pp. xl–xli.

34 I.G.C. Hutchison, 'Anglo-Scottish Political Relations in the Nineteenth Century, c.1815–1914', in *Anglo-Scottish Relations from 1603 to 1900*, ed. by T.C. Smout (Oxford: Oxford University Press, 2005), p. 259.

35 M. Escott, 'Graham, James Robert George (1792–1861), of Netherby, Cumb.', in *History of Parliament, Commons 1820–1832*, www.historyofparliamentonline. org/volume/1820-1832/member/graham-james-1792-1861 (accessed 23 February 2017).

36 BL, MS Graham, 79727, fos 179–181. Sir James Graham to Buccleuch, 28 September 1842.

37 BL, MS Graham, 79666, fos 63–64. Graham to Duncan McNeill, 30 September 1842.

38 See, for instance, NRS, MS Buccleuch, GD224/1031/54/1–2. Graham to Buccleuch, 29 December 1842.

39 BL, MS Graham, 79727, ff. 179–181. Graham to Buccleuch, 28 September 1842.

40 BL, MS Graham, 79666, fos 72–74. Graham to Rae, 29 December 1842.

41 NRS, MS Buccleuch, GD224/1031/54/5–6. Graham to Buccleuch, 31 December 1842.

42 For Aberdeen's career more generally, see M. Chamberlain, *Lord Aberdeen: A Political Biography* (New York: Longman, 1983).

43 BL, MS Aberdeen, 43327, fos 99–101. Lord Aberdeen to Hope, 29 December 1838; BL, MS Aberdeen, 43327, fos 68–69. Aberdeen to Hope, 19 May 1836.

44 BL, MS Aberdeen, 43327, fos 79–81. Aberdeen to Hope, 10 February 1838.

45 Flintshire Record Office, MS Glynne-Gladstone, GG/225, fos 239–241. William Gladstone to John Gladstone, 9 December 1839.

46 For the complex interaction between politics and Scottish religious affairs, see G.I.T. Machin, *Politics and the Churches in Great Britain, 1832–1868* (Oxford: Clarendon Press, 1977).

47 G.I.T. Machin, 'The Disruption and British Politics, 1834–43', *Scottish Historical Review* 51 (1972), pp. 20–51 [p. 21].

48 BL, MS Aberdeen, 43065, fos 391–394. Peel to Aberdeen, 11 November 1849.

49 Hutchison, 'Anglo-Scottish Political Relations', p. 262.

50 BL, MS Peel, 40541, fo. 59. James Blackwood to Peel, 4 March 1844.

51 See, for instance, BL, MS Peel, 40525, fos 1–2. Buccleuch to Peel, 15 February 1843.

52 See, for instance, BL, MS Peel, 40485, fo. 79. Sir James Campbell to Peel, 7 July 1841; BL, MS Peel, 40493, fos 396–397. Robert Lamond to Peel, 2 November 1841; BL, MS Peel, 40318, fos 263–265. Lamond to Peel, 21 June 1841.

53 Hutchison, 'Anglo-Scottish Political Relations', pp. 259–260.

54 For Derby's career as party leader in a broader context, see Angus Hawkins, *The Forgotten Prime Minister: The 14th Earl of Derby: Ascent, 1799–1851* (Oxford: Oxford University Press, 2007).

55 NLS, MS Blackwoods, 30011, fo. 259. Derby to John Blackwood, 30 October 1858. For the relationship between Scotland, the party, and Blackwood's, see J. Shattock, 'The Sense of Place and Blackwood's (Edinburgh) Magazine', *Victorian Periodicals Review* 49 (2016), pp. 431–442.

56 LRO, MS Derby, 920 DER (14)/148/2/49. Lord Eglinton to Derby, 26 April 1852.

57 A. Hawkins, *The Forgotten Prime Minister: The 14th Earl of Derby: Achievement, 1852-1869* (Oxford: Oxford University Press, 2008), p. 15.

58 T. Martin, *Memoir of William Edmonstoune Aytoun* (Edinburgh: William Blackwood & Sons, 1867), p. 135.

59 LRO, MS Derby, 920 DER (14)/148/2/53. Eglinton to Derby, 13 May 1852.

60 J.D. Jones and R.B. Erickson, *The Peelites, 1846–1857* (Columbus: Ohio State University Press, 1972), p. 132.

61 A. Hawkins, *Parliament, Party and the Art of Politics in Britain, 1855–1859* (Stanford: Stanford University Press, 1987), p. 114.

62 LRO, MS Derby, 920 DER (14)/164/17b/15. Buccleuch to Derby, 9 July 1866.

63 See, for instance, *Hansard*, HC Debates, 22 March 1867, vol. 186, cc. 397–399.

64 For broader-context comparisons of the Irish and Scottish unions in this period, see A. Jackson, *The Two Unions: Ireland, Scotland, and the Survival of the United Kingdom, 1707–2007* (Oxford: Oxford University Press, 2012).

65 Omond, *The Lord Advocates of Scotland*, pp. 160, 231.

66 LRO, MS Derby, 920 DER (14)/60/2/15. McNeill to Derby, 5 October 1866.

67 LRO, MS Derby, 920 DER (14)/164/17b/2. Buccleuch to Derby, 12 March 1858.

68 There is a still-flourishing body of work on the NAVSR. The most recent valuable work on this is A. Tyrrell, 'The Earl of Eglinton, Scottish Conservatism, and the National Association for the Vindication of Scottish Rights', *Historical Journal* 53 (2010), pp. 87–107.

69 For parliamentary reform interest in Scotland, see M. Chase, 'The Popular Movement for Parliamentary Reform in Provincial Britain during the 1860s', *Parliamentary History* 36 (2017), pp. 14–30.

70 *Press*, 24 December 1853, quoted in Tyrrell, p. 106.

71 An Edinburgh mass meeting on the issue in 1884, for instance, boasted the Liberal Rosebery and Conservative Marquis of Lothian as speakers. See E. Cameron, *Impaled Upon a Thistle: Scotland since 1880* (Edinburgh: Edinburgh University Press, 2010), pp. 61–62.

72 Edward Bouverie and Arthur Kinnaird, for instance, were Liberal MPs for Kilmarnock Burghs and Perth, and opposed the creation of a Scottish Secretary. See *Hansard*, HC Debates 15 June 1858, vol. 150, cc. 2125–2127; 12 July 1869, vol. 197, c. 1734.

73 Paterson, *The Autonomy of Modern Scotland*, p. 49.

Bibliography

Bagehot, W. *The English Constitution* (Oxford: Oxford University Press, 1945).

Blake, R. *The Conservative Party from Peel to Major* (London: Heinemann, 1997).

Brash, J.I. 'The Conservatives in the Haddington District of Burghs, 1832–52', *Transactions of the East Lothian Antiquarian and Field Naturalists' Society* 11 (n.s. 1968), pp. 37–70.

Brash, J.I., *Papers on Scottish Electoral Politics, 1832–1854* (Edinburgh: T. and A. Constable, 1974).

British Library, MS Aberdeen, 43327, fos 68–69. Aberdeen to Hope, 19 May 1836.

British Library, MS Aberdeen, 43327, fos 79–81. Aberdeen to Hope, 10 February 1838.

British Library, MS Aberdeen, 43327, fos 99–101. Lord Aberdeen to Sir John Hope, 29 December 1838.

British Library, MS Aberdeen, 43205, fos 134–135. Sir William Rae to Sir John Hope, 11 July 1841.

British Library, MS Peel, 40339, fo. 322. Peel to Rae, 19 December 1834.

British Library, MS Peel, 40339, fos 332–333. Henry Home Drummond to Rae, 21 December 1834.

British Library, MS Peel, 40318, fos 263–265. Lamond to Peel, 21 June 1841.

British Library, MS Peel, 40485, fo. 79. Sir James Campbell to Peel, 7 July 1841.

British Library, MS Peel, 40493, fos 396–397. Robert Lamond to Peel, 2 November 1841.

British Library, MS Peel, 40517, fos 14–16. Buccleuch to Peel, 14 October 1842.

British Library, MS Peel, 40525, fo. 1–2. Buccleuch to Peel, 15 February 1843.

British Library, MS Peel, 40541, fo. 59. James Blackwood to Peel, 4 March 1844.

British Library, MS Aberdeen, 43065, fos 391–394. Peel to Aberdeen, 11 November 1849.

Cameron, E. *Impaled Upon a Thistle: Scotland since 1880* (Edinburgh: Edinburgh University Press, 2010).

Chamberlain, M. *Lord Aberdeen: A Political Biography* (New York: Longman, 1983).

Chase, M. 'The Popular Movement for Parliamentary Reform in Provincial Britain during the 1860s', *Parliamentary History* 36 (2017), pp. 14–30.

Craig, F.W.S. *British Parliamentary Election Results, 1832–1885* (London: Macmillan, 1977).

Dyer, M. *Men of Property and Intelligence: The Scottish Electoral System Prior to 1884* (Aberdeen: Scottish Cultural Press, 1996).

Flintshire Record Office, MS Glynne-Gladstone, GG/225, fos 239–241. William Gladstone to John Gladstone, 9 December 1839.

Fry, M. *The Dundas Despotism* (Edinburgh: John Donald, 1992).

Fry, M. *Patronage and Principle: A Political History of Modern Scotland* (Aberdeen: Aberdeen University Press, 1987).

Gash, N. 'The Organization of the Conservative Party, 1832–1846, Part I: The Parliamentary Organization', *Parliamentary History* 1 (1982), pp. 137–159.

Gash, N. 'The Organization of the Conservative Party, 1832–1846, Part II: The Electoral Organization', *Parliamentary History* 2 (1983), pp. 131–152.

Gash, N. *Politics in the Age of Peel: A Study in the Technique of Parliamentary Representation, 1830–1850* (London: Longmans, Green, 1953).

Hansard, HC Debates, 15 June 1858, vol. 150, cc. 2125–2127.

Hansard, HC Debates, 22 March 1867, vol. 186, cc. 397–399.

Hansard, HC Debates, 12 July 1869, vol. 197, c. 1734.

Hawkins, A. *The Forgotten Prime Minister: The 14th Earl of Derby: Ascent, 1799–1851* (Oxford: Oxford University Press, 2007).

Hawkins, A. *The Forgotten Prime Minister: The 14th Earl of Derby: Achievement, 1852-1869* (Oxford: Oxford University Press, 2008)

Hawkins, A. *Parliament, Party and the Art of Politics in Britain, 1855–1859* (Stanford: Stanford University Press, 1987).

Hutchison, I.G.C. 'Anglo-Scottish Political Relations in the Nineteenth Century, c.1815–1914', in *Anglo-Scottish Relations from 1603 to 1900*, ed. by T.C. Smout (Oxford: Oxford University Press, 2005), pp. 247–266.

Hutchison, I.G.C. *A Political History of Scotland 1832–1924: Parties, Elections, Issues* (Edinburgh: John Donald, 1986).

Jackson, A. *The Two Unions: Ireland, Scotland, and the Survival of the United Kingdom, 1707–2007* (Oxford: Oxford University Press, 2012).

Jones, J.D. and R. B. Erickson, *The Peelites, 1846–1857* (Columbus: Ohio State University Press, 1972).

Levitt, I. *Government and Social Conditions in Scotland, 1845–1919* (Edinburgh: Blackwood, Pillans & Wilson, 1988).

Liverpool Record Office, MS Derby, 920 DER (14)/148/2/53. Eglinton to Derby, 13 May 1852.

Liverpool Record Office, MS Derby, 920 DER (14)/164/17b/2. Buccleuch to Derby, 12 March 1858.

Liverpool Record Office, MS Derby, 920 DER (14)/164/17b/10. [?] Smith to Duke of Buccleuch, [April 1859].

Liverpool Record Office, MS Derby, 920 DER (14)/13/7/10. Lord Mansfield to Earl of Derby, 10 April 1859.

Liverpool Record Office, MS Derby, 920 DER (14)/164/17b/15. Buccleuch to Derby, 9 July 1866.

Liverpool Record Office, MS Derby, 920 DER (14)/60/2/15. McNeill to Derby, 5 October 1866.

Machin, G.I.T. *Politics and the Churches in Great Britain, 1832–1868* (Oxford: Clarendon Press, 1977).

Machin, G.I.T. 'The Disruption and British Politics, 1834–43', *Scottish Historical Review* 51 (1972), pp. 20–51.

Martin, T. *Memoir of William Edmonstoune Aytoun* (Edinburgh: William Blackwood & Sons, 1867).

Michie, M. *An Enlightenment Tory in Victorian Scotland: The Career of Sir Archibald Alison* (East Linton: Tuckwell Press, 1997).

Millar, G.F. 'The Conservative Split in the Scottish Counties, 1846–1857', *Scottish Historical Review* 80:1 (2001), pp. 221–250.

Mitchell, J. *Governing Scotland: The Invention of Administrative Devolution* (London: Palgrave Macmillan, 2003).

Morton, G. *Unionist Nationalism: Governing Urban Scotland, 1830–1860* (East Linton: Tuckwell Press, 1999).

National Library of Scotland, MS Blackwoods, 30011, fo. 259. Derby to John Blackwood, 30 October 1858.

National Library of Scotland, MS Makgill, GD82/472/5. Archibald Campbell Swinton to George Makgill, 25 February 1867.

National Records of Scotland, MS Buccleuch, GD224/1031/4/18–19. Drummond to Buccleuch, 30 December 1834.

National Records of Scotland, MS Buccleuch, GD224/1031/5/7–9. Buccleuch to Sir Robert Peel, 12 January 1835.

National Records of Scotland, MS Buccleuch, GD224/1031/54/1–2. Graham to Buccleuch, 29 December 1842.

National Records of Scotland, MS Buccleuch, GD224/1031/54/5–6. Graham to Buccleuch, 31 December 1842.

National Records of Scotland, MS Drummond of Hawthornden, GD230/580/18. Buccleuch to Sir Francis Drummond, 1 June 1835.

National Records of Scotland, MS Lothian, GD40/9/326/3. Colonel Macdonald to Lord Lothian, 4 January 1835.

Omond, G.W.T. *The Lord Advocates of Scotland. Second Series, 1834–1880* (London: Andrew Melrose, 1914).

Paterson, L. *The Autonomy of Modern Scotland* (Edinburgh: Edinburgh University Press, 1994).

Shattock, J. 'The Sense of Place and Blackwood's (Edinburgh) Magazine', *Victorian Periodicals Review* 49 (2016), pp. 431–442.

Somerset Heritage Centre, MS Hylton, DD\HY/24/16/179. Duke of Montrose to Jolliffe, 11 April 1859.

Tyrrell, A. 'The Earl of Eglinton, Scottish Conservatism, and the National Association for the Vindication of Scottish Rights', *Historical Journal* 53 (2010), pp. 87–107.

Whetstone, A. *Scottish County Government in the Eighteenth and Nineteenth Centuries* (Edinburgh: John Donald, 1981).

7 Union Street

More than simply a metaphor for the coming together of Plymouth's Three Towns?

Kim Stevenson and Judith Rowbotham

Introduction

Until 1914, the city of Plymouth comprised three separate towns when consequent to the Admiralty's anticipation of the exigencies of the Great War, the Three Towns of Plymouth, East Stonehouse and Devonport were forced to amalgamate. Unsurprisingly, there was significant local hostility to this development as each of the Three Towns took pride in their own discrete identities. While there is substantial evidence in their nineteenth-century history suggesting an apparent high degree of disunion within these communities and desire to remain separate and autonomous, this does not necessarily represent the daily realities of life across the Three Towns. As this chapter reveals, despite the deeply rooted schisms within what was already an urban conglomeration at the beginning of the nineteenth century, there are interesting and tangible indications of the extent to which the potential and aspirations for unification co-existed with that evidence of disunion. This was physically represented in the aptly named Union Street, an important thoroughfare that ran through all Three Towns and which had been deliberately designed and constructed to link them. Today, Union Street still exists, but the explicit reference to 'unity' in the street name is mostly ignored underlining the tradition of the persistence of separation within the city. Few Plymothians know or have any appreciation of the historic significance and strategic importance of this once renowned thoroughfare, or how its history signifies both the disunion and the union of the borough of Plymouth, the town and parish of East Stonehouse, and the county borough of Devonport. This chapter focusses on the symbolism surrounding the creation and development of Union Street in the context of the history of the Three Towns, exploring the impact of the concepts of union and disunion on their cultural heritage.

At the start of the nineteenth century, from an external government perspective, the separation into Three Towns of the still-important commercial port of Plymouth itself, the Marine establishment in East Stonehouse and the naval base of Plymouth Dock (soon to become Devonport) made little sense. Physically, as local maps illustrate, the Three Towns were effectively contiguous at one point, where the narrow shoreline at Stonehouse was flanked by Plymouth to the north and Devonport to the south. For the Admiralty, charged with the responsibility of the blockade of the English Channel to French ships during the Napoleonic Wars, the division between the towns was a challenge to the efficient management of replenishing the stores to be shuttled out to the ships patrolling there.[1] Plymouth's continuing importance in Britain's defence planning strategies endured into the twentieth century as evidenced by the mid-nineteenth-century construction of the Palmerston forts and in its control of the empire, including the commercial dimensions. The separation, therefore, continued to make little sense at both the national and county levels. What this chapter explores are the attempts to overcome local opposition and instead, promote union. It also aims to estimate the degree of unity that practically developed as the contiguity between the Three Towns forced increasing degrees of accommodation and institutional sharing across their boundaries, including the role played by Union Street itself.

A starting point is the journalist J.C. Trewin's comment from the 1970s to the effect that civic unity was *forced* on Plymouth in 1914 through amalgamation, with the choice of name being dictated by the view that the town of Plymouth was more familiar to the rest of the country than either Stonehouse or Devonport.[2] This forced amalgamation took place in the context of the outbreak of war, when the Admiralty informed the government that it would seriously hinder the war effort as a unified enterprise if the different administrations and petty jealousies of the three separate towns were allowed to interfere with the effective policing of the area and dockyards.

Historical background to the Three Towns

It is worth briefly outlining the complicated background to the emergence of the Three Towns' scenario. In the 1300s, Plymouth had become a town, as opposed to a village, by virtue of the granting of a right (from 1253) to hold markets, it became a borough in 1439 enjoying all the rights and privileges attached to that status.[3] Originally a fishing and commercial port, as the importance of naval defences for the realm became established from the late fifteenth and sixteenth centuries, there was an increased fortification of the borough to resist any attack on the emerging Royal Navy and its resources when in harbour there.[4] From the early modern period, however, Plymouth prided itself on being a borough that tolerated dissent, both religious and political.[5] The borough showed this aspect most strongly by supporting Parliament in a county that was substantially Royalist during the Civil War. For four years, Plymouth uncompromisingly resisted Royalist attempts to control it.[6] The post-Restoration construction of the Royal Citadel on Plymouth's waterfront further underlined Plymouth's contumacious nature. The stronghold had guns not only facing out to sea to defend against foreign invaders but also trained on Plymouth itself so that, as Worth commented, it could 'hold in check the liberal views of the Plymouthians should civil disturbances again arise'.[7] As the Georgian town grew and prospered, it also became a crowded and not always salubrious place to live but retained a sense of pride in itself and its radical traditions. It is no coincidence that Protestant Nonconformity remained strong in the borough and was a key feature of its urban identity in the nineteenth century.[8]

Adjoining the borough was the old Domesday Manor of East Stonehouse, owned by the Edgcumbe family, which essentially remained a village into the seventeenth century. Unlike Plymouth, and despite the resource of Stonehouse Pool (later utilised by the Navy), what enriched the people of East Stonehouse as it grew from a village to a small rural town was wool. If Plymouth in the sixteenth to the late eighteenth century was a major player in the export wool trade, it was East Stonehouse that raised the sheep and produced the woollen cloth in its local mills. East Stonehouse shared the tradition of 'belonging' to a local gentry family,[9] but it also had a population of new urban workers associated with both the old wool trade and the defence industry that increasingly replaced it and was careful not to align itself with the more radical Plymouth. Instead, it continued to identify much more strongly with county interests and was predominantly Anglican in outlook, exploiting Plymouth and neighbouring Devonport as a source of profit but distinguishing itself from the former and, to a slightly greater extent, with its nouveau neighbour to the south. Though it also became a county borough in recognition of its increased urban profile and size, Stonehouse remained in many ways, including its gentry-dominated local governance, a village at heart, despite the numbers of sailors and marines living there in barracks or lodgings, which were cheaper though seen as slightly more salubrious than Plymouth.[10]

The southern neighbour to both was Devonport, whose origins lie in the settlement that grew up around a new naval dockyard built to expand the country's naval resources during the reign of William and Mary. The harbour in the parish of Stoke Damerel (the old village was slightly inland) was chosen for the defence-related development that started in 1690, taking advantage of the River Tamar as opposed to the River Plym, substantially to distance the new naval resource from the dubious neighbourhood of Plymouth and its unreliable loyalties to the Crown. The naval base continued to be refined and expanded, consequently the new settlement acquired a different name, Plymouth Dock, one gifted by the navy rather than its inhabitants. The designation of 'Plymouth Dock' essentially underlines that the Royal Navy, as a national institution, viewed its older resources in Plymouth (victualling, and other shipboard supplies) alongside the newer resources being built in Devonport as part of a contiguous whole.[11]

By the late eighteenth century the town that had emerged from the original higgledy-piggledy settlement clustered around the naval dock saw things rather differently. It was not, unlike neighbouring Stonehouse, associated with the tradition of due deference from belonging to the tenantry of a gentry family but with the deference associated with the hierarchy of Crown service.[12] There were, of course, obvious links to the land-owning gentry class of England (and Ireland) given how many younger sons entered the navy. The town that coalesced during the course of the eighteenth century developed a sense of pride based not on the kinds of ancient traditions that Plymouth rejoiced in but one rooted in the sense of their modernity on the one hand, and their loyalty to Crown and Country on the other.[13] As Samuel Johnson opined, Plymouth society was 'very good', but he expressed his displeasure at the expanding town of Plymouth Dock, 'this new and rising town could not but excite the envy and jealously of the old ... I am a Plymouth man' he declared, these 'dockers' are merely 'upstarts and aliens'.[14] Consequently, the inhabitants of Plymouth Dock resented its name because it implied a union with nearby Plymouth for which they had no appetite and needed no citadel with the guns trained on themselves. The town successfully petitioned George IV to permit a change of name, to Devonport, a nomenclature chosen for its overtones of association with the famously loyal county, rather than with its neighbouring radical borough, underlining its patriotism. Established as a town, Devonport became a municipal borough in 1837, hugely increasing its sense of self-importance and pre-eminence over Plymouth, looking down on it not just geographically but with a confidence in its own cultural superiority.

Reshaping the towns: continuing the jealousy?

One of the features of the burgeoning townscapes of the nineteenth century was the growth in buildings intended to demonstrate local civic pride. The most spectacular architectural manifestations found in the Three Towns up to the early nineteenth century had either been government constructions (Royal Citadel, the Barbican, Royal Marine Barracks), places of worship or the surrounding houses of the local landowners such as Saltram House or Mount Edgcumbe. But Devonport's success in ridding itself of the nomenclature link with Plymouth spurred on the inhabitants of both the ancient and the new boroughs to take action to demonstrate their pride of identity through distinctive public buildings. Plymouth, for example, constructed the Athenaeum according to the design of architect and founding member John Foulston, in operation from 1819. Foulston had already been responsible for the new, neo-classical Theatre Royal, which opened its doors for performances in 1813. Then in the 1820s, Devonport succeeded in luring Foulston's attention away from the ancient borough, to take the opportunity of designing new central public buildings to celebrate its renaming. The result was the construction of the Devonport Guildhall and its accompanying column, bigger, better and more striking buildings than Plymouth's recent additions and self-consciously advertising the town's 'public spirit and the loyalty of its inhabitants'.[15] As Jewitt confirms, 'Plymouth became dissevered from its dock, and a large part of its inhabitants'.[16]

The symbols of local government were maintained by all Three Towns but cherished particularly by Plymouth and Devonport as channels through which power and authority could be expressed by their local elites. The Municipal Reform Act 1835 reshaped the Plymouth Corporation, endowing it with six wards electing councilmen as well as having two Members of Parliament. Devonport followed suit in 1837 when it received its deed of incorporation. Lacking borough status but having township status under the 1835 reform, Stonehouse had fewer such institutions but jealously guarded those it had. Each town also had their own petty sessions (magistrates' courts) and police establishments though Stonehouse's was less independent as it was constituted as Division H of the Devon County force. Plymouth and Devonport had not only their own local borough police forces but also their own Watch Committees who could decide how best to spend the police fund element of ratepayer money on local policing strategies that reflected each town's individuality. Devonport's Watch Committee was dominated by retired naval men, many of them younger sons of local Devon gentry families. The Committee's attitudes towards policing priorities were powerfully influenced by the naval experience of the town's councillors, particularly the boundaries of unacceptable behaviour and knowledge of what sailors got up to, on and off duty, and whether it constituted 'good' conduct in that light. This contrasted very strongly with Plymouth's Watch Committee, where instructions for policing strongly reflected the intolerance in the borough for disorderly conduct that arose from drunkenness and immorality.

Policing in Stonehouse was managed by the county's Police Committee, which being gentry-dominated in its thinking, inclined more towards the Devonport style of policing expectations than the more moralistic Plymouth thinking. As merely a division of the Devon County force, Stonehouse District was vulnerable to both amalgamation and poor resourcing. At the Devon Midsummer Sessions in 1861 councillor J.W. Wilson challenged the County Chief Constable Gerald de Courcy Hamilton, expressing concern that Stonehouse had become the 'resort of thieves and disreputable characters' who were able to escape the more effective policing in Devonport and Plymouth because of the greater size of their forces. Stonehouse had more committals than either Plymouth or Devonport but its force was considerably smaller, led, according to the County Chief Constable, by one 'very effective' Superintendent, one Sergeant and eight constables, but only one man was on duty in the area at any one time.[17] Two years later in 1863, Sir John Duckworth, the Government Inspector of Police, 'considered it desirable that Stonehouse, chiefly from the peculiarity of it being situated between two jurisdictions, should be made into a separate district', recommending an increase in establishment of just four constables.[18] In comparison, Devonport District had started with twelve constables in 1839 rapidly increasing to nearly sixty by the 1880s.[19] Similarly, Plymouth had nearly 100 by the end of the century.[20]

This separation in thinking about policing strategies was also reflected in the petty sessions operating in each of the Three Towns. In Plymouth, the magistracy was dominated by the solid citizens of Plymouth with the Mayor acting as Chair of the Bench. The Devonport and Stonehouse magistracies were very different: being led by local gentry families, living contiguously to but not physically residing within these towns. In Devonport, the occupant of the role of Surgeon General, based in the port, was an automatic member of the Bench, testifying to the reality that many of the individuals appearing before the court would be sailors enlisted in the Navy. Stonehouse, despite the presence of the Royal Marines, had no automatic judicial role and instead relied regularly on County magistrates to ride in and fill the Bench. The disunion between the Three Towns over the management of public disorder and the ratepayer choices made to fund police prosecutions is also apparent in the types of prosecution brought by the local citizenry and the reactions of the local magistrates.

A brief survey of public petitions also gives a sense of the different perspectives of the Three Towns towards alcohol control. Almost immediately after the enactment of the Beer Act 1833 all three petitioned for its repeal or alteration in significantly higher numbers than, for example, Portsmouth. The Devon towns individually returned relatively consistent figures of around 1,300 each. Portsmouth returned just 258 indicating a much more tolerant approach (Liverpool returned 855).[21] Equally, in 1836 when Portsmouth sent 2,459 petitions calling for the repeal of additional duty on spirituous liquors, Devonport sent just 353; when added to Plymouth's 348 and Stonehouse's 352 this represents less than half the opposition of Portsmouth.[22] In 1850, a further demonstration of Plymouth's harsh attitude is evident when it overwhelmingly supported reducing the number of beerhouses with 9,873 in favour and 1,027 against. No returns from Devonport or Stonehouse are recorded. Llewellynn Jewitt asserted in his local history in 1873, that Plymouth had become 'remarkably healthy and pleasant in every respect' implicitly referring to its more 'respectable', less drink-fuelled environment and virtual elimination of cholera.[23]

A high level of separation is also indicated by the extent of replication in the organisation of local leisure activities. Each town insisted on maintaining their own societies and launching their own programmes of cultural events during the year, providing another example of disunion between the Three Towns. As a result, many of these societies and local branches of national institutions were short-lived due to the refusal of each town to combine with either of its neighbours to enhance viability. The history of the local profile of the national system of mechanics' institutes is instructive. These institutes were well regarded and, in many towns, they were extremely successful, promoting working-class self-education through night-schools and employer-release schemes. Each of the Three Towns had its own branch. The Devonport mechanics' institute opened first in 1827, closed in 1838, reopened in 1845 and closed finally in 1881 because it was no longer financially viable. The Stonehouse mechanics' institute opened in 1845 and closed in 1853. The Plymouth mechanics' institute lasted the longest, opening in 1827 and not closing until 1899 when its assets merged with the Plymouth Institute, now the Athenaeum. What is striking is the extent to which the programmes offered by these separate but geographically close institutes shared a similarity. For example, on 19 November 1852, according to the *Western Courier*, Mr D. Low gave the second of two lectures on tobacco and the history of its manufacture, including pipes and other accessories. The report makes it clear that both lectures had been delivered separately to, and the lecturer paid separately by, the Plymouth mechanics' institute.[24] Therefore, it cannot be claimed that the interests of the audiences differed, the same topics appealed across the Three Towns but the Stonehouse institute, once it ran out of funds, closed rather than amalgamating with either neighbour. It could be speculated that neither neighbour was willing to accept adding Stonehouse to its existing town-based name. Alternatively, that Stonehouse itself preferred demise to amalgamation, unfortunately there is no specific information on this.

Running on parallel lines? The railway

Something that unequivocally displays the jealous guarding of their independence by these neighbouring towns, and the consequent obstinate zeal in pursuing a local focus at the cost of wider efficiencies and sensible collaboration relates to the arrival of the railway in the middle of the century. Most urban conglomerations that were the size of Plymouth seized the opportunity to construct striking stations to demonstrate to travellers the importance and civic pride possessed by their destination. Visitors today, looking at the unlovely 1960s architecture of Plymouth's current main station, might presume that an original, grand Victorian station had either been a victim of Second World War bombs or pulled down by iconoclastic 1960s planners. However, there never was a single main station in Plymouth, because of a lack of agreement at the highest level of local politics, complicated by railway company rivalries.[25] In the late 1840s, companies looking for opportunities to extend the network identified Plymouth as the likely 'chief station of Foreign Packets', or the main departure point for foreign mails to the colonies, making it a particularly desirable location for a terminus. Equally, there was recognition of the military value of linking Devonport and Portsmouth.[26] But there was no specific reference as to where within Plymouth that should be. In 1856 and 1857, reportage of the South Devon Railway (SDR) meetings regularly mentioned the need for an expanded Plymouth station and ongoing 'negotiations with landowners' for the purchase of land 'on satisfactory terms', especially in view of the extension of the line into Cornwall.[27] Nevertheless, a close survey of local newspapers reveals there was no planned collaboration to create a unitary grand terminus for the Three Towns.

The first company to build a line to Plymouth was the SDR, which between 1847 and 1848 laid track from Exeter to a temporary depot in Laira, extended the following year to Millbay, but this was essentially intended to serve the commercial traffic of Plymouth.[28] Subsequently, with demands from Devonport (especially the naval authorities) and Stonehouse, a number of small railway companies emerged and merged, building a variety of stations such as Plymouth Millbay, Devonport Albert Road, Marsh Mills and the current main Plymouth station, originally North Road. This sparked the first debates about the construction of a rail terminus to serve the Three Towns. By the 1870s, these small lines had been absorbed by the Great Western Railway (GWR). In that decade, another major player entered the scene, in the shape of the London and South Western Railway (LSWR) which finally achieved its ambition of building a rival to the GWR line, advertising its aim of serving Devonport 'properly' with a terminus at Plymouth Friary and another set of stations on the way. It was the arrival of this line that spurred the construction of North Road to serve the lines of both companies.

In the 1870s, the rivalry between the GWR and LSWR meant a reinvigoration of the discussion over where a Plymouth main terminus should be located. Both railway companies were increasingly conscious of the unsustainability of so many small and often cramped stations with poor facilities.[29] Yet not one of the towns was willing to cede in favour of the other two, preferring divergence to convergence. Agreement seemed within reach on a greenfield site at the edge of Roborough that was part of Stonehouse parish but easily accessible to the other two boroughs. Ultimately, Plymouth and Devonport councillors were obstinately resistant to committing their ratepayers to funding part of the cost of a grand station and Stonehouse was unable to pay for it alone. Another difficulty was its name: Plymouth was the obvious choice externally but neither Devonport nor Stonehouse could accept that. This was the final nail in the coffin of a Three Towns' grand station. Nineteenth-century Plymouth never achieved that symbol of Victorian civic unity, an architecturally impressive main railway station. The significance of this should not be overlooked, grand station buildings acted as the modern gateway to towns and cities symbolising their membership of the modern age.[30]

Union Street: a practical union?

This emphasis on disunion can be taken too far. On closer examination, what the issues and incidents highlighted above relate to are the power struggles and rivalries between local elites within the towns and hinterland. This suggests that consciousness of separateness was powerful among those local bigwigs who were determined to guard jealously their authority against potential encroachment. The practical realities, however, were that the borough of Plymouth relied heavily for its prosperity on selling marine stores and associated commodities to the Navy. This meant that, in turn, Devonport was dependent on Plymouth due to its flourishing commercial sector. Stonehouse, where many of the distilleries and breweries were located, needed a robust market to flourish. All of this focusses attention on the ordinary inhabitants who lived and worked across all Three Towns, regardless of the power struggles at the highest level. Should these citizens find themselves before one of the three petty sessions, they might be conscious of local difference in the ways that each Bench treated drunkenness, immorality and disorder. For the most part though, they simply lived their lives and communicated across town boundaries in ways that suggest a sense of union was stronger than disunion among the working-class elements of each at least.

The practicalities of communication are particularly revealing of union, given the clear need that locals had for travelling between the towns on a regular basis. Water transport had been the main form of travel between the towns in their early days, but the development of usable road links was a key feature of late-eighteenth-century development. The Victorian local historian Richard Worth, lauding the improved state of infrastructure in the mid-century, recalled the days when '[land-based] communication between Dock and Plymouth was of a miserable description, consisting of a road by Mill bridge, and a ferry, the boats of which were pulled by ropes from Stonehouse'.[31] The area connecting all three was called Sourpool because of the surrounding marshland, with its unpleasant smell from the stagnant pools contaminated with effluent from Stonehouse. After sunset it became a notoriously desolate and dark place, which gave opportunistic thieves a chance to make a profit from unwary travellers. It was thought prudent for anyone who wanted to cross to either Devonport or Plymouth after dark to wait until a strong enough group who could fight off any marauding thieves or attackers had assembled.[32] New techniques in road and bridge building, allied to new funding strategies, encouraged private enterprise across the country, including the potential income from the increasing amount of travel between the dockyards and Three Towns. First came the replacement of the ferry by the new Stonehouse toll bridge, completed in 1773. This was fed by a new turnpike road opened in 1784 that provided a link at one end to Plymouth and at the other to Devonport. It was dubbed Union Road, almost certainly for the purely practical reason that the road on either side of the Stonehouse bridge provided a link bringing all Three Towns together and enabling travellers to pass swiftly over the tarmacked road surfaces and solid stone bridge. The provision of tollhouses on the bridge and the road also provided greater security to users.

The new road was so popular that traffic increased to a level where bridge and road both had to be widened to accommodate users. As part of this widening process in 1815, a short section was constructed across the marshes, and an extension added called New Road, leading into Stonehouse. Over the next thirty years, despite the consciousness of separate identity, a project to link the Three Towns came into being, seeking to provide a facility through which the people could move freely for work, commercial and leisure opportunities. This was the development of Union Street, deliberately named to symbolise the importance of an easy linkage between the Three Towns. Substantially, the vision was that of local architect, John Foulston. If the bones of Union Street were there by 1815, it was his mid-1820s vision that made it of local significance. His concept was of a grand street, broad in width and running all the way from the heart of Plymouth up to the centre of the new Devonport. At a mile and a half it was thought by contemporary admirers to be the longest street in England. Foulston conceived his grand project as the construction of what became known as a boulevard which terminated outside his Devonport Guildhall (which easily outshone Plymouth's medieval Guildhall).[33] The positioning of the new Devonport column was to be aligned with the axis of Union Street. At the heart of this visionary upmarket street was The Octagon, intended by Foulston to be the harmonious fulcrum where all Three Towns met. It was estimated that by the 1860s, some 26,000 people passed daily through The Octagon, with 15,000 going over the bridge from both Plymouth and Stonehouse into Devonport to work and returning home at night (see Figure 7.1 for detail from a map of 1845).[34]

Union Street's heyday was represented by the opening of Rendle's Botanical Gardens in August 1850, when 6,000 visitors of 'the highest respectability' including foreign ambassadors flocked to the Three Towns to witness the event. They were entertained by the bands of the Royal Marines and Royal Welsh Fusiliers and in that upbeat mood, were invited to admire its archery field, pleasure promenade, peach and pine houses, and melon and cucumber pits.[35] It explicitly presented an example of collaboration between all Three Towns in that the mayors of Plymouth and Devonport were joint presidents of the Gardens, and of the eight Vice-Presidents, four were from Stonehouse.[36]

It is easy to point out that Foulston's grandiose plans were, from the beginning, compromised. Plans to establish a locomotive steam carriage

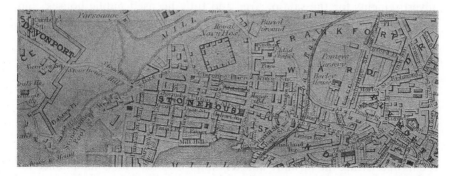

Figure 7.1 Detail showing Union Street from R. Brown, 'Plan of Plymouth, Stonehouse and Devonport', in *Route Book of Devon: A Guide for the Stranger & Tourist* (1845; new edition: Exeter: Henry Besley, 1850), pp. 282–283. Image courtesy of the University of Plymouth.

from Plymouth to Devonport adjacent or along Union Street were rejected in 1836; however, by 1871 a tramline had been constructed, improving communication.[37] By 1895 one local commentator asserted that 'notwithstanding, its extraordinary length ... its effect is mean and unimpressive to a degree'.[38] From the twentieth-century perspective, Trewin wrote acerbically that Foulston 'had little luck with Union Street which was always the family's awkward child and has never known what to do with itself'.[39] It must be admitted that even at the time of the grand opening of the Botanical Gardens, Union Street had become locally notorious in epitomising the social problems associated with drunkenness and immoral behaviour across the Three Towns. Yet a case can be made that because of its strategic location, Union Street unconsciously played a significant, if not formally recognised, role in paving the way for later unification.

The key thoroughfare

The newly named Union Street was more than just a physical bridge, as its name implies its purpose was to expressly unify the Three Towns. A few Union Streets can be found in other towns and cities including Aberdeen, Bristol, Manchester, Cardiff, Southport, Kendal, Torquay and there is the 'Great' Union Street in London renamed from Duke and Queen Street in 1813, but none were as deliberately designed to promote a coming together of communities. What, on the one hand, made the management of Union Street more difficult but, on the other hand, more important, was the development of Millbay Docks in the 1840s and the opening of the Millbay railway station on 2 April 1849 making Union Street, and in particular the Stonehouse section, the main commercial hub for the Three Towns. This was now its busiest part, 'awash with hatters, milliners' and clothing stores for the wealthy.[40] After the enactment of the Beerhouse Act 1830 it also became increasingly awash with beer and alcohol with a constant stream of advertisements for the sale of 'free and fully licensed public houses' and beerhouses.[41] By the late nineteenth century, there were around 100 public houses in Stonehouse alone, sixty of which were either on or within 100 yards of Union Street.[42]

The denigrators of the value of Union Street, at the time and subsequently, pointed out that though the shops may have attracted a respectable clientele, the pubs inevitably attracted sailors bringing with them incidents of drunkenness, prostitution and associated forms of petty crime. Immorality was rife as brothel keepers along its length or on neighbouring streets would maintain the façade of legitimacy by applying for beer licences for their downstairs rooms and letting the upstairs quarters to prostitutes who companioned local sailors (naval and commercial) while on shore leave. By the 1860s there were 154 brothels, most with beerhouse licences, and over 100 prostitutes in just two streets leading off Union Street adjacent to the Stonehouse barracks.[43] Any attempt to limit the supply of alcohol on or contiguous to the street presented another dilemma for contemporaries, as councillor Samuel Elliott informed the 1868 Select Committee on the Sale of Liquors on Sunday Bill. Outlining Plymouth's position on the proposed ban on sale of alcohol on Sundays he confirmed that many of the town's 3,000 visiting sailors, when on shore leave, were housed not just in lodging houses and in some cases the more respectable seamen's missions but in rooms above inns and alehouses. The need for somewhere comfortable to spend their leisure hours, especially in bad weather, ensured the popularity of the taprooms where men could smoke and drink, play cards and make music to sing or dance to. The seamen's missions were more sober and so a less inviting milieux for such enjoyments, the reality as Elliott pointed out, was that these licensed establishments made a significant contribution to 'the commerce of the town'.[44]

Managing the disorder associated with a thoroughfare that passed through three different policing and petty session jurisdictions was always going to be difficult and could certainly be perceived as a sign of disunion and separation. Plymouth's notoriously puritanical Chief Constable, Joseph Sowerby, expressed particular frustration about the impossibility of policing the Plymouth end of Union Street, which he identified as 'The most difficult street to manage'.[45] Under his supervision were eighteen fully licensed houses, twenty-two indoor beerhouses and six off-licences as well as a number of other leisure-associated establishments including restaurants and entertainment venues. In office from 1892, Sowerby, unlike his predecessor Arthur Wreford, was a self-declared and active temperance supporter like many of the Plymouth local elite. He was sponsored by them in adopting a vigorous approach to the regulation of licensed premises and consumption of alcohol, and sought, with only moderate success, to encourage the other jurisdictions to do the same. To an extent, he succeeded. A close examination of the newspaper reportage of incidents suggests that in the period up to 1914, policing practices along Union Street became more consistent and despite the delineation in jurisdiction, the situation advanced to a position where police officers would voluntarily and often be compelled to cross their force boundary to assist each other. For example, in 1895 the Stonehouse police came to the assistance of the Plymouth police who were trying to quell an affray involving a number of drunken sailors.[46] The provision of such mutual aid and necessity of combining strength to deal with such incidents undoubtedly paved the way for the successful amalgamation, in 1914, of all three forces into one Plymouth Police Force under Sowerby's direction.

Temperance and totality

Linked to policing and the evidence of growing harmonisation between practice in the Three Towns, there was also evidence of growing union in terms of the management of leisure activities, with a growth of support among women and local clergy in particular for temperance initiatives. At one level, the responses of the Three Towns reflected their differing religious

profiles. As mentioned above, Plymouth had been long noted for its Nonconformity and strong presence of Baptist chapels, various Methodist churches,
as well as Congregationalists and Unitarians. There were Nonconformist
places of worship found across all Three Towns but there was undoubtedly
a heavier concentration in Plymouth and with larger congregations. Devonport was part of the parish of Stoke Damerel. At the start of the nineteenth
century, outside the parish church of St Andrew and St Mary, the only Anglican place of worship was within the naval base, but developments during
the 1840s ensured the construction of five daughter parishes.[47] In Stonehouse, there was only one Anglican parish church: St George's, but again a
number of Nonconformist churches and chapels. Many of the womenfolk
belonging to prominent families in all Three Towns were powerfully in favour of at least temperance, if not of teetotalism. The elite male inhabitants
of Devonport, because of its naval presence, took a more relaxed approach
than did Plymouth, and those of Stonehouse were even more tolerant, given
how highly dependent the town was on the liquor trade (eleven of Plymouth's
sixteen local breweries operated or had outlets on or near to the Stonehouse
section of Union Street).[48]

Ironically, it was Devonport that would become identified as the leading
town in the cross-Three Towns temperance efforts thanks to Dame Agnes
Weston, familiar to all as 'the Sailor's Friend'. While she did not neglect
the commercial port, her main focus was on the Royal Navy's seamen. The
Plymouth and Stonehouse Seamen's and Soldiers' Friend Society set up
in 1820 on Castle Street focussed on the commercial marine industry. In
comparison, Devonport did not provide any equivalent missions until Miss
Weston arrived, full of fervour. With support from women across the Three
Towns she founded the Devonport Seamen's Mission and the first Royal
Sailors' Rest next to the Dockyard gates in May 1876, replicating similar
Christian rest homes she had set up in Portsmouth.[49]

It can also be argued that it was the combined moral pressure from
Plymouth and Devonport upon Stonehouse in this cause that subconsciously
drew the towns together. It is no coincidence that Union Street was the focal
point for the public manifestation of the temperance cause with regular meetings and processions held along the street and in adjacent buildings encouraging people to sign the pledge of abstinence or teetotalism. In 1871, the British
Medical Association along with the local temperance societies held its thir-
ty-ninth Annual Meeting at different locations in Plymouth and Devonport
including a temperance breakfast on the final day in acknowledgement of
their equal importance.[50] The determination of the conjoined Plymouth and
Devonport campaigners reached its climax in September 1887 with the so-
termed 'Grand Monster Temperance Demonstration' where all those pledg-
ing personal abstention gathered including The Blue Ribband Army, Church
of England Temperance Society, Total Abstinence society and 'other kindred
organisations that operate within the Three Towns united'.[51] In a further
example of union, Aggie Weston was now President of the tripartite Plymouth, Stonehouse and Devonport Ladies Temperance Association. Starting in

Devonport Park the procession made its way along Union Street to Plymouth with a rhetoric of unification that called upon 'all good citizens ... to combine their electoral influences, so as to secure to the people in their separate localities the power to banish the liquor traffic from their midst'.[52] Presenting the National Temperance League annual report later that month at Exeter Hall in London, the Bishop of London publicly praised Weston and her friends for their work that year in taking 3,952 pledges and distributing 700 cards of medals and awards to sailors and soldiers in Devonport and Portsmouth who had kept the pledge for between one and twenty years. The temperance campaign therefore started a process of unification both expressly and implicitly that had an effect on all classes across the Three Towns. By 1895, for instance, Miss Weston's Ladies Temperance Association was being referred to as the Three Towns Temperance Association.[53]

But in terms of evidencing this link it is the list of the leading members of the Plymouth Temperance Society dated 1894 which really underlines the influence of the elite temperancers in supporting and promoting amalgamation between the Three Towns. These included the well-respected Joseph Sowerby, the dynamic Chief Constable of Plymouth City Police, and another prominent figure in Plymouth social and political circles, Henry Whitfield. This 'smart up to date editor of the *Western Independent*' regularly 'preached amalgamation' in his newspaper.[54] It also featured Joseph Arthur Bellamy, chairman of the Plymouth Chamber of Commerce and a director of the lucrative Sutton Harbour Company. Later as mayor of Plymouth, he would lead the negotiations for amalgamation across the Three Towns in 1914 (see Figure 7.2 for an early-twentieth-century postcard view of Union Street).

Figure 7.2 A view of Union Street from a postcard in W.H. Smith's Kingsway Real Photo series. Image courtesy of James Gregory.

Conclusion

What this chapter has revealed is that in understanding issues of union and disunion within communities, it is important to look beyond the headlines suggesting the dominance of one or other of these forces. Evidence of disunion across the Three Towns during the nineteenth century is particularly easy to find as it featured in and characterises much of the newspaper reportage of that era. However, looking beyond this evidence, to the mass of the everyday population of this urban conglomeration it becomes clear that a *de facto* social and community unification had already emerged in the late nineteenth century. Typically, men and women lived in one and worked in another of the towns as a matter of course. They shopped according to taste and purse across all three, and as Union Street's commercial (if not aesthetic) success underlines, they drank and enjoyed entertainments with scant regard for the formal boundaries of separation paving the way for an easier formal Corporation in October 1914.[55] Shared aims also drew together the women of the Three Towns in particular, with charitable, religious, and temperance associations gradually unifying to strengthen the impact of their public messages and reform agendas.

Sixty years later, Trewin reflected that the modern residents of the unified city of Plymouth still acknowledged a consciousness of being parts of such different traditions and heritage. The 'geographical accident that had jammed them together on a roughly serrated peninsula between two rivers' might, once unity had been forced on them, have 'made one city of them'. Instead, he surmised, 'they have kept their own personalities, voices and loyalties'.[56]

However, too much emphasis should not be placed on this kind of nostalgia. While the separate identities can and have endured, what is at least equally powerful is the sense of unity among the ordinary people of Plymouth.

Notes

1 C. Hall, *British Naval Strategy in the Napoleonic War 1803–1815* (Manchester: Manchester University Press, 1992), pp. 38–41.

2 J.C. Trewin, *Portrait of Plymouth* (London: Hale, 1973), p. 89.

3 C. Gill, *Plymouth: A New History* (Newton Abbot: David and Charles, 1966).

4 D. Loades, *The Tudor Navy: An Administrative, Political and Military History* (Abingdon: Routledge, 2013).

5 R. Worth, *The History of Plymouth from the Earliest Time to the Present Time* (Plymouth: Brendon, 1873), pp. 162–169.

6 Worth, *The History of Plymouth*, pp. 62–64.

7 Worth, *The History of Plymouth*, p. 90.

8 D. Johnson, *The Changing Shape of English Nonconformity 1825–1925* (Oxford: Oxford University Press, 1999); J. Bradley, *Religion, Revolution and English Radicalism: Nonconformity Eighteenth Century Politics and Society* (Cambridge: Cambridge University Press, 2002), p. 397; D. Coomer, *English Dissent under the Early Hanoverians* (London: Epworth, 1946), p. 14.

9 A. Collins, *The Peerage of England; containing a Genealogical and Historical Account of all the Peers of that Kingdom*, 7 vols (London: Woodfall, 1768), vol. 7, p. 279; W. Burt, *Review of the Mercantile, Trading and Manufacturing State, Interests and Capabilities of the Port of Plymouth* (Plymouth: Nettleton, 1816), p. 177.

10 'Market Towns of Devon: Stonehouse, 1842', *Penny Cyclopedia of the Society for the Diffusion of Useful Knowledge*, 27 vols (London: Charles Knight, 1833–1844), vol. 14, p. 12.

11 L.F.W. Jewitt, *A History of Plymouth* (London: Simpkin Marshall, 1873), p. 270; R. Worth, *History of the Town and Borough of Devonport, Sometime Plymouth Dock* (Plymouth: Brendon, 1870).

12 The land on which much of Devonport was built belonged to the St Aubyn family who took a keen interest in the town; Stonehouse was largely land-owned by the Edgcumbe family; the Earls of Mount Edgcumbe (related to the St Aubyns) also took care to be involved in local Stonehouse politics.

13 Worth, *History of the Town and Borough of Devonport*.

14 Z. Mudge, *Mudge Memoirs* (Truro: Netherton and Worth, 1883), p. 86.

15 'Devonport Column', *Caledonian Mercury*, 21 August 1824.

16 L. Jewitt, *History of Plymouth* (Plymouth: Luke, 1873), p. 397.

17 'Devon Midsummer Sessions', *Exeter Flying Post*, 3 July 1861. County average was one constable per 1,600/1,700 population; Torquay was 1 to 2,000.

18 'Devon Midsummer Sessions', *Exeter Flying Post*, 1 July 1863.

19 Parliamentary Papers, *Reports of Inspectors of Constabulary to Secretary of State, 1880–81* (1882), p. 24.

20 *Reports of Inspectors of Constabulary to Secretary of State, 1880–81*, p. 245.

21 Plymouth 1,387, Stonehouse 1,301, Devonport 1,146, Parliamentary Papers, *General Index for the Report of Public Petitions 1833–1852, 1854–55* (Cmnd 381, 1855), pp. 34, 35.

22 *General Index for the Report of Public Petitions 1833–1852, 1854–55*, pp. 909–910.

23 1854: 59 cases in Plymouth and 15 in Stonehouse; 1866: 13 cases in Plymouth and 0 in Stonehouse. Parliamentary Papers, *Report of the Cholera Epidemic of 1866 in England by William Farr* (Cmnd 4072, 1868), p. 9. See also Jewitt, *History of Plymouth*, p. 478.

24 'Stonehouse', *Western Courier*, 24 November 1852.

25 See, for example, 'Railways. Rival Westerns', *Exeter and Plymouth Gazette*, 24 January 1846.

26 'South Devon Railway', *Exeter and Plymouth Gazette*, 3 March 1849; 'Extension of the Narrow Gauge to Plymouth', *Exeter and Plymouth Gazette*, 16 July 1853.

27 See, for example, 'South Devon Railway', *Exeter and Plymouth Gazette*, 1 March 1856.

28 'The South Devon Railway to Laira', *Exeter and Plymouth Gazette*, 13 May 1848; 'South Devon Railway: Completion of the Line into Plymouth', *Exeter and Plymouth Gazette*, 7 April 1849. The SDR later amalgamated with the GWR.

29 'Devon and Cornwall Railway Bill', *Exeter and Plymouth Gazette*, 24 April 1872; 'The South Devon, and Devon and Cornwall Railway Bills', *Exeter and Plymouth Gazette*, 20 June 1872; 'The London and South Western Railway', *Exeter and Plymouth Gazette*, 13 February 1877.

30 P. Dobraszczyk, *Iron, Ornament and Architecture in Victorian Britain: Myth and Modernity, Excess and Enchantment* (Abingdon: Routledge, 2014), pp. 230–231.

31 Worth, *The History of Plymouth*, p. 32.

32 Trewin, *Portrait of Plymouth*, p. 89.

33 This was replaced by the current French Gothic construction in 1879.

34 Councillor J.W. Wilson quoted in 'Devon Midsummer Sessions', *Exeter Flying Post*, 3 July 1861.

35 'Opening of the Plymouth Royal Botanical Gardens', *Illustrated London News*, 3 August 1850; Trewin, *Portrait of Plymouth*, p. 89.
36 'South Devon Botanical and Horticultural Society', *Western Courier*, 29 January 1851.
37 Jewitt, *History of Plymouth*, p. 481.
38 H.W. Brewer, 'Plymouth: Or the Three Towns', *The Graphic*, 3 August 1895.
39 Trewin, *Portrait of Plymouth*, p. 89.
40 C. Robinson, *Union Street* (Plymouth: Pen & Ink, 2000), p. 20.
41 *Western Morning News*, 16 July 1887.
42 Robinson, *Union Street*, p. 62. The Beerhouse Act 1830 virtually allowed anyone to set up a public house or off-licence.
43 *Royal Cornwall Gazette*, 14 December 1865.
44 Parliamentary Papers, Select Committee on Sale of Liquors on Sunday Bill, Special Report, paper 402 (1867–1868), pp. 242–245.
45 *Western Times*, 6 April 1904.
46 *Western Weekly News*, 30 November 1895.
47 With a member of the St Aubyn family always holding the living of Stoke Damerel, they were determined to hang on to their moral and ecclesiastical authority by ensuring the new churches of Devonport were not independent parishes but still linked to and dependent on Stoke Damerel and so to the St Aubyns.
48 Robinson, *Union Street*, p. 72.
49 Plymouth and West Devon Record Office, Reference 750, The Royal Sailors' Rest in Portsmouth was not built until 1881.
50 *Western Morning News*, 12 August 1871.
51 *Western Weekly News*, 24 September 1887.
52 *Western Morning News*, 22 September 1887; *Western Weekly News*, 24 September 1887.
53 *Western Morning News*, 22 March 1895.
54 *Western Morning News*, 23 September 1902.
55 The population of nearly 214,000 became a single entity under the mayoralty of Sir Thomas Baker, or as Trewin concludes, like Malaprop's Cerberus 'three gentleman at once', Trewin, *Portrait of Plymouth*, p. 95.
56 Trewin, *Portrait of Plymouth*, p. 95.

Bibliography

Anon., 'Devonport Column', *Caledonian Mercury*, 21 August 1824.
Anon., 'Market Towns of Devon: Stonehouse, 1842', *Penny Cyclopedia of the Society for the Diffusion of Useful Knowledge*, 27 vols (London: Charles Knight, 1833–1844), vol. 14.
Anon., 'Opening of the Plymouth Royal Botanical Gardens', *Illustrated London News*, 3 August 1850.
Anon., 'South Devon Botanical and Horticultural Society', *Western Courier*, 29 January 1851.
Brewer, H.W. 'Plymouth: Or the Three Towns', *The Graphic*, 3 August 1895.
Burt, W. *Review of the Mercantile, Trading and Manufacturing State, Interests and Capabilities of the Port of Plymouth* (Plymouth: Nettleton, 1816).
Collins, A. *The Peerage of England; Containing a Genealogical and Historical Account of all the Peers of that Kingdom*, 7 vols (London: Woodfall, 1768).
Coomer, D. *English Dissent under the Early Hanoverians* (London: Epworth, 1946).

Dobraszczyk, P. *Iron, Ornament and Architecture in Victorian Britain: Myth and Modernity, Excess and Enchantment* (Abingdon: Routledge, 2014).

Exeter and Plymouth Gazette.

Exeter Flying Post.

Gill, C. *Plymouth: A New History* (Newton Abbot: David and Charles, 1966).

Hall, C. *British Naval Strategy in the Napoleonic War 1803–1815* (Manchester: Manchester University Press, 1992).

Jewitt, L.F.W. *A History of Plymouth* (London: Simpkin Marshall, 1873).

Jewitt, L.F.W. *A History of Plymouth* (Plymouth: Luke, 1873).

Johnson, D. *The Changing Shape of English Nonconformity 1825–1925* (Oxford: Oxford University Press, 1999).

Loades, D. *The Tudor Navy: An Administrative, Political and Military History* (Abingdon: Routledge, 2013).

Mudge, Z. *Mudge Memoirs* (Truro: Netherton and Worth, 1883).

Parliamentary Papers, *General Index for the Report of Public Petitions 1833–1852, 1854–55* (Cmnd 381, 1855).

Parliamentary Papers, *Report of the Cholera Epidemic of 1866 in England by William Farr* (Cmnd 4072, 1868).

Parliamentary Papers, *Reports of Inspectors of Constabulary to Secretary of State, 1880 – 81* (1882).

Parliamentary Papers, Select Committee on Sale of Liquors on Sunday Bill, Special Report, Paper 402 (1867–1868).

Plymouth and West Devon Record Office, Reference 750.

Robinson, C. *Union Street* (Plymouth: Pen & Ink, 2000).

Royal Cornwall Gazette.

Trewin, J.C. *Portrait of Plymouth* (London: Hale, 1973).

Western Courier.

Western Morning News.

Western Times.

Western Weekly News.

Worth, R. *History of the Town and Borough of Devonport, Sometime Plymouth Dock* (Plymouth: Brendon, 1870).

Worth, R. *The History of Plymouth from the Earliest Time to the Present Time* (Plymouth: Brendon, 1873).

Part IV

Union and disunion in the United States of America

8 The union of enslaved couples during the disunion of the nation

Love, discord and separations in US slavery and thereafter

Emily West

Unions and disunions worked on many different levels in the nineteenth century. The US Civil War of 1861–1865 wrenched the country apart and the American Union survived only because of the Northern (Unionist) victory, after which the defeated Southern states lost their dream of a new *Confederate* United States. They subsequently endured being forced back into a Union they had wanted to leave because of their desire for continued slaveholding and increased states' rights. Such meta-narratives of Union and disunion are well known, but this chapter takes a different approach in pursuing the meanings of union and disunion through people's intimate lives at a time of national upheaval.

Focussing on enslaved people in the US South, mostly those from South Carolina, who experienced the war first hand, this chapter explores the way in which enslaved people in the Southern states of the United States negotiated their marriages in late antebellum times and during the era of the Civil War and emancipation. It is difficult for historians to probe these more intimate lives of enslaved people, so often lacking in written testimony and hard to decipher from surviving evidence. Significantly, as non-citizens of the United States, the law did not recognise enslaved people's marriages as valid, but tradition, custom and predominantly Christian religious practice meant that wider Southern society recognised that enslaved people should (and did) enter wedlock. Profit-hungry enslavers had every reason to encourage these marriages since every child born to enslaved women they owned added to their wealth. So slaveholders frequently became involved in their enslaved people's intimate relationships, their interventions ranging from arranging religious services and celebrations at marriage ceremonies (whether wanted or not), to more coercive attempts to persuade, cajole and sometimes even to force, their enslaved people into wedlock. Slaves challenged this involvement. Rebecca Fraser has uncovered the ways in which enslaved people fought for the ability to engage in courtship on their own terms in North Carolina. Even wedding ceremonies themselves, where couples often jumped over a broom, were contested events between the enslaved and slaveholders according to research by Thomas Will and Tyler Parry.[1]

The institution of slavery unsurprisingly caused problems for enslaved people's marriages and meant that a state of union could easily tip over unto disunion. Issues facing enslaved couples included their relative lack of control over visiting arrangements when their marriages crossed farms or plantations, the ultimate authority of enslavers to physically control people (and sexually assault enslaved women), and the impact of sale and separations upon an institution allegedly sacred under God. Moreover, the Civil War and emancipation brought a new range of problems for couples seeking to preserve their matrimonial unions. The Thirteenth Constitutional Amendment of 1865, which legally abolished slavery in the United States, presented freedpeople with more issues around their marriages' legitimacy and even their desirability, within an already complicated context of wedlock.

Despite all the complications that entering the union of matrimony under bondage might cause, enslaved people undoubtedly wanted to marry because wedlock provided a bulwark against the oppression of slavery and enabled intimate partners with the ability to support one another in difficult times. Prioritising the evidence of enslaved and formerly enslaved people themselves, this chapter explores the changing nature of friction between enslaved and free couples from antebellum times through the Civil War and emancipation. It suggests that clearly defined gendered roles constituted the main source of tensions between enslaved spouses in the antebellum era. While both partners worked together with their wider familial networks to survive the regime, a failure to fulfil one's gendered domestic chores often resulted in significant marital strife. Intimate partner abuse also caused marital upsets, although most enslaved people cajoled into wedlock grew to love their spouses over time.

Negotiating marriages under slavery was hard enough, but the Civil War years presented enslaved couples with new sources of tensions, especially for those families seeking refuge behind Union army lines. Army officials often had expectations of gendered roles that did not fit the typical familial dynamics of enslaved people. War understandably exacerbated spousal antagonisms and conflicts, as well as providing men and women with different routes to freedom. The chapter concludes with an exploration of the ways in which emancipation in 1865 affected the marital relationships of formerly enslaved people. The majority chose to validate their marriages under American law as they could now legally do so, while others linked personal freedom with the wider process of emancipation and chose to leave those to whom they were unhappily wed. Individual manifestations of union and disunion hence replicated in microcosm the broader upheavals endured by the United States as a whole.

Historiographical context

Historians have thankfully now moved away from 'matriarchy versus patriarchy' debates about whether men or women dominated enslaved people's households largely based upon their own preconceptions and white paradigms about household structure.[2] But until fairly recently, the nature of the intimate unions between enslaved spouses was relatively neglected. Most previous research on enslaved people's community lives focussed on camaraderie and support networks along, rather than across, gendered lines because spousal relationships have proven rather more difficult to probe and questions about the nature of enslaved people's intimacies under the regime remain.[3] For example, it is now accepted that the majority of enslaved people appear to have settled into heterosexual marital relationships and spent a good deal of time with their spouses once work for slaveholders had been completed. However, a lack of primary evidence means same-sex intimate relationships are likely to remain something for historians to speculate on.[4]

Historians such as Larry Hudson, and John D'Emilio and Estelle B. Freedman, have drawn parallels between wedlock under slavery and in pre-capitalist agricultural communities elsewhere in the world. Romantic love in marriage unions came secondary to practical and pragmatic considerations that facilitated survival, including physical strength, health, and technical and mental ability.[5] Conversely, I have argued elsewhere that enslaved people were early pioneers in marrying for romantic love because they had nothing to gain or lose materially.[6] Tera Hunter's recent book on nineteenth-century African-American marriage argues enslaved marriage was ultimately tautological – neither prohibited nor legally possible. She argues marriages during – and after slavery too – complicated forms, and has brought depth and nuance to understandings of enslaved couples' heterosexual relationships.[7]

Spousal hostilities, sexual or domestic abuse and adultery within slave marriage have been rather neglected in historical analysis until fairly recently. Jeff Forret's *Slave against Slave* claims that disputes and violence within enslaved communities often revolved around notions of honour and constructions of masculinity and femininity that displayed parallels with those of white society. It is harder still to find evidence about sexual assaults within enslaved communities rather than those inflicted by white slaveholders although some historians are tackling black-on-black sexual violence within the context of wider patriarchal structures. This research draws upon the pioneering theoretical works of Susan Brownmiller on rape and Darlene Clark Hine's 'culture of dissemblance' whereby women's reluctance to divulge details of black-on-black sexual violence meant many cases of domestic sexual violence simply never made it to the historical record.[8]

Because evidence is missing from historical records it does not necessarily correlate that it did not happen. This chapter therefore assesses disunion within marriage from the antebellum era of slavery through to the early days of freedom, especially using Works Progress Administration (WPA) interviews with formerly enslaved people from the late 1930s and published autobiographies written before emancipation. It also uses various kinds of evidence from slaveholders when they became involved in their slaves' domestic relationships, including plantation rulebooks, letters and diaries. But the chapter also offers some speculations about feelings and emotions in the past – highly relevant sentiments when considering romantic relationships and their changing nature over time. The historian Stephanie Camp writes:

> documentation does not indicate significance; indeed many social truths are unspoken and therefore undocumented … we [historians] can also employ the imagination, closely reading our documents in their context and speculating about their meaning.

Hence the idea that archives have 'silences' that historians should address has increasingly gained credence, especially among historians of subaltern women, for whom few written sources remain.[9]

Antebellum-era marriages and gendered expectations

Most antebellum-era enslaved couples found their marriages a place of refuge and a mechanism of support under adversity but their partnerships were also subject to complex issues of discord. These included the tiredness caused by performing hard labour for slaveholders as well as working on behalf of their families; the stresses caused by trying to raise children within an institution of bondage; the everyday threat of sale and separation; the loneliness suffered by those living within cross-plantation families (most of whom only saw their spouse once or twice a week unless they risked 'illicit' visits without a written pass) and sexual assault upon enslaved women by white men.[10]

Enslaved couples' disputes often revolved around onerous domestic responsibilities, including cooking, cleaning, fishing, hunting, washing, making and repairing clothes or utensils; making goods that could be sold to supplement the family's income; raising children and sometimes tending animals. The separation of these tasks reveals marked gender divisions. Men fished and hunted, and they were more often able to leave their plantations and to acquire the skills needed to make and sell supplementary goods to support their families.[11] Husbands and enslavers expected women to raise the children, cook, clean, wash and repair.[12] So women lived in a more restricted and geographically contained domestic space than their male partners. However, the most common exception to manifestations of these gendered roles was found within the South Carolina and Georgia Lowcountry coastal regions, where enslavers made use of a 'gang' labour system to grow cotton and rice that permitted enslaved people a small amount of time to themselves at the end of the day when all their 'tasks' had been completed. The task system hence differed from the more common 'gang' system of labour utilised elsewhere in the slave South, where people simply laboured from 'sundown to sunup' under the watchful eye of an overseer or driver. Importantly, the task system enabled enslaved people to tend their own small plots of land known as 'patches' where men, women and children all worked together in a collective enterprise growing provisions and supplementing their meagre and monotonous diets.[13]

Life was undoubtedly hard for all enslaved people whether they worked under the task or gang system, but all women had extra burdens placed upon them because they were expected to bear and raise valuable children in *addition* to performing work for slaveholders and household chores for their families, increased their levels of exhaustion, and contributed to friction between spouses. Female slaves worked a 'double day' before other women in American society, a point that puts the notion of African-American households as America's first 'modern' families in a rather more negative light.[14] WPA interviews with formerly enslaved people supports this assertion of a 'double day' of labour. Chana Littlejohn recalled that slaveholders excused sick women from fieldwork but had to do domestic chores instead.[15] Benjamin Russell described enslaved mothers devoting Saturday afternoons to domestic work such as washing. Enslavers thus granted female fieldworkers with children 'time off' on a Saturday afternoon, but only to 'wash' and care for their children, and owners revoked this 'freedom' at busy times of year such as during the annual harvest.[16]

Enslaved communities did not tolerate any perceived 'laziness' among women or men when it came to domestic responsibilities. The autobiographer Charles Ball related the story of an enslaved woman, Lydia, who was married to a man who 'maintained ... a kind of lazy dignity at home'. He also beat his wife.[17] Ball attributed the behaviour of Lydia's husband to his unusual background; apparently he was an African prince. Ball's comments therefore implicitly suggest that the norm among most American-born slaves was towards spousal support; conflict and disunion only ensued when a partner 'failed' in their household responsibilities. Ball hence drew a distinction between himself, American born and virtuous, and the African-born man, who was not, a tactic he no doubt hoped would endear him to his largely abolitionist, Northern readership.

Enslaved people placed a great deal of emphasis on these gendered roles because the system of bondage worked to undermine them. Slaveholders, not husbands, provided food, shelter and clothing for families. Likewise, enslavers dually exploited enslaved women as labourers and reproducers – expecting them to engage in hard physical labour as well as bear and rear valuable children – and their labour undermined contemporary notions of femininity within wider white society that emphasised piety, purity, submissiveness and domesticity.[18] In short, enslaved women's work enabled white women, especially those who lived on wealthy plantations with many enslaved people, to use their race-based privilege to live lives full of leisure and luxury, albeit within a narrowly defined sphere of 'ladylike' femininity. Writing to her sister-in-law, Maria, Amelia Lines (known as 'Jennie') mentioned that without 'help': 'I could never look nice myself, keep my baby or my house clean'.[19] Consequently then, the use of traditional 'masculine' and 'feminine' roles among enslaved people therefore served as an indirect means of resistance because couples worked together in their attempts to strengthen wider gender conventions that the institution of slavery constantly undermined.

In more intimate realms of life, marital disharmony sometimes arose as a consequence of white men's sexual assaults upon enslaved women, although enslaved men commonly responded to such violence by attempting to help or protect abused women, again operating within a prism of more conventional gendered norms.[20] But sometimes men rejected women when they felt they had engaged in 'voluntary' sexual relations with white men rather than simply being victims of white men's sexual violence. Henry Bibb described in his autobiography how he believed his wife, Malinda, had consensual sex with her master. He wrote: 'She has ever since been regarded as theoretically and practically dead to me as a wife'.[21] Significantly, Bibb did not mention the extent to which his wife may have been forced into such a relationship, and that women's responses to white men's sexual violence can be placed on a spectrum. Obviously, the power dynamic involved in women's relationships with their enslavers meant that their sexual relationships could never be purely loving and consensual.

Conforming to wider nineteenth-century behavioural norms, slaveholders sanctioned enslaved men's use of violence to control their wives, sometimes in an official capacity, but otherwise more informally. For example, the rulebook of John Miller's Cornhill plantation contained the entry: 'No man must whip his wife <u>without my permission</u>'.[22] Miller's recording of such a rule suggests that he expected at least some level of domestic violence among his enslaved people. The South Carolinian slaveholder Emily Wharton Sinkler briefly alluded to marital disharmony in a letter to her mother when she said that her enslaved man, Mollo, had complained that his wife was continually 'fighting and scratching' him.[23] John Springs, of York County, South Carolina, believed one of his enslaved men took his own life because his wife was a 'merciless woman'.[24]

A case of alleged domestic abuse by her slave Jim, upon his wife, Maria, caused great concern for Elizabeth Franklin Perry of Greenville, South Carolina. In a letter to her husband, she wrote that Jim had apparently beaten Maria. Elizabeth then went to their cabin, where she found Maria with 'everything about her filthy, the floor not even swept, the beds, pails etc... all dirty … I talked to her and gave her some good advice about doing better'. Jim admitted he had struck Maria 'about three blows', that she was 'obstinate... and lazy and dirty, that she will not clean the house, wash his clothes or mend them, or even wash hers'. Mrs Perry thus told her husband: 'I want her sold to the first trader who passes... Now I have done with Maria … I have never liked her'.[25] The violence towards Maria was seen as justifiable because she was not adept in her role as homemaker and Elizabeth had no empathy for her.[26]

Sexual violence and enslaved people's marriages

Violence and discord within enslaved people's marriages sometimes took sexual forms.[27] So nineteenth-century patriarchal power structures within which societies had a more general acceptance of husbands' right to use violence to control their wives and ensure their own sexual satisfaction meant that some enslaved women endured years of sexual violence within wedlock, although evidence on these sensitive, intimate themes is understandably scant. Only in the second half of the twentieth century was rape within marriage recognised in the United States, meaning the phenomenon is hard for historians to locate in surviving sources. If one adds to this the archival challenges present when researching slavery this makes the topic harder still to investigate.[28]

However, a careful reading of available testimony throws up some instances of enslaved marriages characterised by men's sexual violence towards women, and slaveholders often enabled these abusive relationships through forcing women into forms of 'wedlock' with men they did not love, men who then forced themselves upon their new 'wives'. Enslavers had a vested interest in encouraging sexual relationships among their chattel (even if not consensual) as part of their pronatalist policies designed to increase their number of enslaved children, because children grew into valuable adults. For example, Mary Gaffney told her WPA interviewer she hated the man that her enslaver forced her to marry: 'I would not let him touch me and he told Master, and Master gave me a real good whipping, so that night I let him have his way'.[29] Perhaps Gaffney's husband believed it was his right to impose himself on his new wife. Gaffney herself also seemed resigned to the fact that she would have to submit to him.

Similarly, in an often-quoted example of sexual violence within wedlock, Rose Williams, of Texas, explained how her master, Hawkins, told her, at just sixteen, how she had to set up home with a man named Rufus. Rose assumed, naively, but understandably considering her youth, that Hawkins expected her to perform domestic work for Rufus, but the reality was more chilling. Rose only realised Rufus's intentions when he climbed into her bed at night; she then fought him off with a poker. However, Hawkins subsequently threatened Rose with a whipping if she did not relent. Rose henceforward allowed Rufus to have sex with her so she would not be punished, and her heartbreaking dilemma reveals something of the anguish of enslaved women forced to make horrendous pragmatic choices in life when all their options were undesirable. Rufus's voice is also lacking here. No doubt he felt his expectation of sexual relations with a woman deemed to be his wife was reasonable, in this sense, of course, both were victims of the power of slaveholders, a point made more broadly by the historian Thomas Foster.[30]

Enslaved marriages during the Civil War

Moving chronologically from antebellum times to the Civil War and era of emancipation, the great conflict that wrenched the United States in two undoubtedly made enslaved men's and women's lives more complicated and more different to each other. As men departed for the battlefront, slave women often remained alone with white women on plantations and farms on what Laura Edwards has described as the 'second home front'.[31]

Unions and disunions in the nation as a whole hence again played out in microcosm within white and black southern homes and communities.

War separated married couples both black and white. The Confederate army first attempted to enforce enslaved men into the military at state level, followed by the Confederate Impressment Law in 1863. Left alone with white women on farms and plantations, women had to support themselves both practically and emotionally. Abraham Lincoln's Emancipation Proclamation of 1863 which freed all enslaved people in states that had seceded from the Union also led, unsurprisingly, to a rush by formerly enslaved men to join the Union forces, just as Lincoln hoped it would. Couples not separated by men's departure to the battlefront sometimes fled slavery together, seeking the relative safety of Union forces within their makeshift camps. Behind Union lines, black couples found their relationships challenged in new ways. The Union forces provided black men with work, and expected them to provide for their families. But this was both unfamiliar and simply impossible for black men who had previously lived under slavery. Couples ended up confined within overcrowded and unsanitary refugee camps where they lacked adequate food, clothing and shelter in conditions sometimes materially worse than slavery itself.[32]

Moreover, black women in Union camps were not treated as subjects in their own right and were perceived only as the *wives* of contraband men. Union attitudes were inherently ironic because no slave women had been fully dependent, in a material sense, upon their husbands. But Union policy was based upon free white middle-class notions of female dependency.[33] So black women in camps, displaying the same sense of initiative as they had during antebellum days, relied on their enterprising spirits, for example, by selling or bartering their own produce. For example, WPA respondent Ellen Campbell, again conveying typically gendered roles, recalled women travelling from the camp to rivers to wash the troops' clothes in return for money or produce.[34] Such additional work undoubtedly added to the marital strains couples already faced.

Susie King Taylor, an African-American nurse in the Civil War who later published her memoirs, likewise remembered black women's enterprising spirit in using gendered expectations to find new forms of work to support their families after Union forces occupied the South Carolina lowcountry area from 1861 onwards:

> There were about six hundred men, women and children on St. Simon's, the women and children being in the majority....The first colored troops did not receive any pay for eighteen months, and the men had to depend wholly on what they received from the commissary, established by General Saxton. A great many of these men had large families, and as they had no money to support them, their wives were obliged to support themselves and children by washing for the officers of the gunboats and the soldiers, and making cakes and pies which they sold to the boys in camp.[35]

Aside from creating a situation where enslaved couples in camps were unable to provide for themselves, Union forces also rather naively saw legal marriage as a solution to this problem. Legal wedlock proved to be a contentious issue for Union authorities, and black responses to their policies also varied. The Union army saw marriage as a solution to the alleged 'dependency' of black women within their camps. Legal wedlock would render black women reliant upon their husbands, they mistakenly believed, *not* Union troops. But black women had their own views and acted on their own initiative. Some *wanted* to partake in the legal marriage ceremonies conducted by Union army clergymen. Enslaved wedlock had been illegal under American law, but *not* custom and practice, so some regarded the legal legitimisation of their marriages as very important. Other women, however, questioned why this was necessary. Former slaves who had undergone wedding ceremonies conducted by a religious leader simply felt their marriages were already legal in the eyes of God. Historian Stephanie McCurry hence argues that regardless of whether they lived in Union or Confederate territory, enslaved men and women took very different paths to emancipation. The route of men was mostly military, but women's road was marital.[36] Furthermore, as persuasively argued by Tera Hunter, marriage served as an instrument of war as policy-makers grappled with the roles of black men and women within marriages that had no legal standing under enslavement.[37]

Emancipation and thereafter

The Thirteenth Constitutional Amendment of 1865 ended slavery in the United States, and this had important ramifications for previously enslaved couples, some of whom linked emancipation in a legal, universal sense, with a more personal sense of what freedom meant. Legal practice varied across the South. Some states required formerly enslaved couples to register their relationships but others did not, and not all couples chose to go down this route anyway.[38] While one meta-narrative of emancipation related to formerly enslaved couples using Union army clergymen and others to formalise their marriages, another strand of this journey into freedom related to formerly enslaved women who used emancipation to *escape* unhappy wedlock. Leslie Schwalm has detailed the experiences of women who complained to the Freedmen's Bureau (set up after the war to assist freedpeople in their new lives) about abusive husbands from whom they wished to separate. She notes that couples in disunion separated for a variety of reasons, including ill treatment and a failure to grant support for spouses and children.[39] Freedwomen increasingly expected husbands to provide.

Lucy Skipwith also used freedom's opportunities to leave her unsatisfactory marriage in Alabama. Unusual in that she wrote letters to her master during slavery and after, Skipwith described in 1865 how she had lived a 'life of trouble' with her enslaved spouse, Armistead, possibly including physical and/or sexual abuse:

Hopewell, [Alabama,] December 7 1865

My dear Master:

I received your letter a few days ago. I was truly glad to see that you were still alive & not gone the way to all the Earth. I was sorry that I had to part with Armistead but I have lived a life of trouble with him, & a white man has ever had to Judge between us, & now to be turned loose from under a master, I know that I could not live with him in peace, therefore I left him. If you have any hard feelings against me on the subject, I hope that you will forgive me for Jesus sake.[40]

Similarly, the formerly enslaved Texan woman Rose Williams left her 'spouse', Rufus, after the war. She told her WPA interviewer she never married, conveying how she never really accepted her relationship with him as legitimate because her slaveholder forced her into an intimate relationship with Rufus.[41]

In contrast, most formerly enslaved couples who had been forced or otherwise cajoled into forms of wedlock by their enslavers more commonly tended to find that their relationships moved in the reverse direction: what was once disunion became more solidly a sense of union and continuities was more significant than changes for these couples. WPA testimony suggests formerly couples simply grew to accept (and sometimes even to feel affection for) each other, and they remained together after emancipation, raising their families in pragmatic fashion. This conveys a clear awareness of the impact of the slave regime upon intimate relationships because couples blamed their former slaveholders for forcing them together rather than each other. In this sense, they recognised their spouses as fellow victims of white enslavers' power and privilege to abuse. These views also subsequently fed into a more collective memory of sexual assault under slavery that minimised the violence women received at the hands of black men precisely because the rapes they endured by white men were so endemic and systemic.

Mary Gaffney therefore chose to stay with Paul through emancipation, and the couple raised five children together.[42] Lizzie Grant, also interviewed by the WPA about her life while enslaved in Virginia, described her wedlock as follows:

Master said it was cheaper to raise slaves than it was to buy them ... I was about 17 years old when I was given to my young Master, me and the man that I called my husband. So our young Master put us to live together to raise from just like you would stock today. They never thought anything about it either. They never cared or thought of our feelings in the matter, of course we got used to one another and never thought anything about the way they put us to live.

Lizzie and her husband had nine children together and their marriage survived emancipation and her husband's subsequent death at the end of the nineteenth century. She never 'married' again.[43]

Conclusions

The majority of enslaved marriages were characterised by great affection, with wedlock serving as a bulwark against the oppression of the regime, and marital relationships were supportive. However, it is also true that marriages were subject to significant tensions, some of which have affected all couples in intimate relationships across time and space while others were specific to slavery itself. Marriage could and did sometimes erupt into violence, or lead spouses to seek solace elsewhere. Enslavement added a unique set of burdens and pressures to the lives of people seeking to make a shared life together despite the arduous nature of their work, the threat of sale and or separation, and the fear of violence – sexual or otherwise. Moreover, tracking the changing dynamics of marriage from slavery through the Civil War to the era of freedom exposes how these burdens and pressures changed, but did not necessarily lessen. New forms of racial subjugation brought new challenges. Despite some diverse experiences, this is essentially a story about continuities of racial oppression for black couples from the antebellum era to the time of Reconstruction despite their attempts to seek intimate unions on their own terms.

Notes

1 For more on enslaved courtship and weddings, see R. Fraser, *Courtship and Love among the Enslaved in North Carolina* (Jackson: University of Mississippi Press, 2007); E. West, *Chains of Love: Slave Couples in Antebellum South Carolina* (Urbana: University of Illinois Press, 2004); T.E. Will, 'Weddings on Contested Grounds: Slave Marriage in the Antebellum South', *The Historian* 62 (Fall 1999), pp. 99–117; T.D. Parry, 'Married in Slavery Time: Jumping the Broom in Atlantic Perspective', *Journal of Southern History* 81:2 (2015), pp. 273–312. The best overview of nineteenth-century black marriage is Tera Hunter's recent book, *Bound in Wedlock: Slave and Free Black Marriage in the Nineteenth Century* (Cambridge, MA: Belknap Press, 2017).

2 Writing in the 1950s, Kenneth Stampp stressed the emasculation of enslaved fathers, unable to 'protect and provide' for their wives and families. Writers of the 1970s, notably Herbert Gutman, reacted against this 'myth of matriarchy' and stressed the strong role played by enslaved men as heads of households. In reaction, Deborah White questioned how far the pendulum should swing in favour of patriarchy. She also suggested that the loaded term 'matriarchy' be replaced with 'matrifocal' – mother-centred rather than mother-dominated. However, more than a decade before this, Angela Davis had demolished the

entire matriarchy thesis when she noted how enslaved women's 'release' from contemporary ideals of femininity and integration into a productive workforce *in addition* to performing reproductive labour simply meant more work for them to perform outside the usual sphere of dull, boring monotonous domestic chores that have characterised the lives of so many women across time and space. See K.M. Stampp, *The Peculiar Institution* (New York: Knopf, 1956); H.G. Gutman, *The Black Family in Slavery and Freedom, 1750–1925* (New York: Pantheon, 1976); D.G. White, 'Female Slaves: Sex Roles and Status in the Antebellum Plantation South', *Journal of Family History* 8 (1983), pp. 248–261, especially p. 249 and p. 256; A. Davis, 'Reflections on the Black Woman's Role in the Community of Slaves', *The Black Scholar* 3:4 (1971), pp. 2–15.

3 Some historians have used the conceptual tools of historians of enslaved women to probe notions of masculinity under the regime, including the homosocial worlds of enslaved men, and also the impact sexual abuse had upon them. See S. Lussana, *My Brother Slaves: Friendship, Masculinity, and Resistance in the Antebellum South* (Lexington: University Press of Kentucky, 2016); D. Doddington, *'Are You Men?': Contesting Manhood in the Slave South* (New York: Cambridge University Press, 2018); T.A. Foster, 'The Sexual Abuse of Black Men under American Slavery', *Journal of the History of Sexuality* 20:3 (2011), pp. 445–464 and T.A. Foster, *Rethinking Rufus: Sexual Violations of Enslaved Men* (Athens: University of Georgia Press, 2019).

4 Recent emphasis on overcoming archival silences offers exciting opportunities to explore same-sex desire under bondage. Orlando Patterson notes that since homosexuality has existed in other societies across time and space, the same would have been true of US slavery. See O. Patterson, *Rituals of Blood: Consequences of Slavery in Two American Centuries* (New York: Basic Civitas, 1998), p. 289. See also A.I. Abdur-Rahrman, '"The Strangest Freaks of Despotism": Queer Sexuality in Antebellum African American Slave Narratives', *African American Review* 40:2 (2006), pp. 223–237.

5 See L.E. Hudson Jr., *To Have and To Hold: Slave Work and Family Life in Antebellum South Carolina* (Athens: University of Georgia Press, 1997), pp. 157–158. John D'Emilio and Estelle B. Freedman have also claimed that, in their marriage patterns, slave communities resembled certain preindustrial and peasant societies. See J. D'Emilio and E.B. Freedman, *Intimate Matters: A History of Sexuality in America*, 2nd edn (Chicago: University of Chicago Press, 1997), p. 97. See also D.G. White, *Ar'n't I a Woman? Female Slaves in the Plantation South* (New York and London: W. W. Norton, 1985), p. 150.

6 West, *Chains of Love*, p. 25.

7 Hunter, *Bound in Wedlock*, chapters one and two, especially p. 77.

8 J. Forret, *Slave Against Slave: Plantation Violence in the Old South* (Baton Rouge: Louisiana State University Press, 2015); E. West, 'Tensions, Tempers and Temptations: Marital Discord among Slaves in Antebellum South Carolina', *American Nineteenth Century History* 5:2 (2004), pp. 1–18; and 'Reflections on the *History and Historians* of the Black Woman's Role in the Community of Slaves: Enslaved Women and Intimate Partner Violence', *American Nineteenth Century History* 19:1 (2018), pp. 1–21; D. Doddington, 'Manhood, Sex, and Power in Antebellum Slave Communities,' in *Sexuality and Slavery: Reclaiming Intimate Histories in the Americas*, ed. by L. Harris and D.R. Berry (Athens: University of Georgia Press, 2018), pp. 145–158; S. Brownmiller, *Against Our Will: Men, Women and Rape* (Harmondsworth and New York: Penguin, 1975), especially pp. 153–173; D.C. Hine, 'Rape and Their Inner Lives of Black Women in the Middle West: Preliminary Thought on the Culture of Dissemblance', *Signs: Journal of Women in Culture and Society* 14:4 (1989), pp. 912–920.

9 S. Camp, *Closer to Freedom: Enslaved Women and Everyday Resistance in the Plantation South* (Chapel Hill: University of North Carolina Press, 2004), p. 95. See also B. Connolly and M. Fuentes, 'Introduction: From Archives of Slavery to

Liberated Futures?', *History of the Present: A Journal of Critical History* 6:2 (2016), pp. 106–116; S.V. Hartman, 'Venus in Two Acts', *Small Axe* 12:2 (2008), pp. 1–14.

10 For more on cross-plantation marriages, see West, *Chains of Love*, chapter two.

11 For example, Charles Ball made wooden trays and bowls that he sold in order to support financially the family he lodged with. See *Fifty Years in Chains; or, The Life of an American Slave* (New York: Dover Publications, [1859], 1970), p. 134. The ways in which men could acquire skills more easily than women is also considered in West, *Chains of Love*, p. 92.

12 On female roles within the slave home, see West, *Chains of Love*, pp. 100–101.

13 Tending gardens or patches of land had become common in South Carolina from the 1820s onwards among slaves on both large and smallholdings. See Hudson, *To Have and To Hold*, p. 10, pp. 32–33; D.A. Pargas, *The Quarters and the Fields: Slave Families in the Non-Cotton South* (Gainesville: University of Florida Press, 2010); J. Saville, *The Work of Reconstruction: From Slave to Wage Laborer in South Carolina, 1860–1870* (Cambridge: Cambridge University Press, 1994), p. 7; B. Wood, *Women's Work, Men's Work: The Informal Slave Economies of Lowcountry Georgia* (Athens: University of Georgia Press, 1995), p. 41.

14 Leslie Schwalm has warned historians against romanticising the family life of enslaved women, writing that their 'social and reproductive' labour should be examined as critically as the work they performed for their owners. See L. Schwalm, *A Hard Fight for We: Women's Transition from Slavery to Freedom in South Carolina* (Urbana: University of Illinois Press, 1997), p. 47. Deborah White noted how the absence of 'ownership' among enslaved men contributed to women's independence from them, meaning enslaved families were 'unusually egalitarian'. See *Ar'n't I a Woman?*, p. 153, p. 158.

15 WPA Slave Narrative Project, North Carolina Narratives, Vol. 11, Pt. 2, p. 57. Federal Writers Project, United States Work Projects Administration; Manuscript Division, Library of Congress: http://memory.loc.gov/ammem/snhtml/snhome.html

16 WPA Slave Narrative Project, South Carolina Narratives, Vol. 14, Pt. 4, p. 52; WPA Slave Narrative Project, North Carolina Narratives, Vol. 11, Pt. 2, p. 114 and p. 179.

17 Ball, *Fifty Years in Chains*, p. 197.

18 See B. Welter, 'The Cult of True Womanhood, 1820–1860,' in *Major Problems in American Women's History*, ed. by M.B. Norton and R. Alexander (Lexington, MA: D. C. Heath, 1996), p. 115. For more on the polarity between ideologies of black and white womanhood under slavery, see H. Carby, *Reconstructing Womanhood: The Emergence of the Afro-American Woman Novelist* (Oxford: Oxford University Press, 1987), chapter two, and E. Fox-Genovese, *Within the Plantation Household: Black and White Women of the Old South* (Chapel Hill and London: University of North Carolina Press, 1988), pp. 50–51; Davis, 'Reflections', p. 7.

19 Letter from Jennie to Maria, December 2nd, 1862, in A.A. Lines, *To Raise Myself a Little: The Diaries and Letters of Jennie, a Georgia Teacher, 1951–1886*, ed. Thomas Dyer (Athens: University of Georgia Press, 1982), p. 193.

20 The systematic sexual abuse of enslaved women by white men has been well documented by historians. Angela Davis defined the rape of black women by white men under slavery as a form of 'institutional terrorism' as early as 1971. See 'Reflections'. Other key literature on the sexual assaults of enslaved women by white men includes S. Block, *Rape and Sexual Power in Early America* (Chapel Hill: University of North Carolina Press, 2006); Hine, 'Rape and The Inner Lives of Black Women'; W. King, '"Prematurely Knowing of Evil Things": The Sexual Abuse of African American Girls and Young Women in Slavery and Freedom', *Journal of African American History* 99:3 (2014), pp. 173–196; D.M. Sommerville, *Rape and Race in the Nineteenth Century South* (Chapel Hill: University of North Carolina Press, 2004).

21 Bibb did however later explain that 'I bring no charge of guilt against her, for I know not all the circumstances connected with the case'. See *Narrative of the Life and Adventures of Henry Bibb, An American Slave* (New York, published by the author, 1849), pp. 162–163.

22 'Negro Rules for Government', Cornhill Plantation Book, 1827–1873, [Plantation of John B. Miller], McDonald-Furman Papers, William R. Perkins Library, Duke University, Durham, North Carolina.

23 Emily Wharton Sinkler, letter to her mother, 11 December 1843, Emily Wharton Sinkler letters, South Caroliniana Library, University of South Carolina, Columbia South Carolina.

24 John Springs, Letter to John Blackstone, 13 November 1845, Springs Family Papers, Southern Historical Collection, University of North Carolina, Chapel Hill, North Carolina.

25 Letter to Benjamin Franklin Perry from Elizabeth Perry, 11 May 1846, Benjamin Franklin Perry Papers, South Caroliniana Library.

26 Thavolia Glymph argues persuasively that white women were 'co-masters' who were complicit in the regime. See T. Glymph, *Out of the House of Bondage: The Transformation of the Plantation Household* (Cambridge: Cambridge University Press, 2008), pp. 5, 123.

27 Some of these arguments appear in West, 'Reflections on the *History and Historians*'.

28 By 1993 rape within marriage was deemed a crime in all 50 US states. It became illegal in England and Wales in 1991. See R.K. Bergen, *Wife Rape: Understanding the Response of Survivors and Service Providers* (Thousand Oaks, CA: Sage, 1996), p. 4. See also E.B. Freedman, *Redefining Rape: Sexual Violence in the Era of Suffrage and Segregation* (Cambridge, MA: Harvard University Press, 2013), p. 282; Block, *Rape and Sexual Power*, pp. 78–79.

29 G.P. Rawick, *The American Slave: A composite Autobiography, Supplement Series 2*, Vol. 5, Pt. 4, Texas Narratives (Westport, CT: Greenwood Press 1979), p. 1453.

30 WPA Slave Narrative Project: *Texas Narratives*, Vol. 16, Pt. 4, pp. 176–178; Foster, 'The Sexual Abuse of Black Men', p. 457.

31 See L. Edwards, *Scarlett Doesn't Live Here Anymore: Southern Women in the Civil War Era* (Urbana: University of Illinois Press, 2004), 'Introduction'.

32 J. Downs, 'The Other Side of Freedom: Destitution, Disease and Dependency among Freedwomen and Their Children during and after the Civil War,' in *Battle Scars: Gender and Sexuality in the American Civil War*, ed. by C. Clinton and N. Silber (Oxford: Oxford University Press, 2006), p. 79.

33 S. McCurry, *Confederate Reckoning: Power and Politics in the Civil War South* (Cambridge, MA: Harvard University Press, 2010), p. 273.

34 WPA Slave Narrative Project: Georgia Narratives, Vol. 4, Pt. 4, p. 225.

35 S.K. Taylor, *Reminiscences of My Life in Camp: An African American Woman's Civil War Memoir* (Athens and London: University of Georgia Press, [1902], 2006), pp. 14–16.

36 McCurry, *Confederate Reckoning*, p. 9, p. 266.

37 Hunter, *Bound in Wedlock*, chapter five, especially p. 166.

38 Hunter, *Bound in Wedlock*, p. 213.

39 Schwalm, *A Hard Fight for We*, p. 234, pp. 260–266.

40 Letter from Lucy Skipwith to her master, quoted in Dorothy Sterling (ed.), *We are Your Sisters: Black Women in the Nineteenth Century* (New York: W. W. Norton, 1984, 1997), p. 310.

41 WPA Slave Narrative Project: Texas Narratives, Vol. 16, Part 4, p. 174.

42 Rawick, *The American Slave: Supplement Series 2*, Vol. 5, Pt. 4, Texas Narratives, p. 1453.

43 Rawick, *The American Slave: Supplement Series 2*, Vol. 5, Pt. 4, Texas Narratives, pp. 1553–1567.

Bibliography

Abdur-Rahrman, A.I. '"The Strangest Freaks of Despotism": Queer Sexuality in Antebellum African American Slave Narratives', *African American Review* 40:2 (2006), pp. 223–237.

Ball, C. *Fifty Years in Chains; or, The Life of an American Slave* (New York: Dover Publications, [1859], 1970).

Bergen, R.K. *Wife Rape: Understanding the Response of Survivors and Service Providers* (Thousand Oaks, CA: Sage, 1996).

Bibb, H. *Narrative of the Life and Adventures of Henry Bibb, An American Slave* (New York, published by the author, 1849).

Block, S. *Rape and Sexual Power in Early America* (Chapel Hill: University of North Carolina Press, 2006).

Brownmiller, S. *Against Our Will: Men, Women and Rape* (Harmondsworth and New York: Penguin, 1975).

Camp, S. *Closer to Freedom: Enslaved Women and Everyday Resistance in the Plantation South* (Chapel Hill: University of North Carolina Press, 2004).

Carby, H. *Reconstructing Womanhood: The Emergence of the Afro-American Woman Novelist* (Oxford: Oxford University Press, 1987).

Connolly, B. and M. Fuentes, 'Introduction: From Archives of Slavery to Liberated Futures?', *History of the Present: A Journal of Critical History* 6:2 (2016), pp. 106–116.

Davis, A. 'Reflections on the Black Woman's Role in the Community of Slaves', *The Black Scholar* 3:4 (1971), pp. 2–15.

D'Emilio, J. and E.B. Freedman, *Intimate Matters: A History of Sexuality in America*, 2nd edn (Chicago: University of Chicago Press, 1997).

Doddington, D. *'Are You Men?': Contesting Manhood in the Slave South* (New York: Cambridge University Press, 2018).

Doddington, D. 'Manhood, Sex, and Power in Antebellum Slave Communities,' in *Sexuality and Slavery: Reclaiming Intimate Histories in the Americas*, ed. by L. Harris and D. Ramey Berry (Athens: University of Georgia Press, 2018), pp. 145–158.

Downs, J. 'The Other Side of Freedom: Destitution, Disease and Dependency among Freedwomen and Their Children during and after the Civil War,' in *Battle Scars: Gender and Sexuality in the American Civil War*, ed. by C. Clinton and N. Silber (Oxford: Oxford University Press, 2006), pp. 78–103.

Edwards, L. *Scarlett Doesn't Live Here Anymore: Southern Women in the Civil War Era* (Urbana: University of Illinois Press, 2004).

Forret, J. *Slave against Slave: Plantation Violence in the Old South* (Baton Rouge: Louisiana State University Press, 2015).

Foster, T.A. 'The Sexual Abuse of Black Men under American Slavery', *Journal of the History of Sexuality* 20:3 (2011), pp. 445–464.

Foster, T.A. *Rethinking Rufus: Sexual Violations of Enslaved Men* (Athens: University of Georgia Press, 2019).

Fox-Genovese, E. *Within the Plantation Household: Black and White Women of the Old South* (Chapel Hill: University of North Carolina Press, 1988).

Fraser, R. *Courtship and Love among the Enslaved in North Carolina* (Jackson: University of Mississippi Press, 2007).

Freedman, E.B. *Redefining Rape: Sexual Violence in the Era of Suffrage and Segregation* (Cambridge, MA: Harvard University Press, 2013).

Glymph, T. *Out of the House of Bondage: The Transformation of the Plantation Household* (Cambridge: Cambridge University Press, 2008).

Gutman, H.G. *The Black Family in Slavery and Freedom, 1750–1925* (New York: Pantheon, 1976).

Hartman, S.V. 'Venus in Two Acts', *Small Axe* 12:2 (2008), pp. 1–14.

Hine, D.C. 'Rape and Their Inner Lives of Black Women in the Middle West: Preliminary Thought on the Culture of Dissemblance', *Signs: Journal of Women in Culture and Society* 14:4 (1989), pp. 912–920.

Hudson Jr., L.E. *To Have and To Hold: Slave Work and Family Life in Antebellum South Carolina* (Athens: University of Georgia Press, 1997).

Hunter, T. *Bound in Wedlock: Slave and Free Black Marriage in the Nineteenth Century* (Cambridge, MA: Belknap Press, 2017).

King, W. '"Prematurely Knowing of Evil Things": The Sexual Abuse of African American Girls and Young Women in Slavery and Freedom', *Journal of African American History* 99:3 (2014), pp. 173–196.

Lines, A.A. *To Raise Myself a Little: The Diaries and Letters of Jennie, a Georgia Teacher, 1951–1886*, ed. *Thomas Dyer* (Athens: University of Georgia Press, 1982).

Lussana, S. *My Brother Slaves: Friendship, Masculinity, and Resistance in the Antebellum South* (Lexington: University Press of Kentucky, 2016).

McCurry, S. *Confederate Reckoning: Power and Politics in the Civil War South* (Cambridge, MA: Harvard University Press, 2010).

'Negro Rules for Government', Cornhill Plantation Book, 1827–1873, [Plantation of John B. Miller], McDonald-Furman Papers, William R. Perkins Library, Duke University, Durham, North Carolina.

Pargas, D.A. *The Quarters and the Fields: Slave Families in the Non-Cotton South* (Gainesville: University of Florida Press, 2010).

Parry, T.D. 'Married in Slavery Time: Jumping the Broom in Atlantic Perspective', *Journal of Southern History* 81:2 (2015), pp. 273–312.

Patterson, O. *Rituals of Blood: Consequences of Slavery in Two American Centuries* (New York: Basic Civitas, 1998).

Letter to Benjamin Franklin Perry from Elizabeth Perry, 11 May 1846, Benjamin Franklin Perry Papers, South Caroliniana Library, University of South Carolina, Columbia South Carolina.

Rawick, G.P. *The American Slave: A composite Autobiography, Supplement Series 2*, Vol. 5, Part 4, Texas Narratives (Westport, CT: Greenwood Press, 1979).

Saville, J. *The Work of Reconstruction: From Slave to Wage Laborer in South Carolina, 1860–1870* (Cambridge: Cambridge University Press, 1994).

Schwalm, L. *A Hard Fight for We: Women's Transition from Slavery to Freedom in South Carolina* (Urbana: University of Illinois Press, 1997).

Emily Wharton Sinkler, letter to her mother, 11 December 1843, Emily Wharton Sinkler letters, South Caroliniana Library, University of South Carolina, Columbia South Carolina.

Sommerville, D.M. *Rape and Race in the Nineteenth Century South* (Chapel Hill: University of North Carolina Press, 2004).

John Springs, Letter to John Blackstone, 13 November 1845, Springs Family Papers, Southern Historical Collection, University of North Carolina, Chapel Hill, North Carolina.

Stampp, K.M. *The Peculiar Institution* (New York: Knopf, 1956).

Sterling, D. (ed.), *We are Your Sisters: Black Women in the Nineteenth Century* (New York and London: W. W. Norton, 1984, 1997).

Taylor, S.K. *Reminiscences of My Life in Camp: An African American Woman's Civil War Memoir* (Athens: University of Georgia Press, [1902], 2006).

Welter, B. 'The Cult of True Womanhood, 1820–1860,' in *Major Problems in American Women's History*, ed. by M.B. Norton and R. Alexander (Lexington, MA: D. C. Heath, 1996), pp. 115–121.

West, E. *Chains of Love: Slave Couples in Antebellum South Carolina* (Urbana: University of Illinois Press, 2004).

West, E. 'Tensions, Tempers and Temptations: Marital Discord among Slaves in Antebellum South Carolina', *American Nineteenth Century History* 5:2 (2004), pp. 1–18.

West, E. 'Reflections on the *History and Historians* of the Black Woman's Role in the Community of Slaves: Enslaved Women and Intimate Partner Violence', *American Nineteenth Century History* 19:1 (2018), pp. 1–21.

White, D.G. *Ar'n't I a Woman? Female Slaves in the Plantation South* (New York: W. W. Norton, 1985).

White, D.G. 'Female Slaves: Sex Roles and Status in the Antebellum Plantation South', *Journal of Family History* 8 (1983), pp. 248–261.

Will, T.E. 'Weddings on Contested Grounds: Slave Marriage in the Antebellum South', *The Historian* 62 (1999), pp. 99–117.

WPA Slave Narrative Project, Federal Writers Project, United States Work Projects Administration; Manuscript Division, Library of Congress: http://memory.loc.gov/ammem/snhtml/snhome.htm

Wood, B. *Women's Work, Men's Work: The Informal Slave Economies of Lowcountry Georgia* (Athens: University of Georgia Press, 1995).

9 Attempting disunion

Mutable borders and the Mormon experience with the United States, 1846–1858

Pearl T. Ponce

Introduction

On 23 June 2016, concerned by the free flow of goods, services and, especially, people, more than seventeen million votes were cast for the United Kingdom to leave the European Union.[1] Since then, Brexit – as this disunion from the European Union has been nicknamed – has dominated British politics. Although the choice to leave or remain was simple, the process of the United Kingdom disentangling herself from Union has been arduous. Negotiations have been particularly fraught, in part because the goal has not been obliterating all ties. Instead, the United Kingdom has sought a more limited connection, striving to keep the best aspects of union while remaining at a remove. But over two years after this historic vote and after a firm date of departure had been set by law, Brexit has become a riveting spectacle shaped by regrets and recriminations and the boundaries of a new relationship remain frustratingly amorphous.

While it is tempting to believe disunion is rare, nineteenth-century examples abound. In 1861, for example, the United States refused to accede to the severance of its union, resulting in civil war and a loss of life so staggering that it immediately comes to mind more than 150 years later.[2] The eleven states that formed a competing union of their own, the Confederate States of America, lost their effort at disunion in 1865 because the United States proved too powerful. However, the fact that they were able to fight off a forced reunion for four years was indicative of a degree of parity their own union had even in defeat. Today, while not all British citizens are appreciative of their choices as they see Brexit through to the end, they do have choices. They are able to negotiate from a position of relative power, although how well they can bring that power to bear in peaceful negotiations remains to be seen.

But entities seeking disunion do not always have sufficient power to dictate their own fate. Such is the case with a lesser known example of American disunion in the nineteenth century. In 1846, a religious group, the Church of Jesus Christ of Latter-day Saints (LDS), also known as the Mormons, attempted disunion. Unlike these two better-known cases of disunion, however, the Mormons were state actors with insufficient power for leverage. Although their act of disunion was fleeting, lasting a mere two years, over the subsequent decade from 1848 to 1858, the Mormons nonetheless attempted to manage the conditions of their forced reunion, gaining some concessions, but ultimately pushing so hard that the Union pushed back during the so-called Utah War of 1857–1858.

Disunion and reunion

The Mormons resorted to disunion because they could find no safety in their home country. Founded in New York in 1830, many Americans were drawn to this new religion; among a people searching for meaning during the Second Great Awakening, it was, as Daniel Walker Howe has argued, an 'authoritative and authoritarian solution'. But soon, Mormons faced prejudice and persecution and thus moved westward, first to Ohio and then to Missouri on the country's western frontier. But they encountered new problems as Missourians were taken aback by Mormons' 'mutual economic cooperation, their suspicious overtures to the Indians, and the presence of a few free black Latter-day Saints in a slave state that wished to exclude free black settlers'. The frontier provided insufficient refuge; by October 1838, Governor Lilburn Boggs had declared them 'enemies' who 'must be exterminated or driven from the state'. After forty Mormons died, they left Missouri for Illinois.[3]

In Illinois, helped by the legislature's grant of a self-government charter, the Mormon settlement of Nauvoo prospered, but local residents became concerned by the power Smith was accruing. He was 'mayor of the town, commander of its militia, city planner, recorder of deeds, and chief justice of the municipal court', and even ran for president in 1844. When a dissident Mormon group published an article about Smith's belief in plural marriage, two local militias converged on Nauvoo believing he 'had exceeded his legal authority and become a dangerous despot'. Although an armed conflict was averted by the intervention of Illinois Governor Thomas Ford, an anti-Mormon mob nonetheless murdered Smith and his brother on 27 June 1844.[4] After this devastating loss, LDS leadership decided to leave the United States entirely for neighbouring Mexico.

In February 1846, the first group of Mormons departed for the Pacific coast but settled instead around the Great Salt Lake Basin. Although this region belonged to Mexico, it was on that country's northern reaches while the majority of its citizenry lived more than a thousand miles away in the Yucatán. Independence would be an ideal outcome but, if nothing else, its isolation would allow them to establish religious communities in peace, away from both a hostile United States and a Mexico too distant to interfere. Unfortunately for their plans, the United States declared war on Mexico three months later. In the 1848 Treaty of Guadalupe Hidalgo that ended the Mexican-American War, Mexico ceded the southwest region where the Mormons had settled in the United States.

Managing reunion after a failed disunion

With a stroke of a pen, Mormons were once more a part of the country they had fled. They were enveloped by the United States so their disunion could no longer be a physical act of geographic distance. Mormons would have to effect disunion on a more limited scale from within, to ameliorate their now failed disunion by seeking concessions to improve their situation now that they were returned to the fold. More significantly, they tested the limits of their influence by an outright refusal when the United States tried to implement policies not to their liking.

Mormons first attempted to control their forced reunion by shaping their re-entry. Striving to stake out the strongest position possible, they asked to re-join the union as a state after first contemplating, then rejecting, a request for territorial status because doing so would leave them unable to select their leaders. To increase the likelihood their request would be accepted, they presented the United States with a fait accompli: in March 1849, Mormons created the state of Deseret, complete with a constitution, and petitioned for admission.[5] In 1850, when Congress organised the Mexican Cession they did admit a state, but it was California that joined the Union, not Deseret. Moreover, the remaining region – which included the Great Salt Lake Basin – was divided into two territories: New Mexico and Utah. The United States accepted neither the Mormons' proffered state nor their chosen name.

Finding themselves re-joining the Union as a territory rather than a state was disappointing for multiple reasons. First, while territories did become states, it took an average of twelve to thirteen years to do so.[6] Moreover, Mormons would have less control over their fate since territories were considered embryonic states in need of oversight while they matured. There were benefits (Congress provided funds until the territory could sustain itself), but also significant drawbacks, most notably, the electoral restrictions placed on residents. For instance, they would vote for a legislative assembly but not their own governor. And while they were represented in Congress, it was by a non-voting delegate not a full member of the House of Representatives. Finally, Mormons had wanted a say in their leadership, but the president – for whom they could not vote – would appoint their territorial governor and secretary; a chief justice and two associate justices; and a US attorney and a US marshal for the territory. Typically, the president rewarded members of his political party with these appointments rather than local men.[7]

Having failed to become a state, Mormons turned to influencing the upcoming federal appointments via an extensive lobbying campaign. Significantly, this campaign was undertaken by Thomas Leiper Kane, a well-connected philanthropist who although not of the faith was sympathetic to their plight. Through Kane's intervention, the Mormons gained an important concession: President Millard Fillmore appointed Brigham Young, the head of the Mormon Church, as Utah's territorial governor

BRIGHAM YOUNG, THE MORMON PRESIDENT.

Figure 9.1 Brigham Young (1801–1877) from *Gleason's Pictorial*, 1854. Image courtesy of the Library of Congress, LC-USZ62–50426.

(see Figure 9.1). Young had led the great migration out of Illinois and under the provisional (and unrecognised) Deseret state elections, had been elected governor. Furthermore, four of Fillmore's initial seven appointees were Mormon.[8] This was a significant victory – not only were a majority Mormon, but these four had been on a list of preferred territorial officials that Mormon John Bernhisel, who would himself become Utah's territorial delegate to Congress, had sent Kane in September 1850 to present to the president.[9]

On the face of it, including Mormons among these federal appointments made sense. Unlike other territories that developed organically, drawing citizens from diverse regions, religions and ethnicities into a region over a much longer period of time, the Mormon community around the Great Salt Lake Basin resulted from a directed settlement, undertaken for a specific purpose in a short time frame, and thus, its populace was defined by its religion and bonded by a homogenous culture. Although Congress had dismissed Deseret as a state and created Utah Territory instead, Young's appointment to be territorial governor can be seen as a signal that the federal government was sensitive to the reasons the Mormons had sought disunion. In short, it was an easy concession to make and served to reassure the Mormons that even though the land they had settled had been subsumed by the United States, the Union would keep its interests in mind.

In addition, Mormons tried to negotiate their position within the Union by being unrepentant about how their religion deviated from the dominant form of Christianity in the country, evangelical Protestantism. They had pursued disunion in order to practise their religion insulated from the violence that had driven them out of the United States. Now that they were back, they did not want to see the hostility and brutality that had compelled their exit to resume. Nonetheless, Mormons were no longer content to hide their religious practices, no matter how controversial. Having established the Kingdom of God in Utah, they would not regress to a time, for instance, when they had practised plural marriage while publicly diminishing its importance. In 1848, the very year they were drawn back into the union, Mormons insisted that 'the First Amendment protected their practice of polygamy as a "free exercise of religion"'. In keeping with their desire to practise their faith freely, four years later, Young 'proclaimed the doctrine publicly in 1852'.[10] Moreover, they insisted their doctrinal decisions were outside the government's purview, a right their religious identification did not alter. 'If we are Mormons or Methodists, or worship the sun or a white dog, or if we worship a dumb idol, or all turn Shaking Quakers and have no wife', Young asserted, 'it is not their prerogative to meddle with these affairs, for in doing so they would violate the Constitution'.[11] By the time they had fled the United States, 'most gentiles [the term applied by Mormons to those outside the faith] saw Mormonism the way nativists saw Roman Catholicism: as a denial of and a threat to American liberal pluralism'.[12] While this had created problems within the United States, in Utah, Mormons were dominant, and thus, central tenets of their religion, including plural marriage, baptism of the dead and ongoing revelation, were not aberrant and Mormons insisted on being transparent in their practices.

But the difficulties that Mormons had faced from 1830 until their disunion of 1846 returned to haunt their efforts to control their fate as a territory. Although they had gained some concessions from Fillmore regarding their territorial governing team, they had not been entirely successful. Now it was the unbelievers who were polluting the community with their beliefs and behaviour and, in Utah, they were the outliers. As such, Mormons fought to ensure non-Mormon appointees either conformed or were replaced. Not surprisingly, conflicts quickly arose within the territorial team between the four who were part of the LDS Church and the three who were not. Soon the secretary, chief justice and an associate justice had fled the territory arguing that they could not perform their duties and, in an ironic turnabout, that the community was hazardous for them. As one of these so-called runaway officials explained to the Secretary of State, returning 'would be not only to subject myself to renewed indignity, insult, [and] mortification, but to place my life in extreme peril'.[13]

Back in Utah, Young complained to President Fillmore that these men had come to Utah solely to '*watch for iniquity*, [...] to spy out our liberties, and by manifold misrepresentation, seek to prejudice minds against us'.[14] Indeed Young charged these officials with 'entertaining *defective* and *disloyal* sentiments toward the Government'.[15] But if, as Young charged, these officials had come to Utah to propagate prejudice, they shared the bigotry of the Americans who had driven the Mormons out of the Union and such attitudes had not dissipated. In late 1856, for instance, a self-designated 'concerned citizen' wrote to the president to complain that 'the civil laws of the Territory are overshadowed and neutralised by a so-styled ecclesiastical organisation, as despotic, dangerous and damnable, as has ever been known to exist in any country'.[16] Similarly, in a pamphlet published a year later, Hugh Briggs, while complimenting the 'industrious' Mormons, nonetheless argued that they had established a 'self-styled religious despotism' which 'has shaded out the morals, and choked the domestic institutions belonging to the age and generation, and is now bearing fruits so novel that language, itself, is at a loss in giving them a name or designation'.[17] This erosion of democracy was all the more significant because civil government, as Briggs charged, had 'been substantially annihilated, paralyzed, or perverted by their ecclesiastical organizations and by their theocratic government'.[18] As such, every element of Utah's government was infused with and answering to Mormonism. In short, Briggs believed 'the civil duties and powers of Governor are regarded as mere attributes of the Priesthood'.[19]

The idea that the territorial government was a theocracy was troubling because, if true, it violated the traditional American separation between church and state. Fillmore's selection of Young for governor rather than a typical political operative was fraught *because* he headed the church and had not been asked to resign as a condition of his appointment. As indicated by the violent reception with which communities across the country had greeted migrating Mormons, Americans were deeply threatened by this religion. Moreover, it was a similar melding of civil and religious roles in the person of Joseph Smith that had led to riots and murder in Nauvoo, Illinois. Now not only had a new territory consisting largely of Mormons been created, but President Fillmore had elevated their religious leader to the highest position of civil authority.

Since Brigham Young's initial four-year appointment in 1850, discussions on replacing him had become routine, especially during presidential campaigns since a new executive would probably want to name his own team. In 1852, for instance, the *Milwaukee Daily Sentinel* argued that the 'fierce, fanatical, and persecuted' Mormons were dangerous because 'The Mormon

Prophet [has been] made the Civil Governor [...]. – This is not indeed a union of Church and State, but far worse'.[20] In fact, the winner of that year's presidential election, Democrat Franklin Pierce, did try to replace Young after he was inaugurated in 1853, but Young was retained for a second term when the new president's nominee declined the post.[21] Four years later, the next president would also look closely at the territorial governor.

President James Buchanan versus Brigham Young

Democrat James Buchanan came to office in 1857 and promptly demonstrated a lack of sentimentality towards incumbents by removing Kansas Territorial Governor John Geary. This was surprising because he hailed from the president's home state of Pennsylvania, his able handling of 'Bleeding Kansas' had facilitated Buchanan's 1856 electoral victory, and his replacement would be Kansas's fourth governor in its three years as a territory. If Geary was expendable, surely Young was as well, especially since he had governed Utah for all seven years of its existence and had no ties to Buchanan. If anything, Utah was a more pressing issue. Unlike in Kansas, where controversial territorial laws, voter fraud and bloodshed had drawn national headlines and overthrown several governors, Young's position was undermined by the steady stream of negative reports emanating from the territory.

The worrisome reports began with the aforementioned runaway officials. For instance, when territorial secretary Broughton D. Harris left Utah he argued that all Mormons should be removed from office because 'no matter what their position, theoretically & practically [they] regard their obligation to [...] the Church as paramount to all other obligations'.[22] Disagreements with the governor and legislature over financial policy left Harris threatened with 'violence and assassination'.[23] But rumours of financial irregularities were not the only ones circulating. Some were merely strange – whispers that the Mormons had their own alphabet and had created their own money for use as legal tender – while others – such as charges that Mormons had burnt the library, destroyed federal court records and were interfering in the government's relationship with the Indians – were troubling.[24] Even more disconcerting were reports that the territorial government was failing at its primary responsibility, the protection of residents. Not only had a US surveying team of eight been massacred in 1853, but an emigrant party of more than 120 individuals heading for California had been as well. Given tense relations with native tribes, this Mountain Meadows Massacre of 1857 was tragic but not out of the realm of possibility. What was of tremendous concern, however, was that the Indians implicated in it acknowledged their culpability but insisted that they had done so at the Mormons' instigation and with their participation.[25] Thus, Young's removal seemed both inevitable and increasingly urgent. But in the Mormons' most overt attempt to bend the United States to its will by rejecting the federal government's decisions, when the new president decided to remove the governor, Young simply refused to go.

According to the president's memoirs, when he came to office Buchanan was

> confronted by an open resistance to the execution of law in the Territory of Utah. All the officers of the United States, judicial and executive, except two Indian Agents, had found it necessary for their personal safety to escape from the Territory.

Thus, Buchanan justified his decision by arguing that the only existing government in Utah was 'the Mormon despotism of Brigham Young'.[26] And as the *Charleston Mercury* noted, Young 'could not be stripped of his priesthood, or of his gifts for prophecy, by the secular authorities but his political and military rule' could 'be modified'.[27] To do so, Buchanan would send to Utah both a new governor, Alfred Cumming, and the US army to help execute civil law.[28] Such military force was necessary because territorial officials had fled Utah and the local population was resisting the law. But it is also likely that Buchanan suspected, correctly as it turned out, that Young would not willingly be displaced. Indeed, Young was alleged to have said 'he intended to stay in his place until the Lord should say to him, "Brigham, I don't want you to be governor of Utah any longer"'.[29]

Regardless of what the Lord wanted, by the time Young learnt of his removal, the army and Cumming were on their way. The only decision left was whether he would prove Buchanan right by his response to the army. Young was suspicious of Buchanan's motives as this show of force recalled the events that precipitated their disunion. After all, Mormons had previously trusted the US government 'only to be scorned, held in derision, insulted and betrayed'. As Americans, protected by the constitution, Young was convinced that religious bigotry drove the president's actions and that the army was not in the territory to execute the law, but to 'accomplish our destruction'. Yes, rumours of malfeasance had reached Washington but unlike in Kansas the year before, the government had simply accepted these charges, which stemmed from 'anonymous letter writers', rather than send a congressional committee to investigate 'as is customary'. The president had dispatched an 'armed, mercenary mob' against which they had asserted, they had a right to self-defence. Young declared martial law; forbade armed forces from entering Utah; restrained the movement of those already present and required permits to enter, exit or move within the territory.[30]

To prevent their anticipated destruction, Mormons attacked federal forces, destroying wagons and forts, harassed the army encamped in the mountains one hundred miles from Salt Lake and burned available grazing areas that the army, having unwisely arrived in mid-winter, desperately needed. Such actions led to awkward exchanges such as when the newly arrived governor, encamped outside the city, was forced to write to the former governor, still occupying his office, about the destruction of federal property. Cumming reported that he had

> found many acts of violence have been committed on the highways in the destruction & robbery of property belonging to the United States. These acts which indicate that the Territory is in a state of rebellion are ascribed, how truly I do not know, to yourself.[31]

In another missive, Cumming reassured sceptical residents that he was in Utah at the behest of 'a just and firm administration', with 'no prejudices or enmities'. Instead, he hoped 'to command your confidence. Freedom of conscience, and the use of your own peculiar mode of serving God, are sacred rights' which would not be interfered with. He asked Utah's residents to disarm; if not, they would be 'subject [...] to the punishment due traitors'.[32]

But Young disputed any notion that they were traitors. In his December 1857 annual message to the territorial legislature, he asserted that Mormons were 'peacefully, loyally and lawfully occupying American soil'. The stand-off in the territory stemmed from the fact that Buchanan and his cabinet 'had yielded to the rabid clamor raised against Utah by lying editors, corrupt demagogues, heartless office hunters and the ignorant rabble' and sent an army to force them to 'abandon their religion [...] or be expelled from the country, or exterminated'. From the start, all Mormons had wanted from the union was '*good* men for officers', men such as these would have been 'cordially welcomed and obeyed'. Instead, they had been subject to 'the abuse and misrule meted by official villains', men who 'were so sunken in degradation as to have utterly lost sight of those pure and just principles embodied in the Constitution'. According to Young, the president could only dispatch the army 'for the safety and welfare of the people [...];' however, the army was in Utah 'unconstitutionally to oppress the people'. Mormons were not traitors but were instead defending the nation by opposing an army whose very existence in the territory was the true act of treason.[33]

This continued defiance of federal authority led Buchanan to proclaim that a 'strange system of terrorism' reigned in Utah Territory on 6 April 1858. In recalling events since the organisation of the territory, the president noted that residents had become so alienated from the federal government that no one could 'express an opinion favorable to the government, or even propose to obey its laws, without exposing his life and property to peril'. Federal forces were thus necessitated to put down a rebellion against the nation (see Figure 9.2). Mormon resistance had 'not only been expressed in words but manifested in overt acts of the most unequivocal character'. In his proclamation, Buchanan reminded Utah's 'fellow-citizens' that contrary to Young's assessment, he had sent the army to enforce federal law, not to engage in a religious crusade. He reminded residents that they owed allegiance to the United States and that by 'levying war', they were guilty of treason.[34]

Figure 9.2 'The March across the Plains in a Snow Storm' [General Albert Johnston's march to Camp Scott, Utah Territory], *Harper's Weekly*, 24 April 1858, p. 265. Courtesy of the Library of Congress, LC-USZ62–438.

While Mormons once might have imagined that they could achieve disunion by leaving the country, the Mexican-American War had ended that dream. Now a decade later, circumstances had changed – independence was unlikely and there was nowhere left to go on the continent.

> If you have calculated upon the forbearance of the United States – if you have permitted yourselves to suppose that this government will fail to put forth its strength and bring you to submission – you have fallen into a grave mistake,

Buchanan bluntly told them.

> You have settled upon territory which lies geographically in the heart of the Union. The land you live upon was purchased by the United States and paid for out of their treasury. The proprietary right and title to it is in them, and not in you. Utah is bounded on every side by States and Territories whose people are true to the Union. It is absurd to believe that they will or can permit you to erect in their very midst a government of your own, not only independent of the authority which they all acknowledge, but hostile to them and their interests.

Buchanan proceeded to outline the federal government's patience with the territory and assured them that despite their actions, the Mormons had his forbearance. Because he was 'anxious to save the effusion of blood', the president offered 'a free and full pardon to all who will submit themselves to the authority of the federal government'. To ensure they remembered that authority, forces would remain in Utah until residents demonstrated 'a proper sense of duty'. In closing, Buchanan urged the people of Utah to seriously consider the ramifications of rejecting his 'tender of peace and goodwill'.[35]

This offer of a presidential pardon was reinforced by the new governor's proclamation two months later. On 14 June 1858, Cumming reiterated Buchanan's terms and emphasised that '*All* criminal offences associated with, or growing out of, the overt acts of Sedition and Treason *are merged in them*, and are embraced in the "*free and full pardon*" of the President'. He noted that '*Peace is restored to our Territory*' and congratulated residents for this outcome. In fact, it had been peaceful in part because Thomas Kane, who had been so helpful in garnering the governorship for Young in 1850, had come west to help mediate the conflict. That said, the former governor also took credit for having used his 'powers of reason, and my influence to teach the people not to do what they believed to be their imperative duty'. Having done so, Young looked 'forward in hope that all matters will be amicably adjusted, and we shall be in peace here'.[36]

The limits of influence without power

Ultimately, the so-called Utah War was largely fought on paper and through Young's bellicose statements, sermons and proclamations. In the end, the Mormons' last, most overt attempt to manage the terms of the Union by refusing Young's replacement had been too drastic. The presence of the US army in Utah had made it clear that Young served at the pleasure of the president. Nonetheless, Young remained the head of the church and continued to try to effect change. Three years later when the United States was experiencing a more serious disunion, Young could not resist trying to manage this relationship once more. As he wrote to William Hooper, Utah's territorial delegate, in early 1861, 'in these hurrying times, Utah after patiently waiting so long, may not feel disposed to again trouble Congress with a petition for admission'.[37] Young was even more explicit three months later when he instructed Hooper that 'a hint that Territories as well as States are liable to become restive in these exciting times' might help President Abraham Lincoln make appropriate choices for Utah's leadership team.[38] Yet while he could not resist needling the government during its time of crisis, such insinuations were just that because Buchanan's 1857–1858 show of force had accomplished its goal: it had severed the Mormons' religious leadership from the civil government.

In trying to manage their reunion, Mormons wrestled with a fundamental problem: they were content to be Americans so long as they were left alone. In 1851, Young had informed President Fillmore 'that no people exist who are more friendly to the Government of the United States, than the people of this Territory. The Constitution they revere, the Laws they seek to honor'.[39] Yet when President Buchanan replaced Young as was his prerogative, Mormons fought to ensure their preferred governor remain in place. Having already been driven out of the United States by bigotry and outright violence, they were determined to make a stand when they felt threatened once more. And for the Mormons, having a gentile governor was a threat to their way of life.

Being in distant Utah had given them time to grow their communities and strengthen the militia. However, although they had been largely left alone for a decade, when conflict came and the federal government brought its power to bear on the territory, the truth was revealed: the Mormons were not as independent and isolated as they had believed. Although the Mormon militia inflicted damage and hardship on federal forces, their resistance to both Cumming and the army merely delayed the inevitable. They only escaped greater retribution because the army refrained from retaliating long enough for Brigham Young to recognise that a direct engagement would be too consequential. As he himself admitted, without 'the influence I have over this people', who knows where the army then within its borders would have gone?[40] While he meant the statement to emphasise his own importance, in truth, for the sake of his people, Young had to accept a new governor and the proffered pardon for treasonable crimes. While war did not officially break out, Mormons had caused hundreds of thousands of dollars of damage to federal property for which they were liable. Buchanan's pardon was an olive branch on the part of the federal government while the Mormons' acceptance of it was an acknowledgement of their subordinate status within that union.

The Mormons' initial disunion failed because of the fortunes of war. They could not have known that two months after they began their migration out of the country, the United States would declare war on the neighbouring country into which they moved. But the Mormons' fall-back position of fighting for greater control within the union also failed, perhaps because they were conflicted about their place in it. They wanted to have it both ways: to be a part of the United States but separate from most of its citizenry. In part, this was a legacy of the experiences that had led directly to disunion. As Elder James Ferguson declared before a Mormon gathering in Liverpool in 1855, the Mormons' history with the United States was 'one continued chain of alternate insult and abuse'. Driven out, they had 'like the Pilgrim founders', written a constitution for their

> mutual preservation. But they scoffed at our pretensions. We asked them for a State Government. They mocked us with an Organic act for a Territory [...]. We asked from them bread, from the Store-house of Freedom, and they gave us a stone, quarried from the crumbling pile of an old despotism, to grind us to the dust.[41]

Reunited, the federal government remained a 'they' and the Mormons were more likely to feel acted upon then part of a collective. When conflict came, they readily identified their fellow citizens as the enemy. As Ferguson's speech indicates, reunion did not dim the memory of their persecution nor did their small victories in managing their relationship cleave them tighter to the union.

This tendency to maintain an antagonistic relationship with the United States that I have been tracing is most evident in the Mormons' relationships with the tribes within Utah. In early 1857, Superintendents of Indian Affairs were assigned to four territories where governors had held both positions, including Utah.[42] That December, Indian Agent Garland Hunt reported that the Piede Indians, who were accused of committing the Mountains Meadows Massacre, claimed 'that Mormons, and not Indians had killed the Americans'; that John D. Lee, a prominent Mormon leader, had told them that 'the Americans were very bad people, and always made it a rule to kill Indians whenever they had the chance', before encouraging the attack, assuring them that 'if they were not strong enough to whip them, the Mormons would help them'. Moreover, the chief of the Utah Indians had also reported that that the governor had been 'trying to bribe them to join in rebellion against the United States, by offering them guns ammunition and blankets' if they would oppose the army.[43] At the very least, it is clear that in making connections with the Indians, the Mormons spoke of their fellow Americans as distinct from themselves.[44]

This outreach to the Indians is reflective of a Mormon effort to build alliances that might help protect them. Although Joseph Smith had spoken out against slavery, in 1852, Utah legalised slavery having come to see the benefits of allying themselves with Southerners. In particular, they believed states' rights ideology could 'protect their respective "peculiar institutions" from outside attack'. In fact, Mormon Jedediah M. Grant argued that, like Southerners, they were 'opponents of centralization'; in addition, other LDS members 'applauded' the Dred Scott decision, in which the Supreme Court ruled that Congress could not exclude slavery from the territories, as 'establishing a principle favorable to polygamy'.[45]

Mormons were willing to be a part of the union, but only on their own terms. Initially, they had some success in achieving limited goals. While they had not been admitted as a state in 1850 when Congress had organised the territory, President Fillmore had been persuaded to name Brigham Young its territorial governor. Moreover, Mormons believed the distance they had placed between themselves and most Americans by settling around Salt Lake would be sufficient, but that distance was purely illusory. As Buchanan demonstrated, an army could – albeit with great cost, hardship and deprivation – transcend that distance. After the conflict ended, William E. Phelps wrote to Thomas Kane asking for help in securing a new postmaster, indicating that while trouble still remained (especially in terms of some federal appointees), he was optimistic. 'I see nothing to prevent an amicable chain of friendship, and reciprocity uniting the children of Utah to Uncle Sam's policy; – *the more room, the more rest'*.[46] Tellingly, even after the conflict's resolution, this relationship still required room to prosper.

Moreover, like distance, the anomaly of Utah's territorial government – having a governor who was simultaneously head of a church – could easily be revised and with it, perhaps, their original goals of safety and self-determination. Brigham Young's dual role in Utah was reassuring for the territory's Mormon residents and reflected their desire to maintain control even when reunion significantly tempered that control. There is no denying that the nature of the Mormon religion contributed to many Americans' discomfort with having their religious leader simultaneously serve as governor. The Mormons' very homogeneity was a problem because the commonalities that made them first a community and then a territory were already at odds with mainstream America. Had Young been a Protestant evangelical, would his dual role had been more palatable? In 1854, after all, the contentious debate over the Kansas-Nebraska bill had brought politics to pulpits across the nation.[47] But Mormonism was out of step with nineteenth-century America and, significantly, when Utah finally did become a state in 1896, it was only after the LDS Church eliminated plural marriage. Nonetheless, although Utah remains majority Mormon, their 'otherness' in the larger United States has also remained. As Mitt Romney's 2012 presidential campaign made clear, many evangelical Americans still view Mormonism with suspicion, not even recognising it as an offshoot of Christianity.

Conclusion

As the Mormons learnt in the nineteenth century, disunion is difficult to achieve under most circumstances, but especially when the entity seeking to leave a union is not an equal partner. Thus, the Mormons had to negotiate their compelled reunion from a subordinate position, and, for a decade, they did fairly well. However, when the territory balked at the government's plan to replace their Mormon governor with a gentile, the United States demonstrated how little actual power they had. When they pushed the union too far, the union pushed back, sending the army and revealing that the Mormons' independence within it was severely limited. The end result was the transformation of Utah into a more typical territory, one with a traditional separation of church and state. Despite the Mormon's initial successes, they learnt that when a significant power differential exists, there are limits to enjoying the benefits of union while remaining at a remove.

Britain undertakes disunion in a better position than the Mormons did in 1846 but they too are learning that union cannot be had piecemeal. Moreover, the discourse around Brexit has definite echoes of the Mormons' 'us versus them' mentality. It seems the British are just as conflicted about their status within the European Union as the Mormons were about their relationship with the United States. However, while the Mormons had clearly been persecuted and understood Brigham Young's removal as territorial governor from that perspective, the damages Britain has suffered (or not) as a part of the European Union is contested. Nonetheless, as President Buchanan stated in his 1858 proclamation in regard to American democracy, 'Human wisdom never devised a political system which bestowed more blessings or imposed lighter burdens'.[48] Only time will tell whether the burdens felt by almost fifty-two per cent of voters in 2016's referendum outweighed the blessings of being affiliated with the European Union. Yet both examples demonstrate that disunion, like union, is rarely static and simple.

Notes

1 The 'Leave' voters won with 51.9 per cent of the votes cast to 48.1 per cent for 'Remain'. See 'Results', www.bbc.com/news/politics/eu_referendum/results (accessed 31 December 2018).

2 For more on American disunion and Civil War, see J. McPherson, *Battle Cry of Freedom: The Civil War Era* (New York: Oxford University Press, 1988); W. Freehling, *The Road to Disunion, vol. I: Secessionists at Bay, 1776–1854* (New York: Oxford University Press, 1991) and *The Road to Disunion, vol. II: Secessionists Triumphant, 1854–1861* (New York: Oxford University Press, 2008); D. Potter, *The Impending Crisis: America before the Civil War, 1848–1861*, rev. ed. (New York: HarperPerennial, 2011); C. Dew, *Apostles of Disunion: Southern Secession Commissioners and the Causes of the Civil War* (Charlottesville: University of Virginia Press, 2001); and E. Foner, *This Fiery Trial: Abraham Lincoln and American Slavery* (New York: W. W. Norton & Co., 2010).

3 D.W. Howe, *What Hath God Wrought: The Transformation of America, 1815–1848* (New York: Oxford University Press, 2007), pp. 316–319.

4 Howe, *What Hath God Wrought*, pp. 723–726.

5 D.L. Bigler, *Forgotten Kingdom: The Mormon Theocracy in the American West, 1847–1896* (Spokane, WA: Clark, 1998), pp. 45–47.

6 P.T. Ponce, *To Govern the Devil in Hell: The Political Crisis in Territorial Kansas* (DeKalb: Northern Illinois, 2014), pp. 116–117.

7 For more on territorial policies, see Ponce, *To Govern the Devil in Hell*, chapters 2 and 3.

8 Bigler, *Forgotten Kingdom*, p. 49, n. 15.

9 Letter from John M. Bernhisel to Thomas L. Kane, 11 September 1850, The Thomas Leiper Kane Papers, Beinecke Rare Book and Manuscript Library, Yale University.

10 Howe, *What Hath God Wrought*, pp. 730–731. The Supreme Court dismissed this claim.

11 Brigham Young, *Deseret News*, 31 August 1856, quoted in *Cleveland Plain Dealer*, 12 November, 1856.

12 Howe, *What Hath God Wrought*, p. 726.

13 Broughton D. Harris to Daniel Webster, 3 May 1852, Broughton D. Harris Papers, Church History Library, Salt Lake City, Utah.

14 Brigham Young to Millard Fillmore, 29 September 1851, Series 242, Executive Book A, Utah State Archives, Salt Lake City, Utah.

15 Brigham Young to Elisha Whittlesey, 31 January 1852, Series 242, Executive Book A, Utah State Archives, Salt Lake City, Utah.

16 W.F.M. Magraw to President Pierce, 3 October 1856, in US House of Representatives, 35th Congress, 1st Session, *Ex. Doc. No. 71: The Utah Expedition: Message*

from President of the United States, Transmitting Reports from the Secretaries of State, of War, of the Interior, and of the Attorney General, relative to the military expedition ordered into the Territory of Utah (Washington, 1858), p. 3.

17 H.L. Briggs, *A Lecture on the Moral, Social, and Political Condition of Utah Territory* (N.P., 1857), pp. 6–7.

18 Briggs, *A Lecture*, p. 14.

19 Briggs, *A Lecture*, pp. 14–15.

20 'From our N. Y. Correspondent,' *Milwaukee Daily Sentinel*, 31 May 1852.

21 *Charleston Mercury*, 14 May 1856; Anon., 'Utah and the Mormons: A Brief Sketch of Mormonism, and the Recent Difficulties in Utah,' *The Tribune Almanac and Political Register for 1859* (New York: Greeley, 1859), p. 39.

22 Broughton D. Harris, draft letter c. January 1852, Broughton D. Harris Papers.

23 Broughton D. Harris to James Guthrie, 30 September 1853, Broughton D. Harris Papers.

24 See William E. Phelps to Thomas Kane, 25 June 1852, Thomas Leiper Kane Papers; United States House of Representatives, 32nd Congress, 1st Session, *Ex. Doc. No. 25: Utah. Message from President of the United States. Transmitting Information in reference to the condition of affairs in the Territory of Utah. January 9, 1852* (Washington, 1852); and 'Utah and the Mormons,' p. 39.

25 Garland Hurt to Jacob Forney, 4 December 1858, Jacob Forney Letterbook 1, Church History Library.

26 James Buchanan, *Mr. Buchanan's Administration on the Eve of the Rebellion* (1865; Freeport, NY: Books for Libraries Press, 1970), pp. 232–233.

27 *Charleston Mercury*, 30 April 1857.

28 Buchanan, *Mr. Buchanan's Administration*, p. 233.

29 Brigham Young, quoted by Thomas Benton in 'The Presidency: Speech of Col. Benton in St. Louis – Birdseye View of the Pierce Administration and Cincinnati Convention,' *New York Herald*, 27 June 1856.

30 Brigham Young, 'Proclamation of the Governor,' 15 September 1857, Graham Collection, Huntington Library, San Marino, California.

31 Alfred Cumming to Brigham Young, 21 November 1857, Series 242, Executive Book B, Utah State Archives.

32 Alfred Cumming, 'Proclamation of Governor Gumming,' 21 November 1857, Series 242, Executive Book B, Utah State Archives.

33 Brigham Young, 'Governor's Message to the Legislative Assembly to the Territory of Utah,' 15 December 1857, Series 242, Executive Book B, Utah State Archives.

34 *By James Buchanan, President of the United States: A Proclamation*, 6 April 1858, HM 470193, The Huntington Library, San Marino, California.

35 *By James Buchanan, President of the United States: A Proclamation*, 6 April 1858, HM 470193, The Huntington Library, San Marino, California.

36 Brigham Young speech, 25 April 1858, Vault MSS 792, Kane Family Papers; Tom Perry Special Collections; Harold B. Lee Library, Brigham Young University, Provo, Utah https://contentdm.lib.byu.edu/digital/collection/p15999coll22/id/304 (accessed 21 December 2018).

37 Brigham Young to William Hooper, 3 January 1861, Brigham Young Letters, Beinecke Rare Book and Manuscript Library, Yale University.

38 Brigham Young to William Hooper, 25 April 1861, Brigham Young Letters. Beinecke Rare Book and Manuscript Library, Yale University.

39 Brigham Young to Millard Fillmore, 29 September 1851, Series 242, Executive Book A.

40 Brigham Young speech, 25 April 1858, Kane Family Papers.

41 *The LDS' Millennial Star*, n. 48, vol. XVII (1 December 1855).

42 See D.L. Morgan, 'The Administration of Indian Affairs in Utah, 1851–1858', *The Pacific Historical Review* 17:4 (1948), pp. 404–407.
43 Garland Hunt to Jacob Forney, 4 December 1857, Jacob Forney Letterbook 1; *Ex. Doc. No. 71*, pp. 203–204.
44 See C.L. Craig to David H. Burr, 1 August 1856, in *Ex. Doc. No. 71*, p. 116. This is a recurring comment from both surveyors and Indian agents in the territory.
45 N.G. Bringhurst, 'The Mormons and Slavery: A Closer Look,' *Pacific Historical Review* 50:3 (1981), pp. 332–333. Bringhurst argues that the limitations placed by the Utah territorial legislature on slaveholders would necessarily limit the growth of the institution (pp. 334–335).
46 William E. Phelps to Thomas Kane, 10 February 1859, Thomas Leiper Kane Papers.
47 For how the debate on the Kansas-Nebraska bill animated political action by clergy, see Ponce, *To Govern the Devil in Hell*, chapter 1.
48 *By James Buchanan, President of the United States: A Proclamation*, 6 April 1858.

Bibliography

Alfred Cumming to Brigham Young, 21 November 1857, Series 242, Executive Book B, Utah State Archives.

Anon. 'Utah and the Mormons: A Brief Sketch of Mormonism, and the Recent Difficulties in Utah', in *The Tribune Almanac and Political Register for 1859* (New York: Greeley, 1859), pp. 37–42.

Bigler, D.L. *Forgotten Kingdom: The Mormon Theocracy in the American West, 1847–1896*, (Spokane, WA: Clark, 1998).

Briggs, H.L. *A Lecture on the Moral, Social, and Political Condition of Utah Territory* (N.P., 1857).

Brigham Young to Millard Fillmore, 29 September 1851, Series 242, Executive Book A, Utah State Archives, Salt Lake City, Utah.

Brigham Young to Elisha Whittlesey, 31 January 1852, Series 242, Executive Book A, Utah State Archives, Salt Lake City, Utah.

Brigham Young, 'Proclamation of the Governor,' 15 September 1857, Graham Collection, Huntington Library, San Marino, California.

Brigham Young, 'Governor's Message to the Legislative Assembly to the Territory of Utah,' December 15, 1857, Series 242, Executive Book B, Utah State Archives.

Brigham Young speech, 25 April 1858, Vault MSS 792, Kane Family Papers; Tom Perry Special Collections; Harold B. Lee Library, Brigham Young University, Provo, Utah. https://contentdm.lib.byu.edu/digital/collection/p15999coll22/id/304 (accessed 21 December 2018).

Brigham Young to William Hooper, 3 January 1861, Brigham Young Letters, Beinecke Rare Book and Manuscript Library, Yale University.

Brigham Young to William Hooper, 25 April 1861, Brigham Young Letters. Beinecke Rare Book and Manuscript Library, Yale University.

Bringhurst, N.G. 'The Mormons and Slavery: A Closer Look,' *Pacific Historical Review* 50:3 (1981), pp. 329–338.

Broughton D. Harris, draft letter c. January 1852, Broughton D. Harris Papers, Church History Library, Salt Lake City, Utah.

Broughton D. Harris to Daniel Webster, 3 May 1852, Broughton D. Harris Papers, Church History Library, Salt Lake City, Utah.

Broughton D. Harris to James Guthrie, 30 September 1853, Broughton D. Harris Papers, Church History Library, Salt Lake City, Utah.

Buchanan, J. *Mr. Buchanan's Administration on the Eve of the Rebellion* (1865; Freeport, NY: Books for Libraries Press, 1970).

By James Buchanan, President of the United States: A Proclamation, 6 April 1858. HM 470193, The Huntington Library, San Marino, California.

Dew, C. *Apostles of Disunion: Southern Secession Commissioners and the Causes of the Civil War* (Charlottesville: University of Virginia Press, 2001).

Foner, E. *This Fiery Trial: Abraham Lincoln and American Slavery* (New York: W. W. Norton & Co., 2010).

Freehling, W. *The Road to Disunion, vol. I: Secessionists at Bay, 1776–1854* (New York: Oxford University Press, 1991).

Freehling, W. *The Road to Disunion, vol. II: Secessionists Triumphant, 1854–1861* (New York: Oxford University Press, 2008).

Garland Hurt to Jacob Forney, 4 December 1858, Jacob Forney Letterbook 1, Church History Library.

Howe, D.W. *What Hath God Wrought: The Transformation of America, 1815–1848* (New York: Oxford University Press, 2007).

Letter from John M. Bernhisel to Thomas L. Kane, 11 September 1850. The Thomas Leiper Kane Papers, Beinecke Rare Book and Manuscript Library, Yale University.

McPherson, J. *Battle Cry of Freedom: The Civil War Era* (New York: Oxford University Press, 1988).

Morgan, D.L. 'The Administration of Indian Affairs in Utah, 1851–1858', *The Pacific Historical Review* 17:4 (1948), pp. 383–409.

New York Herald, 27 June 1856.

Ponce, P.T. *To Govern the Devil in Hell: The Political Crisis in Territorial Kansas* (DeKalb: Northern Illinois, 2014).

Potter, *The Impending Crisis: America before the Civil War, 1848–1861*, rev. ed. (New York: HarperPerennial, 2011).

The Charleston Mercury, 14 May 1856.

The Charleston Mercury, 30 April 1857.

The Cleveland Plain Dealer, 12 November 1856.

The LDS' Millennial Star, 1 December 1855.

The Milwaukee Daily Sentinel, 31 May 1852.

United States House of Representatives, 32nd Congress, 1st Session, *Ex. Doc. No. 25: Utah. Message from President of the United States. Transmitting Information in reference to the condition of affairs in the Territory of Utah. January 9, 1852* (Washington, 1852).

United States House of Representatives, 35th Congress, 1st Session, *Ex. Doc. No. 71: The Utah Expedition: Message from President of the United States, Transmitting Reports from the Secretaries of State, of War, of the Interior, and of the Attorney General, relative to the military expedition ordered into the Territory of Utah* (Washington, 1858).

William E. Phelps to Thomas Kane, 25 June 1852. The Thomas Leiper Kane Papers, Beinecke Rare Book and Manuscript Library, Yale University.

William E. Phelps to Thomas Kane, 10 February 1859. The Thomas Leiper Kane Papers, Beinecke Rare Book and Manuscript Library, Yale University.

10 The South Carolina jeremiad

Reinterpreting John C. Calhoun's legacy in the 1850s

Lawrence T. McDonnell

What good was a dead Calhoun? In the spring of 1850, at the height of an unparalleled political crisis, American sectionalists and unionists both suddenly faced that cynical question, straining to turn tragedy into opportunity. For four decades, John C. Calhoun had towered over national politics as Congressman and Senator, Vice President, Secretary of War and of State, the guiding spirit of the South as a unified force in Washington. But now, as the country stood deadlocked over a tangle of political issues related to slavery's place in the country's future, death had snatched him away (see Figure 10.1). For a range of Calhoun's enemies, from William Lloyd Garrison to Thomas Hart Benton, news of his demise brought a heartfelt 'good riddance'. Yet for most seeking a solution to the growing sectional crisis, Calhoun's absence seemed desperately destabilising. Congress had fallen into bitter paralysis over the future status of Western territories won from Mexico precisely because the Southern prophet had been ignored. Calhoun had counselled the nation against the inevitable consequences of a war he opposed. He had searched for compromise protecting the South's power as a sectional minority in the federal union. He had warned against the growing danger of political extremists aiming to overthrow the safeguards of the Constitution itself. Few listened. And now, without him, would crisis spill over into calamity?[1]

Hardly: Congress found its way – for better or worse – to compromise, and for the past fifty years historians have argued that Calhoun dead proved more lingering annoyance than liberating avatar. From Nullification onward, had he embodied anything more than the self-seeking, foot-dragging, and legalistic talk, talk, talk that simultaneously eroded national unity and crippled Southern sectionalism?[2] Debilitated by tuberculosis, drained by debt, and long past his political prime, even unto the end Calhoun could not relinquish the vain hope that America would turn back to his leadership, calling him finally to the presidency he so coveted. What could have been more errant and self-deceiving than his final 'address' to the Senate, when he was carried into the chamber on a stretcher, placed before the Speaker's chair, and lay coughing, gasping, and gesticulating while George Mason of Virginia read page after page of his leaden prose? The moment must have

THE LATE J. C. CALHOUN, ESQ.

Figure 10.1 John C. Calhoun, engraving in obituary notice in *Illustrated London News*, 20 April 1850, p. 269. Image courtesy of James Gregory.

been delicious, nonetheless: few men or women get to play the corpse at anything so near unto their own funeral. Calhoun's finale was 'a culmination' in personal terms, historian David Potter allowed, but the rigmarole of mourning and burying the man, short weeks later, stole time and energy from the nation's task of achieving rapprochement. 'If I could have but one hour to speak in the Senate', the Carolinian grieved on his deathbed, 'I could do more good than on any previous occasion in my life'. The tragedy is that perhaps he meant it. But the gesture was futile, historians declare, and the judgement flawed. Calhoun was a 'man beaten by the clock', in William Freehling's fine phrase, 'trapped in the 1830s'. Now that his hour had come, Southern partisans' gaze remained fixed on the political crisis, as he claimed to have wished. New giants were already waiting in the wings – Stephen Douglas, Jefferson Davis and more – along with watercarriers like Robert Barnwell Rhett and Robert Toombs who longed for their turn in the spotlight. Now they would have to clean up the mess that Calhoun had done so much to create across his career, battling according to their best instincts.[3]

According to scholars like John McCardell and Eric Walther, this was a moment of generational transition, when new minds and voices surged forth to champion the South's cause. Although their roots lay in the era before

1850, they focussed unremittingly on the external threat the antislavery North posed to their civilisation, and the need to shape their own fate in years to come. As to Calhoun, militants could only count him among the fallen, 'bury him with honours – and rush on past his grave'. There was no political value to be gained from any other course. Across the 1850s, they fought abolitionists and Republicans toe-to-toe, and when at last the national Democratic Party collapsed and the presidency was lost, they took that final, fatal step that Calhoun could never resign himself to, seceding from the Union.[4]

But that narrative seems quite mistaken – not least because it excuses Calhoun from the political disasters of the 1850s that brought on secession and civil war, to boot. There was no getting around the arguments he had devised and the strategies he had unleashed, down to the hour of disunion and beyond. Although it is too much to say that Calhoun caused the Civil War by the choices he made during his lifetime, Calhoun dead remained a powerful and malign presence, steering the South steadily towards self-destruction. Disunion's ironic triumph cannot be understood apart from that ghost story and its central element, the South Carolina jeremiad.

In April 1850, Calhoun's death struck both friends and foes of Southern sectionalism alike as momentous. Both sides had courted him in life and now seemed deprived of their strongest potential patron. Both sides united in elaborate ceremonies of public mourning, stretching from Washington to Charleston. Both sides spent the years to come battling over Calhoun's legacy: the meaning of his speeches and actions, the astonishing trove of unpublished writings he left, and the collected works and tributes to his legacy published in 1854 and 1857. 'Calhoun is the only man whom the South can rely on as a leader', many believed; only he could plead a unifying course to save a divided nation. Even before the Compromise of 1850, most of the old titans of the Early Republic had been eclipsed – Webster, Clay, Van Buren – but Calhoun's example and influence shaped Southern action at every turn, rendering sectional conflict entirely irrepressible. This chapter examines that remarkable – and often quite dishonest – struggle, demonstrating how unionists and disunionists both learnt to use the dead Calhoun to advance proximate political goals, and also how they found themselves mastered by that usage. Dead he surely was after 1850, but Calhoun in his afterlife saw no rest.[5]

The common ground between these contending forces was a Calhounist version of what Sacvan Bercovitch called *The American Jeremiad*. Few books so short have explained so much so profoundly about the nation's character and ideological trajectory. At the core of Bercovitch's argument is the Puritan appropriation of the structure and content of the claims of the Biblical prophet Jeremiah, and its application to a wide range of problems and situations by American leaders and movements across the political spectrum from the first settlers down to the present day. For John Winthrop as for Jeremiah, Bercovitch explains, it was clear that his people were the Chosen of God, and that temporal misfortunes befell them as a consequence of having broken their special covenant with the Almighty. Turning back to the paths of righteousness would restore that bond and bring their just reward. That was the message the original colonists heard aboard the *Arbella*; that was the lesson of the Gettysburg Address. Martin Luther King Jr. announced it in his 'I Have a Dream' speech, and Ronald Reagan trumpeted it as 'Morning in America'. However degraded, it persists in contemporary demands to 'Make America Great Again'.[6] Left, right, and centre, America is a nation that believes in its special destiny, understands momentary defeat as a requirement for cosmic course correction, and anticipates blue skies and a home on high in return for dutiful submission to an adjusted reading of God's plan.[7]

To understand how King or Lincoln or Winthrop could persuade their followers of such an extraordinary perspective requires us to remember how desperate were the crises they sought to resolve. People pushed to the brink will embrace unlikely interpretations of where they stand, as recent political events suggest. But scholars have failed to recognise how, in the late 1840s, Calhoun appropriated and repurposed the American jeremiad as a mechanism for achieving political unity and advancing his own fortunes. Likewise, they have neglected the central role of the jeremiad in shaping Southern political thought and action in the decade after Calhoun's death. Strikingly, instead, they have understood the two decades between the Nullification controversy in South Carolina and the eruption of Southern nationalism at the Nashville Convention of 1850 as the natural growth of class consciousness and political militancy within an aristocratic slaveocracy. According to most scholars on these years, when an aggressive abolitionist minority and an increasingly rebellious enslaved population of African Americans needled the planter class, it struck back hard, and looked for new ways to expand its empire to the south and west. Across the 1850s, Southern unity undergirded radical intransigence, leading straight to secession and war.

In 1974, historian James Banner summed up this perspective in his essay, 'The Problem of South Carolina'. From 1820 down to Lincoln's election, he noted, South Carolina was distinctive among Southern states for its commitment to the defence of slavery and its remarkable political unity. 'Nowhere else', Banner argued, 'did the 'fire-eaters' gain such an early ascendancy and maintain such a lasting hold'. Cohesive militancy, he explained, derived from the state's distinctive political culture: a party system never flourished there. Other scholars, extending and criticising Banner's argument, rooted that anomaly in the long-term stability of a planter elite, its common ground and compromises with a yeoman class, and the dominance of republican ideology. In almost all cases, however, research has accepted Banner's basic point: South Carolina's distinctive militancy derived from its political unity.[8]

But Banner's premise fundamentally misunderstood the relation between internal unity and South Carolina's hotheadedness. 'The Problem of South

Carolina' was a think-piece for a festschrift, not the product of extensive documentary research. Although it succeeds in describing a question for historical analysis, it could do little more than sketch a broad hypothesis by way of answer. That is perhaps one reason that John C. Calhoun hardly figures in Banner's argument. More surprising, though, is the way that subsequent scholarship blurs and ignores all kinds of specific local conflicts in order to paint South Carolina as unified and cohesive. In the same way, historians of slaveholding militancy and disunion have portrayed proslavery 'fire-eaters' as conscious, unified, and potent, Southern Apostles leading their lambs towards the true faith – and the slaughter that followed thereafter.[9] That was hardly so, especially in South Carolina.

Closer inspection reveals a very different political trajectory. By the late 1820s, South Carolina's relations with the federal government had become increasingly fractious, engendering bitter divisions between Nullifiers and Unionists across the state, complete with paramilitary Minute Men groups and ferocious mob battles. The defeat of the Nullification movement saw radicals humiliated, unionists ostracised, and Calhoun politically wounded. The months and years after the Compromise of 1833 were a period of vicious internal score-settling, as hardnosed Calhoun loyalists simultaneously demoted radicals like James Hamilton and Robert Barnwell Rhett, on the one hand, and obliterated naysaying Whigs like Waddy Thompson and Joel Poinsett. When impatient underlings tried to seize power through the so-called Beaufort Movement of 1840–1843, Calhoun struck them down and banished his own brother-in-law, Frank Pickens, for siding with the plotters. As these examples show, unity in South Carolina after 1830 was forged, not foreordained. If there was, by 1838, something like a one-party system in the state, that was the product of arm-twisting, veiled threats, and corruption, not cohesion of outlook. Thereafter, too, there were always factions, cliques, and budding conspiracies working to explode social unity. Politically, the situation was more volatile than in states like Georgia or Alabama that presented stable party conflict between Democrats and Whigs precisely because so many conflicts and manoeuvres in South Carolina remained half-hidden. And in large part, that instability was the consequence of Calhoun's efforts, however unintentional their outcome.[10]

As these examples suggest, South Carolina politics after 1833 was far more inward-looking than has been recognised. Fascinated by the concurrent majority theory Calhoun developed in his *Disquisition on Government*, and by his efforts to win the presidency across the 1840s, historians have paid inordinate attention to the state's relations with Washington and the North during this period. A glance at local newspapers or personal manuscripts, however, shows that different questions were uppermost in the minds of Carolinians – banking and railroad expansion, growing larger crops of cotton and rice, gaining better representation in the state legislature – and these all focussed political activity at the local and state levels.[11]

Certainly, by the mid-1840s, Calhoun was focussed on the creation of a unified Southern Party, aiming to defend slavery and state rights principles. From his perspective, the long-term preservation of the planters' world depended on adherence to a set of principles that is best understood as a variant of Bercovitch's *American Jeremiad* – a distinctly South Carolina jeremiad. First enunciated in Charleston in 1847, in the years after his death Calhoun's words were shaped by both unionists and disunionists into an agreed-upon set of presuppositions, warnings, and promises meant to guide political action. The curse was that Calhoun's medicine was both curative and toxic, depending on how it was administered. The South Carolina jeremiad insisted on internal unity above all else – but whether towards or away from national disunion, none could rightly say. That deliberate imprecision, which was a pillar of strength during Calhoun's life, rooted men in bitterly divided cliques after his death. Indeed, by the hour of secession in 1860, it was less Lincoln's election which drove the radical separatist movement than a determination to resolve the internal contradictions of party and caucus Calhoun's political injunctions had fomented. Secession, it turned out, had less to do with achieving disunion from the North than winning a final, lasting union among the various factions within South Carolina. And so the war came.

What I call the South Carolina jeremiad was the moral, social, and political ethic which came to shape white attitudes across the 1850s, first within the state and finally across the Deep South. Underlying Calhoun's discussion of politics was a dread of internal division, subversion, and the rise of self-interested factions. In his last public speech in Charleston in 1847, Calhoun articulated this fear with special clarity, calling for a unified Southern Party to oppose northern abolitionists.

> Henceforward, let all party distinction among us cease, so long as this aggression on our rights and honor shall continue, on the part of the non-slaveholding States.... As they make the destruction of our domestic institution the paramount question, so let us make, on our part, its safety the paramount question; let us regard every man as of our party, who stands up in its defense; and every one as against us, who does not, until aggression ceases. It is thus, and thus only, that we can defend our rights, maintain our honor, ensure our safety, and command respect.[12]

The benefits of this course would soon become clear, Calhoun promised. 'If we should prove true to ourselves and our peculiar institution [slavery], we shall be great and prosperous, let what will occur'. The alternative imperilled the South and the Union alike. 'Delay, indecision, and want of union among ourselves', Calhoun warned, 'would in all probability, in the end, prove fatal' to section and nation both.[13]

As this prophecy made clear, the South Carolina jeremiad identified the gravest threat to southern civilisation as internal, not external. The party spirit and 'spoilsmanship' that pluralism engendered would do more to abolish slavery than all the Frederick Douglasses and John Browns the North could muster. To be secure in his property and place in society required each Carolinian to stand with his neighbours 'as A BAND OF BROTHERS', putting aside differences and keeping a close eye on his neighbours' loyalty in the bargain. Sincerity, fidelity, and the skill to see through the traitor's disguise were crucial here. The 'noblest of destinies' hinged on southerners' determination to be 'true to ourselves', politicians warned. But what that requirement meant, what duties it entailed, remained quite uncertain.[14]

Calhoun's speech promoted solidarity as a strategy both nationalist and sectionalist, preserving the Union and saving the South. It was a superb device to knit together dissonant factions in South Carolina, increasingly eager to refight the battles of Nullification and win status on the local political scene. Throughout his career, Calhoun had championed an ideal of statesmanship over spoilsmanship, denouncing the evil influence of faction and personal interest in politics. To be sure, there was much in his own conduct that made mock of that stance, and by the end of his career Calhoun's strength within the state derived primarily from his role as a broker of local political networks, dispensing favour and adjudicating disputes. As referee, linchpin, and idol, he was essential to maintaining political order – if never peace – within the state. When Calhoun died three years after his Charleston speech, tensions exploded into the open and politicos learnt to harness the jeremiad against their opponents. The consequence was a self-regenerating cycle of conflict and a death spiral of extremism cloaked as loyalty to the values of the fallen Calhoun.[15]

It was South Carolina's failure to rally on a strong substitute for Calhoun that unleashed this dismal train of events. 'While Mr. Calhoun lived', one old-timer recalled,

> the only lesson either taught or comprehended, from the parish school to the senate chamber, was to obey orders! We did this implicitly and kept up the appearance of a solid column! We were drilled in the lockstep, but the instruction was merely mechanical... Well, our great chief, for he was essentially great, is among the dead, and he has left no one to administer upon his political estate.[16]

That was the upshot of an awful series of political failures that only South Carolina politicians could have conspired to manufacture. First, Calhoun's replacement to the US Senate, the powerful but ill-suited Frank Elmore, promptly died. The ambitious governor then slotted in a lesser light – inoffensive Robert W. Barnwell – in hopes of winning the seat for himself a few months hence. Instead, the legislature chose fractious Robert Barnwell Rhett, erstwhile Calhounist and chieftain of sectionalism. But even that appointment did not last: by 1852, Rhett had resigned his seat on principle, declaring that his personal politics strayed too far from the spirit of the state he represented. That pretty much out-Calhouned Calhoun himself in terms of adhering to the code of statesmanship, but it also deprived South Carolina of any single dominant leader. That put power up for grabs and the jeremiad into play as never before.[17]

Across the 1850s, Carolina politicians adapted Calhoun's exhortation to further conflicting goals. When the dream of a Southern Party capsized after 1852, upcountry Congressman James L. Orr argued that southerners could shape national destiny by seizing control of the Democratic Party. That had been Calhoun's chief aim, and few men knew better how the prospect of potential profits from railroad growth might allay sectional tensions. Orr's National Democrats warned that secessionists only injured the South's cause. Instead of raising impossible demands, they should hew to the party line and hush up.[18]

But, to 'State Rights' extremists, Orr's bloc had everything backwards. *Their* leader was 'the most pernicious enemy' of slaveholding society, *his* policy 'portentous of all evil'. In Washington, one Carolina stalwart after another had abandoned principle in hope of high office and a share of the 'loaves and fishes'. All too soon Yankee 'demons on one side, and false friends on the other' would thrust aside these inconstant sentries to ravish the South. After one term of Republican rule, Governor James Adams predicted, self-interest and factionalism would be so rampant in South Carolina that

> we will find in our midst an organized *Freesoil Party*, backed and upheld by the overshadowing power and patronage of the Federal Government.... Abolition presses, under the false pretence of giving the new Administration a fair showing, will spring up among us. The Post Office will be in the hands of the enemy. Its mission will become one of poison – poison to be infused into our system through a thousand secret channels. Our enemy knows too well his game for an open assault. Sapping and mining will be the process of our ruin.

To avert this fate, States'-Righters had to rally on principle, not party. 'Do your duty', ordered Maxcy Gregg, 'and leave the consequences to God'. Duty, of course, would be defined by the fire-eaters: immediate secession, reopening the slave trade, and God knew what else. Dissent from this world-saving course was tantamount to treason.[19]

Between these warring camps, moderates tried to straddle a broad middle ground. To Senator James Hammond, the 'minor distinctions' of party seemed 'factitious and factious, gotten up by cunning men for selfish purposes, to which the true patriot and honest man should be slow to lend himself'. He would champion neither National Democrats' manipulation nor States' – Rights Democrats' brinkmanship. '[T]he Constitution, strictly construed and faithfully carried out' was the flag he followed. 'I will make my fight', Hammond declared, 'by the side of any man, whether from the

North, South, East or West who will do the same'. That was a credo bland enough to unite both Orrites and secessionists, moderates hoped, but as Hammond's warlike language suggested, here too promises were coupled with threats. Those who abandoned sectarian principles were patriots. Those who would not were traitors to be vanquished.[20]

By 1860, then, Carolinians across the political spectrum shared a dynamic set of political premises subject to broad and clashing interpretation. Southern safety required internal unity, all agreed. Those who betrayed that unity, said the jeremiad, whether from self-seeking or shortsightedness, were turncoats to be hunted, exposed, and destroyed. In this view, politics was the constant testing and scrutinising of loyalties, a deathless demand for internal cohesion, and an unending war against dissenters. After Calhoun's passing, Carolinians could never agree on what the basis of solidarity should be, and so were never able to achieve anything like internal unity, however abstract and transitory. Subversion threatened on all sides, yet vigilance never crossed over to the safety of single-mindedness.

Southern society in the 1850s showed nothing except double-mindedness: the variance between plantation society and what some historians have unfortunately called modernisation, the contradictions of honour and respectability, and the innumerable internal conflicts slavery engendered. Politically, bribery and all forms of crookedness became subsumed under the category of 'Calhounery' in South Carolina politics. So long as the right names showed up in the right columns on election night, and no important heads wound up broken in the process, all was well.[21]

That peculiar calculus was just why secession finally came off in 1860 in just the most unlikely place – the conservative epicentre of the most saber-rattling, do-nothing state in Dixie – to the consternation of all. Since 1828, South Carolina had howled about its violated rights, its blighted prospects, and its radical plans. Again and again it had approached the precipice – then stepped back. No other Southern state, for good reason, had ventured close by its side. But then Calhoun died, and by the very uncertainty of his political legacy, cut out the middle ground of South Carolina politics. In the wake of Lincoln's election, at street level in Charleston, everything depended on personal performance and political spin. Men wore badges, marched in parades, mounted flags, and sang songs, which aimed to put them on the right side of the South Carolina jeremiad. But falling faithfully into ranks here for the first time put them on a disastrously radical course.[22]

Nothing so clearly demonstrated the power of the South Carolina jeremiad in 1860, and the double-minded character of South Carolina's political movement in November 1860 as the performance enacted in Charleston's federal courthouse on the morning after Lincoln's electoral victory was announced. Almost all of the principal actors were conservatives and nationalists, members of what locals called the 'Broad Street Clique'. Outside the courthouse that morning, angry men displaying blue cockades, shouting, and waving flags cursed the news of Republican victory. Stepping up to the bench, federal District Attorney James Conner and grand jury foreman Robert Gourdin chose to present no cases and retired their offices. Judge Andrew G. Magrath, a vastly popular political figure, both because and in spite of his only nominally Irish identity, went a step further. Standing up melodramatically, he pulled off his robes and declared the court closed. By nightfall, men were painting banners depicting Magrath rending his garments like an Old Testament prophet and cursing the federal union. Was that not what any Southern statesman would do, according to the dictates of the South Carolina jeremiad, in this hour of crisis?[23]

'When Charleston is ready for action', radical John Cunningham crowed in late November 1860,

> you may take it as an indication that the State is ready for action, and when such a man as Judge Magrath tells you it is time for action, I tell you there must follow him the only influence in the city of Charleston that might cause you to doubt as to what course you might take.

There was now no mistaking the sentiment of the people, James Conner agreed.

> We in Charleston have felt the fever – we have caught the excitement; and I wish you all had been with us last night and witnessed the manifestations, not only greater than I have ever seen, but greater than those older than I have had the opportunity to witness. It was an excitement that pervaded the whole community. It manifested itself in no wildness. It was earnest but determined. It discussed little; passed few resolves, but sent back one loud echo, that the day for deliberation is passed and that the hour of action is at hand. Charleston, which has been at times considered lukewarm, and by virtue of her commercial interests conservative in an eminent degree, has been the first to move.[24]

And that had won the day. As much as he deplored radicalism, Conner, like all Carolinians, craved unity. Performance had trumped discourse; symbols had replaced speech. Discussion of secession itself symbolised the failure of unity and militancy and needed to be suppressed. It was the empty sound he celebrated – 'one loud echo' – not the meaning of the words themselves.[25]

Two days later, Charleston rallied at the newly christened 'Secession Hall'. Formerly the showplace of reformist enterprise and moderates favoured meeting place, now the South Carolina Institute was commandeered pointedly by local radicals. 'The solid men of the city were there *en masse*', the *Mercury* noted, and nearly two hundred were appointed vice presidents or secretaries. Some, like J.J. McCarter and Henry Gourdin, were well-known Unionists, and others notoriously 'slow', but that was no matter. All were present and passive. With that, the melodrama could proceed.[26]

'We will have no division', Magrath warned gravely. 'Whoever leads my State in the path of honor and duty, is the leader for me'. Lincoln went quite unmentioned here; factionalism was secession's sternest foe. 'We must be true to the high destiny', George Elliott told cheering crowds outside the hall, 'let no distracting councils divide the State, but let us all... carry out the great drama you have inaugurated'. Whatever men thought about secession, the cause of the jeremiad would not be denied.[27]

For moderates, too, dwelling on disunion was not so important. Power for the conservative Broad Street Clique and their peers had ever been their cause. Across more than a decade they had ridden into office on money, men, brave words, and social fears – anything that came to hand. Even now it seemed likely that Clique men like Magrath and Conner would lead the state, provided that they mouthed the correct phrases. Once in power, they would steer things as suited them best, as they always had, under the aegis of Calhoun. But this time they were riding the tiger.

The finale of Charleston's 'great drama' was enacted on the same stage on November 15, just a week after the first angry improvisation. Now the 'vast hall was beautifully decorated with banners and palmetto branches, and a live palmetto was planted at the entrance'. Crowds jammed every corner and spilled into the street, welcoming the city's representatives home from Columbia. 'Torches and fireworks lit up the front' of the Institute, the *Mercury* wrote, 'and the continual explosion of crackers reminded us that the new "Independence Day" is at hand'.[28]

First, Mayor Macbeth addressed the throng, amid 'loud cheers and waving of hats', applauding the respect for 'law and order' that all had shown while pressing the cause of revolution forward. It had not always been thus, radicals remembered. Then Calhounist Robert Gourdin spoke, congratulating fellow citizens 'on the unity of opinion and purpose' they showed. 'Harmony in counsel and unity in action are... essential to our political deliverance and independence', he affirmed. Senator William Dennison Porter sounded the same themes.

> Your danger lies not in isolation, but... in the effort to patch and tinker up this quarrel, and save the Union from the perils into which it is now plunged.... In the position you have assumed, you cannot retreat. You must go forward or be utterly degraded and disgraced.[29]

Charleston had been 'the herald and pioneer' of the revolution, he exulted. Now '[w]e must have faith in each other and charity in each other, for the heart of every Carolinian is true. Let there be one party, and that party the city against a common foe'. Could Calhoun himself have offered a better benediction?[30]

One after another, Charleston politicos hammered that message home, declaiming the themes of the jeremiad like a disunionist Apostles' Creed. Demagogues like Michael O'Conner and William Whaley whipped up the crowd, begging it to 'hand me a rifle and assign me a place' in the line of battle. Cooperationists ate crow, bowing to the will of the people. 'We [are] now all cooperationists', Joe Pope plagiarised, 'and all secessionists'. What else could he say? 'He who would advise [men] to hesitate and deliberate now', Charles Simonton warned, 'was a traitor to their best interests'.[31]

And so the most conservative city in the South swung into line with the most radical political faction in the South. Political ideology had nothing to do with the shift. Slavery mattered nothing particularly in the drive towards conformity. Political and existential consequences went mostly unconsidered. The calculus men made – in pinning on a secessionist blue cockade, in marching in a disunionist parade, in casting a radical ballot, and in joining a militant Minute Man company – rested instead on the performative imperatives of the South Carolina jeremiad. Young men have long made such stupid, disastrous choices, hastening them to strange, sudden deaths in un-American sounding places like Antietam and Khe Sanh and Fallujah. Were that the end of it, it would be bad enough. But the South Carolina jeremiad morphed into the most virulent strain of Lost Cause ideology, the most conservative aspect of anti-capitalist thought in the wake of the Great Depression, and the central theme of the Southern Manifesto opposing desegregation. John C. Calhoun, as it turns out, hadn't nearly died. Like Frankenstein's monster he has been reanimated, again and again, weaponised to purposes that a moderate, rational, slaveholding man like himself could never have foreseen.[32]

Notes

For advice and criticism, I am indebted to Kathleen M. Hilliard and Orville Vernon Burton.

1 The best biography of Calhoun remains C.M. Wiltse, *John Calhoun*, 3 vols (Indianapolis: Bobbs-Merrill, 1944–1951). On his opposition to the Mexican War, see E.M. Lander, Jr., *Reluctant Imperialists: Calhoun, the South Carolinians, and the Mexican War* (Baton Rouge: Louisiana State University Press, 1980). The Crisis of 1850 is well studied in A. Nevins, *The Ordeal of the Union*, 8 vols (New York: Scribners, 1947–1971), vols. 1–2, H. Hamilton, *Prologue to Conflict: The Crisis and Compromise of 1850* (New York: W. W. Norton, 1966), and in S.E. Maizlish, *A Strife of Tongues: The Compromise of 1850 and the Ideological Origins of the American Civil War* (Charlottesville: University Press of Virginia, 2018). Calhoun's death is best traced through R.L. Meriwether, et al., eds, *The Papers of John C. Calhoun*, 28 vols (Columbia: University of South Carolina Press, 1959–2003), vol. 28.
2 The Nullification movement (1827–1833), with little support beyond South Carolina's borders, insisted on the right of individual states to prevent collection of federal customs duties that were imposed inequitably or had a broadly deleterious effect on their constituents. Political leaders of this movement ('nullifiers') such as Calhoun feared that the imposition of tariffs that bore especially heavily on the South would provide a constitutional rationale for abolitionist efforts to destroy slavery through federal legislation. 'Nullifying' those taxes by state legislation or direct action, *à la* the Revolutionary patriots of the Boston Tea

Party, challenged the Federalist interpretation of the Constitution itself. W.W. Freehling, *Prelude to Civil War: The Nullification Controversy in South Carolina, 1816 – 1836* (New York: Harper and Row, 1966).

3　D.M. Potter, *The Impending Crisis, 1848 – 1861* (New York: Harper and Row, 1976), p. 107; Meriwether, et al., eds, *Papers of John C. Calhoun*, 28, p. 251; L.R. Bailey, *A Short Notice of the Death and Character of Mr. Calhoun* (Philadelphia: L.R. Bailey, 1850), p. 3; W.W. Freehling, *The Road to Disunion: Secessionists at Bay, 1776 – 1854* (New York: Oxford University Press, 1990), p. 516.

4　E.H. Walther, *The Fire-Eaters* (Baton Rouge: Louisiana State University Press, 1992); J. McCardell, *The Idea of a Southern Nation: Southern Nationalists and Southern Nationalism, 1830 – 1860* (New York: W.W. Norton, 1981); Freehling, *Road to Disunion*, p. 519. C.f., Tulane University [hereafter, TU] Colcock Family Papers, William Ferguson Colcock to Mary Woodward Hutson Colcock, 30 January 1850].

5　TU Colcock Family Papers, William Ferguson Colcock to Mary Woodward Hutson Colcock, 29 January and 14 February 1850; University of South Carolina, South Caroliniana Library, Washington Peace Papers: Washington Peace to Anna M. Hoover, 9 April 1850.

6　P. Miller, *Errand Into the Wilderness* (Cambridge, MA: Belknap Press, 1956), esp. pp. 1–15; G. Wills, *Lincoln at Gettysburg: The Words that Remade America* (New York: Simon and Schuster, 1992); C.B. Jones and S. Connelly, *Behind the Dream: The Making of the Speech that Transformed a Nation* (New York: St. Martin's Press, 2011); G. Troy, *Morning in America: How Ronald Reagan Invented the 1980s* (Princeton, NJ: Princeton University Press, 2006); D.J. Trump, *Crippled America: How to Make America Great Again* (New York: Threshold Editions, 2015).

7　S. Bercovitch, *The American Jeremiad* (Madison: University of Wisconsin Press, 1978).

8　J.M. Banner, Jr., 'The Problem of South Carolina,' in *The Hofstadter Aegis: A Memorial*, ed. by Stanley Elkins and Eric McKitrick (New York: Alfred A. Knopf, 1974), pp. 60–93. C.f. J. Haw, '"The Problem of South Carolina" Reexamined: A Review Essay,' *South Carolina Historical Magazine* 107 (2006), pp. 9–25. Important studies following in this tradition include R.M. Weir, 'The South Carolinian as Extremist,' *South Atlantic Quarterly* 74 (1975), pp. 86–103; L.K. Ford, Jr., *Origins of Southern Radicalism: The South Carolina Upcountry, 1800 – 1860* (New York: Oxford University Press, 1988); D. Moltke-Hansen, 'Protecting Interests, Maintaining Rights, Emulating Ancestors: U. S. Constitution Bicentennial Reflections on 'The Problem of South Carolina', 1787 – 1860,' *South Carolina Historical Magazine* 89 (1988), pp. 160–182; S. McCurry, *Masters of Small Worlds: Yeoman Households, Gender Relations, and the Political Culture of the Antebellum South Carolina Lowcountry* (New York: Oxford University Press, 1997).

9　On 'fire-eaters', the proslavery radicals who advocated secession from the American union both as a *sine qua non* for the South's safety from abolitionism and Northern values and as a progressive step leading to the construction of a superior and expansionist slave-based civilisation, see especially J.T. Carpenter, *The South as a Conscious Minority, 1789–1861* (New York: New York University Press, 1930); U.B. Phillips, *The Course of the South to Secession* (New York: D. Appleton-Century Company, 1939); D.S. Heidler, 'Fire-Eaters: The Radical Secessionists in Antebellum Politics' (unpublished doctoral thesis, Auburn University, 1985); E.H. Walther, 'The Fire-Eaters, the South, and Secession' (unpublished doctoral thesis, Louisiana State University, 1988).

10　C.S. Boucher, 'Sectionalism, Representation, and the Electoral Question in Ante-Bellum South Carolina,' *Washington University Studies* 4 (1916), pp. 3–62;

H.S. Schultz, *Nationalism and Sectionalism in South Carolina, 1852 to 1860* (Durham, NC: Duke University Press, 1950); Freehling, *Prelude to Civil War*; J.B. Edmunds, Jr., *Francis W. Pickens and the Politics of Destruction* (Chapel Hill: University of North Carolina Press, 1986); W.C. Davis, *Rhett: The Turbulent Life and Times of a Fire-Eater* (Columbia: University of South Carolina Press, 2001); L.T. McDonnell, *Performing Disunion: The Coming of the Civil War in Charleston, South Carolina* (New York: Cambridge University Press, 2018).

11 In the late 1840s, Calhoun sought to resolve the problem of how a proslavery sectional minority's political rights could be secured within an increasingly anti-slavery federal union. His solution – which remained private until after his death and endlessly revised and contested thereafter – was to provide the South with a collective veto over Congressional legislation. With regard to ameliorating or abolishing slavery, then, passage of federal laws would require not only the assent of a majority of representatives and senators, plus the president's signature, but the concurrence of a Southern majority. D.M. Potter, *The South and the Concurrent Majority* (Baton Rouge: Louisiana State University Press, 1972); L.K. Ford, Jr., 'Recovering the Republic: Calhoun, South Carolina, and the Concurrent Majority,' *South Carolina Historical Magazine* 89 (1988), pp. 146–159.

12 *The Works of John C. Calhoun*, ed. R.K. Crallé (Charleston: Walker and James, 1851–1856), vol. 4, pp. 394–396.

13 *The Works of John C. Calhoun*, vol. 4, pp. 394–396.

14 *Charleston Mercury*, August 10, 1835; P. Della Torre, *Is Southern Civilization Worth Preserving?* (Charleston: Southern Rights Association, 1851); South Carolina Historical Society, Charleston, South Carolina, Chesnut-Miller-Manning Papers. W.S. Lyles to James Chesnut, Jr., 1 July 1851.

15 W.W. Freehling, 'Spoilsmen and Interests in the Thought and Career of John C. Calhoun,' *Journal of American History* 52 (1965), pp. 25–42; K.S. Greenberg, 'Representation and the Isolation of South Carolina, 1776–1860,' *Journal of American History* 64 (1977), pp. 723–743.

16 Southern Historical Collection, University of North Carolina [hereafter, SHC] William Porcher Miles Papers. Letter from Alfred Huger to William P. Miles, 1 June 1860.

17 J. Barnwell, *Love of Order: South Carolina's First Secession Crisis* (Chapel Hill: University of North Carolina Press, 1982); K.S. Greenberg, *Masters and Statesmen: The Political Culture of American Slavery* (Baltimore, MD: John Hopkins University Press, 1985), esp. pp. 3–22.

18 *Proceedings of the Democratic State Convention, Held at Columbia, 5th and 6th of May 1856, for the Purpose of Electing Delegates to the Democratic National Convention to Meet at Cincinnati in June* (Columbia, SC: R.W. Gibbs, 1856); T.Y. Simons, Jr., *Speech of Col. Thomas Y. Simons, in Favor of South Carolina Being Represented in the Democratic Convention, Held in Hibernian Hall, Feb. 26, 1860* (Charleston, SC: A.J. Burke, 1860); D.H. Breese, 'James L. Orr, Calhoun, and the Cooperationist Tradition in South Carolina,' *South Carolina Historical Magazine* 80 (1979), pp. 273–285.

19 [Maxcy Gregg, ed.], *An Appeal to the State Rights Party of South Carolina: In Several Letters on the Present Condition of Public Affairs* (Columbia, SC: Southern Guardian, 1858), pp. vii, ix, 2, 8, 10, 35, 36.

20 J.H. Hammond, *Speech of Hon. James H. Hammond, Delivered at Barnwell C. H., October 29th, 1858* (Charleston, SC: Walker, Evans, and Company, 1858), esp. 9.

21 SHC, Pettigrew Family Papers. See variously Franklin Gaillard to James J. Pettigrew, 18 October 1858; Robert F.W. Allston to James J. Pettigrew, 21 October 1858; James J. Pettigrew to William S. Pettigrew, 24 October 1858.

22 McDonnell, *Performing Disunion*.

23 McDonnell, *Performing Disunion*, p. 316; *Charleston Mercury*, 8 November 1860; *Charleston Daily Courier*, 8 November 1860.
24 SHC, William Ferguson Colcock Autobiography, undated entry, p. 38.
25 *Charleston Mercury*, 11 November 1860.
26 *Charleston Mercury*, 11 November 1860; Library of Congress, Washington, DC. J[ohn] J. McCarter Journal, undated entry, pp. 22–24.
27 *Charleston Daily Courier*, 13 November 1860.
28 *Charleston Mercury*, 16 November 1860.
29 *Charleston Mercury*, 16 November 1860; *Charleston Daily Courier*, 16 November 1860.
30 *Charleston Mercury*, 16 November 1860; *Charleston Daily Courier*, 16 November 1860.
31 *Charleston Mercury*, 16 November 1860.
32 That problem, considering the afterlife of Calhoun from 1850 to 2018, is the subject of my book in progress, *The Death and Rebirth of John C. Calhoun*.

Bibliography

Bailey, L.R. *A Short Notice of the Death and Character of Mr. Calhoun* (Philadelphia, PA: L.R. Bailey, 1850).

Banner, J.M., Jr., 'The Problem of South Carolina,' in *The Hofstadter Aegis: A Memorial*, ed. by S. Elkins and E. McKitrick (New York: Alfred A. Knopf, 1974), pp. 60–93.

Barnwell, J. *Love of Order: South Carolina's First Secession Crisis* (Chapel Hill: University of North Carolina Press, 1982).

Bercovitch, S. *The American Jeremiad* (Madison: University of Wisconsin Press, 1978).

Boucher, C.S. 'Sectionalism, Representation, and the Electoral Question in Ante-Bellum South Carolina,' *Washington University Studies* 4 (1916), pp. 3–62.

Breese, D.H. 'James L. Orr, Calhoun, and the Cooperationist Tradition in South Carolina,' *South Carolina Historical Magazine* 80 (1979), pp. 273–285.

Armistead Burt Papers, Duke University, Durham, North Carolina.

Carpenter, J.T. *The South as a Conscious Minority, 1789–1861* (New York: New York University Press, 1930).

Charleston Daily Courier.

Charleston Mercury.

Chesnut-Miller-Manning Papers, South Carolina Historical Society, Charleston, South Carolina.

Colcock, W.F. Autobiography, Southern Historical Collection, University of North Carolina, Chapel Hill, North Carolina.

Colcock Family Papers, Tulane University.

Crallé, R.K. ed. *The Works of John C. Calhoun* (Charleston: Walker and James, 1851–1856).

Davis, W.C. *Rhett: The Turbulent Life and Times of a Fire-Eater* (Columbia: University of South Carolina Press, 2001).

Della Torre, P. *Is Southern Civilization Worth Preserving?* (Charleston, SC: Southern Rights Association, 1851).

Edmunds, Jr. J.B. *Francis W. Pickens and the Politics of Destruction* (Chapel Hill: University of North Carolina Press, 1986).

Ford, Jr. L.K. *Origins of Southern Radicalism: The South Carolina Upcountry, 1800–1860* (New York: Oxford University Press, 1988).

———. 'Recovering the Republic: Calhoun, South Carolina, and the Concurrent Majority,' *South Carolina Historical Magazine* 89 (1988), pp. 146–159.

Freehling, W.W. *Prelude to Civil War: The Nullification Controversy in South Carolina, 1816–1836* (New York: Harper and Row, 1966).

———. *The Road to Disunion: Secessionists at Bay, 1776–1854* (New York: Oxford University Press, 1990).

———. 'Spoilsmen and Interests in the Thought and Career of John C. Calhoun,' *Journal of American History* 52 (1965), pp. 25–42.

Greenberg, K.S. *Masters and Statesmen: The Political Culture of American Slavery.* (Baltimore, MD: Johns Hopkins University Press, 1985).

———. 'Representation and the Isolation of South Carolina, 1776–1860,' *Journal of American History* 64 (1977), pp. 723–743.

[Gregg, M. ed.]. *An Appeal to the State Rights Party of South Carolina: In Several Letters on the Present Condition of Public Affairs* (Columbia, SC: Southern Guardian, 1858).

Hamilton, H. *Prologue to Conflict: The Crisis and Compromise of 1850* (New York: W. W. Norton, 1966).

Hammond, J.H. *Speech of Hon. James H. Hammond, Delivered at Barnwell C. H., October 29th, 1858* (Charleston: Walker, Evans, and Company, 1858).

Haw, J. '"The Problem of South Carolina" Reexamined: A Review Essay,' *South Carolina Historical Magazine* 107 (2006), pp. 9–25.

Heidler, D.S. 'Fire-Eaters: The Radical Secessionists in Antebellum Politics' (unpublished doctoral thesis, Auburn University, 1985).

Jones, C.B. and S. Connelly. *Behind the Dream: The Making of the Speech that Transformed a Nation* (New York: St. Martin's Press, 2011).

Lander, Jr. E.M. *Reluctant Imperialists: Calhoun, the South Carolinians, and the Mexican War* (Baton Rouge: Louisiana State University Press, 1980).

Maizlish, S.E. *A Strife of Tongues: The Compromise of 1850 and the Ideological Origins of the American Civil War* (Charlottesville: University Press of Virginia, 2018).

McCardell, J. *The Idea of a Southern Nation: Southern Nationalists and Southern Nationalism, 1830–1860* (New York: W. W. Norton, 1981).

McCarter, J.J. Journal, Library of Congress, Washington, DC.

McCurry, S. *Masters of Small Worlds: Yeoman Households, Gender Relations, and the Political Culture of the Antebellum South Carolina Low Country* (New York: Oxford University Press, 1997).

McDonnell, L.T. *Performing Disunion: The Coming of the Civil War in Charleston, South Carolina* (New York: Cambridge University Press, 2018).

Meriwether, R.L., et al., eds, *The Papers of John C. Calhoun*, 28 vols (Columbia: University of South Carolina Press, 1959–2003).

William Porcher Miles Papers, Southern Historical Collection, University of North Carolina, Chapel Hill, North Carolina.

Miller, P. *Errand into the Wilderness* (Cambridge, MA: Belknap Press, 1956).

Moltke-Hansen, D. 'Protecting Interests, Maintaining Rights, Emulating Ancestors: U. S. Constitution Bicentennial Reflections on 'The Problem of South Carolina', 1787–1860,' *South Carolina Historical Magazine* 89 (1988), pp. 160–182.

Nevins, A. *The Ordeal of the Union*, 8 vols (New York: Scribners, 1947–1971).

Washington Peace Papers, South Caroliniana Library, University of South Carolina, Columbia, South Carolina.

Pettigrew Family Papers, Southern Historical Collection, University of North Carolina, Chapel Hill, North Carolina.

Phillips, U.B. *The Course of the South to Secession* (New York: D. Appleton-Century Company, 1939).

Potter, D.M. *The Impending Crisis, 1848–1861* (New York: Harper and Row, 1976).

———. *The South and the Concurrent Majority* (Baton Rouge: Louisiana State University Press, 1972).

Proceedings of the Democratic State Convention, Held at Columbia, 5th and 6th of May 1856, for the Purpose of Electing Delegates to the Democratic National Convention to Meet at Cincinnati in June (Columbia, SC: R. W. Gibbes, 1856).

Schultz, H.S. *Nationalism and Sectionalism in South Carolina, 1852 to 1860* (Durham, NC: Duke University Press, 1950).

Simons, Jr. T.Y. *Speech of Col. Thomas Y. Simons, in Favor of South Carolina Being Represented in the Democratic Convention, Held in Hibernian Hall, Feb. 26, 1860* (Charleston, SC: A. J. Burke, 1860).

Troy, G. *Morning in America: How Ronald Reagan Invented the 1980s* (Princeton, NJ: Princeton University Press, 2006).

Trump, D.J. *Crippled America: How to Make America Great Again* (New York: Threshold Editions, 2015).

Walther, E.H. *The Fire-Eaters* (Baton Rouge: Louisiana State University Press, 1992).

Walther, E.H. 'The Fire-Eaters, the South, and Secession' (unpublished doctoral thesis, Louisiana State University, 1988).

Weir, R.M. 'The South Carolinian as Extremist,' *South Atlantic Quarterly* 74 (1975), pp. 86–103.

Wills, G. *Lincoln at Gettysburg: The Words that Remade America* (New York: Simon and Schuster, 1992).

Wiltse, C.M. *John Calhoun*, 3 vols (Indianapolis: Bobbs-Merrill, 1944–1951).

Part V
Family division and union

11 Family union and the discharge of infanticidal married mothers from Broadmoor Criminal Lunatic Asylum, 1863–1895

Alison Pedley

The murder of a child is an act which, by its very nature, can tear apart even the strongest of marriages and families. The Victorian view of motherhood was that a normal mother would instinctively nurture her children and could never commit such a heinous and unnatural act as child-murder. Yet when an ordinary, respectable mother acted completely out of character and was driven to kill her child, popular and official opinion was consistently compassionate towards her.[1] One 'acceptable' explanation for the mother's unconscionable behaviour lay in a diagnosis of insanity. Although the term 'infanticide' was usually associated with the murder of infants within a year of the birth, it was popularly used in the period to describe the killing of children of all ages up to early teens. Within this chapter the term is not only used in this context but also used to include other violent assaults on young children.[2] The main focus of my survey is a cohort of married mothers who had been detained in Broadmoor between 1863 and 1895, 'until her Majesty's pleasure be known'. As 'criminal lunatics' the women were incarcerated indefinitely, only able to leave by Home Office authorised discharge (with or without particular conditions for care attached) or by death. In this chapter, I concentrate on those women who were discharged to the guardianship of their families and specifically, to their husbands.

The Broadmoor Hospital Archive is held at the Berkshire Record Office, where the admission and discharge books, administrative records and various individual case files are available for study. The personal case files are a rich source containing draft medical reports, Home Office papers, letters and other personal ephemera.[3] The Archive has been used for research into a range of topics to do with patients in Victorian Broadmoor, and the work of Jonathan Andrews is particularly relevant to this chapter.[4] His research was carried out over fifteen years ago when the archive was still held at Broadmoor, and he was able to access records which are now closed.[5] Andrews reviewed discharges of female infanticidal patients from two criminal lunatic facilities, Broadmoor and the Perth Criminal Lunatic Department in Scotland. Many of his points about the circumstances and background to the release of women from Broadmoor are relevant here.[6] Andrews's survey covered a wide range of issues considered by the authorities when they reviewed a case for possible discharge. I concentrate on one factor in particular, that of family and spousal unity and investigate the impact that social and cultural standards may have had on those discharge decisions.

The crime had a social impact on the families and friends of the infanticidal mothers, and long-term confinement could profoundly affect family dynamics. Although they did not comprehend the motives behind the murder, family and partners of the mentally ill mothers would actively seek their release from Broadmoor and would offer support and care. When reaching their discharge decisions, the clinicians at Broadmoor and officials at the Home Office reviewed not only the patient's mental and physical health, but also the social and domestic circumstances of the proposed guardians. The authorities would only be willing to pass on responsibility for the patient's care if the family and friends were considered capable of providing for and protecting a mentally fragile person. As an illustration of the success or otherwise of the discharge decisions, I include, where possible, a brief resumé of the lives of the women after discharge from the Asylum. I conclude the chapter with a case study to illustrate the importance of strong marital union and family unity in the decision-making process, both at the Asylum and at the Home Office.

Discharge from Broadmoor

Between 1863 and 1895 there were 235 mothers admitted to Broadmoor for murdering or violently assaulting their children. The main focus for this chapter is the 197 women of the group who were married or widowed. As shown in Table 11.1, 53 per cent of this smaller group were discharged and

Table 11.1 'Discharges Removals & Deaths'. Married mothers who had murdered their children – Admissions between 1863 and 1895

Discharges from Broadmoor for Admissions between 1863 and 1895

To the Care of:	No.	% of Total	% of Discharges
Husband	45		43
Siblings	12		11
Parents	11		10
Children (adult)	9		9
Other Relatives	7		7
Total to Family care	84		80
Other Asylums	19		18
Employers	2		2
Discharges – total	105	53	100
Died in Asylum	92	47	
Total 'Discharges Removals & Deaths'	197	100	

Source: BRO D/H14/D/1/15/1, Discharge register: 1863–1900. I have identified 235 such cases for the period 1863–1895.

47 per cent died in the Asylum. Of the 105 patients who were released 84 were released to care of family members and of that number, 45 were discharged into their husbands' care.

Obtaining a discharge from Broadmoor was a long, complicated process. All patients in Broadmoor were 'criminal lunatics' and therefore under the control of the State, so the role of the medical superintendent and his medical staff in the discharge process was that of expert medical advisors. The initial impetus or petition for release could come from the patient, their family, or any interested third party, but in all cases, the request had to be made to the Home Secretary. The authorities at the Asylum could only sanction the release of patients in concert with other parties, although their advice and recommendations were of paramount significance. A discharge from Broadmoor required the agreement of not only the Home Office and the medical superintendents but also the Lunacy Commissioners. To this end, there was a full assessment of the patient's potential future living circumstances from such parties as local dignitaries and employers, and full reports from the medical superintendents and their staff.[7]

The system for discharge at Broadmoor was not routinely explained to interested parties: it appears to have been given on a 'need to know' basis. It also differed from that of a county lunatic asylum, where a family could make a direct request to the superintendent for the release of a relative. As in the state criminal lunatic asylum, the asylum doctors in county asylums had little say in who was *admitted* to the asylum, but in the county asylums, they did have a profound influence over who was discharged and the ultimate discharge decision lay in their hands.[8] Perhaps because they regarded the medical superintendent at Broadmoor as all-powerful in such matters, there were cases of relatives following the 'normal' route and appealing directly to the Broadmoor authorities. These demands and requests were invariably answered by the medical officers with a reminder to the relatives that the decision was not theirs to make and that Whitehall must be petitioned. Despite this, many families persisted in their direct hounding of the medical superintendent using different strategies. The family of Mary Bennett frequently requested that she be released and stated that they would come and collect her when the Medical Superintendent of Broadmoor gave them a time.[9] Dr William Orange reminded them, on each occasion, that only the Home Office could sanction her release.[10] There is a sense of exasperation in Orange's reply that 'it is only right that I tell you... to save you needless trouble... the question of liberation of persons from this asylum... rests solely with the Secretary of State for the Home Dept (sic)'.[11] The process was protracted and painstaking because, after all, the patients were murderers and although one concern was the patient's future care, the authorities had to consider public safety. A major consideration was whether they could be assimilated back into normal life, and therefore the lives and circumstances of potential guardians were examined in great detail (Figure 11.1).

Figure 11.1 'Female Dormitory', *Illustrated London News*, 7 September 1867, p. 209.
Source: Berkshire Record Office, Coley Avenue, Reading.

Husbands and matrimonial unity

The education and the social circumstances of the husband mattered to both the asylum authorities and the Home Office. The efforts of those men who tried to better themselves and perhaps change their lifestyle, so they could have their wives back, were respected. This is apparent in the official responses to Annie Nicholls's husband, Richard. Annie Nicholls was committed to the Asylum in December 1871 for the murder of her four-month-old son by vitriol. Although she was found 'not guilty but insane' by the courts, Annie did not display many symptoms of insanity when on remand in prison nor in Broadmoor. It was noted on her prison transfer document from Durham Gaol to Broadmoor in 1871, that '[she] has been free of any symptom since admission. Good health'.[12] In 1873 Richard Nicholls wrote the first of many letters asking whether it would be worth him petitioning the Home Secretary for his wife's release. He did not doubt her sanity, writing, 'I need only say that from the manner of her writing she seems to be quite recovered' but also that he would defer to the opinion of the Medical Superintendent, 'but of that [her recovery] I leave to yourself to judge'.[13]

Dr Orange replied that 'there has been no change in the state of her health and she may still be considered sane'.[14] Nicholls advised Orange that he was considering emigration to which end he had taught himself French and German. His reason for doing so was that although he was comfortably provided for at home, receiving wages of three shillings a week, he believed that there were fair prospects in 'leaving this country for a number of years', and that then he would be in a position to provide well for his wife.[15] As he had found regular employment in the United States, in 1878 Orange endorsed the petition for Annie's discharge to Nicholls's care.[16] By 1900 they had had three more children and were living in Trumbull, Ohio.[17]

Despite the best of intentions from the husband, sometimes his intellectual abilities and economic circumstances were viewed as a potential risk to his wife's future welfare. When the women were admitted to the Asylum their levels of literacy were recorded and played a part in the assessment of suitability for discharge. Similarly, the educational background and intelligence of their husbands, and extended families, appeared to be of significance in the authorities' decisions about the families' capabilities as potential guardians.[18] In the case of Emma Luke, officials at both the Home Office and Broadmoor doubted her husband's ability to protect her and guard against potential relapse. They were particularly concerned by the possibility of another pregnancy. On 25 October 1875 Emma had murdered her four-week-old daughter by cutting her throat and was discovered by neighbours soon afterwards attempting to commit suicide. After her trial at Warwick Assizes, she was admitted to Broadmoor in December 1875. In court it was said that she was suffering from puerperal mania at the time of the crime and had not been conscious of her murderous and suicidal actions.[19] Puerperal mania or insanity was a widely used diagnosis for a debilitating mental illness suffered by women after childbirth. Mothers who were said to be puerperally insane could be violent towards themselves, their families and their babies and unaware of or unable to control such tendencies.[20] Applications for Emma Luke's release began within a few months of her admission but met with little success. Thomas Luke, her husband, was a nail caster and they lived in a poor area of Aston, Birmingham. Despite the humble state of their home-life, the couple were regarded as respectable people in the local community. Thomas Luke was described as a 'respectable mechanic', but it was noted that he was rather short of employment at the time of the murder.[21] The medical officers at the Asylum disparaged him and his domestic situation. One medical report described Luke as not 'possessing the necessary degree of intelligence which would enable him to have his wife properly taken care of', and said that he was not in 'sufficiently good circumstances' to prevent 'the future possibility of violence on her part'.[22] Emma was discharged in 1878 into the care of friends, eventually returning to her husband sometime before 1881.[23] The Lukes would have five more children, and Emma died in 1929 at the age of 75.[24] The Luke household was regarded as respectable by their local community and Emma was described as 'a fond mother' and good housewife, both important social virtues.[25] While the officials at Broadmoor and the Home Office may have had doubts about the Lukes, their friends and neighbours did not. The support of their peers helped in securing a quick release and illustrates the socio-cultural importance of the role of extended family and community for the Victorian poor.[26]

In November 1875 Martha Baines, the wife of a chemist and druggist from Kendal, murdered her five-month-old baby by feeding him bleach. At the inquest, it was stated that she was suffering from puerperal mania and for that reason she had been attended by a doctor since the birth. Her doctor had suggested she should go into an asylum to rest, but her husband, Thomas, resisted the idea.[27] She was sent into Appleby Gaol but, as she was obviously insane, the prison surgeons applied to the Home Office for direct admission into Broadmoor, avoiding a trial by jury. It was said that Martha needed compassionate treatment rather than punishment.[28] Within a few days of her admission Thomas Baines was writing to the Broadmoor authorities pleading for her return. He wrote, 'I have 3 children left who are very much attached to her. No-one was a better mother and wife than she was, she was completely wrapped up in her children'.[29] Orange at that point replied that although she was recovering from the state of mental depression she was not 'strong in body or in mind but is likely to improve'.[30] The desperation to obtain Mrs Baines's discharge might also be seen in an economic as much as a loving context. Without friends or family to look after young children, a lone parent might find it difficult to look after a household. Unlike in the assessment of Thomas Luke, Thomas Baines's ability to care for his wife was not questioned. The medical staff were less critical of Baines's financial and domestic situation. He was a respectably employed semi-professional man and perceived as able to support his wife. The Baines's middle-class household and the social expectations of their life would be familiar to the educated officials at both Broadmoor and the Home Office. In his report to the Home Office recommending her release, Dr Orange wrote '[s]he is in a respectable position in life and her husband is able and willing to provide for her'.[31] The social status of the family, and in particular the status of Thomas Baines, was instrumental in her early discharge. In August 1877 after just thirteen months in the Asylum, Martha was discharged, 'her sanity now ... re-established'.[32] She returned home to Kendal, where she had two more children and lived until her death in 1925.[33]

Other husbands travelled abroad to seek a new life, a move which was sometimes viewed unfavourably by the medical officers. Andrews suggests that this moving away to seek employment was viewed as a 'careless semi-abandonment'.[34] This was not necessarily the case if the move proved successful in securing a good future for the family. The main concern of the authorities was that a discharged patient should have a secure and 'comfortable' future outside Broadmoor. Sometimes emigration and the ensuing change in prospects were viewed as a positive move in securing a safe release for the patient, as in the case of Annie and Richard Nicholls. The Asylum authorities applauded Richard Nicholls's efforts to establish a new life by educating himself and finding steady employment, albeit in the United States. Orange wrote in his report to the Home Office that Annie Nicholls 'might without unwarrantable risk, be discharged to the care of her husband who is prepared and anxious for her to share the comforts of his home in America'.[35] However, the idea that a husband might be avoiding responsibility for his wife by working abroad was mooted in other cases.

Lucy Keary's husband was absent and working in India as a railway engineer when she drowned one of their daughters and attempted suicide near her parents' home in London. From the time of her admission in 1878, he was in regular contact with the Broadmoor authorities seeking his wife's discharge.[36] Despite good references from his employer affirming Edward Keary's trustworthiness and assurances that there was a support network of friends in Bombay, the doctors refused to recommend Lucy's release to his care while he was in India.[37] The Asylum authorities together with the Home Office could not see their way to recommending Lucy Keary's discharge if her husband remained abroad. Once it was agreed that she had recovered sufficiently to warrant discharge, the officials and clinicians would only consider her release to the care of her brother. Keary appeared to be aggrieved at the decision, writing in 1886 that 'there is no chance of my coming to England to seek employment as I could not get such a situation'.[38] Lucy's discharge was eventually made possible only with the support of family in England, Keary's employers in India and a local MP's intervention. She was discharged to her brother's care in 1886 and then allowed to go out to Bombay to join her husband.[39]

The risk of relapse was of major concern to the medical staff in the discharge process. This was particularly relevant to those women who had been diagnosed as suffering from puerperal insanity and other manias related to childbearing.[40] In a letter from the Broadmoor to the Home Office about Lucy Keary, for instance, Dr Orange wrote, 'she is 35 years old ... There would be considerable risk of her relapsing ... unless she were detained until she had passed the childbearing age'.[41] The ability of husbands to guard against future attacks of insanity was often questioned. Although not officially documented as a condition of discharge, case file notes indicate that the husbands would be made aware of the risks caused by pregnancy and childbirth. They were urged to be cautious in this regard to protect their wives' mental well-being. Annie Howell was described as 'not at all unlikely to relapse into insanity more especially in the event of her becoming pregnant'.[42] It was advised that her husband, Captain James Howell, 'should be clearly informed of the risk of the occurrence of a relapse into insanity and that suitable provision should be made for taking necessary steps to avert danger'.[43] Some husbands were very aware of the reasons behind their wife's collapse and accepted that it was important to guard against any possibility of relapse into insanity. As John Ashley wrote to Orange in 1879 '[If] she [his wife Louisa] be restored to us ... there is little probability of her having more children ... [so] ...would be free from those cares which were the cause of her mind giving way'.[44] Ashley understood that it would be his responsibility to protect his wife from the possibility of future insanity. In the event, Louisa Ashley did not recover sufficiently in medical opinion to be released to her husband. She was transferred to Claybury Asylum in 1904 as 'fit for an ordinary asylum' where she died in 1905.[45]

The authorities looked for the involvement of husbands, and there was an expectation that they would shoulder the responsibility for the patient's mental and physical welfare if she were discharged. In their observations of the domestic circumstances of their patients, the asylum medical officers seem to adhere to the contemporary, arguably middle-class, cultural ideal that a wife and mother's place was in the centre of her family.[46] This did not mean that they were unaware of the threat of domestic violence in the homes of some of their patients and they did recognise the significant effect that domestic disunion and violence could have on a woman's mental state.[47] They would not necessarily release the women to their husbands irrespective of the domestic situation, and as far as possible they sought to protect the vulnerable. Blame was laid on spouses for their wives' mental deterioration through not fulfilling their expected masculine role of guardian, provider and carer.[48] Sarah Beagley was admitted to Broadmoor in 1882 after strangling her child, her attack of insanity attributed to 'Lactation and domestic trouble ... husband was unfaithful ... acknowledged being with other women'. In Sarah Beagley's case file, it was explicitly stated and acknowledged that her treatment by her spouses and her domestic circumstances lay at the root of her mental illness.

> She appears to have lived very unhappily with her husband ... was a wife and mother at 14, [in Canada] 1st husband dead, married to 2nd husband 13 years ... has always suffered from headaches; both husbands have struck her about the head.[49]

In 1890, an application for Sarah Beagley's release from her husband was refused after Dr Nicolson received a letter from her son which accused his father of drinking to excess and of being the cause of all the family problems.[50] Eventually, in 1895, Sarah was released to the care of her 'respectably employed' son.[51]

However, not all women in this type of situation had alternative places to go. Family needs often seemed to override potential domestic problems. Dr Orange himself wrote, '[i]t is a sad thing for a wife and mother to be separated from her family', articulating perhaps a fundamental view of a woman's place in Victorian society, in the home caring for her family.[52] The key role women played in childcare and in the home meant that pragmatic motivation often played a large part in discharge decisions. Rebecca Loveridge's husband was described as 'brutish' and 'the cause of her trouble, he drank and ill-used her'.[53] However, he was described as being 'most attentive' during her time in Broadmoor and because he 'promise[d] well ... and ... quite prepared to sign an undertaking' to care for her, Rebecca was released to his guardianship.[54] Rebecca Loveridge's case highlights some of the inconsistencies that could exist between discharge cases. There were occasions when the authorities appeared to believe that the need for the mother to return to run the home and family took priority over her welfare. Rebecca Loveridge returned to the family home in Kingsteignton, Devon, where she lived until her death in 1922.[55]

In other cases, the medical officers were more protective, especially if it were believed that the husbands were unreasonably demanding. As Medical Superintendent, Dr Orange could be particularly protective in his interactions with patients. In the mid-nineteenth century, the medical superintendent's role was seen as the benevolent father at the head of his asylum family.[56] William Orange was very much in this mould, described as 'ever sympathetic with those in trouble and ready to help when appealed to', a protector and mentor to his patients.[57] Elizabeth Harris was admitted to Broadmoor on 10 January 1872 having been found 'not guilty but insane' of assaulting Sarah and Mary Harris 'with intent to do some grievous bodily harm'.[58] She had attacked her daughters with a razor, slashing them on their arms. Doubts were expressed from the outset about her purported insanity, and her mental state was attributed to 'exhaustion caused by profuse haemorrhaging accompanying abortion'.[59] In contemporary usage, the term 'abortion' meant a naturally occurring miscarriage. Elizabeth was released from Broadmoor in March 1872 but a month later she wrote to Dr Orange saying that she was 'not nearly as well as ... when I left'.[60] She was readmitted in a state of exhaustion and depression. It was arranged that she should go to work for the Anglican sisters at the House of Mercy in Clewer, near Windsor, as a convalescent patient undertaking light tasks to help prepare her for return to her home.[61] Her husband, Richard Harris, was very exacting and demanding, and his attitude towards his wife was not liked by the asylum staff, nor by the Sisters.[62] Dr Nicolson wrote in August 1872 that since Harris's visits, Elizabeth had 'been growing gradually more depressed'.[63] Following one visit to Clewer, Richard Harris wrote demanding her release saying,

> considering the length of time I have been neglected, I say again if she is quite well which I believe she is ... it is her duty as a noble and honnest (sic) woman to return to her domestic duties.[64]

In Elizabeth's case file notes Dr Nicolson wrote, 'The husband although evincing much affection is far from judicious ... it would not be prudent to trust her to his care'.[65] The hospital authorities were protecting their patient from domestic circumstances which could cause a slide back into depression and insanity. Elizabeth Harris did eventually return to her family in 1873 and stayed in correspondence with Orange until her husband's death in 1881.[66]

Family unity

For one reason or another some husbands disappeared, or decided they could not be responsible for a mentally fragile wife. Charles Oldman was an attentive husband, regularly visiting and writing to his wife Ellen after her admission in 1878. Although initially he seemed willing to take responsibility for her on discharge, in 1882 when the final decision came to be made, he admitted that he felt unable to cope with her care.[67] Ellen Oldman's father had written to Dr Orange in April 1880 offering to look after his daughter, an offer which was accepted after the Asylum received Charles Oldman's refusal.[68] Extended family unity, in the absence of supportive spousal care, was an important consideration in the decision-making process surrounding discharge of infanticidal mothers. Any proposed guardian was expected to show willingness to care for the patient with kindness and patience, and to protect them by looking out for any incipient signs of relapse. Orange was concerned that Ellen Oldman's parents were 'somewhat advanced in years' although 'anxious to do what they can for her'.[69] They were accepted as guardians because they were considered respectable people and able to 'provide her with a comfortable home'.[70] The moral and social conditions of the families themselves were among the most important considerations for the authorities.[71] These, of course, were not impartial criteria, being highly prone to cultural biases.

In the assessments for suitability as guardians, significant importance was attached to the social respectability of a patient's family members. Respectability in the Victorian period was a gauge by which people could be perceived and their behaviour understood. Most levels of society strove for respectability and people were judged in communities through diverse criteria such as whether the father was in employment, whether the wife kept a clean house, whether the children were cared for and fed. Significantly for married women, this invariably meant displaying good mothering and housekeeping skills. Working-class mothers were seen as the fulcrum of the home, taking pride in capably managing children and the domestic economy – keeping a respectable home was considered an essential quality.[72] Emma Luke was described in a local newspaper as having 'always borne a character amongst her neighbours for industry and respectability', two valued virtues in her community.[73] There is an argument that suggests that asylum treatment existed to instil and restore womanly virtues of modesty, deference and docility in female patients; that the aim of the institution was to re-form its female patient along the lines of the middle-class ideal of womanhood.[74] This ideal was of a caring, dependent, emotional and passive woman, 'looking on the outside world from the safety of her domestic realm'.[75] Whether or not the medical superintendents were influenced by such beliefs, this concept of acceptable and respectable female behaviour seemed to filter through into the Asylum and consequently impacted on the decisions made about the female patients.

The social stigma of a family member being in an asylum was hard for many families to bear.[76] In 1881, Kate Barrow was admitted into Broadmoor after drowning her baby in the bath; she had apparently suffered mental derangement for 'nearly six months after [its] birth'.[77] The family was considered very respectable, and her husband was a grocer and provision merchant in Slough. However, letters in her file indicate that the business was lost 'owing to reverses in trade' and her husband had broken under the pressure: the stigma of his wife being found criminally insane added to that pressure.[78] Charles Barrow, helped by support from prominent public figures, successfully petitioned for his wife's release and she was discharged in 1888.[79] The Barrows moved away from Berkshire to Leamington Spa, presumably to make a fresh start. A usual condition of discharge was that the guardian should submit periodic reports on the progress of the former patient to Broadmoor, countersigned by a person of authority such as a local doctor or minister. In 1892 Charles Barrow wrote to Dr Nicolson requesting that this condition be dropped as he felt 'it is not necessary for our new society to be aware of our circumstances'.[80] The request was formally declined, but Barrow gave up furnishing the reports anyway. Without informing Broadmoor, he moved his family to Birmingham which action culminated in a police search. Eventually their whereabouts and circumstances were reported to Broadmoor by the Chief Constable of Birmingham Police. He wrote explaining that 'Mr Barrow is in a terrible state of anxiety... he appeared to think that Mrs Barrow should not be obliged to return to Broadmoor if she lost her reason again'.[81] This was accepted by the authorities and Kate Barrow was allowed to remain with the family in Warwickshire.

The perception of insanity as a shameful stain on a family's reputation can be seen in other cases. Thomas Baines bemoaned the fact that his wife's name 'should be bandied about for that which she had not the power to avoid'.[82] Agnes Morris's family and friends distanced themselves from her after she was admitted in 1877. Despite having the funds for a comfortable life, she convinced herself that she would be better in a private asylum nearer her home in Liverpool.[83] This move was vigorously opposed by her family and friends, ostensibly to protect her other children and it was noted in her case file that, 'Her own family (do not) make any move about her release'.[84] The guardian of her surviving children requested that her communications to them be monitored as the children had been greatly disturbed by her letters.[85] Even in America, Annie Nicholls's husband requested that his wife's insanity be kept secret, albeit for different reasons. He told Dr Orange that 'there is a great jealousy in the minds of the American people against the importation of invalids and... I desire to keep as secret as possible the circumstance connected with my wife's confinement in Broadmoor'.[86]

While great care was exercised in trying to ensure that the future situation of discharged infanticidal mothers would be appropriate, all officials involved in assessing suitability for discharge were conscious of the risk of relapse.[87] As shown with the cases of Annie Howell and Louisa Ashley, one of the clinicians' prime anxieties was the potential risk attached to any future pregnancy. Former patients were readmitted, but among the cases reviewed none of the relapses were for that particular reason. Readmissions, in the main, were of those women who wanted to return because they felt vulnerable and unable to cope with life outside the asylum. Others could be readmitted because their guardians felt they were no longer able to manage their charge. In 1885 Sarah Newman was discharged to the guardianship of her husband, Daniel but in 1900 he wrote to Broadmoor saying, 'I can no longer be answerable for my wife's safety or my own as I live in fear of my life ... her threats and behaviour are past all bounds, she cannot be restrained'.[88] A former patient was also supposed to return to the Asylum in the event of the death of their guardian. Whatever the circumstances were surrounding readmission, a patient could be re-released if their physical and mental states were suitable. In all situations, whether with a change of guardian or not, the domestic circumstances and capabilities were reviewed and assessed to ensure a 'safe' discharge. The integrity of the family and home were of great importance as a factor in the decisions to discharge the infanticidal mothers. Through what they viewed as thorough investigation and assessment, the asylum authorities and government officials tried to ensure that the future welfare of the discharged women would be protected.

Sarah Bates

The story of Sarah Bates is an example of the impact that a strong marital bond, together with the support of a united family, had on the discharge process. It also illustrates some of the reasons behind readmissions. In this case, Sarah, her husband, James, their children and her father were instrumental in obtaining her discharge on two separate occasions. James Bates was a skilled shoe finisher working for a prestigious boot and shoe company in Northampton. In January 1880, Sarah Bates was tried for the murder of their six-month-old daughter, Florence, by suffocation.[89] She was admitted to Broadmoor on 10 February, the cause of her insanity being attributed to severe melancholia brought on by over-lactation.[90] In February 1881, James Bates began enquiring about the worth of petitioning for release, eventually receiving a positive answer in 1884.[91]

In many cases of discharge, the patronage of outside agencies in support of a family added weight to an application for a patient's release. While not being mandatory, Home Office approval was often assisted by the submission of references from employers and local dignitaries. Favourable third-party confirmation of the husband's capacity to be responsible for the wife and about the quality of the circumstances of family and home was considered desirable by all officials. Bates's campaign was backed by local community leaders and his employer. A local Wesleyan minister wrote of James Bates that 'the man has conducted himself so as to gain true esteem ... his life is free from reproach and the children always appearing clean and neat and comfortable'.[92] Bates's employer wrote 'I have always found him to be a very industrious & honest man' adding that 'they always lived very happily together' and that the 'home was a very comfortable one'.[93] In 1886 when writing to the Home Office in support of Sarah's release, Dr Orange advised that, 'her husband and father are ... in a position to give her a good home and their respectability is testified by the Mayor of Northampton'.[94]

Sarah Bates was discharged from Broadmoor in June 1886, but soon returned after her husband asked for help from the medical staff at Broadmoor. She had said to him that 'she had the same feeling come over as when she destroyed the child' and requested that she be returned.[95] For the next fourteen years the family, and Sarah herself, sought permission for another release. Sarah wrote to Dr Orange requesting that she be restored to her 'Dear Husband & Darling Children', adding, 'What I will know you carnt (sic) do all for me but you kindly do what you can'.[96] In 1904 she was discharged again, this time to the care of her daughter and son-in-law.[97] At her own request, she was transferred to the care of James but unfortunately this did not work and she returned to Broadmoor in 1905, following an attempt at suicide.[98] She then remained in Broadmoor until her death in 1911 (see Figure 11.2 for an image of the asylum in this era). Although each time her discharge was requested the authorities took great care in ensuring release was right, as Dr David Nicolson said, 'her great joy at being at home pressed upon her and caused her mind to become unhinged & deranged once again'.[99]

Figure 11.2. The female airing court at Broadmoor Asylum, from an undated photographic postcard, undated but probably early twentieth century.
Source: Berkshire Record Office, Coley Avenue, Reading.

Conclusion

If discharge was considered, all domestic and economic social circumstances were reviewed to ensure that the family and friends were capable of providing safe and correct care for vulnerable patients. Throughout the case files in the correspondence between the Broadmoor authorities and the Home Office, there is official acknowledgement of families' willingness to help the patient on her release: 'her parents and friends are both able and anxious to do what they can for her', and 'her father and married brother are willing and anxious to make what provision they can for her'.[100] If the authorities felt a patient was well enough and that the proposed domestic circumstances were favourable and protective, they would support a discharge. The important factor was that the future guardians would be responsible enough to ensure against potential relapse.

The majority of infanticidal mothers discussed here were from a working-class background and, to an extent, social status played a part in the way the women and their home circumstances were perceived. Respectability was a shared point of reference for both middle-class and working-class culture, although each class had its own ideas of what this constituted.[101] It is clear that respectability and the moral condition of the family were significant to both the asylum authorities and the Home Office. If the circumstances of family, neighbours and friends were confirmed as favourable by outside patrons, officials at both the Home Office and Broadmoor would agree to release. From the statistics, the husband was often the preferred guardian and, for that reason, reports into his employment, conduct and general attitude to life were required. Occasionally the educational background of the family and husband was questioned as making them unsuitable to act as guardians and, while the medical officers at Broadmoor placed value on the emotional bonds of a family, there was occasionally a lack of appreciation for the socio-economics of poorer families. If it were shown that the husband and the patient's extended family were offering a respectable domestic environment together with caring companionship, discharge would be allowed. A husband's desire to care for his wife was viewed as an indication of marital union and was a key consideration in the release process. Those discharges which were, at least initially, successful occurred where there was a good network of spouses, family and friends who were willing and able to support, and protect, the discharged patient.

Notes

1 D.J.R. Grey, '"No Crime to Kill a Bastard-Child": Stereotypes of Infanticide in Nineteenth-Century England and Wales', in *Intersections of Gender, Class, and Race in the Long Nineteenth Century and Beyond*, ed. by B. Leonardi (Cham: Palgrave Macmillan, 2018), especially pp. 50–53.
2 R. Smith, *Trial by Medicine: Insanity and Responsibility in Victorian Trials* (Edinburgh: Edinburgh University Press, 1981); T. Ward, 'The Sad Subject of

Infanticide: Law, Medicine and Child Murder, 1860–1938', *Social and Legal Studies* 8 (1999), pp. 163–180.

3 See variously Berkshire Record Office [henceforth BRO], D/H14/D/1/15/1, Broadmoor Hospital Archive: Discharge Register – Males and Females 1863–1900; BRO D/H14/D1/1/1/1 and BRO D/H14/D1/1/1/2 Broadmoor Hospital Archive: Admissions Registers, 1863–1900; BRO Broadmoor Hospital Archive: Patients' Case Files: Females D/H14/D2/2/2.

4 See J. Andrews, 'The Boundaries of Her Majesty's Pleasure: Discharging Child-Murderers from Broadmoor and Perth Criminal Lunatic Department, *c.*1860–1920', in *Infanticide: Historical Perspectives on Child Murder and Concealment, 1550–2000*, ed. by M. Jackson (Aldershot: Ashgate, 2002), pp. 216–248; A. Pedley, 'The Emotional Reactions of Judges in Cases of Maternal Child Murder in England, 1840–1890', in *Judgment in the Victorian Age*, ed. by J. Gregory, D.J.R Grey and A. Bautz (Abingdon: Routledge, 2019), pp. 83–99; J. Shepherd, 'Victorian Madmen: Broadmoor, Masculinity and the Experiences of the Criminally Insane, 1863–1900' (unpublished doctoral thesis, Queen Mary University of London, 2013); L. Williams and B. Godfrey, *Criminal Women 1850–1920* (Barnsley: Pen & Sword, 2018).

5 Asylum records are closed to researchers until 100 years after a patient's death. The records for discharged patients whose date of death is unknown are opened 160 years after their birth date.

6 Andrews, 'The Boundaries of Her Majesty's Pleasure'.

7 Andrews, 'The Boundaries of Her Majesty's Pleasure', p. 224.

8 L. Hide, *Gender and Class in English Asylums, 1890–1914* (Basingstoke: Palgrave Macmillan, 2014), p. 142; D. Wright, 'The Discharge of Pauper Lunatics from County Asylums in Mid-Victorian England', in *Insanity, Institutions & Society 1800–1914*, ed. by J. Melling and W. Forsythe (London: Routledge, 1999), p. 107.

9 BRO D/H14/D2/2/2/111. Case file of Mary Bennett. See variously: letter from Mary Bennett to Dr Orange (undated); letter from H. Spence to Dr Orange, 30 July 1867; letter from E. Cooper to Dr Orange, 9 December 1875; letter from A. Stokes (M.P.) to Dr Orange, September 1876.

10 Orange was Deputy Medical Superintendent 1862–1870, then Medical Superintendent 1870–1886 at Broadmoor.

11 BRO D/H14/D2/2/2/111. Letter from Dr Orange to Mrs E. Cooper 21 December 1875.

12 BRO D/H14/D2/2/2/188. Case File of Annie Nicholls. See Schedule A, 26 December 1871. The 'Schedule A' was a pro forma included in each file containing details of the crime, verdict, general health and the cause of insanity.

13 BRO D/H14/D2/2/2/188. Letter from Richard Nicholls to Dr Orange, 10 March 1871.

14 BRO D/H14/D2/2/2/188. Report from Dr Orange to Home Office, 15 March 1871.

15 BRO D/H14/D2/2/2/188. Letter from Richard Nicholls to Dr Orange, 10 March 1871.

16 BRO D/H14/D2/2/2/188. Warrant of Discharge, 12 March 1878.

17 United States Federal Censuses 1880, Pittsburgh, Allegheny. Roll 1093 p.199A ED135. 1900 Trumbull, Ohio Roll T623_1326 p4B ED 0123 & 1910 Gogebic, Michigan. Roll T624_627 p.5A ED0081.

18 Andrews, 'The Boundaries of Her Majesty's Pleasure', p. 236

19 'The Birmingham Murder', *Belfast Telegraph*, 23 October 1875.

20 H. Marland, *Dangerous Motherhood. Insanity and Childbirth in Victorian Britain* (Basingstoke: Palgrave Macmillan, 2004), pp. 3–7.

21 *Worcestershire Chronicle*, 18 October 1875.

22 BRO D/H14/D2/2/2/252. Draft report for Home Office by Dr J. Isaacs, May 1877.

23 England, Wales & Scotland Census 1881 Aston, Warwickshire. Class RG11. Folio 65 p.38.

24 England & Wales, Civil Registration Death Index, 1916–2007. June 1929 Vol 6d p.39.

25 *Worcestershire Chronicle*, 23 October 1875.

26 E. Ross, *Love and Toil: Motherhood in Outcast London, 1870–1918* (Oxford: Oxford University Press, 1993).

27 'Extraordinary Occurrence in Kendal', *Kendal Mercury*, 6 November 1875.

28 BRO D/H14/D2/2/2/251. Case File of Martha Baines. See Medical Certificate, 20 November 1875.

29 BRO D/H14/D2/2/2/251. Letter from Thomas Baines to Medical Superintendent, Broadmoor, 30 December 1876.

30 BRO D/H14/D2/2/2/251. Report from Broadmoor to Home Office, 3 January 1876.

31 BRO D/H14/D2/2/2/251. Report from Broadmoor to Home Office, 25 January 1877.

32 BRO D/H14/D2/2/2/251. Report from Broadmoor to Home Office, 24 July 1877.

33 England, Wales & Scotland Census.1901 Kendal. Class RG16. Folio 121 p.19 and England & Wales, National Probate Calendar (Index of Wills and Administrations), 1858–1995 Wills & Administration 1925, p. 123.

34 Andrews, 'The Boundaries of Her Majesty's Pleasure', p. 237.

35 BRO D/H14/D2/2/2/188. Report from Dr Orange to Home Office, 10 February 1878.

36 BRO D/H14/D2/2/2/284. Case File of Lucy Keary. See various letters 1879–1886.

37 BRO D/H14/D2/2/2/284. Letter from Bombay, Baruda & Central India Railway, Parel Works, 16 October 1879 and letter from Edward Keary to Dr Orange, 28 February 1883.

38 BRO D/H14/D2/2/2/284. Letter from Edward Keary to Broadmoor, 21 August 1886.

39 BRO D/H14/D2/2/2/284/32. Warrant of Discharge, 6 October 1886.

40 Other 'manias' relating to childbearing included lactational insanity and insanity of pregnancy. See Marland, *Dangerous Motherhood*, pp. 3–7.

41 BRO D/H14/D2/2/2/284. File note for medical report for Home Office June 1885.

42 BRO D/H14/D2/2/2/290. Case File of Annie Howell. Draft medical report to Home Office, 10 July 1879.

43 BRO D/H14/D2/2/2/290. Letter from Broadmoor to the Home Office, 6 August 1879.

44 BRO D/H14/D2/2/2/244. Case File of Louisa Ashley. Letter from John Ashley to Dr Orange, 30 March 1879.

45 BRO D/H14/D2/2/2/244. Medical Certificate, 16 December 1903.

46 J. Tosh. *A Man's Place: Masculinity and the Middle-Class Home in Victorian England* (New Haven: Yale University Press, 1999), pp. 79–101.

47 S. D'Cruze, *Crimes of Outrage: Sex, Violence and Victorian Working Women* (London: UCL Press, 1998).

48 G.S. Frost, *Living in Sin: Cohabiting as Husband and Wife in Nineteenth-Century England* (Manchester: Manchester University Press, 2008).

49 BRO D/H14/D2/2/2/344. Case File of Sarah Beagley. See copy of medical report to Home Office, 26 June 1885.

50 BRO D/H14/D2/2/2/344. Letter from Pvt J. Beagley to Dr Nicolson, 21 February 1890. Dr David Nicolson was Deputy Medical Superintendent 1872–1886 at Broadmoor, then Medical Superintendent 1886–1896.

51 BRO D/H14/D2/2/2/344. Warrant of Discharge, 12 August 1895.
52 BRO D/H14/D2/2/2/257. Case File of Elizabeth Cole. See copy of report to Home Office by Dr Orange, 26 September 1877.
53 BRO D/H14/D2/2/2/365. Case File of Rebecca Loveridge. Memorandum to Home Office signed WO and DN, 3 June 1884.
54 BRO D/H14/D2/2/2/365. See memorandum to Home Office signed DN, 30 September 1885 and Warrant of Discharge 4 November 1885.
55 England & Wales, Civil Registration Death Index, 1916–2007. March 1922, Vol. 5b, p. 211.
56 Hide, *Gender and Class*, p. 42.
57 'Obituary: William Orange, CB, MD, and FRCP', *British Medical Journal*, 13 January 1917, p. 67.
58 *Old Bailey Proceedings Online* (www.oldbaileyonline.org, version 8.0, 21 January 2019), January 1872, trial of Elizabeth Harris (35) (t18720108-156).
59 BRO D/H14/D2/2/2/189/20. Case File of Elizabeth Harris. Copy of memorandum to Home Office August 1872.
60 BRO D/H14/D2/2/2/189. See Warrant of Release, 21 March 1872. Letter from Elizabeth Harris to Dr Orange, 16 April 1872.
61 The Community of St John the Baptist was an Anglican religious community in Clewer, Windsor, which ran the House of Mercy, a home for unmarried mothers and 'fallen women'.
62 BRO D/H14/D2/2/2/189/12. Letter from Sister Frances Constance to Dr Nicolson, 1 August 1872.
63 BRO D/H14/D2/2/2/189/20. Copy of memorandum to Home Office, August 1872.
64 BRO D/H14/D2/2/2/189/11. Letter from Richard Harris to Dr Orange, 16 July 1872.
65 BRO D/H14/D2/2/2/189/20 Copy of memorandum to Home Office, August 1872.
66 BRO D/H14/D2/2/2/189. Letter from Elizabeth Harris to Dr Orange, 16 January 1881.
67 BRO D/H14/D2/2/2/274. Case File of Ellen Oldman. Letter from Charles Oldman to Dr Orange, 16 March 1881.
68 BRO D/H14/D2/2/2/274. Letter from Samuel Rainbird to Dr Orange, April 1880.
69 BRO D/H14/D2/2/2/274. Report on mental and physical health for Home Office, 14 March 1881.
70 BRO D/H14/D2/2/2/274. Report for Home Office, 14 March 1881.
71 Andrews, 'The Boundaries of Her Majesty's Pleasure', p. 224.
72 Ross, *Love and Toil*, pp. 69–72.
73 *Worcestershire Chronicle*, 23 October 1875.
74 A. Shepherd, *Institutionalizing the Insane in Nineteenth-Century England* (London: Pickering & Chatto, 2014), pp. 9–10.
75 Hide, *Gender and Class,* p. 8.
76 Andrews, 'The Boundaries of Her Majesty's Pleasure', p. 244.
77 BRO D/H14/D2/2/2/330. Case file of Kate Barrow. See Warrant for Reception, 2 November 1881.
78 BRO D/H14/D2/2/2/330. Memorandum from Dr J. Isaacs to Dr D. Nicolson, 11 July 1891.
79 BRO D/H14/D2/2/2/330. See letter from Viscount Curzon, 10 October 1887 and Warrant of Discharge, 20 November 1888.
80 BRO D/H14/D2/2/2/330. Letter from C. Barrow to Dr Nicolson, 5 January 1892.
81 BRO D/H14/D2/2/2/330. Letter from Chief Constable, Birmingham Police to Dr Nicolson, 19 August 1895.

82 BRO D/H14/D2/2/2/251. Letter from Thomas Baines to Medical Superintendent, Broadmoor, 12 March 1876.
83 BRO D/H14/D2/2/2/261/6. Case File of Agnes Martha Morris. Letter from Laces, Bird, Newton & Richardson (Solicitors) to Dr Orange, 15 January 1877.
84 BRO D/H14/D2/2/2/261/55. Memorandum from Dr Orange to Home Office, 4 April 1885.
85 BRO D/H14/D2/2/2/261/22. Letter from Rev. R Gough to Dr Orange, 23 May 1878.
86 BRO D/H14/D2/2/2/188. Letter from Richard Nicholls to Dr Orange, 5 May 1877.
87 Andrews, 'The Boundaries of Her Majesty's Pleasure', p. 225.
88 BRO D/H14/D2/2/2/568. Case File of Sarah Newman. Letter from Daniel Newman to Dr R. Brayn, 5 January 1900.
89 *Northampton Mercury*, 17 January 1880.
90 BRO D/H14/D2/2/2/303. Case File (1) of Sarah Bates. Warrant for Admission, 3 February 1880.
91 BRO D/H14/D2/2/2/398. Case File (2) of Sarah Bates. See letter from J. Bates to Dr Orange, 19 July 1881 and letter from Dr Orange to J. Bates, 27 August 1884.
92 BRO D/H14/D2/2/2/398. Letter from Rev. G. Harrison, 29 July 1884.
93 BRO D/H14/D2/2/2/303. Letter from Thomas Britten to Dr Orange, 7 July 1882.
94 BRO D/H14/D2/2/2/398 Annual Report to Home Office, 25 May 1886.
95 BRO D/H14/D2/2/2/398. Letter from J. Bates to Dr Orange, 9 July 1886.
96 BRO D/H14D2/2/2/398/78. Undated letter from Sarah Bates to Dr Orange.
97 BRO D/H14/D2/2/2/661. Case File (3) of Sarah Bates. Warrant of Conditional Discharge, 6 July 1904.
98 BRO D/H14/D2/2/2/661. See letter from Sarah Bates to Dr Brayn, 19 December 1904 and Revocation of Warrant, 14 January 1905.
99 BRO D/H14/D2/2/2/661. Letter from Dr Nicolson to Home Office, 11 July 1886.
100 See variously BRO D/H14/D2/2/2/219. Case File of Martha Bland; and BRO D/H14/D2/2/2/440. Case File of Elizabeth Hillier.
101 L.A. Jackson, *Child Sexual Abuse in Victorian England* (London: Routledge, 2000), pp. 40–41.

Bibliography

Andrews, J. 'The Boundaries of Her Majesty's Pleasure: Discharging Child-Murderers from Broadmoor and Perth Criminal Lunatic Department, *c.* 1860–1920', in *Infanticide: Historical Perspectives on Child Murder and Concealment, 1550–2000*, ed. by M. Jackson (Aldershot: Ashgate, 2002), pp. 216–248.
Belfast Telegraph, 'The Birmingham Murder', 23 October 1875.
Berkshire Record Office Broadmoor Hospital Archive: Admissions Registers 1863–1900 D/H14/D/1/1/1/1 & 2.
Berkshire Record Office Broadmoor Hospital Archive: Discharge Register – Males and Females 1863–1900, D/H14/D1/15/1.
Berkshire Record Office Broadmoor Hospital Archive: Female Patient Case Files Series D/H14/D2/2/2.
British Medical Journal, 13 January 1917.
D'Cruze, S. *Crimes of Outrage. Sex, Violence, and Victorian Working Women* (London: UCL Press, 1998).
England & Wales Census, 1881, 1901, 1911.
England & Wales, Civil Registration Death Index, 1916–2007.

Frost, G.S. *Living in Sin: Cohabiting as Husband and Wife in Nineteenth-Century England* (Manchester: Manchester University Press, 2008).

Grey, D.J.R. '"No Crime to Kill a Bastard–Child": Stereotypes of Infanticide in Nineteenth-Century England and Wales', in *Intersections of Gender, Class, and Race in the Long Nineteenth Century and Beyond*, ed. by B. Leonardi (Cham: Palgrave Macmillan, 2018), pp. 41–66.

Hide, L. *Gender and Class in English Asylums, 1890–1914* (Basingstoke: Palgrave Macmillan, 2014).

Jackson, L. A. *Child Sexual Abuse in Victorian England* (London: Routledge, 2000).

Kendal Mercury, 6 November 1875.

Marland, H. *Dangerous Motherhood: Insanity and Childbirth in Victorian Britain* (Basingstoke: Palgrave Macmillan, 2004).

Northampton Mercury, 17 January 1880

Old Bailey Proceedings Online (www.oldbaileyonline.org, version 8.0, 21 January 2019), January 1872, trial of Elizabeth Harris (35) (t18720108-156).

Pedley, A. 'The Emotional Reactions of Judges in Cases of Maternal Child Murder in England, 1840–1890', in *Judgment in the Victorian Age*, ed. by J. Gregory, D.J.R Grey and A. Bautz (Abingdon: Routledge, 2019), pp. 83–99.

Ross, E. *Love and Toil: Motherhood in Outcast London, 1870–1918* (Oxford: Oxford University Press, 1993).

Shepherd, A. *Institutionalizing the Insane in Nineteenth-Century England* (London: Pickering & Chatto, 2014).

Shepherd, J. 'Victorian Madmen: Broadmoor, Masculinity and the Experiences of the Criminally Insane 1863–1900' (unpublished doctoral thesis, Queen Mary University of London, 2013).

Smith, R. *Trial by Medicine: Insanity and Responsibility in Victorian Trials* (Edinburgh: Edinburgh University Press, 1981).

Tosh, J. *A Man's Place. Masculinity and the Middle-Class Home in Victorian England* (New Haven: Yale University Press, 1999).

United States Federal Census, 1880, 1890 and 1910.

Ward, T. 'The Sad Subject of Infanticide: Law, Medicine and Child Murder, 1860–1938', *Social and Legal Studies* 8 (1999), pp. 163–180.

Williams, L. and Godfrey, B. *Criminal Women. 1850–1920* (Barnsley: Pen & Sword, 2018).

Worcestershire Chronicle, 18 October and 23 October 1875.

Wright, D. 'The Discharge of Pauper Lunatics from County Asylums in Mid-Victorian England', in *Insanity, Institutions & Society 1800–1914*, ed. by J. Melling and W. Forsythe (London: Routledge, 1999), pp. 93–112.

12 Unity or disunity? The trials of a Jury in *R v John William Anderson*

Newcastle Winter Assizes 1875

Helen Rutherford

On 30 August 1875, in the crowded room of the *Durham Ox* public house in Clayton Street, the coroner for the town and borough of Newcastle upon Tyne held an inquest into the death of 29-year-old Elizabeth Anderson. Her cause of death was 'stabs in the back and side'.[1] There were seven wounds to her back, chest, shoulder and near the hip.[2] This was not an inquest to identify an unknown assailant. The perpetrator, Elizabeth's husband, had presented himself at the Laurel Street police station two nights previously and informed the sergeant on duty that he had stabbed Elizabeth to death. On 22 December 1875, the same coroner held an inquest into the death of John William Anderson, pursuant to the 'Act to provide for carrying out Capital Punishment within prisons'. There was also no doubt as to the cause of death or the perpetrator. Anderson's cause of death was recorded as 'lawfully hanged for murder'.[3]

In the period between the two inquests, Anderson was tried and found guilty of the murder. Yet detailed examination of the trial revealed a disquieting series of events leading to his conviction and execution. Newspaper reports and the Home Office file demonstrate that many residents of Newcastle, despite the seeming brutality of the crime, were united in a vain attempt to obtain mercy for Anderson. There is an unusually comprehensive set of original documents in this case. Court papers for trials in the nineteenth century are often scantily preserved and spread across a number of archives. In this case, the Home Office file contains much material relevant to the trial and execution. The folder preserved in the National Archives contains the coroner's depositions, the judge's trial notes, newspaper cuttings, correspondence relating to the planning and carrying out of the execution, two petitions for mercy, the judge's notes from the trial and related correspondence.[4] The file reveals a complex scenario and illuminates contemporary debates about capital punishment, provocation and the role of judge and jurors in murder trials.[5] An analysis of these papers reveals a complex dynamic in the jury's deliberations, unrevealed in contemporary reportage.[6] Did the noise of a crowded court; the timidity of a jury foreman; and a misunderstanding, lead to a miscarriage of justice? Alternatively, was this, as the judge, Mr Justice Denman, suggested, a very clear case of murder?

This chapter examines the legal process in the Anderson case and considers whether he was the victim of a miscarriage of justice. The theme of union and disunion is adopted in a micro-historical examination of the nineteenth-century interpretation of the law relating to murder and manslaughter in the context of a provincial trial.[7] The Home Office file offers a tantalising glimpse of usually sacrosanct deliberations by the jury and an opportunity to examine this case from perspectives that are rarely available. The sanctity of the jury room was breached in a very particular and mediated format. This case allows consideration of the dynamics of the relationship between judge, jury and the wider community, and offers a troubling insight into nineteenth-century justice.

United in matrimony and acrimony

In a last hurrah for the execution broadside genre, an unnamed poet wrote of the crime: 'The fearful executions | Shows the sad increase of crime, | The dreadful scene has been enacted | At [...] Newcastle-on- Tyne'.[8] The doggerel told the cautionary tale of the crimes, trials and executions of two men who killed their wives in the summer of 1875 in the North East of England.[9] One man, Richard Charlton, shot his estranged wife.[10] The other, the subject of this chapter, John William Anderson, stabbed his wife to death with a butcher's knife following a quarrel and fight. Anderson and Charlton, united in the ballad, were executed on consecutive days in December. Neither crime generated much interest outside the immediate area. The *Manchester Evening News* classified the murders as 'smaller fry'.[11] In fact, Anderson was the first person hanged behind the walls of Newcastle gaol, following the abolition of public execution in England. The events that led to the gallows were short and brutal.

It is difficult to reconstruct a clear picture of John and Elizabeth Anderson. They left scant details in the official records. Newcastle in the 1870s was a prosperous town with a population in the region of 140,000.[12] The events of 28 August 1875 took place in an area populated by the skilled working class. The Andersons lived alongside printers, boiler-smiths, coachbuilders and joiners.[13] However, John was not of the same class as his neighbours. He was born in Gateshead in 1843 to a middle-class family and 'once occupied a respectable position'.[14] He married Elizabeth Walker, the daughter of a stonemason from Cockermouth, at St John's Church, Newcastle, on 31 March 1866.[15] Anderson was 'well educated' and literate; Elizabeth, by contrast, could not sign her name in the marriage certificate.[16] A former soldier, at the date of his marriage he was an 'agent'.[17] As a clerk he earned a reasonable wage because he was on the burgesses' roll for 1875 and could vote in local elections. However, at the time of the crime, John was out of work. The couple owned a small provisions shop, although contemporary newspaper reports suggest Elizabeth ran it. Perhaps the fall into unemployment was in part the catalyst for the murder.

The 1871 census records the Andersons living with Elizabeth's parents at 58 and 59 Mitford Street.[18] Mitford Street was one of a number of close-built terraces leading down to the industrial heartland of the river Tyne, dominated by Armstrong's Elswick armaments factory. By 1875 the couple had moved with their youngest son to a house at the end of Mitford Street in which they inhabited one room.[19] An older boy lived with Anderson's father. A plan in the Home Office file shows the layout of the premises. The front room was the shop and the back room was the living quarters.[20]

John Anderson had served with the 98th Regiment of Foot and when he appeared in court, sported a 'heavy military moustache' suggesting pride in his military background. However, Elizabeth's father gave evidence at trial that Anderson was bought out of the army by his wife.[21] The lure of a military life was obviously strong: Anderson was a member of the Northumberland Militia and trained with them in the summer of 1875.[22] Thus Anderson had been respectably employed and served his country, but at the time of the murder the newspapers described him as 'a man of idle and dissipated habits'.[23] Respectability was fundamental to Victorian society and involved 'maintaining a steady income, preserving the respect of the local community, and avoiding the workhouse and a pauper's funeral'.[24] Yet, in the words of Carolyn Conley, 'criminals were not respectable and respectable persons were not criminals'.[25] Evidence at the inquest and at trial showed Anderson was fond of a drink and on the evening of the murder he had been drinking, though it is unclear whether it was this that had meant he lost his job or drinking was a response to unemployment. Elizabeth's drinking habits are less clear. A number of witnesses suggested she too had been drinking but her father suggested she was 'never given to drink'.[26] Anderson was 'a good-looking man of middle height'.[27] The judge, Mr Justice Denman, notes him as 'a strong powerfully built man in the prime of life'.[28] Elizabeth was described as a 'delicate woman'.[29] Whether the union was happy or tempestuous was a matter for speculation among the couple's family and neighbours. Whatever the truth, any resentments and disagreements came to a head on 28 August 1875.

On the evening of 28 August, the Andersons were in good spirits and spent time with their neighbours Benjamin and Bridget Danskin. Benjamin was an ex-army colleague. The couple returned home at about 9.30 pm and John helped Elizabeth shutter the shop. For some reason he bolted the bottom half of the door to prevent his wife from leaving and his son from coming into the house.[30] A disagreement turned into a quarrel, and Anderson accused his wife of being a 'dirty woman'.[31] Although the newspapers speculated that Elizabeth was physically abused by her husband and this was echoed by a comment from the judge, Elizabeth's father stated Anderson did not 'ill use her' and indicated during the trial that he had no idea the relationship had deteriorated.[32] Other witnesses testified that the couple quarrelled when they had both been drinking.

It was a warm summer evening and there were plenty of people around Mitford Street to hear a loud argument, the sound of a slap and, possibly,

Anderson shouting 'you bitch if you hit me I will stab you'.[33] Anderson told the police that Elizabeth picked up a bacon knife from the counter and a fight ensued.[34] A local newspaper reported that the Andersons' son saw his mother pick up the knife.[35] However, the child gave no evidence at the inquest or the trial. Witnesses gave evidence of screams and something falling. As one of the petitions for mercy pleaded, no one except Anderson could explain exactly what happened and thus it was 'impossible for him to prove the whole of the provocation he had received'. Anderson did not try to cover up his deed and walked immediately to the police station in nearby Laurel Street. He showed the police officer a profusely bleeding wound on his hand and was 'excited' but not drunk, although he had clearly had a drink.[36] Sergeant Kennedy gave evidence at trial that Anderson explained: 'the knife I stabbed her with is the knife she struck me with'.[37] The facts seemed to be that Elizabeth had shouted at John, he had shouted back; she had hit him and picked up the knife. He had taken the knife from her, cutting his hand on the blade, and then lost control and stabbed her. Whatever the catalyst, the evidence of the medical witnesses was stark that the injuries required immense violence. Anderson was right handed and possibly held the knife 'over hand' to stab Elizabeth, his army training perhaps coming into play to wield the knife like a bayonet.[38]

United in condemnation

Anderson was indicted for murder. The trial lasted a full day at the New-castle Winter Assizes on 1 December 1875. The public galleries of the court were packed to excess with the usual noisy and curious crowd. The law stated that the felony of murder required an intention to kill on the accused's part. Like most defendants on a charge of murder, Anderson pleaded not guilty, since murder carried a mandatory death sentence and there was always a chance a jury would return a 'not guilty' verdict. Anderson's barrister, Charles Skidmore, was confident that this was a case of manslaughter on the basis of provocation. Slovenly housekeeping, drunkenness and shrewish behaviour by wives, which pushed men to the limits, had been sufficient to prevent other homicides from being found to be murder. Skidmore hoped that the jurors would accept Anderson had been provoked by a drunken, lazy, 'wretched' and violent wife.[39]

The barristers David Steavenson and Thomas Granger worked hard to prosecute the case and Skidmore noted in court that the defence was am-bushed by extra evidence in the hours leading up to the trial. The extent and nature of this evidence is unclear, but likely to have been the 'extra witness evidence (not called)' mentioned in the Home Office file. A number of wit-nesses gave evidence who had not been called at the preliminary hearing in the police court.[40] Skidmore suggested that the defence had not been al-lowed time to adequately deal with the witnesses produced.[41]

Justice George Denman was a regular judge on the Northern Cir-cuit.[42] His obituary suggests an undistinguished judge, but his judgements, correspondence and evidence to parliamentary committees suggest a man who carefully considered his words and was unafraid to express unpopular opinions.[43] He opened his evidence to the 1864–1866 Royal Commission on Capital Punishment by claiming a particular interest in capital punishment.[44] He did not believe the punishment provided a deterrent and thought that even murderers could be reformed and returned to society to lead useful lives.[45] His view was that the penalty was a strong weapon in the hands of defence barristers and inimical to certainty of punishment. He considered that the outcome of murder trials was most dependent upon the judge trying the case.[46]

Martin Wiener has written in detail about the development of the attitude of courts and juries to the law relating to provocation in the nineteenth century.[47] The raising of doubt in the Anderson case merits a mere footnote from Wiener.[48] However, closer examination of the Anderson case offers an interesting perspective on these issues. It is necessary to outline the law before analysing the treatment of provocation in the Anderson case.[49] Murder in the nineteenth century, as now, was a common law offence.[50] The classic definition is that of Lord Coke: 'Where a person of sound memory and discretion – unlawfully killeth – any reasonable creature in being – and under the Kings peace – with malice aforethought, either express or implied'.[51] The only sentence available to a judge following a verdict of murder was hanging.[52]

In the latter part of the nineteenth century, the appetite for executions was waning. From 1864 to 1866, the Royal Commission investigated whether those guilty of murder were often instead acquitted because of the jury's distaste for capital punishment. As *Archbold*, the leading legal manual, made clear, the law presumed 'every homicide to be murder, until the contrary appears'.[53] The defendant had to prove that the offence did not amount to murder. This was not straightforward because the defendant could not give evidence in their own defence. They were dependent upon the skill of defending counsel in cross-examination and the address to the jury at the end of the trial. Nor did the law accept any provocation could result in justifiable homicide.[54] So if it was not murder then it must be manslaughter. *Archbold* set out the position: 'If the provocation was great, and such as must have greatly excited [the defendant], the killing is manslaughter only'.[55] The police officer who first spoke to Anderson used this precise word and stated he was 'excited' at the police station.[56] Despite earlier decisions to the contrary, by 1875 it was judicially accepted that words, however inflammatory, were insufficient to amount to provocation.[57] However, as Wiener has established, many juries took a different view of verbal provocation.[58]

A complicating factor in Anderson's case was the butcher's knife. *Archbold* makes clear, if a deadly weapon was used, the provocation must be very great indeed to reduce murder to manslaughter. However, if the provocation itself was with a weapon, then that might be sufficient to lead to a manslaughter verdict.[59] The evidence, not strongly pressed at trial, but certainly raised by Anderson immediately after the killing, was that Elizabeth had been the first to pick up the knife and attack. A further criterion to reduce murder to manslaughter was that the violence must immediately follow the provocation with no 'cooling off' period. North East juries interpreted the cooling off period very widely, but this was unnecessary in this case: Elizabeth was killed within minutes of the quarrel. Skidmore, on consulting *Archbold*, must have felt confident that this was manslaughter.[60] There was provocation, with words, slap and knife, and all of the events took place in a short period.

At the trial, Skidmore attempted to establish that Anderson's wife had verbally and physically attacked John Anderson and suggested, when addressing the jury, that the multiple stabbing should be viewed as one event arising from a loss of control. The explanation for such a defence might be found in legal treatises setting out that degree of provocation necessary to reduce a homicide to manslaughter, heating the blood 'to a proportional degree of resentment, and keep[ing] it boiling to the moment of the fact; so that the party may rather be considered as having acted under a temporary suspension of reason than from any deliberate malicious motive'.[61] Skidmore told the jury that Anderson's mind had been affected by 'something …causing anger suddenly to arise against his wife'. Whether this was 'only a fancy' or not, this 'would enable them to reduce the crime from murder to the lesser one'. If Elizabeth Anderson had been about to strike him with a knife then 'he was so aggravated, that he lost, for the moment, control over his actions he would not be responsible for the amount of injury inflicted'.[62]

The judge's notes were detailed. He drew a picture in the margin showing how the knife had been held. In cross-examination, the physician who had stitched the cut agreed that the deep wound to Anderson's hand could have been caused by Elizabeth striking him. Denman, as he explained to the Home Secretary, did not accept this view.[63] Skidmore was unable to make any more of the point but could only hope that the jury had noted that the defendant was attacked first with the knife. After the witnesses had been examined and cross-examined, counsel for both sides addressed the jury. The prosecution presented their case dispassionately. Skidmore appealed to the jury's fairmindedness and common sense and suggested that the correct verdict would be manslaughter. This appeal flattered the sensibilities of the jurors and thus encouraged them to see the truth of the defence's plea.[64]

After praising the barristers for their fairness and skill, Denman summed up the evidence and explained to the jury the legal difference between murder and manslaughter. This included a direction on provocation. Unfortunately, the precise direction is unrecorded in his notes, although to the Home Secretary Denman emphasised that he carefully explained the difference between the offences.[65] However, it is likely that Denman would have adopted a regular form of words. In 1872 in the murder case at Durham Assizes Denman explained the difference in full, and this was reported in the newspapers.[66] He told the jury that if words spoken by his wife could have provoked anger and hot blood from John Grant then that would reduce the offence to manslaughter. If they had been mere words, and not a real threat, then it would be murder. In contrast, the *Newcastle Journal* noted some of Denman's summing up regarding the case, which seemed to leave no doubt as to his view:

> If they [the jury] were satisfied beyond reasonable doubt that with this knife the prisoner killed his wife and inflicted violence upon her, and that none of the evidence they had heard would enable them to say that what he did was short of **a brutal, a malignant, barbarous attack** upon her to kill her, he would be guilty of wilful murder. If upon the other hand they felt that upon all the facts of the case there was enough to warrant them in saying that there was enough to warrant them in saying that there was such provocation that he must be considered to be **absolved from that kind of barbarity, ferocity, determination, and malignity** which constituted the crime of wilful murder, it would be competent for them upon that indictment to find him guilty of manslaughter.[67]

This is a more strident direction than that reported in the Durham trial, where the jury returned a verdict of manslaughter.[68] Perhaps Denman, who had sentenced Grant to penal servitude for life, decided to be less nuanced in Anderson's case. The jury had to decide whether words, and a slap and/ or a threat with a knife, were sufficient provocation to reduce the crime to manslaughter.

A disunion of jurors

The jury room is a mysterious place and only the jurors are privy to the discussions, disagreements and grounds on which the verdict is reached. A jury is instructed by the judge to try the matter based only on the evidence in court but they are appointed from the local community with local knowledge and trusted to apply common sense. The choice between guilt and innocence in this case was a decision between life and death for the accused. Although the precise deliberations can never be known, the newspaper reports and surviving documents throw light on the jury decision-making.

The verdict of the jury, as now, save in the rarest circumstances, had to be unanimous as to guilt. The jury had to be united in their condemnation. Even in capital cases a nineteenth-century jury took little time to reach a verdict.[69] Denman himself noted, despite the speed of most decisions in most cases, for the sake of form and decorum, it was usual to retire for at least fifteen minutes.[70] Anderson's jury retired for much longer: there was clearly a problem. Approximately an hour after leaving the courtroom, the Court Bailiff returned and requested pens, ink and paper. There was no precedent for the fulfilment of such a request, and the judge called the jury back into court.

When they had taken their places in the jury box, the foreman indicated that they could not agree. This caused the judge a problem. He cut the foreman short and said that he did not want to know anything of the dispute in the jury room. The foreman asked for further explanation of the difference between 'aggravated manslaughter' (sic) and 'wilful murder'. Denman explained that there was no offence of aggravated manslaughter and once again, in relation to provocation, said that they had to consider the amount of provocation, the force used and the number of wounds and whether there was an intention to kill.[71] The judge appeared exasperated and stated that he could not explain any more clearly without going through the evidence once more. The jury retired again and returned to the court after twelve minutes, at 6.47 pm. At this point, events took an odd turn. The official record notes that the jury found Anderson guilty with a recommendation to mercy due to provocation and lack of premeditation. The reports of the event and the judge's notes suggest that Denman was careful to question the foreman about the recommendation to mercy, as to whether this was on grounds of provocation. Denman noted the reply: 'we think he intended to kill but it was not long premeditated'.[72] Denman had fulfilled his role of explaining the law and leaving the decision up to the jury.

The newspaper reports make clear that the court was in an uproar. The acoustics in the Moot Hall are poor and it is possible that the judge and the jury were speaking at cross-purposes. This is important to bear in mind when considering the letters in the Home Office file, discussed below.[73] The judge explained the verdict to Anderson who, as was his right, addressed the courtroom. He said that Elizabeth was his wife and he loved her. In 'a frenzy' he had committed 'the rash act' – he did not expect any mercy.[74]

Why did Anderson become the first man in Newcastle for twelve years to pay the ultimate penalty? The carrying out of the sentence was by no means a foregone conclusion. There was much local optimism that the sentence would be commuted, despite the fact, as Wiener has established, there was a general movement away from mercy for male-on-female violence. The *York Herald* reflected this optimism when, reporting the date of the execution it qualified it, '[s]hould it really take place'.[75]

The campaign to save Anderson began as soon as the verdict was known. Petitioning for mercy was common after a sentence of death. The government expected petitions in all capital cases, and it was a notable fact when these were unforthcoming.[76] There was a particularly strong campaign for Anderson with two weighty petitions. One was co-ordinated by Jonathan Joel, Anderson's legal representative at the police court hearing. Signatures included local MPs, clergymen, coroner, and many other 'persons of position and influence in the neighbourhood as well as the grand and common juries who heard the case'. [77] The letter sending the petition emphasised that the coroner had signed, perhaps to underline the fact that his court had heard the evidence immediately after the crime. Coroner Hoyle's participation was uncommon and perhaps reflected a sense of the justice of the plea. The Earl of Ravensworth, erstwhile MP for Northumberland and North Durham in Parliament, sent the second petition. This referred to the 'influential position of the Parties whose names are attached to the petition coupled with the unanimous recommendation to mercy by the jury which tried the case'.[78] The letter also underlined the prisoner's good character and the 'great provocation' to which he was subjected.

The popular view was not wholly united, for not everyone was convinced that Anderson should be saved. The *Newcastle Journal* was unremitting and explained that Denman's reasoning was 'more cogent than the scruples that seem to have swayed the minds of some of those who united at last in this verdict'.[79] However, the *Journal* was mistaken in speaking of a united jury. The jury was *not* united. Noise in the court, the confusion and misunderstanding between the judge and the timid foreman, may have led to a miscarriage of justice and thus to Anderson's death. The jury's recommendation for mercy, and the pleas in the petitions, is supplemented by correspondence that gives a unique insight into events in the jury room. The impression given in reports of the trial and the official notes from Denman is that the conclusion that Anderson was guilty of wilful murder was the unanimous verdict required by the law. The correspondence gives an alternative and troubling view.

The concluding exchange in court between the judge and the jury was not as simple as the official record suggests. When Denman wrote to the Home Secretary following the trial, he enclosed his detailed notes of the evidence. He put on record the care taken to explain to the jury the difference between murder and manslaughter and what could amount to provocation, as he had

> seen a growing disposition, especially in these Northern Counties to believe that any the slightest provocation however feeble in the nature of a defensive blow given even by a woman to a man is enough to reduce the crime to manslaughter.[80]

He would have been aware that capital punishment was rarely carried out in Newcastle. From 1831 until 1875, there had only been three executions. There had been eighteen in the neighbouring assize court of Durham, a striking comparison since there was common legal personnel at these North East legal venues. Perhaps the jurymen of Newcastle reflected a local distaste for the death penalty.[81]

Denman's notes, together with what he accepted was a 'tolerably accurate' newspaper account of the trial, are retained in the Home Office file along with two letters addressed to the Home Secretary. The first, from Christopher Anderson, a wine and spirits merchant from Gateshead, was 'on behalf of a juror'.[82] The second was from James Dellow, a member of the trial jury.[83] Dellow ran a hairdressing establishment on Northumberland Street, in the centre of Newcastle.[84] These letters alleged that one, or perhaps two, of the jury had doubts about the verdict and these doubts should have been acted upon the second time the jury returned to speak to the judge. Rather than leading to a verdict of guilty of murder, the conversation between the foreman and the judge should have led to further discussion before a final verdict. Dellow referred to 'an error by the jury or judge or both' and stated that the jury was not unanimous.[85]

It is unclear whether the man referred to in the letter from the wine merchant was Dellow, or whether there were two jurors worried that the verdict was wrongly returned. It is more likely that there were at least two dissenting jurors who felt compelled to contact the Home Secretary and sufficiently concerned to break the sanctity of the jury room. Both men explained that the foreman had misunderstood the judge's questions when he asked for the verdict. The foreman had not meant to indicate unanimity but to explain that the jury disagreed regarding provocation. After this conversation with the judge the foreman should have consulted the jury again and thus potentially returned a different verdict.

The word 'pressing', written in red on the face of these letters, is particularly poignant. Anderson was found guilty on 1 December, and executed on 22 December. The letters are each stamped 'received 20 December': the decision to be taken by the Home Secretary was indeed 'pressing'. The letter from Christopher Anderson asserted that there would be a miscarriage of justice if Anderson were hanged. Dellow explained he thought the verdict should be manslaughter and that the verdict was anything but unanimous. Dellow indicated that he believed that the deed was unpremeditated and committed from 'one impulse only' and thus the verdict should have been manslaughter.[86] In order to clarify his point, Dellow explained in some detail what happened in the jury room. The first vote taken was five to seven – with seven votes for 'guilty of murder'. This division caused the jurors to request pens and paper and resulted in the foreman telling the judge that a verdict could not be agreed. Why were pens and paper required: to draw diagrams or ensure anonymity by ballot, or for a juryman to explain his view? The next time the jury came into court, the judge accepted the responses of the foreman as a guilty verdict. However, Dellow's letter suggests that this was a second attempt by the jury to obtain clarification on the distinction between murder and manslaughter, and to consider the nature of provocation and premeditation. When the foreman asked for clarification, he was nervous and agreed that the jury had unanimously agreed a verdict of murder when this was not the case. Denman specifically explained to the Home Secretary that he advised the jury that there was no offence of 'aggravated manslaughter' and asked questions to make sure it was a verdict of murder.[87] Denman does not indicate any uncertainty but in the light of the letters he may have been at cross-purposes with the foreman.

Christopher Anderson's letter makes clear that the juror

> was and is yet of opinion that it was manslaughter, so also are others of the jury, they had misunderstood the Judge in his question to them and their foreman instead of again consulting with the other jurymen answered and caused a miscarriage of justice.[88]

A horrifying revelation in the circumstances of a capital trial, yet the letters carried no weight with the Home Secretary, who turned down the mercy pleas.

Although Anderson stated that he had no expectation of mercy, he must have held out some hope. A paper read to the Statistical Society in March 1880 reviewed statistics relating to indictable offences in England and Wales, demonstrating that in the period 1872–1876 only 35 per cent of those committed to trial for murder were convicted. The proportion of executions relative to the number of convictions in the same period was 51 per cent.[89] In Anderson's case, with clear doubt as to the verdict and petitions for mercy signed by many important and influential citizens, why was there no mercy? One reason might be a political concern about domestic violence, especially in working-class communities.[90] Wiener has suggested that in this period mercy was withheld to bring the tendency to violence in the working classes under control.[91] Yet Anderson was not a working-class offender. The Home Secretary was Richard Assheton Cross, a liberal Conservative who had been a barrister on the Northern Circuit and had often appeared in the Newcastle Courts. He was concerned about violence in communities and in 1874 sent a circular to all police forces, courts and judges to seek views on flogging for brutal crimes.[92] There was a general appetite to enforce the ultimate punishment to help contain violence in the country.[93]

A further reason for mercy's absence in this case might be the judge's influence. Denman thought that the outcome of murder trials was most dependent upon the judge hearing the case. Although the petitions and correspondence did not sway Cross, the explanatory letter from the judge had great influence.[94] In addressing the court at the end of the trial, Denman had explained that if the law of England was to hold that Anderson's crime was not murder, then a precedent endangering the protection of human life would be established. He dismissed any idea that the wound to Anderson's hand was defensive and asserted it was sustained when Anderson attacked Elizabeth. Denman's appraisal of the evidence as to Anderson's wound predated the communications revealing juror disunity. Would it have made any difference to his appraisal had he read the letters from the hairdresser and the wine merchant? What had happened to Denman's view in 1864, that even a murderer could be rehabilitated and returned to society to live a useful life?[95] Perhaps the North East of England exasperated him in 1875. After Newcastle, he travelled to Durham Assizes where he delivered a blistering opening speech about the serious nature of the calendar he faced and emphasised the influence of liquor on the accused: he may well have had Anderson's drunkenness in mind.[96]

Conclusion

An appraisal of the case, with the benefit of hindsight, suggests that Anderson committed the murder: the provocation was insufficient to reduce the offence to manslaughter. Nevertheless, the impact of provocation was a matter of judgement reserved for a jury and it is clear that the certainty necessary for a proper verdict was compromised by inadequate communication between judge and jury. Although there was little official acknowledgment of the impact of provocation, the broadside ballad reflected a common view that murdered women were complicit in their deaths, and 'it was hard words that brought these men to their unhappy end'.[97] An alternative interpretation offered here is that despite well-supported petitions, the views of clergymen, MPs, jurors, and the local coroner and magistrates, the trial judge could not support the recommendation to mercy. It was Denman's harsh words that ensured John Anderson was the first prisoner to be executed in the yard of the gaol in Newcastle. Jury recommendations to mercy fell on stony ground. Anderson's execution left an interesting legacy in the locality. The jurors of Newcastle, despite the failure to save Anderson, managed to ensure that there was no further execution in Newcastle until 1886 when Patrick Judge was executed for the murder of his wife.[98]

Notes

1 Death Certificate: Elizabeth Anderson.

2 The National Archives [hereafter TNA], HO 45/9395/49945. *R. v. Anderson*. Evidence of Dr May recorded in Mr Justice Denman's notes, 1 December 1875.

3 Death Certificate: John William Anderson. The hangman was William Marwood.

4 TNA HO 45/9395/49945. *R. v. Anderson* and TNA ASSI 44/192 Assizes: Northern and North-Eastern Circuits: Indictment Files (1875). The Home Office file contains depositions from the coroner's court and a note that the additional depositions taken before the magistrates were returned in February 1876 to the clerk of the Northern Circuit. They must have then been mislaid or misfiled, as neither these nor copies of the coroner's depositions that would normally also be kept by the clerk seem to have survived. Defendants could not testify in their own defence until the Criminal Evidence Act 1898 and therefore Anderson's voice is muted in the records. Defence counsel could cross examine witnesses, and the words are often recorded in newspaper accounts which provide information that cannot be obtained elsewhere.

5 See M.J. Wiener, 'Judges v. Jurors: Courtroom Tensions', *Law and History Review* 17 (1999), pp. 467–506.

6 Newspaper accounts of the exchange between the judge and jury differ slightly but there is no indication of the turmoil revealed in the letters.

7 For an examination of micro-histories in relation to law and crime, see essays in A.M. Kilday and D. Nash (eds) *Law, Crime and Deviance since 1700: Micro-Studies in the History of Crime* (London: Bloomsbury, 2016).

8 *Double Executions: John William Anderson, at Newcastle and Richard Charlton, at Morpeth, both for murdering their wives*, copy from Kenneth Goldstein Collection, Special Collections, University of Mississippi Libraries. Crime broadsides, printed locally and often with woodcut illustrations, were an important means of recording and disseminating news about serious crimes and punishments. The increased availability of cheap newspapers after mid-century caused their decline: Anderson's is thus a late example. See R. Crone. *Violent Victorians: Popular Entertainment in Nineteenth-Century London* (Manchester: Manchester University Press, 2012).

9 Wiener incorrectly suggests that broadsides relating to the earlier trial of Wainwright in 1875 were the last produced in a murder case, *Men of Blood: Violence, Manliness and Criminal Justice in Victorian England* (Cambridge: Cambridge University Press, 2004), note 73, p. 144.

10 On the Charlton case, see *Morpeth Herald*, 18 December 1875.

11 *Manchester Evening News*, 3 December 1875.

12 *A Vision of Britain through Time*, www.visionofbritain.org.uk/unit/10139466/cube/TOT_POP (accessed 1 October 2018).

13 Census: Mitford Street.

14 *Sunderland Daily Echo*, 30 August 1875.

15 Marriage certificate of John William Anderson and Elizabeth Walker.

16 Gaol Calendar.

17 'John Anderson', census return for Jackson Street, Gateshead, 1851.

18 Census: Mitford Street.

19 Anderson is registered on the ward list of burgesses in 1875: Tyne and Wear Archives D.NC/D/2/1/1875.

20 TNA HO 45/9395/49945. Plan of the house at Mitford Street.

21 TNA HO 45/9395/49945. Inquest deposition of Ashley Walker, 31 August 1875.

22 TNA HO 45/9395/49945. Inquest deposition of Ashley Walker, 31 August 1875.

23 *York Herald*, 30 August 1875.

24 J.F.C. Harrison, *The Common People: A History from the Norman Conquest to the Present* (London: Fontana, 1984), p. 302.

25 C.A. Conley, *The Unwritten Law: Criminal Justice in Victorian Kent* (Oxford: Oxford University Press, 1991), p. 6.

26 TNA HO 45/9395/49945. Inquest deposition of Ashley Walker, 31 August, 1875.

27 *Newcastle Journal*, 21 December 1875.

28 TNA HO 45/9395/49945. Denman to Home Secretary, 5 December 1875.

29 TNA HO 45/9395/49945. Denman to Home Secretary, 5 December 1875.

30 TNA HO 45/9395/49945. Evidence given by a number of witnesses.

31 TNA HO 45/9395/49945. Benjamin Danskin, evidence at trial noted by judge.

32 TNA HO 45/9395/49945. Walker's evidence at the inquest and trial was conflicting as to whether the relationship was violent.

33 TNA HO 45/9395/49945. Evidence of a witness also named Elizabeth Anderson.

34 *Morpeth Herald*, 4 September 1875.

35 *Sunderland Daily Echo*, 30 August 1875.

36 *Morpeth Herald*, 4 September 1875.

37 TNA HO 45/9395/49945. Inquest deposition, 31 August 1875.

38 TNA HO 45/9395/49945. Evidence of Dr May recorded in Denman's notes of the trial.

39 *Double Executions* referred to Elizabeth as 'wretched'.

40 TNA HO 45/9395/49945. Document headed 'Additional Evidence'.

41 *Newcastle Journal*, 21 December 1875.

42 A.B. Schofield, *Dictionary of Legal Biography 1845–1945* (London: Rose Publishing, 1998), p. 120. The Northern Circuit, prior to 1876 when it divided into the Northern and North Eastern Circuits, comprised all North England and included Assize courts in Yorkshire, Lancashire, County Durham, Westmoreland, Cumberland, and Northumberland.

43 Denman's obituary notice, *The Times*, 22 September 1896.

44 *Royal Commission on Capital Punishment. Report of the Capital Punishment Commission: Together with the Minutes of Evidence and Appendix* (London: Eyre and Spottiswoode, 1866), p. 78.

45 *Royal Commission on Capital Punishment*, p. 99.

46 *Royal Commission on Capital Punishment*, p. 91.

47 Wiener, *Men of Blood*, pp. 170–200.

48 Wiener, *Men of Blood*, p. 183.
49 On early and mid-nineteenth-century judicial opinions of provocation in wife-murder cases, see D.J.R. Grey 'Importing Gendered Legal Reasoning from England: Wife Murders in Early Colonial India, 1805–1857', *Cultural and Social History* 14: 4 (2017), pp. 483–498.
50 W. Bruce, *Archbold's Pleading and Evidence in Criminal Cases. With the Statutes, Precedents of Indictments, &c., and the Evidence Necessary to Support Them*, 17th edn (London: H. Sweet, 1871). *Archbold* as the leading practitioner text would have been consulted by lawyers in this case.
51 E. Coke, *The Third Part of the Institutes of the Laws of England: Concerning High Treason, and Other Pleas of the Crown, and Criminal Causes*, 6th edn (London: Thomas Basset, 1680), p. 47.
52 Judges lost the power to merely record sentence of death when the Offences against the Person Act 1861 abolished the death penalty for all offences except murder and high treason.
53 Bruce, *Archbold*, p. 621.
54 Bruce, *Archbold*, p. 633.
55 Bruce, *Archbold*, p. 631.
56 TNA HO 45/9395/49945. Deposition of P.C. Dixon to Coroner 30 August 1875.
57 See discussion in Bruce, *Archbold*, pp. 633–634.
58 No provocation, however great, could extenuate or justify a homicide where there was evidence of express malice.
59 Bruce, *Archbold*, p. 631.
60 Bruce, *Archbold*, p. 623.
61 E.H. East, *A Treatise of the Pleas of the Crown* (London: J. Butterworth, 1803), p. 238.
62 *Morpeth Herald*, 4 December 1875.
63 TNA HO 45/9395/49945. Denman to Home Secretary, 5 December 1875.
64 'Common sense' is not value-neutral even if frequently claimed to be so. See T. Ward, 'Law, Common Sense and the Authority of Science: Expert Witnesses and Criminal Insanity in England, 1840–1940', *Social & Legal Studies* 6: 3 (1997), pp. 343–362.
65 TNA HO 45/9395/49945. Denman to Home Secretary, 5 December 1875.
66 On the Grant case, see *Newcastle Journal*, 17 December 1872.
67 *Newcastle Journal*, 23 December 1875. My emphasis.
68 See *The Times*, 18 December 1872.
69 Denman mentioned this in his evidence to the Royal Commission in 1864, see *Royal Commission on Capital Punishment*, p. 79.
70 *Royal Commission on Capital Punishment*, p. 79.
71 TNA HO 45/9395/49945. Denman trial notes, 1 December 1875.
72 TNA HO 45/9395/49945. Denman trial notes, 1 December 1875.
73 TNA HO 45/9395/49945. Letter from James Dellow to Home Secretary, 18 December 1875, and letter from Christopher Anderson to Home Secretary, 19 December 1875.
74 *Morpeth Herald*, 4 December 1875.
75 *York Herald*, 10 December 1875.
76 *Prerogative of Mercy. Return of Instances since 1869 in Which Appeal has been Made on behalf of Persons Convicted of Capital Offences to the Home Secretary, for the Exercise of the Royal Prerogative of Pardon or Mitigation of Sentence; Setting Forth the Names, Dates of Conviction, Crimes, Sentences, Dates of Appeal to the Secretary, and the Result; with Summary of Total Number of Such Applications Refused or Granted in Whole or Part*. House of Commons Sessional Papers, 1881, vol. LXXVI, p. 391. This includes reference to a petition in the 1863 murder case of *R*. v. *George Vass*, there was no petition.

77 The first time a prisoner appeared in court to answer to a criminal charge was in the police court, where the magistrates decided if there was sufficient evidence to send the case to the assize court.
78 TNA HO 45/9395/49945. Letter from the Earl of Ravensworth to Home Secretary, 6 December 1875.
79 *Newcastle Journal*, 3 December 1875.
80 TNA HO 45/9395/49945. Denman to Home Secretary, 5 December 1875.
81 See the report of an exasperated judge informed by the foreman of a Newcastle jury that a recommendation to mercy was 'on account of an objection to capital punishments,' *Newcastle Journal*, 24 February 1849.
82 TNA HO 45/9395/49945. Christopher Anderson to Home Secretary, 19 December 1875. There is no way of establishing whether he was a relation of the accused.
83 TNA HO 45/9395/49945. James Dellow to Home Secretary, 18 December 1875.
84 *Newcastle Journal*, 31 December 1872.
85 TNA HO 45/9395/49945. Dellow to Home Secretary, 18 December 1875.
86 TNA HO 45/9395/49945. Dellow to Home Secretary, 18 December 1875.
87 TNA HO 45/9395/49945. Denman to Home Secretary, 5 December 1875.
88 TNA HO 45/9395/49945. Christopher Anderson to Home Secretary, 19 December 1875.
89 L. Levi, 'A Survey of Indictable and Summary Jurisdiction Offences in England and Wales, from 1857 to 1876, in Quinquennial Periods, and in 1877 and 1878', *Journal of the Statistical Society of London* 43: 3 (1880), pp. 423–461.
90 For detailed consideration and discussion of 'expected' middle-class behaviour, see S. D'Cruze, *Crimes of Outrage: Sex, Violence and Victorian Working Women* (London: UCL Press, 1998) and B. Griffin, *The Politics of Gender in Victorian Britain: Masculinity, Political Culture and the Struggle for Women's Rights* (Cambridge: Cambridge University Press, 2014).
91 Wiener, *Men of Blood*, p. 194.
92 *Reports to Secretary of State for Home Department on State of Law relating to Brutal Assaults*, 1875. Command Paper C.1138, vol. 61, p. 29. On Cross, see J.P. Parry, 'Religion and the Collapse of Gladstone's First Government, 1870–1874', *The Historical Journal* 25 (1982), pp. 71–101.
93 Wiener, *Men of Blood*. See also M.L. Shanley, *Feminism, Marriage, and the Law in Victorian England* (Princeton, NJ: Princeton University Press, 1993).
94 On the reluctance of Home Secretaries to overrule judges, see R. Chadwick, *Bureaucratic Mercy. The Home Office and the Treatment of Capital Cases in Victorian Britain* (New York: Garland, 1992), p. 151.
95 *Royal Commission on Capital Punishment*, p. 99.
96 *Shields Daily Gazette*, 14 December 1875.
97 *Double Executions*.
98 For details of the crime and trial, *Newcastle Evening Chronicle*, 16 July 1886 and on the execution, *Newcastle Evening Chronicle*, 16 November 1886.

Bibliography

'John Anderson', Census Return for Jackson Street, Gateshead, Durham (HO107/2402, folio 289, 1851), p. 38.

A Vision of Britain through Time, www.visionofbritain.org.uk/unit/10139466/cube/TOT_POP (accessed 1 October 2018)

Bruce, W. *Archbold's Pleading and Evidence in Criminal Cases. With The Statutes, Precedents of Indictments, &c., and the Evidence Necessary To Support Them*, 17th edn London: Sweet, 1871).

Census Return for Mitford Street, Elswick, Newcastle upon Tyne, Northumberland, (RG10/5081, folio 11, 1871).

Certified Copy of Death Certificate for Elizabeth Anderson, 1 September 1875 (Newcastle upon Tyne Register Office, 1875).

Certified Copy of Death Certificate for John William Anderson, 24 December 1875 (Newcastle upon Tyne Register Office, 1875).

Certified Copy of Marriage Certificate for John William Anderson and Elizabeth Walker, 31 March 1866 (Newcastle upon Tyne Register Office, 1866).

Chadwick, R. *Bureaucratic Mercy. The Home Office and the Treatment of Capital Cases in Victorian Britain* (New York and London: Garland, 1992).

Coke, E. *The Third part of the Institutes of the Laws of England: Concerning High Treason, and Other Pleas of the Crown, and Criminal Causes*, 6th edn (London: Thomas Basset, 1680).

Conley, C.A. *The Unwritten Law: Criminal Justice in Victorian Kent* (New York and Oxford: Oxford University Press, 1991).

Crone, R. *Violent Victorians: Popular Entertainment in Nineteenth-Century London* (Manchester: Manchester University Press, 2012).

D'Cruze, S. *Crimes of Outrage: Sex, Violence and Victorian Working Women* (London: UCL Press, 1998).

Double Executions: John William Anderson, at Newcastle and Richard Charlton, at Morpeth, Both for Murdering their Wives (n.d., December 1875) [copy in Kenneth Goldstein Collection, Special Collections, University of Mississippi Libraries].

East, E.H. *A Treatise of the Pleas of the Crown* (London: J Butterworth, 1803).

Grey, D.J.R. 'Importing Gendered Legal Reasoning from England: Wife Murders in Early Colonial India, 1805–1857', *Cultural and Social History* 14:4 (2017), pp. 483–498.

Griffin, B. *The Politics of Gender in Victorian Britain: Masculinity, Political Culture and the Struggle for Women's Rights* (Cambridge: Cambridge University Press, 2014).

Harrison, J.F.C. *The Common People: A History from the Norman Conquest to the Present* (London: Fontana, 1984).

Kilday, A.M. and D. Nash, eds, *Law, Crime and Deviance since 1700: Micro-Studies in the History of Crime* (London: Bloomsbury, 2017).

Levi, L. 'A Survey of Indictable and Summary Jurisdiction Offences in England and Wales, from 1857 to 1876', *Journal of the Statistical Society* 43:3 (1880), pp. 423–456.

Manchester Evening News.

Morpeth Herald.

Newcastle Daily Journal.

Parry, J.P. 'Religion and the Collapse of Gladstone's First Government, 1870–1874', *The Historical Journal* 25:1 (1982), pp. 71–101.

Prerogative of Mercy. Return of Instances since 1869 in Which Appeal has been Made on behalf of Persons Convicted of Capital Offences to the Home Secretary, for the Exercise of the Royal Prerogative of Pardon or Mitigation of Sentence; Setting Forth the Names, Dates of Conviction, Crimes, Sentences, Dates of Appeal to the Secretary, and the Result; with Summary of Total Number of Such Applications Refused or Granted in Whole or Part. House of Commons Sessional Papers, 1881, vol. LXXVI, p. 391.

Ramsey, C.B. 'Provoking Change: Comparative Insights on Feminist Homicide Law Reform', *Journal of Criminal Law & Criminology* 100:1 (2010), pp. 33–108.

Reports to Secretary of State for Home Department on State of Law relating to Brutal Assaults, Command Papers C1138 1875, vol. LXI, p. 29.

Return of Appeals on behalf of Persons Convicted of Capital Offences to Home Secretary, for Exercise of Royal Prerogative of Pardon or Mitigation of Sentence, 1861–1880, (London: House of Commons Papers, 1881).

Royal Commission on Capital Punishment. Report of the Capital Punishment Commission: Together with the Minutes of Evidence and Appendix (London: Eyre and Spottiswoode, 1866).

Schofield, A.B., *Dictionary of Legal Biography 1845–1945* (London: Rose Publishing, 1998).

Shanley, M.L. *Feminism, Marriage, and the Law in Victorian England* (Princeton, NJ: Princeton University Press, 1993).

Shields Daily Gazette.

Sunderland Daily Echo and Shipping Gazette.

The National Archives, HO45/9395/49945. Home Office File *R.* v. *John William Anderson.*

The National Archives, ASSI 44/192. Assizes: Northern and North-Eastern Circuits: Indictment Files (1875).

Tyne and Wear Archives, D.NC/D/2/1/1875. Newcastle Electoral Registers, Ward List of Burgesses in 1875.

Ward, T. 'Law, Common Sense and the Authority of Science: Expert Witnesses and Criminal Insanity in England, c.1840–1940', *Social & Legal Studies* 6:3 (1997), pp. 343–362.

Wiener, M.J. *Men of Blood: Violence, Manliness and Criminal Justice in Victorian England* (Cambridge: Cambridge University Press, 2004).

Wiener, M.J. 'Judges v. Jurors: Courtroom Tensions in Murder Trails and the Law of Criminal Responsibility in Nineteenth Century England'. *Law and History Review* Fall, 17:3 (1999), pp. 467–506.

York Herald.

13 Establishing the poor law unions under the New Poor Law

Karen Rothery

Introduction

The poor relief system established from Elizabethan times in England and Wales came under increasing pressure at the turn of the nineteenth century and in 1834 was replaced by the New Poor Law (officially known as the Poor Law Amendment Act of 1834).[1] Under the Old Poor Laws more than 16,000 local parishes were responsible for providing help to those in their community who fell on hard times. However, this system came under increasing strain and criticism. Practices varied throughout England and Wales: some felt the poor law system encouraged idleness and immorality and did not encourage the poor to help themselves. In addition, the cost of poor relief in England and Wales was escalating and had increased from approximately £690,000 in the middle of the eighteenth century to around £7 million by 1820. Population numbers were increasing, and significant migration to new urban centres put further pressure on the system. The burden of poor relief was perceived to be most acute in rural areas. The New Poor Law saw the creation of new administrative units, known as poor law unions; these were made up of a number of parishes, administered by a locally elected Board of Guardians. This law also saw the widespread introduction of the deterrent workhouse, accommodation so basic and unattractive as to make it the place of last resort for those in need of help. The payment of out-relief (relief in cash or kind outside of the workhouse) was discouraged. One of the key principles of the new system was 'less eligibility', that is, a pauper claiming relief from the parish would not be better off than a local working man.

This new welfare system was not implemented overnight. It was rolled out over the next eight years under the direction of the Poor Law Commission aided and abetted by a team of itinerant Assistant Poor Law Commissioners.[2] The new administrative districts – the poor law unions – were central to the New Poor Law's operation. A poor law union was a group of contiguous parishes formally brought together to administer the provision of poor relief within the boundaries of that union. Individual poor law unions were not defined within the Act, but were planned and organised locally by the

Assistant Poor Law Commissioners following representations to the central commissioners. Unionisation forced coterminous parishes in England and Wales to unite, creating new administrative and spatial relationships within the local landscape. There were three stages to implementing the New Poor Law: first the appointment of the central Poor Law Commission, second the appointment of itinerant Assistant Poor Law Commissioners and finally a phased programme of local enactment facilitated by the assistant commissioners throughout England and Wales.

This chapter explores the process of creating the poor law unions and, in particular, the role of the Assistant Poor Law Commissioners. It begins with a look at the Commission before looking at the Assistant Poor Law Commissioners, it then focusses on the process of local enactment and examines the methodology for establishing the new poor law unions.

The Poor Law Commission

Within nine days of the Poor Law Amendment Act being passed the Poor Law Commissioners Thomas Frankland-Lewis, J.G. Shaw Lefevre and George Nicholls were sworn in. Edwin Chadwick was appointed as secretary to the commissioners. Chadwick was very knowledgeable about poor law matters; he had worked on the Royal Commission which had investigated the operation of the poor laws between 1832 and 1834 and had co-authored the subsequent *Poor Law Report* with Nassau Senior, a leading political economist and government advisor. The Poor Law Commission was set up as a centralised administrative body independent of central government.[3] Like the new law itself the Commission was not universally popular; the three board members held extensive and previously unseen powers of inspection, intervention and authority over local administrators.[4] Opposition came from many quarters including individuals on both sides of the political divide, radical campaigners, the radical press and religious groups.[5] The Commission became the focus of the criticism expressed by those who campaigned against the New Poor Law. The language employed to describe the group and its work was negative and hostile. For example, the commissioners were described as 'the three Bashaws' or 'the three tyrants' of Somerset House and the 'pinch pauper triumvirate', while the workhouses became known as 'Bastilles'.[6] The three members of the commission and their secretary were the focus of much press vitriol. *The Times* was highly critical of the New Poor Law and repeatedly criticised the legislation and the operation of the commission:

> Every day and in every quarter, some fresh shock is given to humanity by the working of the New Poor Law. All that was bad in the measure has been made worse by the imbecility of the Central Board, which has not the faculty of making itself understood upon the simplest point.[7]

The Commissioners had to forge their own path in setting up and managing the administration as a body whose legal and constitutional position was unprecedented.[8] Based at Somerset House in London, the Commission began to assume responsibility for controlling and directing the management and administration of poor relief throughout England and Wales. It was a small team – three commissioners, one secretary, an assistant secretary and three clerks – but their task was enormous. Almost immediately the amount of correspondence between the centre and the parishes overwhelmed them, and they appointed extra clerks who worked through the night.[9] By 1840 staffing levels had increased seven fold; there were two assistant secretaries, one chief clerk and thirty-three clerks.[10] The volume of surviving documentation in the National Archives demonstrates the extent to which they were consulted by union and parish officials as well as by the Assistant Poor Law Commissioners. Closer examination of the correspondence shows that the commissioners relied heavily on the assistant commissioners for information. The London-based Poor Law Commissioners did not visit the provinces themselves, but the Assistant Poor Law Commissioners often visited Somerset House.[11] The Assistant Poor Law Commissioners were the eyes and ears of the Commission and were essential to the implementation of the New Poor Law around the country.

Assistant Poor Law Commissioners

The central commissioners were initially authorised to employ nine Assistant Poor Law Commissioners to implement and manage the New Poor Law throughout the country. This number proved insufficient and they employed a further seven by the end of 1835 and another eight in early 1836. By the middle of 1836 there were twenty-one assistant commissioners under the control of the central Commission.[12] These assistant commissioners, especially the first nine to be appointed, wielded considerable power and greatly influenced how the New Poor Law was administered on the ground and in shaping the poor law geography of England and Wales. They were essential to the process of implementing the New Poor Law and became an important layer in the administrative process during the initial phase although their importance and influence declined after the unions were fully established.[13]

The Royal Commission of Inquiry into the operation of the Poor Law had employed its own assistant commissioners to report on poor law practice and they built up a considerable knowledge of local poor law custom: however, only three of these men became Assistant Poor Law Commissioners.[14] Those who acted as assistant commissioners to the Royal Commission were said to be 'philanthropically minded amateurs [...] motivated by a sense of the need to do something about the Poor Law'.[15] The authors of the *Poor Law Report* said they were men who had made 'a great sacrifice of time and labour [...] followed by much hostility, and accompanied by no remuneration'.[16] The new position of Assistant Poor Law Commissioner was similarly arduous, but with a salary of £700 per annum plus a one guinea per diem and expenses it attracted not just altruistic men of independent means, but over 2,000 applicants.[17]

Those appointed as assistant commissioners in 1834 were well-educated individuals who had held positions of authority and power in their previous occupation or home location. In total thirty-three men served as assistant commissioners in England and Wales from the establishment of the Commission in 1834 until 1847 when it was replaced by the Poor Law Board.[18] Many were barristers or magistrates, some had military training, and some were career civil servants. The first appointment was the colourful Sir Francis Bond Head, a veteran of Waterloo who had travelled extensively; he proved too 'eccentric to make an ideal Assistant Commissioner' and he left after just one year to become the Lieutenant Governor of Upper Canada.[19] Another military appointment was Sir William Edward Parry, an intrepid naval explorer who subsequently held a number of senior naval positions, including Lieutenant Governor of the Royal Greenwich Hospital.[20] More enduring in his appointment was William Henry Toovey Hawley who served as an assistant commissioner (and subsequently as a poor law inspector) for forty years, working first in southern and then northern districts as well as in Ireland. Likewise, Edward Gulson, who had previously served as the Director for the Poor in Coventry, was an assistant commissioner in England and Ireland for thirty-seven years. Forty per cent of this group lived lives recorded in the *Dictionary of National Biography*. This suggests their Victorian contemporaries who compiled this record regarded them as noteworthy individuals. But there are also some who have left little trace of themselves in the surviving records beyond their correspondence files now held in the National Archives.

The role of the Assistant Poor Law Commissioner was initially a peripatetic one as the Commission instigated a programme of unionisation throughout the country. The first nine assistant commissioners were appointed between October and December 1834 and were deployed to set up unions in the southern counties of England where pauperism was perceived to be the most heightened. Table 13.1 shows the number and location of the unions formed up to August 1835 by twelve assistant commissioners. Four counties, Hampshire, Sussex, Kent and Hertfordshire, account for over half of the unions formed in seven months. Unionisation spread northwards into the Home Counties and South Midlands at a rate of over three new unions per week. No unions were formed in large parts of the Midlands, the Southwest, the North or Wales. One year later in August 1836, 363 unions had been formed covering most of the South and Midlands and the first Welsh unions had been set up in Monmouthshire. The counties of Cornwall, Cumberland, Durham and most of Yorkshire and Wales did not see any unions established until 1837.

Table 13.1 Number of Unions and parishes unionised in each county by 8 August 1835

County	Number of Unions	%	Number of Parishes	Names of Assistant Poor Law Commissioners
Hampshire	21	19	274	A'Court, Gulson, Pilkington, Hall
Sussex	16	14	242	Hawley, Pilkington
Kent	14	12	211	Head
Hertfordshire	12	11	140	Adey, Gilbert, Power
Berkshire	11	10	186	A'Court, Gulson, Hall
Northamptonshire	7	6	157	Gulson, Earle
Buckinghamshire	7	6	162	Adey, Gilbert, Earle, Hall
Oxfordshire	5	4	200	Gilbert, Gulson, Earle, Hall
Bedfordshire	4	4	81	Adey, Earle
Suffolk	4	4	129	Mott
Cambridgeshire	3	3	61	Power
Essex	3	3	96	Power, Hall
Wiltshire	2	2	45	A'Court, Gulson, Mott
Norfolk	2	2	68	Parry
Middlesex	1	1	11	Adey, Mott
Gloucestershire	1	1	37	Gulson, Mott
Somerset			1	Mott
Huntingdonshire			2	Power
Warwickshire			2	Gulson
Total	113	100	2105	

Source: British Parliamentary Papers, 1835 (500), XXXV.107. *First Annual Report of the Poor Law Commissioners for England and Wales*, Appendix D.

Management and supervision of Assistant Poor Law Commissioners

The Assistant Poor Law Commissioners' activities were closely managed through meetings, regular correspondence, ad hoc reports and the submission of weekly diaries detailing their activities. Correspondence with the centre was very regular, often daily. Prior to the postal reforms of 1839, the Commission and its assistants enjoyed the privilege of free post; a practice that was sometimes abused as unions routed mail to other unions through the assistant commissioners rather than pay postage on direct correspondence.[21] Assistant commissioners' salaries were paid quarterly, and their expense claims were rigorously scrutinised by Chadwick. In July 1835 Chadwick told assistant commissioner Daniel Goodson Adey to submit a more detailed itemised expense claim suitable to be submitted 'for auditing the public accounts'. In particular Adey was told to travel 'by means of public conveyance'. (Adey had claimed for the hire of a private coach for a return trip to London when he was in poor health, and this had displeased Chadwick who knew that the unpopular commission could not be seen to be wasting public money.) Adey made the point that 'posting is the only mode of moving that can be depended on' and that it was impractical for him to cover the necessary mileage otherwise. Felix Driver has shown the considerable distances travelled by two assistant commissioners by mapping their journeys over a three-month period.[22] But despite this close scrutiny of their expenses by Chadwick, the assistant commissioners had considerable autonomy.

The Poor Law Commissioners relied heavily on feedback from the assistant commissioners. When Poor Law Commissioners received communications directly from the union or parish they wrote to their assistants for an opinion and the assistant commissioner's reply usually formed the basis of the response to the parish. There are many examples in the central correspondence files with the unions held at the National Archives.[23] Original letters were date stamped on receipt and were often annotated with draft responses that would then provide the 'office copy' of the correspondence.[24] Where several opinions have been sought, one letter was overwritten and annotated in many different hands. Eventually, as the central commissioners became more established, this reliance on the assistant commissioners was reduced, but in the initial stages a significant amount of correspondence was referred back to the assistants annotated 'Ask [name of assistant commissioner] for his opinion'. In the early period at least, policy was not just formed within the walls of Somerset House; the assistant commissioner had the capacity to strongly influence the three 'tyrants' and played a role in the interpretation and evolution of poor law policy and systems.

The various assistant commissioners had their own strengths: Adey was regularly consulted for his pedantic eye for detail on bookkeeping and the standardisation of forms. Both he and Charles Mott often suggested how forms could be improved and made more convenient.[25] It has been argued that the assistant commissioners were essential in disseminating and embedding the then novel practice of double-entry bookkeeping that became standard practice in centralised government departments.[26] Power and Gulson were the preferred commentators on medical matters.[27] Kay-Shuttleworth was passionate about education policy and in time became the chief architect of England's education system.[28]

Local enactment

The commissioners and their assistants were in uncharted territory; they had to devise a system for establishing the unions with no framework to follow. Each assistant commissioner travelled to or based himself in the districts he was unionising. It is not clear how they were selected for each area and they often went to areas they were unfamiliar with. For example, assistant commissioner Adey lived in the centre of the area he initially worked on but was subsequently assigned to Southwest England. His colleague Alfred Power, who had previously travelled widely as a Factories Inspector, started work in east Hertfordshire and Eastern England but later moved to the Northern counties and then on to Ireland. In a letter to the commissioners

Adey wrote of his need to make himself 'acquainted with the habits of the County (many of which are quite new to me)'.[29] In their districts the assistant commissioners organised meetings of the local elite, debated the size and location of union boundaries and influenced decisions on the siting of workhouses. Given the limitations on transport and travel in the 1830s this in itself was an arduous task. There were few railways to aid the commissioners in their early work, more likely they would have had to rely on the network of turnpike and parish roads which criss-crossed the country.

The Assistant Poor Law Commissioner's work began with an 'inspection of his district'.[30] On the ground he made enquiries with the local elite including the nobility, gentry and magistrates. He also consulted farmers, overseers and parish clerks. He gathered information from parish records to determine the amount spent on poor relief in each parish in the preceding three years. This calculation was known as 'the averages' and played an important part in apportioning parish liability in the new union. Sometimes simple maps would be drawn to illustrate the geography and juxtaposition of the parishes for a proposed union. At some point the assistant commissioner formed an opinion on which parishes should be united to form a union. The assistant commissioner convened a public meeting for the parishes concerned after which he recommended to the Poor Law Commissioners that a union should be declared. The final recommendation sometimes ignored or overruled local opinion. The union was given a name, usually the name of the market town in which the union administration would take place. The Poor Law Commissioners formally declared a union had been formed after which the process of setting up the administration could begin. This normally followed within a few days.

In his deliberations the assistant commissioner was lobbied and influenced by both pro and anti-unionists. Historians have disagreed about the extent to which the Assistant Poor Law Commissioners were influenced by the local elite. In his study of the Midlands counties and East Anglia, Anthony Brundage found that the influence and cooperation of large landowners were important factors in establishing the new unions, particularly with respect to administrative boundaries, which were more likely to follow the landholdings of great estates than established administrative divisions such as petty sessional divisions.[31] Peter Dunkley, however, argued that a disproportionate number of the major landholders in the area surveyed by Brundage were peers and that elsewhere 'the peerage played no significant part in conducting the relief system'.[32] Ultimately, it was the Assistant Poor Law Commissioner's recommendation alone that went forward to the central commissioners; creating change within the administrative landscape and the social geography of England and Wales. That is not to say that the Poor Law Commission in London was not lobbied directly. Lord Salisbury, whose seat was at Hatfield in Hertfordshire, had been consulted by Chadwick and others in the development of the New Poor Law. When he raised objections to the parish of Hatfield being combined with another union the assistant commissioner backed down.[33]

The market town that became the administrative centre of the union had the potential to disproportionately dominate other local market towns by becoming the centre to which the economic activity of the union gravitated. The poor law unions created by the assistant commissioner were also the framework for the registration districts created by the Births and Deaths Registration Act of 1836. Those establishing the first unions could not have anticipated this additional administrative requirement. The 'union' town's place as the location for the registration of births and deaths added to its importance as an administrative hub. In modern society, towns or organisations might lobby or bid for the right to become an administrative centre or focal point, but there is no sense that these market towns of the 1830s were clamouring to adopt the responsibility of hosting the Board of Guardians' meetings or be the site of a new workhouse. This significant new role was imposed on them as part of a new administrative framework. The oft-cited concept that the poor law unions were centred on a market town appears to be an accidental outcome rather than a planned strategy and derives from the statement in the first annual report:

> The most convenient limit of unions which we have found has been that of a circle, taking a market town as a centre, and comprehending those surrounding parishes whose inhabitants are accustomed to resort to the same market. This arrangement was found highly convenient for the weekly attendances of the parish officers, and some portion of the guardians and other auxiliaries to good management were derived from the town itself.[34]

In smaller unions, which contained only a few parishes, an economically and socially dominant market town may have been an obvious choice, but in larger unions where two or three viable market towns existed the assistant commissioner's decision may have indirectly influenced which towns saw investment and further development in the future.

Other than having a market town at the centre, there were no other guidelines on the size and composition of the unions. Given that the New Poor Law was predicated on having a uniform system for dealing with the poor of all parishes, one might have expected uniformity in the way the poor law unions were arranged. A close examination of the poor law unions in the county of Hertfordshire, the first area to be fully unionised, shows wide variation in the structure of the unions. First, the new poor law unions were not coterminous with any existing administrative units including county boundaries. The 142 parishes of Hertfordshire were distributed across sixteen different poor law unions with between one and twenty-seven parishes in a given union. Unions contained parishes from one or more counties. Table 13.2 illustrates the distribution of Hertfordshire parishes across different unions and the number of parishes included from adjacent unions. The Bishops Stortford union sat on the Hertfordshire/Essex boarder and half of its parishes came from each county. The Royston union had less than

Table 13.2 Distribution of Hertfordshire Parishes into Poor Law Unions

Union Name	Number of Parishes from Each County						Total Number of Parishes
	Herts	Beds	Bucks	Essex	Cambs	Middex	
Barnet	6					3	9
Berkhampstead	8						8
Bishops Stortford	10			10			20
Buntingford	16						16
Hatfield	4						4
Hemel Hempstead	6						6
Hertford	18						18
Hitchin	27	1					28
Royston	9			3	17		29
St Albans	8						8
Watford	6						6
Welwyn	4						4
Edmonton[a] (Middex)	1			1		5	7
Amersham[a] (Bucks)	1		9				10
Luton[a] (Beds)	3	13					16
Total	142	14	9	14	17	8	204

Source: *First Annual Report of the Poor Law Commissioners for England and Wales*, 1835 (500) XXXV.107.

a   These unions are normally reported with the county in parenthesis. Royston was initially reported as a Cambridgeshire union but by the third annual report of the PLC it was recorded as a Hertfordshire union.

a third of its parishes in Hertfordshire, the majority (59 per cent) were in Cambridgeshire and another three were in Essex.

Despite this blurring of the county boundaries, the Poor Law Commission reported data in county divisions in its annual and other ad hoc reports. For the purposes of poor law reporting, both Bishops Stortford and Royston were classed as Hertfordshire unions although Royston was initially classed as a Cambridgeshire union. Table 13.2 also illustrates how the number of parishes brought together as a union was subject to wide variation; there were just four parishes in both the Welwyn union and the Hatfield union, whereas the Royston union had twenty-nine.

The parish was an ancient unit of geography and administration; perhaps the disparity in the number of parishes in a union reflected the need to harmonise the size of the union in another way. Looking at the Hertfordshire example again, a comparison of various measures: population size, area, average poor rate expenditure, population density, expenditure per head of population and the number of guardians provides further disparity in the size and make-up of the unions as shown in Table 13.3.

Table 13.3 The Hertfordshire Poor Law Unions: Population, Area, Guardians and Poor Law Expenditure

Poor Law Union	Number of Parishes	Population 1831	Area (miles²)	No Elected Guardians	No Ex-officio Guardians	Average Expenditure on Poor Relief 1831–1834	Expenditure per Head of Population	Population Density (Per Mile²)
Barnet	9	12,180	40	14	8	£5,486	£0.45	305
Berkhampstead	8	9,871	39	16	9	£7,750	£0.79	253
Bishops Stortford	20	18,012	83	27	9	£17,421	£0.97	217
Buntingford	16	6,327	45	19	4	£4,615	£0.73	141
Hatfield	4	5,933	36	8	7	£3,177	£0.54	165
Hemel Hempstead	6	9,910	40	14	6	£5,672	£0.57	248
Hertford	18	12,155	53	21	13	£8,202	£0.67	229
Hitchin	28	20,639	101	36	10	£12,315	£0.60	204
Royston	29	15,671	94	32	6	£10,232	£0.65	167
St Albans	8	15,883	54	17	14	£8,488	£0.53	294
Ware	15	14,654	55	21	14	£12,131	£0.83	266
Watford	6	15,379	57	16	11	£8,473	£0.55	270
Welwyn	4	1,970	10	5	4	£1,037	£0.53	197
Total	171	158,584	707	246	115	£104,999	£0.66	224

Source: BPP, *Poor Law Amendment Act. Return, showing the size in square miles of the several unions formed, with the population, and number of guardians.* 1837–1838 (236) XXXVIII.539.38, p. 1–5. BPP *First Annual Report of the Poor Law Commissioners for England & Wales.* Appendix D, p. 239, pp. 249–250.

For a system designed to produce a uniform response to poor relief, the initial administrative framework created by the Assistant Poor Law Commissioners and sanctioned by the Poor Law Commission was inconsistent and contained differences from the outset. A more populous union like Hitchin – population 20,639 and spread over 101 square miles – needed to be administered in a different way to its neighbouring union Welwyn with fewer than 2,000 inhabitants in just ten square miles. The dynamics of a Board of Guardians with forty-six members representing twenty-eight parishes was different to a Board with just nine guardians.

Setting up the poor law unions

Before a local union could begin its work a local Board of Guardians had to be assembled. The Board of Guardians was a new tier of local government created by the Poor Law Amendment Act of 1834 with responsibility for managing poor relief provision in a given union. There were two types of guardian: elected and *ex-officio*. Any magistrate who resided in the area covered by the union was entitled to sit on the Board of Guardians as an *ex-officio* guardian. There was no limit on the number of *ex-officio* guardians, and the ratio of *ex-officio* guardians to elected guardians varied widely. Each parish in the union elected at least one guardian to the board, and larger, more populous parishes elected multiple guardians to the board. A ballot was held among the parish rate payers using a plural voting system, which in many areas gave the property-holding elite greater influence. The guardians all sat voluntarily and were the only positions within the poor law bureaucracy who were unpaid. Every other position from the Poor Law Commissioners in London to a workhouse porter in a small rural union was paid.

As previously stated, setting up the new system was breaking new ground with no particular methodology put in place at the outset. In January 1836, Assistant Poor Law Commissioner Adey wrote an extensive report on his personal methodology for the implementation of the new procedures based on his experience of having set up some of the first unions in Bedfordshire, Buckinghamshire and Hertfordshire.[35] In March 1836 the Poor Law Commission issued an instruction to all assistant commissioners that followed Adey's model.[36] They also created a template 'instructional letter' for Boards of Guardians based on Adey's report which was issued as unions were formed.[37] The latter stated it was designed to 'prevent confusion and difficulty' and guided the guardians through the tasks they needed to complete to get the union up and running. Rather optimistically, the Poor Law Commissioners suggested the union could be set up in just three meetings. However, given the interdependency of some tasks (as we shall see below), the work assigned was not feasible in just three meetings. The Commissioners built in an unspecified number of extra meetings to review the claims of paupers already in receipt of relief 'it has been usual to hold meetings twice or three times each week, until the whole of the pauper cases have been

examined'.[38] Reviewing the relief paid under the Old Poor Law was fundamental to implementing and enforcing the New Poor Law. Yet in the Poor
Law Commissioners' programme of events its significance is downplayed.
For those whose relief payments were under review it was a decisive moment
with the potential to bring about a dramatic change in circumstances.

The Assistant Poor Law Commissioner normally attended the inaugural
meeting of the Board of Guardians. The Poor Law Commissioners recommended the first task was to appoint a Chairman and Vice-Chairman of the
Board of Guardians. The Commissioners suggested that 'the gentlemen who
have shown the greatest interest in the measure, and who have distinguished
themselves within the district by promoting improvements, and reducing the
burthens of the rate-payers' made the best choice.[39] In practice, many of the
chairmen were elected from the *ex-officio* cohort on the board; as these were
all magistrates they were already authority figures within the community.
The date, time and place of weekly meetings were fixed; the Commissioners'
recommended venue was the chief workhouse for the able-bodied paupers
and if that was not practical the guardians should avoid meetings in taverns
and public houses. The place, day and time of guardians' meetings was kept
regular in each location and published in newspapers, directories and even on
visiting cards, so that it was known when those in need could make an application for relief. This was particularly important in some of the larger unions
where potential claimants could live several miles from the town where the
guardians met. The first meeting also saw the appointment of a union Clerk
and a Treasurer. The workload of the Clerk depended upon the size and activity within a particular union. For many, though not all, it was a full-time appointment. A 'respectable banker' was the preferred choice as Treasurer, and
the nominated man was required to give security of one-sixth of the annual
rates of the union. Other positions including that of Relieving Officer and
Medical Officers were to be advertised in the newspaper. In theory appointments to these positions should not have been made until those applications
had been received. In practice, the guardians appointed men already known
to them, especially to the role of Relieving Officer who was to be the main
interface between the poor and the board. 'Diligence, firmness, and mildness,
together with a knowledge of the habits of the indigent classes' were considered the necessary qualifications for Relieving Officers and Workhouse
Masters.[40] Former non-commissioned officers in the army and Metropolitan
Police Officers were recommended as having made suitable candidates for
these positions.[41] As unions varied in size, it was sometimes necessary to set
up sub-divisions within the union before appointing various officers and setting up contracts for goods and services to be supplied to the union.

The second meeting focussed on reviewing existing practices and the appointment of paid offices. The Poor Law Commission suggested an appraisal
of workhouse accommodation take place at this time although in practice
this was often discussed at the first meeting. Many parishes did not have a
workhouse under the Old Poor Law and those that did may have had modest

sized buildings. In their instructional letter, the commissioners did not recommend the building of a large central workhouse but suggested permanent accommodation may be required for up to two per cent of the population. The recommended system of segregation or 'classification' of paupers could begin by using separate smaller workhouses for different classes of pauper. For example, children were housed in one workhouse, the able-bodied in another and the elderly elsewhere. In practice, many Boards of Guardians formed sub-committees to review workhouse accommodation outside of the main committee meetings and make recommendations to the board. The vast majority of unions opted to build a new large central workhouse. As a result, there was an institutional building boom that emptied the coffers of the Exchequer Loan Committee within months as many unions obtained loans to build large, new, austere, union workhouses on 'greenfield' sites. The cost of new premises or the alteration of existing buildings had to be met by the union and approved by the Poor Law Commission. Other details in relation to the administration and maintenance of the workhouse including discussions on uniforms, diet and employment in the workhouse would come later.

One of the recommended activities for the second meeting was the examination and review of the existing paupers within the union. In order to do this, the *Pauper Description List* was to be completed by the Relieving Officer. Given that the Relieving Officer could not be appointed until after the position was advertised, he could not have been appointed until the second meeting and as such would not have been able to complete this list. The review of existing arrangements and migrating paupers from the old system to the new system was quite substantial. Individual parishes may have adopted different practices in relation to their treatment of their parish poor and so they collectively reviewed all cases and individual eligibility under the new law. Some unions required all those in receipt of relief to attend a meeting of the Board of Guardians, others worked from lists provided by the parish overseers or the newly appointed Relieving Officers. If a pauper failed to attend a meeting when required their relief was stopped. There were no transitional arrangements; for individual paupers the reduction or withdrawal of relief may have been sudden and immediate. Alternatively, any ongoing relief may have been restricted to a place in the workhouse.

The new pauper description book was a key document in determining relief and the union officials grumbled about the amount of time it took to complete. There were up to twenty columns of data to be completed including basic details such as name, age, marital status and number of dependent children. Child applicants were to be categorised as 'orphan, deserted or bastard'. The earnings of the applicant and his family were recorded along with details of any disability or medical needs. The pauper description books can provide a fascinating insight into the lives of the poor at the point they entered the relief system; unfortunately, very few have survived.[42]

Each union appointed a number of paid officers. All candidates were interviewed and selected by the guardians. Each appointment was ratified or sanctioned by the Poor Law Commissioners. From the mid-1860s registers of paid officers were kept by the Poor Law Board (formed in 1847).[43] In the initial period letters of recommendation were sent to the commissioners but pro forma documents to gather information about applicants began to be used from the late 1830s. Advice on the suitability of the candidates was often sought from the Assistant Poor Law Commissioner.

Unions became large commissioning bodies for goods and services and most contracts for supplies were put out to tender. The guardians were required to evaluate such tenders and engage suppliers for goods such as meat, bread and coal accordingly. For out-relief provision many unions introduced a ticket or token system which saw paupers exchange tokens for goods rather than receive relief in cash.

Until the Board of Guardians sat the union had no income and would not therefore be able to meet any liabilities in relation to relief or other costs, as such the guardians were required to issue orders to the respective parishes in their union to make a contribution to union costs. This contribution was determined by the 'averages' calculated by the Assistant Poor Law Commissioner. Thereafter, contributions were paid quarterly.

The activities described above represent a substantial amount of initial work for the newly appointed guardians. Local records show that the work ran over into several additional or ad hoc meetings. The third meeting outlined in the instructional letter was set aside for the examination of paupers (existing and new cases), considering the education of pauper children, the appointment of a schoolmaster and schoolmistress (if required) and the provision of a nurse. In this context a 'nurse' was a nursery nurse for young children. A ratio of one nurse to fifty children was deemed sufficient.[44] The instructional letter makes no mention of evaluating tenders for goods and service or agreeing some of the important aspects of administering the poor law at a local level; tasks which took considerable time for the guardians and the clerk. In most areas it was not possible to fully implement the requirements of the New Poor Law until a fully functioning workhouse with capacity for the able-bodied relief claimants was available. The process of obtaining a suitable site, getting plans drawn up and approved by the Poor Law Commission, engaging builders and supervising the build took time. In many instances the implementation process took a couple of years to complete. The longest time taken to set up a union workhouse was in the Todmorden union on the Lancashire and Yorkshire borders. Always against the New Poor Law, the Todmorden union refused to build a central workhouse until 1878.[45]

Board of Guardians meetings were formally minuted and many of these minutes survive in local record officers. Correspondence from the guardians to the Poor Law Commissioners and from the Poor Law Commission back to the individual unions has survived in abundance in the series MH12 at the National Archives. The quality and details of the minute taking varies from union to union, but together these documents open a window onto the systems being established at both national and local levels. These records provide evidence of policy queries, confirmation and adaptations as both the unions and the commissioners adopted the New Poor Law.

Conclusion

There was no immediate countrywide impact when the Poor Law Amendment Act was passed in August 1834. A new, and at the time innovative, central department was established before the legislation was gradually implemented throughout the country. This was a significant undertaking and a task concentrated in the hands of just a few men – the centrally based Poor Law Commissioners and their Assistant Poor Law Commissioners. The latter worked out a system for setting up the poor law unions starting in the rural counties of southern England before fanning out into all areas of England and Wales. The methodology used to set up the poor law unions and take over the provision of poor relief from the parishes required a significant amount of input from the locally elected Board of Guardians. The timetable set out by the central authorities for achieving this was unrealistic, nevertheless, between January 1835 and April 1840, the assistant commissioners created 572 poor law unions the length and breadth of the country. In doing so they created a new tier of local administration which was not mapped on to any existing boundaries or divisions, thus setting up new relationships between parishes in many areas. The poor law union became a crucial new administrative unit for local government and formed the basis for the registration districts introduced for the civil registration of births, marriages and deaths in 1837 and the rural sanitary districts in 1875. Once established, the poor law unions became an essential part of a centrally controlled but locally managed welfare system which lasted for almost one hundred years, until the Local Government Act of 1930 abolished the Boards of Guardians and made county and borough councils responsible for poor relief.

Notes

1 The extensive poor law historiography includes: S. Webb and B. Webb, *English Poor Law Policy*, and *English Poor Law History Part II: The Last Hundred Years* (London: Longmans, 1929); M.E. Rose, *The Relief of Poverty, 1834–1914* (London: Macmillan, 1972); F. Driver, *Power and Pauperism: The Workhouse System, 1834–1884*, Vol. 19 (Cambridge: Cambridge University Press, 1993); P. Slack, *The English Poor Law, 1571–1782* (Cambridge: Cambridge University Press, 1995); D. Englander, *Poverty and Poor Law Reform in Britain: From Chadwick to Booth, 1834–1914* (London: Longman, 1998); S. King, *Poverty and Welfare in England, 1700–1850* (Manchester: Manchester University Press, 2000), A. Brundage, *The English Poor Laws 1700–1930* (Basingstoke: Palgrave, 2002); S. Shave, *Pauper Policies: Poor Law Practice in England 1780–1850* (Manchester: Manchester University Press, 2017).

2 In 1842 the Poor Law Commissioners claimed all of England and Wales was 'under the operation of the ... Act' with named exceptions including three unions in

Lancashire that resisted the new law's imposition. British Parliamentary Papers (hereafter BPP), 1842 (389) XIX.1, *Eighth Annual Report of the Poor Law Commissioners, with Appendices*, p. 18.

3 D. Roberts, *Victorian Origins of the British Welfare State* (New Haven, CT: Yale University Press, 1960), p. 133; Driver, *Power and Pauperism*, p. 29.

4 Roberts, *Victorian Origins*, p. 110; Driver, *Power and Pauperism*, pp. 33–34.

5 N.C. Edsall, *The Anti-Poor Law Movement, 1834–1844* (Manchester: Manchester University Press, 1971).

6 G.R.W. Baxter, *The Book of the Bastiles* (London: J. Stephens, 1841); Webb and Webb, *English Poor Law History*, p. 26; Brundage, *The Making of the New Poor Law*, pp. 69–71; G. Himmelfarb, *The Idea of Poverty: England in the Early Industrial Age* (London: Faber and Faber, 1985).

7 *The Times*, 25 November 1834, p. 2.

8 Webb and Webb, *English Poor Law History*, p. 110.

9 A. Brundage, *The Making of the New Poor Law: The Politics of Inquiry, Enactment, and Implementation, 1832–1839* (London: Hutchinson, 1978), p. 80.

10 BPP, 1841 (263) XXI.1. *Poor Law Amendment Act. Return of the Total Amount of Salaries or Other Payments Received in 1840 by the Poor Law Commissioners, Secretaries, and Others; also Amount of Printing Expenses, as far as the Same can be Ascertained*, p. 1.

11 Roberts, *Victorian Origins*, p. 239. See also the Assistant Poor Law Commissioners correspondence files, The National Archives (hereafter TNA) Series MH 32.

12 Three early appointees resigned and were replaced.

13 Driver, *Power and Pauperism*, pp. 29–31, 33–35.

14 Webb and Webb, *English Poor Law History*, pp. 112–113.

15 S.G. Checkland and E.O.A. Checkland, eds, *The Poor Law Report of 1834* (London: Penguin, 1974), p. 30.

16 BPP, 1834 (44) XXVII–XXXIX. *Report from His Majesty's Commissioners for Inquiring into the Administration and Practical Operation of the Poor Laws*, p. 1.

17 Roberts, *Victorian Origins*, p. 164.

18 After 1847 many continued in their posts and were known as Poor Law Inspectors.

19 Brundage, *The Making of the New Poor Law*, p. 80; S.F. Wise, 'Head, Sir Francis Bond,' in *Dictionary of Canadian Biography* (University of Toronto/Université Laval, 2003), vol. 10, www.biographi.ca/en/bio/head_francis_bond_10E.html (accessed 25 June 2015)

20 J.K. Laughton, 'Parry, Sir (William) Edward (1790–1855)', Rev. A.K. Parry, *Oxford Dictionary of National Biography*, Oxford University Press, 2004; online edn, January 2008 www.oxforddnb.com/view/article/21443 (accessed 17 August 2016)

21 The Postal Museum, http://beta.postalheritage.org.uk/explore/history/rowlandhill_(accessed 25 June 2015); TNA, MH 10/2, 6 January 1836 and MH 32/5, 27 December 1835.

22 Driver, *Power and Pauperism*, p. 30, figure 2.1.

23 MH 12 series is catalogued on a union-by-union basis.

24 P. Carter and N. Whistance, *Living the Poor Life: A Guide to the Poor Law Union Correspondence c 1834–1871 Held at the National Archives* (Salisbury: British Association for Local History, 2011), p. 6.

25 TNA, MH 32/5, 1 and 5 November 1835.

26 V. Care, 'The Significance of a "Correct and Uniform System of Accounts" to the Administration of the Poor Law Amendment Act, 1834', *Accounting History Review* 21: 2 (2011), pp. 121–142 [pp. 138–139].

27 Roberts, *Victorian Origins*, p. 238.

28 Roberts, *Victorian Origins*, p. 239. R. Johnson, 'Educational Policy and Social Control in Early Victorian England', *Past & Present* 49 (1970), pp. 96–119.

29 Adey's correspondence with Poor Law Commission, TNA, MH 32/5, 14 September 1835.
30 Brundage, *The Making of the New Poor Law*, p. 80.
31 Brundage, *The Making of the New Poor Law*, ch. 5, pp. 105–144.
32 P. Dunkley, 'The Landed Interest and the New Poor Law: A Critical Note', *The English Historical Review* 88: 349 (1973), pp. 836–841 [pp. 839–840].
33 TNA, MH 32/5 14 Apr 1835 and Hatfield House Manuscript Collection, 2M/I/1/25/36. Letter from William Blake and draft reply, 10 May 1835.
34 BPP, 1835 (500), XXXV.107. *First Annual Report of the Poor Law Commissioners for England and Wales*.
35 TNA, MH 32/5, 7 January 1836.
36 TNA, MH 10/2, 23 March 1836.
37 BPP, 1837 (546.I) (546.II) XXXI.127. *Third Annual Report of the Poor Law Commissioners for England and Wales; Appendix (A.)*, pp. 47–55.
38 BPP, 1837 (546.I) (546.II) XXXI.127. *Third Annual Report of the Poor Law Commissioners for England and Wales; Appendix (A.)*, pp. 47–55, Instructional Letter to Guardians, paragraph 59.
39 Instructional Letter, paragraph 4.
40 Instructional Letter, paragraph 18.
41 Instructional Letter, paragraph 19.
42 Any surviving Pauper Description Books are likely to be in county archives. Gloucester, Kent, Somerset and Bedfordshire record offices have a small number.
43 TNA, MH 9, *Registers of Paid Officers, 1837–1921*. Note: those who were employed before the mid-1860s and were still employed at the time the registers began were recorded, but anyone who had left employment prior to their introduction was not.
44 Instructional letter, paragraph 87.
45 The Workhouse, www.workhouses.org.uk/Todmorden/ (accessed 16 December 2016).

Bibliography

Baxter, G.R.W. *The Book of the Bastiles* (London: J. Stephens, 1841).
British Parliamentary Papers. 1834 (44) XXVII–XXXIX. *Report from His Majesty's Commissioners for Inquiring into the Administration and Practical Operation of the Poor Laws*.
British Parliamentary Papers. 1835 (500), XXXV.107. *First Annual Report of the Poor Law Commissioners for England and Wales*.
British Parliamentary Papers. 1837 (546.I) (546.II) XXXI.127. *Third Annual Report of the Poor Law Commissioners for England and Wales; Appendix (A.)*.
British Parliamentary Papers. 1837–1838 (236) XXXVIII.539.38 *Poor Law Amendment Act. Return, Showing the Size in Square Miles of the Several Unions Formed, with the Population, and Number of Guardians*.
British Parliamentary Papers. 1841 (263) XXI.1. *Poor Law Amendment Act. Return of the Total Amount of Salaries or Other Payments Received in 1840 by the Poor Law Commissioners, Secretaries, and Others; also Amount of Printing Expenses, as far as the Same can be Ascertained*.
British Parliamentary Papers. 1842 (389) XIX.1. *Eighth Annual Report of the Poor Law Commissioners, with Appendices*.
Brundage, A. *The Making of the New Poor Law: The Politics of Inquiry, Enactment, and Implementation, 1832–1839* (London: Hutchinson, 1978).

Brundage, A. *The English Poor Laws 1700–1930* (Basingstoke: Palgrave, 2002).

Care, V. 'The Significance of a 'Correct and Uniform System of Accounts' to the Administration of the Poor Law Amendment Act, 1834', *Accounting History Review* 21:2 (2011), pp. 121–142.

Carter, P. and N. Whistance, *Living the Poor Life: A Guide to the Poor Law Union Correspondence c.1834–1871 Held at the National Archives* (Salisbury: British Association for Local History, 2011).

Checkland, S.G. and E.O.A. Checkland, eds, *The Poor Law Report of 1834* (London: Penguin, 1974).

Driver, F. *Power and Pauperism: The Workhouse System, 1834–1884* (Cambridge: Cambridge University Press, 2004).

Dunkley, P. 'The Landed Interest and the New Poor Law: A Critical Note', *The English Historical Review* 88:349 (1973), pp. 836–841.

Edsall, N.C. *The Anti-Poor Law Movement, 1834–1844* (Manchester: Manchester University Press, 1971).

Englander, D. *Poverty and Poor Law Reform in Britain: From Chadwick to Booth, 1834–1914* (London: Longman, 1998).

Hatfield House Manuscript Collection 2M/I/1/25/36. Letter from William Blake and draft reply, 10 May 1835.

Himmelfarb, G. *The Idea of Poverty: England in the Early Industrial Age* (London: Faber and Faber, 1985).

Johnson, R. 'Educational Policy and Social Control in Early Victorian England', *Past & Present* 49 (1970), pp. 96–119.

King, S. *Poverty and Welfare in England, 1700–1850: A Regional Perspective* (Manchester: Manchester University Press, 2000).

Laughton, J.K. revised A.K. Parry, 'Parry, Sir (William) Edward (1790–1855)', *Oxford Dictionary of National Biography*, Oxford University Press, 2004; online edn, January 2008 www.oxforddnb.com/view/article/21443 (accessed 17 August 2016)

Roberts, D. *Victorian Origins of the British Welfare State* (New Haven, CT: Yale University Press, 1960).

Rose, M.E. *The Relief of Poverty, 1834–1914* (London: Macmillan, 1972).

Shave, S. *Pauper Policies: Poor Law Practice in England 1780–1850* (Manchester: Manchester University Press, 2017).

Slack, P. *The English Poor Law, 1571–1782* (Cambridge: Cambridge University Press, 1995).

The National Archives. MH 9. Registers of Paid Officers, 1837–1921.

The National Archives. MH 10/2. Circular Letters from the Poor Law Commissioners to the Assistant Poor Law Commissioners 1836.

The National Archives. MH 12. Correspondence with Poor Law Unions and Other Local Authorities.

The National Archives. MH 32. Correspondence with Assistant Poor Law Commissioners.

Webb, S. and B. Webb, *English Poor Law History: Part II, the Last Hundred Years* (London: Longmans, 1929).

Wise, S.F. 'Head, Sir Francis Bond,' in *Dictionary of Canadian Biography* (University of Toronto/Université Laval: 2003), vol. 10.

Index